S0-AHS-875

Dennis L. Breo

Extraordinary Care

Chicago Review Press

The articles included in this book originally appeared in *American Medical News,* a publication of the American Medical Association, as follows:

Hitler's final days recalled by physician, October 11, 1985; Hughes' privacy preserved by hospital, April 19, 1976; Aspirin was fatal to Howard Hughes, his physician says, July 13, 1979; Examiner is firm; heart disease fatal to Presley, December 12, 1979; Presley's MD struggles for a new life, December 11, 1981; MDs, hospital ready for Reagan, April 10, 1981; Pope's physicians redeem a request, May 29, 1981; Shah's physician relates story of intrigue, duplicity, August 7, 1981; Ali's key: treatment compliance, October 5, 1984; Tragedy in Guyana, December 8, 1978; Laetrile—the man behind the movement, April 18, 1977; Three-year-old is fugitive from Mass General, February 9, 1979; Controversy surrounds famed laetrile patient, September 7, 1979; Laetrile controversy's central figure dies, October 26, 1979; Convicted of murder, MD continues his struggle, November 4, 1983; Was Hinckley insane?, July 9, 1982; "Insanity" is question for jury, July 9, 1982; Holes in system led to case mishandling, says Vineyard MD, November 23, 1979; Two decisions to reject Allan Bakke defended by admissions head, September 15, 1978; The story of a surrogate mother, July 28, 1978; Marine invasion latest chapter for troubled school on Granada, November 4, 1983; Historic surgery was worth it, March 25, 1983; Barney Clark's MD-son: "I'm ambivalent," April 22/29, 1983; Is Baby Foe transplant worth it? Experts mixed, November 9, 1984; Therapeutic intent was topmost, November 16, 1984; MD lives in Hemingway's shadow, September 13, 1976; Transsexualism therapy debate goes on, October 18, 1976; Renee Richards returning to medicine, September 24, 1982; MD-astronaut tells of space adventure, May 6, 1983; Space travel always risky, March 21, 1986; Photos are tribute to vanished Jews, December 9, 1983; The Pill brought controversy and praise to John Rock, MD, December 5, 1980; Life on the run with MD-author, August 25, 1978; Dr. Percy's diagnosis, November 21, 1977; MD in Ethiopia, March 1, 1985; Alex Comfort, MD, best known for *Joy of Sex* books, February 23, 1979; Castle is dentist's magnificent obsession, October 6, 1978; The MDs and the mountains, May 23, 1977; Driving through a decade of change, June 15, 1984.

Library of Congress Cataloging-in-Publication Data

Breo, Dennis L., 1942–
    Extraordinary care.

    Reprinted from various issues of the American
medical news.
    Includes index.
        1. Celebrities—Medical care.   2. Physicians—Biography.
3. Physician and patient.   4. Medicine—Miscellanea.
I. American medical news.   II. Title.   [DNLM:
1. Delivery of Health Care—collected works.   2. Famous
Persons—collected works.   3. Physician—Patient
Relations—collected works.   W 84.1 B839e]
R703.B69   1986   610   86-18777
ISBN 0-914091-95-6

For those who shared their stories.

Contents

Acknowledgments

Many people have helped in many ways to make this book possible.

First, I want to thank the three editors with whom I have worked at *American Medical News:* Marvin L. Rowlands, who hired me; Larry D. Boston, a man who believed in and encouraged possibilities; and the current editor, Dick K. Walt, who has supported this project.

For a life of chasing stories, a reporter needs two strong allies—a helpful library staff and a helpful travel staff. The superb AMA library staff answered my every silly query, and I especially want to thank Victoria Bigelow Elsner, Mary Jo Dwyer (who speaks several languages and is terrific at translations), Jane Larkin, and George Kruto (who retrieved the articles that comprise this manuscript). The superb AMA meeting and travel staff regularly pulled rabbits out of hats in the way of finding hotel rooms in cities that were oversold and finding airplane connections to places not easily reached. I am especially indebted to Robert Hobart, the director of the AMA Division of Meeting Management and Planning and to Cheryl Herman, one of his able assistants.

Among the many professional organizations that I have joined, there is one that stands out—the American Assn. of Medical Society Executives, or AAMSE. The small AAMSE membership of 700 or so includes the men and women who run the AMA and this nation's county, state, and specialty medical organizations. On many occasions, when stalking a big story, I have turned first to an AAMSE member to find out what is really going on. While only half of all physicians belong to the AMA, the vast majority do join either their county and state medical organizations and/or their specialty group. And the execs for those groups usually are well acquainted with whatever physicians in their area may be in the news—and why. So, I salute AAMSE and, especially, Jim Hickox, the executive director of the Harris County (Tex.) Medical Society in Houston, who first persuaded me to join AAMSE and to edit their quarterly journal, *Medical Executive*. It is one of the wisest decisions I have ever made and the medical execs I have met, including AAMSE executive directors Edward Collins Jr. and Robert Lindley, have been very impressive.

The original publication of many of these articles in *American Medical News* was greatly enhanced by the layout and design abilities of Barbara

Bolsen, our production editor, who has a particularly fine eye for selecting and cropping the best photograph.

And what I didn't learn about photography from Barbara I learned from the AMA's chief photographer, Joe Fletcher, who runs the Association's photo lab, who has photographed thousands of MDs and medical meetings, and who printed most of the photos included in this book.

I thank Curt Matthews, the publisher of Chicago Review Press, for envisioning the publication of this anthology; and also Linda Matthews, for skillfully editing the manuscript.

From the AMA, I thank Scott Schwar, our director of marketing, for sheperding the book through the various stages of production. The AMA general counsel, Kirk Johnson, is one attorney who believes in making things happen, and he provided wise advice and support. Wayne Hoppe handled all the necessary legal details. And, finally, I thank the Association's chief executive officer, Dr. James H. Sammons, who made this book happen.

Foreword

Every month physicians in the United States find their desks flooded with journals, magazines, drug company pamphlets and newspapers, some solicited, many sent gratuitously. Sad to say, most of these publications wind up in the physician's waste basket; often, immediately, sometimes after a few weeks in a pile that the doctor, "means to read as soon as he can get around to it."

In many offices, including mine, the *American Medical News* gets a more select treatment. Each week, when it arrives, I take it home to read and do so promptly, if not within 24 hours certainly within 48 hours. I find that this paper gives me information that is practical, knowledgeable and necessary in an era when medicine is in a state of flux, not only scientifically but politically and economically.

Some articles I only scan but I read many in detail, including, invariably, those by Dennis Breo. I know if the byline is Breo that the article is not only going to be interesting but particularly well written. He not only knows how to dig out all the relevant information but how to ask the right questions of the right people, the questions most doctors would love to ask if they had the opportunity. When he finally writes the story he does so in prose of the first order. His articles are always a pleasure to read.

Rereading Dennis Breo articles in book form confirmed something I had long suspected; Breo usually chooses material that is germane not only for the moment but for years. I am delighted that much of what he has written over the last ten years has now been preserved between hard covers so that it can be enjoyed not only by those—lay persons as well as physicians—who may have missed it the first time around, but by those of us who enjoy rereading journalism of the first order.

Extraordinary Care is an extraordinarily good book.

William A. Nolen, MD

Introduction

It all began, really, on a cold and snowy day in Ottawa, Canada, in January, 1976.

I had been sent into this abominable weather by my editor, Larry Boston, who wanted a report on Canada's system of national health insurance, called "Medicare," which then and now is a talking point for a system of comprehensive, universal health insurance. Today, the idea of national health insurance, or NHI, is as dead as a dodo bird, but in 1976 it was still an attractive idea to liberal politicians, particularly Massachusetts' Democratic Senator Edward M. Kennedy. Since the British version of NHI had all but collapsed, Sen. Kennedy and his colleagues were now pushing the Canadian version. I was sent to the Northlands to find out what the Canadians had to offer—good and bad.

This trip marked my first assignment as the National Affairs Editor of *American Medical News,* a position created to allow me unlimited freedom to chase the big stories and personalities in medicine. Previously, I had slipped my reporting and writing assignments in between my main job of being the paper's "News Editor," in charge of making assignments and supervising the content and layout of the weekly publication. But, clearly, my interests and talents were more in living on the road and writing for the printed page. Larry Boston, an astute editor, realized this, and turned me loose on an assignment that continues a decade later (though Mr. Boston is gone and my title has been changed to "Special Assignments Editor"). Along the way, I have traveled thousands of miles, met scores of memorable people, and reported on hundreds of stories.

But in January, 1976, it was just beginning. I had the NHI story pretty well in hand (the average Canadian likes his health system, but the Canadian doctors think there are too many state controls and that medical education and research are lagging; many Canadian MDs were defecting to the U.S., notably Houston, which was seen as the land of opportunity).

Suddenly, I was confronted with a new opportunity. Reading a newspaper in my room at Ottawa's Chateau Laurier Hotel, I noticed that famed Canadian portrait photographer Yousuf Karsh had just dedicated a new portfolio, "Healers of Our Age," to the many famous physicians he had photographed over the years. I also noticed that Karsh had his internationally renowned studio right here in the Chateau Laurier Hotel, a few floors below my room. The story seemed like a natural, but I was afraid to pick up the phone and call the master. For one thing, I had yet to have a photograph of mine published, although I had brought a camera along in the hopes of photographing the various people I was interviewing. For another, I had no idea what to ask him. I stewed about it for several minutes, reasoning that, what the hell, he was probably off in Africa on a shoot anyway.

Finally, I picked up the phone, dialed the number, and began my laborious pleading for an interview. Never overlook an opportunity, I had convinced myself. The angels were with me. Karsh's wife, it turned out, answered the phone and, to my great amazement and delight, informed me that before marrying the photographer she had been a medical editor herself in Chicago. Furthermore, she knew and respected both the AMA and *American Medical News*. "Mr. Karsh will be pleased to give you the entire afternoon to discuss his photographs of famous doctors," she told me.

The interview went very smoothly. Estrellita did all the talking, with Mr. Karsh merely nodding here and there for emphasis. But then came the moment of truth:

I was going to swing for the fences and attempt to take a photo of the master himself, right in his own studio, posing him right in front of his portrait of Sir Winston Churchill, the photo that adorned his studio wall, and the photo that was on a postage stamp, the photo that had made Karsh famous.

I came to this momentous assignment equipped only with a $3\frac{1}{2}$-inch by 5-inch index card that had been given to me by our photo editor, Barbara Bolsen. On one side, Barbara had drawn a diagram of my Nikon camera, illustrating how to load and rewind the film and pointing out the controls for the shutter and light meter; on the other, she had provided recommendations for setting film speed for indoors and outdoors shots and for changing various camera lenses. I pulled the humble card out of my pocket and showed it to Karsh. Quickly, he snapped his fingers and three assistants emerged from the darkroom to set up various lights at various angles. Then, he and Estrellita posed in front of the massive portrait of Churchhill. I stuffed my card in a pocket, sank down on one knee, looked through my viewfinder, muttered a few words of nervous small-talk, and began snapping off a roll of black-and-white film.

A few days later, back in Chicago, I was astonished to see that I actually had images on the negatives. And, running a story on "Healers of Our Age," the paper published my photo of Estrellita and Yousuf Karsh, who were resolutely smiling at me as a glowering Churchill looked down. This photo ran in the paper along with Karsh's classic photos of physicians Albert

Schweitzer, Francis Moore, Carl Jung, and Helen Taussig (which he had loaned us for the occasion). In keeping with his credit line, "Karsh, Ottawa," mine read "Breo, Chicago."

My first published photograph was in great company, and Mr. and Mrs. Karsh were delighted with the story. He asked for my negatives, which I promptly mailed. A few weeks later, I received back a custom print of my photograph, handsomely mounted on a silver frame. The inscription reads: "To my photographic colleague, Dennis L. Breo, in happy remembrance of your visit to Ottawa. Yousuf Karsh, 1976." Today, when people inquire about my photographic ability, I casually mention that Yousuf Karsh considers me a colleague.

In 1976, I was off to a great start, and, today, I still have the photo on my wall—and the index card in my drawer.

Chasing news stories is a very hectic and a very lonely calling, but the rewards are unique—seeing the images and the words you have created appear on the printed page for other people to enjoy—and, not infrequently, quarrel with.

People make stories, and my approach to covering a controversial personality or a controversial story has always been first to try to draw close to the people and to see them as they present themselves and then to back off and impose perspective on what I have seen. You don't know what you think about a story, I have found out, until you sit down at the typewriter. I have thought of the process as a little bit like being a sponge and soaking up as much water as possible before wringing yourself dry. Or, as falling into a big hole and slowly climbing out. When beginning most stories, I have initially felt almost overwhelmed by the complications and possibilities, but as things proceed and the interviews and research continues, I gradually get to a point where I am beginning to feel a little bit tired of the subject. At that point, I begin to ruminate and sift and outline the story. My greatest pleasure, I have always found, is finally finishing the writing. And it's really true that as a writer you're never satisfied with what you've done. The best story, I've always been convinced, is right around the corner and yet to be written.

The stories in this anthology are all about people and they all were accomplished by getting on a plane and going to medical people in the news and drawing them out on important stories into which they had unique insight. Many reflect the special access and entree I had as the special correspondent for the national newspaper of medicine.

A few months after taking the photo of Karsh, I managed to persuade Jack Titus, MD, to discuss the autopsy he performed on Howard Hughes. To this day, it is the only interview he has given. Three years later, Hughes' personal physician, Dr. Wilbur Thain, gave me an exclusive interview on his medical care of the eccentric tycoon. Similarly, the physicians who cared for Adolf Hitler, Elvis Presley, Muhammad Ali, President Ronald Reagan, Pope John Paul II, and the Shah of Iran would later tell their stories only to me.

Although my persistence and perspicacity played a role in gaining these exclusive interviews, the larger reason is that physicians respect the American Medical Association and what it represents, and they wanted their stories told in a publication that would put considerations of patient care ahead of headlines on the 6 p.m. news. In a sense, I was selling credibility. And, in essence, when you probe deeply into the medical headlines of recent years, what you will find is a group of individual physicians who by and large were trying to care for their individual patients. Sometimes, this meant trying to get an impossible patient off drugs; sometimes, it meant taking the extraordinary steps of implanting a plastic heart or even a baboon heart to replace a failing human heart; sometimes, it meant taking a courageous but unpopular stand. But, usually, the patient came first. And the doctor was a dedicated professional who worked long hours against great odds.

I have also tried to celebrate the special doctors—crusaders and off-beat characters alike—who add so much texture and variety to the world of medicine.

We all know that oral contraceptives have changed the way we live, but it was a special treat for me to drive up the mountains of New Hampshire and talk to the founder of "The Pill," 90-year-old John Rock, a Catholic physician who said he was trying to find a way to cure *infertility*. Finding a cure for fertility was merely a spin-off. Or, interviewing the 86-year-old Dr. Roman Vishniac who for years took photographs with a hidden camera to preserve the "vanished world" of Eastern European Jews. Like Karsh, Dr. Vishniac also gave me a lesson in photography. "Never pose a picture," Dr. Vishniac said. "That is journalistic nonsense. Photograph people as they live."

This collection attempts to humanize the high-tech gloss of medicine by reporting on the people who are behind the headlines and the controversies. All of these stories are based upon original reportage accomplished by going to the scene and providing eyewitness accounts of the people in the news. Their value is that, whether you agree or not with what is being said, you are hearing from those and only those who have been in a position to know the facts of the case.

Dennis L. Breo
Chicago

1. Extraordinary Care

EXTRAORDINARY PEOPLE ARE like the rest of us, best served by ordinary medical care.

This is good news for most of us; normal medical care in America is very good, indeed.

However, the extraordinary patient—the monarch or movie star or tycoon—will often insist on extraordinary care or try to take an extraordinary degree of control over his medical treatment. As we shall see in the following stories, this is generally a tragic mistake. The best of physicians can do little for a strong-willed patient who as an "extraordinary person" feels that he deserves to exert unlimited control over how he is treated—and not treated.

Three of the most remarkable men of our century were "impossible" patients—extraordinary people who refused to do what was medically necessary to protect their health.

Adolf Hitler, Howard Hughes, and Elvis Presley were all isolated from common humanity by their fame, money, and power. Intriguingly, all three were to give their full trust neither to a friend nor to a physician but to an idea: the idea that drugs are magic, that there is a drug for every mood and purpose.

The physicians who tried their best to treat Hitler, Hughes, and Presley spent most of their time supplying their patients with prescription drugs and, simultaneously, trying to control that drug use so that their patients were not harmed.

Hitler's physician, Dr. Theodor Gilbert Morell, believed in the magic of drugs as much as did his *Fuehrer*. In fact, at one time, he owned a number of drug firms. However, Hughes' personal physician, Wilbur Thain, MD, and Presley's personal physician, George C. Nichopoulos, MD, struggled against great odds to try to wean their patients off drugs.

The outcomes were, perhaps, predictably hopeless:

Hitler demanded countless pills, potions, and injections for every bellyache and every sniffle and when the war decisively turned against him, he required from his doctors only the final pill—cyanide.

Hughes, whose wealth endowed state-of-the-art medical research, including kidney disease, died from kidney failure and almost total neglect of his health.

Presley refused to accept the psychological and pharmaceutical advice that might have prolonged his life.

These three extraordinary men all chose their destiny—and their medical care. In consequence, their charisma and fortunes worked against them. Any of the three might have been saved by the ministrations of an average family physician, provided the physician were allowed to do what he knew to be best. But it was not to be. Each of these remarkable patients retreated to a fantasy world made bearable by countless drugs prescribed in good faith by frustrated physicians. Each of the trio was a "medicine junkie." The drugs they took all had potential therapeutic value and they all were prescribed by physicians who sought a therapeutic effect but this was never achieved.

A successful relationship between patient and physician, is, like any other significant relationship, best served by mutual respect and trust. Hitler, Hughes, and Presley were to give their trust to no man.

Hitler refused to undress for physical examinations and dismissed his doctor's plea for x-rays with the haughty disclaimer, "I have never been sick." Hughes refused to be examined, refused to have his rotten teeth repaired, and refused to go near a hospital, even when he knew that it meant he would never walk again. Presley refused to see a psychiatrist, though he badly needed one, and when his personal physician threatened to cut off his drugs, he merely got in his plane and flew off to other cities— and other suppliers.

Millions of words have been written about this trio of extraordinary men and many of those words have been critical of their physicians, implying that had the physicians acted differently their patients might have done better. The fair appraisal, however, is that a fragile thing like a physician-patient relationship is badly served by our national greed for the sensational story.

The doctors in question, Theodor Morell, Wilbur Thain, and George Nichopoulos, all felt that their real choice was either to work under frustrating conditions or to abandon a patient who clearly needed help. The physicians conscientiously worked with deep human concern against the resistance of their extraordinary patients. Nevertheless, the conduct of the physicians was repeatedly called into question, and, on several occasions, into court.

The doctors may, at times, have been blinded by the charisma of their patients, but, ultimately, they knew that medicine is the science of the way of all flesh. There are limits, even liabilities, in the degree of influence the extraordinary man can exert upon his medical care. Perhaps each one of this distinctive trio refused ordinary medical care because he could not admit his common mortality. Perhaps it was a simple fear of physical intrusion and vulnerability, or a desire for instant, simple answers to a complex equation—their own physical and psychological health. Whatever the motive, their complicated and extraordinary natures played them false in regard to what they needed medically.

Their physicians have long held their silence. Now, in exclusive interviews granted to the professional publication of the American Medical Assn., Drs. Thain, Nichopoulos, and others speak out about these extraordinary patients. Dr. Morell died in 1948, but his medical file of Hitler is ably translated by a colleague, Dr. Ernst Gunther Schenck, who was in the Berlin bunker with Hitler and who has made an exhaustive scientific analysis of Hitler's medical care. The words of the physicians who treated Hitler, Hughes, and Presley demonstrate that, indeed, truth is often stranger than fiction.

By contrast with this famous trio, boxer Muhammad Ali got into a different kind of problem with drugs. Ali got into trouble by refusing to take his medication as directed by his doctors. The ex-champion suffers from parkinsonism, a disease of the nervous system brought on in his case by blows to the head from boxing. The cure is simple—medication. The extraordinary Ali, however, apparently does not have time for such an ordinary activity, and, in 1984, this trait helped land him in a New York hospital. Unlike the others, Ali still has time to accept ordinary care.

Two of the world's most popular leaders, President Ronald Reagan and Pope John Paul II, have been lucky enough to receive the life-saving benefit of ordinary emergency medical care. Gunned down in the streets, the two were rushed to the ER much like any common gunshot victim would be. And, like the common victim, they, too, have had an uncommonly good result—complete recovery. This happened because the President and the Pope were treated according to ordinary medical protocols. They were treated as "Peter Smiths." Fortunately, there was no time to shop around for the "best hospital," the "best surgeon." There was only time to do what hospitals ERs do every day—provide the current, standard treatment, the kind of treatment that three million Americans receive every day when they visit a doctor.

Not so lucky was one of the world's richest men—the late Shah of Iran. In a stunning reversal of what many of us assume—that money and power will purchase a higher level of medical care than those of us in the general public will ever experience—the Shah, instead, became a medical vagabond, a helpless pawn in a losing political game. His billions were not able to buy the experimental treatment, the new form of surgery, the miracle drug available only in limited amounts. Instead, he was bounced from country to country—Mexico and Panama each gave him a wrenching choice: either he could pay for the right to have the operation he needed on that country's soil or he would be bartered away to the Ayatollah's minions who were seeking his extradition.

For reasons of statecraft, the Shah shortened and probably sacrificed his life. Doctors on three continents argued over who would have the privilege of treating him, and, in one extraordinarily absurd moment, world-famed surgeon Michael DeBakey, MD, who has pioneered many surgical procedures and who had answered a plea to operate on the Shah in Panama, was dismissed by the jealous Panamanian doctors as "an itinerant surgeon." The Shah did not have the luxury of being a "Peter Smith," of being entitled to ordinary medical care. The sad saga of the Shah's medically chaotic last year is eloquent proof that extraordinary care is not enough.

Finally, we have the gruesome case of the Guyana madman, the "Peoples Temple" leader, Rev. Jim Jones. His friend and doctor, Carlton Goodlett, MD, makes the telling point that ordinary medical care would have cured Jones' tropical lung infection, a disease that in the absence of treatment quite probably had spread to his brain. An ordinary hospital workup to make the proper diagnosis and the taking of some ordinary antibiotics might well have cleared up Jones' state of mind. But, no, this cult madman was too busy for anything that ordinary. His solution to the hammers beating on his brain was much more dramatic—and tragic.

Adolf Hitler

My journalistic instincts were aroused by a single sentence in *Time's* 1985 coverage of the 40th anniversary of D-Day. Near the end of World War II, the magazine reported, Adolf Hitler was a physical wreck. It attributed the description to a Dr. Ernst Gunther Schenck, who reportedly had been in the Berlin bunker with Hitler.

Was this physician still alive and lucid, I wondered. Would he agree to an interview? Was he legitimate? The aftermath of the forged "Hitler diaries" hung heavy in the air.

The AMA library was able to track Dr. Schenck down to an address in Aachen, West Germany. The German Medical Assn. verified that he had, indeed, served in Hitler's bunker. What neither could tell me, however, was that he spent his summers on holiday in Austria. Numerous calls to his Aachen home went unanswered. I sent him a cable, requesting an interview. There ensued a summerlong correspondence, with Dr. Schenck writing in German from Austria and Dr. Edward Petersen of the AMA Dept. of Undergraduate Medical Education doing the translating. "I will be delighted to meet with my AMA colleague," Dr. Schenck wrote.

I called in Dr. Karl Hnilicka, a Chicago interpreter, to arrange the interview. Fortuitously, Dr. Hnilicka is also a historian, specializing in the Nazi occupation of Yugoslavia. "Dr. Schenck is not only one of the few remaining primary sources on the Third Reich," Dr. Hnilicka said, "but he is also an expert on a story never before told—Hitler's medical file, as compiled by the dictator's late personal physician, Theodor Morell."

A date was set for late September, 1985, when Dr. Schenck returned to Germany. I flew to Cologne, where the night before meeting Dr. Schenck I had dinner with the interpreter who would help conduct the interview, Wanda Menke-Gluckert, herself a World War II refugee from Poland. From a restaurant high above the Rhine River, we looked down upon the ancient city. The only other people in the restaurant were a large group of Japanese tourists. "You are very fortunate," she said, "to have persuaded a German of Dr. Schenck's generation to discuss Hitler and the Nazis."

And so I was. Here is his story.

"IT IS A VERY STRANGE THING," said Ernest Gunther Schenck, MD, the only surviving physician who was in the Berlin bunker with Adolf Hitler only hours before the defeated dictator committed suicide. "We were all ready to throw our lives away for Hitler. It cannot be explained in rational terms. I still ask myself, "How was Hitler possible?"

In an exclusive interview at his home in Aachen, West Germany, the 81-year-old Dr. Schenck told *American Medical News* what it was like to be in the Berlin bunker during the last 10 days of the war. This eyewitness account is dramatic, but of more significance are the physician's years of study into the medical file kept on Hitler by the dictator's personal physician, Theodor Morell, MD, who died in 1948.

Dr. Morell kept meticulous records of his care of Hitler, recording every injection and every pill, saving every needle and every observation. His file on Hitler is one of the most complete records ever made of the medical care of a world leader, rivaling the diary kept on Winston Churchill by Lord Moran. The Morell papers, flown out of the Berlin bunker in 50 boxes and now recorded on microfilm in federal archives in West Germany and the United States, have become an obsession to Dr. Schenck in his quest to understand Hitler.

Dr. Schenck's book, the first scientific analysis of the medical file of Adolf Hitler, will be published in German by Bavarian Connection publishers in Stockach, a suburb of Munich. The book, tentatively titled *Patient A—Adolf Hitler and His Private Physician, Professor Theodor Gilbert Morell*, paints a fascinating medical portrait of the man who once terrorized the world. There are no plans at present to publish the book in English.

In two days of interviews with *AMN*, Dr. Schenck described his forthcoming book in detail. The interview was conducted through an interpreter, as Dr. Schenck said, "I forgot how to speak English during my 10 years of captivity in the Soviet Union."

He portrayed Hitler as an anxious and depressed patient who was psychologically dependent upon drugs. As the world fought back and the war turned against him, Hitler increasingly turned to Dr. Morell for staggering numbers of drug injections to fortify his flagging energy; to arrest his anxiety and depression; to calm the painful spasms caused by his colitis and to treat the disease's alternate effects of constipation and diarrhea; and, at the very end, to try to keep in check the conditions of Parkinson's disease and arteriosclerotic heart disease. Either of these last two conditions would almost certainly have soon killed him, had he not cheated the world by taking his own life, only days before the Russians marched into his bunker.

Dr. Schenck said, "As the Red Army marched into Berlin and as

Hitler saw his political obsession turn to disaster, his health broke. In the last six months, he aged 10 years. At the very end, Hitler wanted his physical energy to keep pace with his enormous psychological energy and will-power. He used his physician as he used everybody else—to help him try to achieve his obsession of changing the face of Eurpoe. As the obsession appeared to be slipping from his grasp, he turned to Dr. Morell and the German pharmaceutical formulary, then the greatest in the world, to prop him up for the last rolls of the dice. When he knew the end was near, he no longer needed his drugs. At that point, he needed a doctor for only one thing—to assure that his suicide would be swift and sure."

A fanatic about his health as well as his politics, Hitler was a difficult, almost impossible patient. Dr. Schenck said that the dictator's physician, Dr. Morell, labored mightily—and scientifically, according to the standards of his time—to try to treat a man who refused to undress for medical exams, who refused to be x-rayed, and who declined to have a complete medical check-up with the imperious disclaimer, "I have never been ill." Yet Hitler often needed a drug to get to sleep; a drug to help him get through the twice-daily military briefings with his generals; a drug to enable him to conduct his notorious monologues on into the night, which usually stupefied his listeners; a drug to treat persistent colds; and, again, a drug to help put him back to sleep. "Try treating Hitler!" an exasperated Dr. Morell once wrote in his diary.

Dr. Schenck ruined his eyes poring over the Morell papers, and he came away feeling sympathy toward the physician but continued bafflement toward the patient. "Medicine cannot explain Adolf Hitler," Dr. Schenck said, "but it can offer some fascinating clues." He concluded that Hitler was neither clinically insane nor physiologically addicted. "Medically, Hitler was neither unique nor unusual," Dr. Schenck said. "He was the slave of some very common maladies. Karl Brandt, MD, once Hitler's escort physician and the inspector general of the German Medical Service, thought Hitler's medical problems were largely 'hysterical' in origin. Hitler himself often told Dr. Morell that he thought many of his problems were psychological. Today, I would call many of his complaints 'psychosomatic.'"

And yet, as Dr. Morell treated every sniffle, every bellyache, and every bout of constipation, Adolf Hitler, resolutely determined, dignified—and demonic—continued to give the orders that meant death for at least 50 million soldiers and civilians in Europe. Dr. Schenck fears Hitler's nihilistic spirit may still be among us, "particularly in the Soviet Union, which feels surrounded by enemies, just as Nazi Germany did 40 years ago."

Dr. Schenck, one of the last surviving primary sources of information on the final days of the Third Reich, was there when Hitler requested information about the cyanide capsule that would kill him. He has exhaustively studied the medical record of how Hitler's mental and physical health deteriorated during the war. This, then, is his account of the patient who held Germany in a death grip until the very end.

Berlin, April, 1945.

The order, Dr. Schenck recalled, came at 3 a.m. on April 30, 1945. Dr. Schenck was one of two surgeons in the Berlin bunker who had performed 350 surgeries on wounded German soldiers and civilians in the past seven days. He had just thrown himself on a cot, hoping to gain a little sleep. But "Hitler, like Stalin," he said, "had turned night into day and now was summoning to him the bunker's surgical team."

Dr. Schenck; Werner Haase, MD; and two Red Cross nurses were led by guards from their operating room in the bunker beneath the new Chancellory of the German Reich (the equivalent of the White House) through 100 yards or so of serpentine corridors to the special *Fuhrerbunker* beneath the old Chancellory, or Imperial Palace. Here, 50 feet underground, protected by 16 feet of concrete and six feet of earth, Hitler and his entourage, including Dr. Morell, had been occupying 32 rooms on two levels.

"My surgical gown was matted with blood and perspiration," Dr. Schenck recalled, "and I smelled awful. I was not in a presentable condition."

The surgical team was kept waiting for a few minutes. Then Hitler stepped out of the door of his private living quarters. He walked down a corridor and up two steps to meet his guests. Dr. Schenck stood two steps above, looking down at his Fuhrer.

Dr. Haase reported in, and Dr. Schenck, like the others, snapped to attention and saluted, "Heil Hitler!"

Hitler began, "Excuse me that I have asked you to come at such a late hour."

Dr. Schenck recalled, "I felt cold, feeling paralyzed to my insides as if an icy wind had frozen me. And yet with every pore of my body I was soaking up impressions of the Fuhrer.

"This was not the man I had seen on millions of posters. True, he wore the black trousers, the green shirt, and the gray tunic with gold stitching and the Iron Cross pinned on the left chest. But the human being dwelling within this cloth was incredibly shrunken into himself. His spine was hunched, his shoulder blades protruded from his bent back, and he was lapsed into his shoulders like a turtle. He seemed to be carrying a mountain on his shoulders. His eyes, glaring at me painfully, were bloodshot, and the drooping black sacs under the eyes betrayed fatique and sleeplessness.

"Suddenly, it hit me like a hammer stroke. I was looking at the eyes of death. We all were doomed. I was looking into the eye of death.

"When Hitler looked at Dr. Haase, it was only with great effort and pain that he could raise his head. With great effort, he climbed up two more steps and directed his eyes at me. His stare was dull and glassy and no expression moved in his face. It was the mask of advanced Parkinson's disease. Deeply furrowed wrinkles ran from his nostrils to the corners of his mouth, which remained closed, the lips pressed tightly together.

"The movement with which he requested and shook my hand was but a reflex. This man was still alive, but he was at the lowest level of existence, about to cross the line to where there would be nothing left at all.

"The moon-like landscape of his ravaged face was within inches of mine and it was colored a pale gray-yellow. In a flat voice, he said that he wanted to thank us for attending to the wounded. My physician's heart awakened and became warm, although I knew that everything here was lost and that Hitler would allow no medical help. He was a living corpse, a dead soul. Gone were the powers to charm, to fascinate, to bend others to his steel will. He was a wasted man with hunched shoulders and dead eyes.

"He shook the hand of our nurse, Sister Erna. We had all kept silent, but now she began to repeat hysterically what she had heard a thousand times." 'My Leader, belief in final victory will ultimately destroy enemies. Eternal allegiance. Heil!'

"Hitler stood right next to this agitated creature and watched as Dr. Haase grabbed her arm. Abruptly, she stopped crying, and the silence was deeper than before. Sister Erna's outburst struck me as unseemly, but in Hitler it struck a spark with the little that was still alive in him. In a muffled voice, without addressing anyone in particular, he said, 'One should not want to cowardly evade one's fate!' Then he turned and left, motioning for Dr. Haase to follow him."

As the Third Reich collapsed, so did the discipline in the *Fuhrerbunker*. Dr. Schenck went up the stairs to another room, where he drank coffee and wine with a group of Hitler's top generals and the Fuhrer's bride of 24 hours, Eva Braun. Hitler went downstairs to negotiate his suicide with Dr. Haase.

"The closer the Russians approached (they now were within one-quarter mile of the Chancellory), the closer the camaraderie in the bunker became," Dr. Schenck recalled. "All distinctions of class and rank were disappearing. Secretaries mingled with generals, and the SS guards, who previously had kept their women out of sight, were breaking out champagne for a final orgy.

"I had never heard of Eva Braun or of her relationship to our leader, but now here I was making small talk with her and with Hitler's secretaries. Eva Braun talked of her memories of parties and festivities under blue Bavarian skies. This is a world that was never mine. I had never belonged to the inner circle when they were on the throne at the Obersalzberg (Hitler's Alpine retreat), like a castle of the gods, separated by a ring of clouds from the rest of us mortals.

"But now I belonged to the inner circle, the circle of the doomed. I felt like one of them. I do not remember much of Eva Braun, her clothes, her figure, her phrases. Still burning in my mind was the picture of our destroyed Fuhrer. When the big things are hopeless, who cares about the little? We were all doomed."

Dr. Schenck rose to visit the bathroom, and incredibly, his path led him directly to where Hitler and Dr. Haase were deep in conversation. Hitler's guards were not to be seen. Dr. Schenck recalled, "I saw Hitler sitting there, talking intensely to Dr. Haase, and I decided to take one more look at him to check my first extremely depressing impression.

"In his left hand, he held his reading glasses—the glasses that he never used in public and that were never seen in the thousands of photographs taken of him—and the hand was trembling rhythmically, tapping the glasses against a plate. His left leg was trembling violently, and he had pressed it between a chair leg and a table leg to try to suppress the movement. But it remained very noticeable. I knew that the trembling was typical of Parkinson's disease. He was suffering from a progressive arteriosclerotic disease of the blood vessels in the brain, and this was gradually causing the hardening of the deeper-seated ganglia cells. His bent posture, the head nearing the chest and resting upon a seemingly shortened neck, remained obvious while Hitler was seated. He seemed to be developing the Bechterev Syndrome, in which the spinal column bends. Within a few years, he would have become a cripple, barely able to lift his sight from the floor and the nearest objects.

"Dr. Haase himself was dying from tuberculosis and, now, our Fuhrer was turning to a critically ill doctor to negotiate his own dying, which had to be swift and sure.

"I would later learn that this was to be Hitler's final medical consultation. On April 21, the day after Hitler turned 56, he had had his last visit with Dr. Morell, who wanted to inject him once again with an energy-restoring combination of vitamins, glucose, and caffeine. Dr. Morell had given Hitler hundreds of similar injections, but, on this day, Hitler thought he was being betrayed. He was growing increasingly paranoid, and he believed that Dr. Morell was going to give him morphine to drug him into a state where he would accept his officers' recommendations to flee Berlin and make a final stand at the 'Alpine Fortress' at Obersalzberg. Hitler had decided to die in Berlin.

"Dr. Morrell, 59, was even sicker than Hitler was and had already suffered three small strokes, the most recent at the *Fuhrerbunker* in March, 1945. On April 21, Hitler flew into an explosive rage, screaming at Dr. Morell and threatening to have him shot. He ordered Dr. Morell to go home, take off his uniform as the Chancellor's physician, and 'forget you ever knew me.' Dr. Morell collapsed at Hitler's feet, and he left the bunker later that day.

"Hitler did not like or trust his other escort physician, the giant-like Dr. Ludwig Stumpfegger, and he refused to take injections from him. So, for his final medical consultation, he had only Dr. Haase, who had been Hitler's escort surgeon before the war and who had returned to the Berlin bunker out of loyalty to his patient. Two days earlier, Hitler had consulted Dr. Haase about the efficacy of cyanide poison and had insisted that a capsule be tested on his favorite dog, Blondi, a German shepherd. The dog had died instantly. And now, once again, Dr. Haase was telling the Fuhrer that death from cyanide is almost instantaneous.

"I had seen enough. Deeply depressed, I returned to the operating room, where, within minutes, I was amputating a soldier's leg. We were doing so many surgeries so quickly that they no longer seemed like human beings, but more like bloody pieces of meat. A few hours later, Dr. Haase whispered in my ear, 'Today, at 3 p.m., the Fuhrer will part from life.' I did not react. I said nothing. My mind was blank.

"I slept for a while, and then I returned to surgery. We kept our dirty linen in a corner, and all the surgical gowns were bloody. I tried to find the one that was least bloody. My clothes were stiffened from blood that had turned brown. I had blood on my glasses and my perspiration fogged them even more. Dust and stench hung in the wet and humid air. The toilets would not flush and the stench was becoming overpowering. I felt as though we were on a slave ship from Africa to America. Stinking chaos! The atmosphere in the bunker was very eerie. We were all losing touch with reality. We feared that the bunker would become a mass grave. I wanted to stop and lie down, but I told myself, 'Hang on, we will make it! Our soldiers are still fighting!'

"The Russians were only hours away, and there was a rush to surgery. Soldiers were bringing civilians, civilians soldiers, as well as soldiers bringing soldiers and civilians civilians. Nameless, unknown, they streamed in and out. I had eyes only for the body on my OR table. I focused clear and sharp. There was nothing else to think about. Dr. Haase was gone and, without him to guide me, I had to concentrate very hard to avoid making mistakes. I was not by specialty a surgeon, and Sister Erna had no OR experience either. But there was nobody else. For the wounded, we were it. Things blurred and time ceased to exist.

"Suddenly, Dr. Haase reappeared and gave me a sign to follow him into the other room. I yelled, 'Short break!' and followed him. He lay down on the cot, and he turned on his side and said, 'The Fuhrer is dead!' " It was 3 p.m. on April 30.

"I had no time to think. Hitler's death was history now. I returned to my surgery," Dr. Schenck said.

Hitler had taken no chances, historians tell us. Afraid that he would share the fate of Mussolini—who on April 26 had been hung by his heels, along with his mistress, outside a gas station in Milan—Hitler simultaneously bit into the cyanide capsule and put his 7.65 mm Walther pistol inside his mouth, pointed it toward his head, and pulled the trigger. His bride of 36 hours, Eva Braun, needed only the cyanide to end her life.

The double suicide prompted the last lie told by Propaganda Minister Joseph Goebbels (who had moved into Dr. Morrell's room and subsequently took cyanide, along with his wife, Magda, and their six young children). In his last broadcast to the nation, Goebbels read a message heard by very few: "The Fuhrer, Adolf Hitler, died fighting for the freedom of Germany and Europe, with a gun in his hand."

Dr. Schenck said, "Only the gun was in his hand. We were all disappointed, deeply hurt. The few soldiers who were still in the bunker expected their Fuhrer to lead them, to fight until the bitter end, and we were all ready to follow him and to meet death while fighting the Russians. When necessary, Hitler did not fight. His soldiers did.

"By German tradition, an oath of military loyalty can be released only by death. In 1934, the German Army had sworn an oath of obedience to the Fuhrer. Only with Hitler's death was the spell broken."

Because May 1, or May Day, is a major Russian holiday, celebrating the Bolshevik Revolution of 1917, the Red troops were taking their time in claiming their victory. On the night of April 30, the mortal remains of Adolf and Eva Hitler were—as the Fuhrer had ordered—slowly burned in the Chancellory garden. German soldiers had poured 180 liters of petroleum upon their bodies.

Meanwhile, the Red Army slowly advanced through the rubble of Berlin.

Dr. Schenck described the scene: "As soon as someone in the bunker died, guards would carry the body up two flights of stairs to the emergency exit and dump it on top of the other bodies piling up in the

Chancellory garden. When the Russian fire let up, German soldiers would run into the garden and try to bury the bodies in shallow graves; when the firing and bombing resumed, the soldiers would run for cover."

Dr. Schenck believes that the charred remains of Adolf and Eva Hitler were dug up from their original position in a Russian shell hole and reburied elsewhere in the huge Chancellory garden. Hitler's teeth were recovered by the Russians, autopsies have confirmed. They were rotten, a symptom of his fear of the dentist's drill. Eva Hitler's upper torso was recovered, and pieces of Russian shrapnel were found embedded near her heart. Dr. Schenck believes, however, that Russian claims of having recovered other parts of Hitler's body for an autopsy are propaganda. "I believe his remains are still ashes and dust in the Chancellory garden," the physician said. "Hitler remained a mystery to the very end."

While Hitler burned, Dr. Schenck and the remnants of the Third Reich were planning their escape. "When the news spread that Hitler was dead," Dr. Schenck recalled, "everybody who had sought shelter in the bunker tried to get out as quickly as possible. On April 25, the Red Army and the U.S. Army had joined forces at Torgau on the Elbe River, and the circle of fire was closing in. We had nothing to sustain us but rumors.

"There was a rumor that SS Commander Felix Steiner was collecting the battered army units from the Eastern Front and was forming a fighting force'—'Fighting Force Steiner'—that would relieve Berlin and allow an orderly retreat to the imaginary Alpine Fortress.

"There was a rumor that 'wonder weapons,' bombs and rockets, were being developed just in time to beat back the enemy.

"And almost right up until his death, Hitler had held to the delusion that the Russians and Americans would start shooting each other in a quarrel over Germany, and that this would allow him to arise from the ruins like phoenix from the ashes.

"But they were only rumors. Waffen SS General Wilhelm Mohnke, the commandant of Berlin, decided to try to break out. We were organized into six groups, and instructed to try to make an escape to North Germany. I said my final goodbye to Dr. Haase, who had decided to stay with the sick in the bunker. Briefly, I considered giving morphine to those who were sicker, so that they could have mercy deaths rather than suffer the revenge of the Russians. I looked around the operating room to consider which of the wounded were the better candidates for mercy death, but I finally decided against it. Besides, there was not enough morphine.

"At 11 p.m. on May 1, we made our attempt at escape. I had been asked to look after Hitler's secretaries, and also those of (Martin) Bormann (Hitler's chief of staff). Gen. Mohnke read to us Hitler's last will and political testament, which had been typed on the special Fuhrer typewriter, in the huge letters required for Hitler's failing eyes. Gen. Mohnke said that, if he died, his chief of staff should take the will to Admiral Karl Doenitz (the new Nazi commander-in-chief, designated by Hitler), and that, if the chief of staff died, I should deliver the will. It was unknown to us at the time that the will had been flown from the bunker to Admiral Doenitz three days before.

"Gen. Mohnke led us on an exhausting march through Berlin. It was dark, empty, and smelly. The Red Army was advancing cautiously, and there was little shooting. The rumor spread that an armistice had been negotiated, but nobody knew for sure. The Berliners, who had been hiding in their basements, did not make any unkind remarks when they saw us stumbling by in great fatigue. Nobody said, 'This serves you right!' Women were crying. They brought us food and cigarets and precious water. Nobody knew where the Russians were. Elsewhere in Berlin, there was pure chaos. People were panicked. Germans were shooting Germans out of confusion and fear. In some places, everybody was shooting at everybody.

"The older officers knew that there was no escape, and they were pleading that the idea of a breakthrough to the North be given up. They were sure that it was merely *mort pour mort* (to die for the sake of death), but the younger officers, including me, favored the breakthrough.

"But within a few hours, we too knew it was hopeless. The Russians were everywhere. There was no escape. The order was given to destroy all weapons and make the tanks and heavy guns unusable. A colonel was designated to negotiate a surrender with the Red Army. Our group gathered inside the Berlin brewery, Schultheiss-Patzenhofer. A rumor spread like wildfire that the soldiers were released from their oath to Hitler.

"Some Nazi Party officers had civilian clothes in their bags. This was an offense punishable by death, but they took off their uniforms, changed into civilian clothes, and disappeared into the ruins. Two secretaries, accompanied by an SS officer, also escaped into the darkness. Some members of our group argued that we should not be taken prisoners without a fight, that we should fire at the Russians and then shoot ourselves. I argued against such blind decisions, but I could not persuade a 24-year-old Waffen SS officer named Stehr. He told me that officers of the Waffen-SS should not survive the death of their Fuhrer. Although he was wounded and knew nothing but the war and its hardships, he remained close to Hitler's memory. He had a girlfriend whom he dearly loved, but he did not want to live without his Fuhrer. He shot himself. He was not alone. There was a wave of suicides. For some, the history of Germany ended with Hitler's death.

"But for most of us the early morning hours of May 2 were 'Day Zero,' the last day of war and the first day of peace. Germany had surrendered. All over Berlin the cries of the Red Army resounded: *'Voina kaputt! Gitler kaputt!'* ('The war is over! Hitler is dead!')

"We were captured by the Russians. The Third Reich, created to last 1,000 years, was dead within 12. I had lived through six years of war, and now I had no future. Ahead of me were 10 years in Russian prisons."

In 1945, it took the Allied Army three months to push from Aachen—the ancient capital of Charlemagne, founder of the First German Reich (which *did* last 1,000 years, from 800 to 1806)—to Cologne. Today, it is a pleasant 43-minute train trip to Aachen from Cologne. The Cologne train station is next to the city's magnificent medieval cathedral, now restored, which was partially destroyed by Allied bombing.

Dr. Schenck is now 81 but very alert, lucid, and lively. A Mercedes taxi whisked us from the Aachen train station to the private drive at 23 Lutherweg, where the former Nazi medical officer lives part of the time, preferring to summer at his farm near the Austrian Alps. He cut short his summer sojourn to reminisce about the past. It was a gray and rainy day, and the old physician stood in his driveway, awaiting the taxi, umbrella in hand.

He is a courtly man. The interview was interrupted for coffee and chocolate tortes at 10 and for German wieners and Moselle wine at lunch, served at a restaurant in the town square. Dr. Schenck explained that, because he is an expert in nutrition, he would make this his only heavy meal of the day. He apologized because his wife was in Austria, and a home-cooked meal could not be prepared for his guests.

But time was short, and Dr. Schenck wanted to explain it all, the 10 days in the Berlin bunker in 1945, the 10 years in Soviet prisons, and the years he had spent studying the Morell papers. He had his memorabilia and papers in hand, as well as the manuscript of his new book about Hitler and Dr. Morell. He said he wanted to make a contribution to future generations.

In many ways it was happenstance, the old man explained, that he became an eyewitness to the Nazi collapse. In 1945, he was a 40-year-old Army colonel with the title of "supervisor of nutrition for the armed forces." He was a medical doctor who had specialized in nutrition, and he had previously served in Greece and Russia, supervising the feeding of the Nazi troops. Now he was determined to stay in Berlin to help combat the hunger and famine that would certainly strike the city's three million residents. When Hitler heard that Dr. Schenck was in Berlin, the MD was ordered to the Chancellory.

"I was asked to stockpile food for 3,000 people for 30 days," Dr. Schenck recalled. "I arrived on April 21, driven by a big black Mercedes past various barriers and checkpoints, and finally driven down the Wilhelmstrasse through the Gate of Honor into the Chancellory compound. By mistake, I was first taken into a room in the new Chancellory building that had been Hitler's study."

It was in this and nearby rooms, historians tell us, that Hitler met with his generals, issued war orders, conducted ceremonies, and drafted the secret orders: *Aktion t4* (which authorized the mercy killing of 100,000 elderly, sick, and insane Germans before a protest by the Catholic archbishop stopped the slaughter two years later, in 1943); *Aktion 13f14* (which authorized the killing of 20,000 "anti-state elements," including 2,000 Jews); and the *Endlosung,* Hitler's "final solution" to the Jewish problem—mass exterminations.

It is a sad commentary upon German medicine, Dr. Schenck reluctantly conceded, that Hitler compromised many of his physicians very early in the war. Historians tell us that the first secret killings were of Germans—the old, the sick, and the insane, the ones who could not help Hitler win a war. Hitler wanted to free bed space for his fighting men, and an agency under the supervision of Germany's top government physician, Karl Brandt, MD, was given the general assignment of supervising the killings. A red cross on a patient's hospital chart meant that he was doomed; a blue slash meant the patient would be allowed to live.

The order, cut in 1939 when Germany invaded Poland to begin the European war, involved only passive killing at first. The patients were left to starve in abandoned castles. In short time, however, the Germans had invented "bath establishments for special action," the primitive gas chambers that initiated the SS ritual of killing. By the time Hitler implemented the *Endlosung,* the instruments of death had been greatly refined.

Dr. Schenck ruefully noted that 300 German physicians have been prosecuted for their actions at the concentration camps. One of the few bright spots in medicine's record during the Nazi era, he recalled, was the bold but short-lived protest against Hitler launched by a group of Munich medical students who called themselves the "White Rose Society." After a perfunctory trial, the students and their leader, Hans Scholl, were beheaded.

But as Dr. Schenck stood in Hitler's study on April 21, 1945, he was thinking only of meeting his assignment. Hitler had gone underground on Feb. 1, and he lived in the Fuhrerbunker until his death. But on this day,

Dr. Schenck recalled, the dictator emerged from the bunker to meet in the Chancellory garden with his military officers.

"I looked down from the room where Hitler had dominated and frightened the world, and I saw him meeting with the Nazi high command. Two generals were facing him and listening carefully. Behind the generals stood a circle of lower ranking officers who whispered to each other. I was very close to them, but relieved that I could see only Hitler's back. I was standing in the shadows, and they were standing in the sunlight. Suddenly, the perspiration under my helmet became cold and sticky."

Dr. Schenck had no trouble stockpiling food. "We favored thick, meaty stews, beans, noodles, oatmeal, sausages, and bread. Our supply was nearly inexhaustible. The food was stockpiled throughout the Chancellory, often right next to the ammunition. We lived in constant fear that the ammo, which was also stored outside, would be hit by a Russian shell and explode. Our cooks did their work with helmets on, and most of the people in the bunker would come upstairs to the Chancellory to eat. I do not know why nobody had thought to stockpile food before, but I knew that we had plenty. The war could not last another 30 days."

Dr. Schenck arrived at the Chancellory on the day Hitler threw Dr. Morell out of the *Fuhrerbunker*. The day before, his 56th birthday, Hitler had made his final public appearance, decorating several young German soldiers who had destroyed a Soviet tank.

On April 24, while helping to carry a wounded German soldier down to the bunker operating room, Dr. Schenck met Dr. Haase—who, wheezing with tuberculosis, was operating on the German wounded. Since Dr. Stumpfegger, Hitler's escort surgeon, confined his medical activities to looking after Hitler and since Dr. Morell had been banished, only Dr. Hasse and two nurses remained to deliver medical care to the rank and file.

"I had very little surgical experience," Dr. Schenck said, "but I told Dr. Haase, 'If you need me and if you will be patient with me, I will do my best.' "

Dr. Haase replied, "You will be greatly appreciated."

Dr. Schenck put on a surgical gown and, for the next seven days, he and Dr. Haase performed 350 surgeries, interrupting his marathon schedule for only a few hours' sleep and occasional forages into Berlin for food and medical supplies.

The physician said he was proud of two actions he ordered in his capacity as food supervisor.

"A Berliner came into the bunker one day and asked for flour from the Chancellory's stockpile. He said he was baking bread for the people of

Berlin and giving it away right in the center of the city. I did not believe that there could be a bakery in the rubble of Berlin, so I had to see for myself. He was telling the truth. People would emerge from their basements, dodge Russian fire and shells, and run to this makeshift bakery to grab a loaf of bread. This man got his flour.

"Another time, I was asked to adjudicate a dispute between the SS and the civilian owners of a food warehouse. The SS wanted to confiscate the food for the military; the warehouse owners wanted to give it to the people who were trapped in their homes. As the military's food czar, I ordered that the precious food be kept in civilian hands."

Another decision was less fortunate. "We decided not to destroy our food warehouses," Dr. Schenck recalls, "because, although they might be seized by the Russians, we thought that it was more important that the population of Berlin have food. But in saving the food, we also saved our supplies of alcohol—beer, wine, and spirits. The Russians found the alcohol, and some of the worst Russian atrocities against German civilians happened under the influence of our liquor."

Dr. Schenck's 10-day stay at the "Citadel," the code name for the Chancellory, came to an end when the Russians captured him. He was released in December, 1955, upon the occasion of a visit to Moscow by West German Chancellor Konrad Adenauer.

"At one point (of captivity), I looked like a skeleton," he said. "I was down to 100 pounds (from a normal weight of 160), and I was very weak. But I am an expert on survival nutrition. Actually, you can go 28 days or so without food; it's the thirst that can kill you. Three days without water and you're in trouble. But my greatest danger came when I refused to go to East Berlin to help the Russians set up a nutrition center. All my family and friends were in West Germany, and I did not want to be a communist for the rest of my life. They threatened to shoot me, but they never did."

After his release from imprisonment, Dr. Schenck worked for a German pharmaceutical company and compiled his memoirs of World War II. First written in 1970, the memoirs were published only in German, and only a few thousand copies were distributed in Germany by the publishing house, Nicolai Verlag, near Munich, before the book quickly went out of print. It was titled, *I Saw Berlin Die*.

Dr. Schenck never gave up on the book, however, and, in 1985, Bavarian Connection published a rewritten edition, retitled *1945: As Physician in Hitler's Bunker*. Neither version of the memoirs has ever been available outside Germany. The physician, now retired, described and expanded on them for *AMN*.

His real passion for the past few years, however, has been tracking the remarkable relationship between Hitler and his long-suffering physician,

Dr. Morell, the descendant of French Huguenots who came to Germany to escape persecution. "I had to wade through 15,000 pages on microfilm," the physician said, "and much of it, unfortunately, was irrelevant—Morell's romances, his business empire, the times he prevailed upon the Fuhrer to keep open a favorite restaurant that was failing. But much is also relevant: Hitler's entire medical file has been preserved."

Leafing through the pages of his Morell manuscript, Dr. Schenck added, "It has probably ruined my eyes, but it is worth it. Morell's papers contain very commonplace details that reveal Hitler to have been the poor slave of his medical complaints and not their master. Many of his symptoms were psychosomatic. Almost daily, he complained to Morell about numerous pains. He demanded injections of invigorating and tranquilizing drugs, complained of headaches, stomach aches, constipation and diarrhea, constant colds, insomnia, and many other discomforts. He described every pain very carefully and he complained bitterly."

This first detailed look at his medical file shows that Adolf Hitler—the iron-willed apostle of hate and war who demanded that his troops be "pitiless supermen" and "fight to the last bullet"—himself required constant coddling, and drug injections, to continue functioning.

To Dr. Morell, Hitler was "Patient A." (Later, Italian dictator Benito Mussolini would become his "Patient C.") Dr. Schenck said that Hitler was introduced to the physician by another patient, Heinrich Hoffmann, who was the official photographer of the Nazi era. "Dr. Morell was a urologist with a bent for psychology," Dr. Schenck said. "Hitler's initial complaints were the colitis that had bothered him for years, a mild kidney problem, and a problem with leg injury suffered during World War I. Dr. Morell helped him with all three problems. From that date in 1937 until April 21, 1945, Hitler had absolute confidence in Dr. Morell. Only Hitler could overrule Dr. Morell when it came to Hitler's health, and Dr. Morell was always available for Hitler."

They were an odd couple, the obsessed German chancellor and Dr. Morell, who was fat, homely—and very powerful. "Hitler would make medical demands," Dr. Schenck said, "and, in return, Dr. Morell would ask for favors. He was the vitamin czar of Germany, and at one time he owned 11 drug firms. He built up quite a medical empire, and because of this and his monopoly of vitamins, I did not at the time think very highly of him. I thought he was a quack who was simply building a personal empire."

Hitler and his physician declined together, Dr. Schenck said. "Dr. Morell was always sick. He had chronic kidney problems, was extremely overweight, had high blood pressure, and, under the stress of the war, suffered several strokes. The physician was in worse shape than his patient.

"But he was always available for Hitler. Once, in 1943, he received permission from Hitler to attend his brother's funeral. While he was gone, Hitler developed stomach cramps from his colitis, and he began to scream at his generals. When Dr. Morell returned to headquarters, Hitler screamed at him for not being available. The generals were even more upset with Dr. Morell. But with that exception and the last encounter on April 21, the two got along very well. Dr. Morell wrote in his diary that his relationship with Hitler was 'extremely brotherly.' He described the April 21, 1945, incident this way: 'The Fuhrer got mad at me as never before!' "

Because Hitler refused to be x-rayed or thoroughly examined, Dr. Schenck explained, his physician's primary method of treatment was drugs. "Hitler refused to be treated like other patients," Dr. Schenck said. "He would not, for example, allow compresses to be put on his legs because he refused to undress and be seen in a way that he thought made him look ridiculous or undignified. He would never do anything that he thought was beneath his dignity. He did allow blood and urine tests, and these Dr. Morell recorded as normal."

At 5 feet 10 inches and 150 pounds, Hitler maintained ideal body weight. He neither smoked nor drank, and he stuck to a strict vegetarian diet. Other than head colds, he had no serious infections, indicating a healthy immune system. The son of a peasant family, he had the physical sturdiness of the peasant, and, until the war went wrong, he coped remarkably well with his stresses.

Dr. Schenck said, "Hitler had three major illnesses: the colitis, which probably represented the irritable bowel syndrome and which included constipation and diarrhea; the arteriosclerotic heart disease; and the Parkinson's disease. The colitis had bothered him from before the war, but the heart disease and parkinsonism did not become a problem until very late. Dr. Morell performed an electrocardiogram in December, 1944, that showed evidence of advanced arteriosclerotic heart disease, and the parkinsonism tremors also showed up for the first time in 1944.

"Dr. Morell treated him with drugs for these three illnesses, and he also used drugs to combat his colds, restore his energy, and treat his anxiety/depression/sleeplessness. Hitler's basic treatment was pharmacological, and, by today's standards, the amounts are incredible. But Hitler believed, as did many Germans of the time, in the magic of medicine, and Dr. Morell was glad to oblige him. Of the 92 different medications prescribed for Hitler during the war years, 20 were manufactured by firms owned by Dr. Morell, and of the 39 preparations that went out of use at least a generation ago, 18 were manufactured by Dr. Morell firms. Some of them were used on Hitler before being scientifically tested.

"Hitler was not a drug addict in the strict sense of the term," Dr. Schenck said. "He used many drugs, but he never became addicted to any one, including morphine, which was administered to him 25 times during 1943–44, for his stomach cramps. But he was psychologically dependent upon the *idea* of drugs as magic."

Dr. Schenck answered one rumor. "Hitler did *not* have syphilis, nor did Mussolini. All great men in history are at one time or another associated with syphilis, but Dr. Morell tested both Hitler and Mussolini for syphilis, and the tests were negative."

On seven sheets of paper, Dr. Schenck had summarized every injection and every pill Hitler received from Dr. Morell during the period 1941–45. "During those 52 months," Dr. Schenck said, "Dr. Morell used 29 different kinds of injections (administered intravenously in the arms and intramuscularly into the buttocks) and 63 different kinds of oral tablets and skin applications to treat Hitler. The use went up dramatically after 1943, when the war in Russia began to turn against Germany. Of those 92 different drug treatments, 85 occurred after 1942. During the 28 months of 1943 through April 1945, Hitler had 778 *separate* injections just to treat his colds (21) and to restore his energy (757). That's one injection almost every day. All this was in *addition* to 32 pills for his colds, four for his invigoration, and the daily multivitamin pills made only for him by Dr. Morell. These special pills for the Fuhrer were wrapped in gold paper like chocolates, and he was instructed to take four or six or eight every day."

Dr. Schenck emphasized, "These were the medicines he took just to treat his minor complaints. The serious problems, like the colitis cramps and sleeplessness, required painkillers like morphine and strong barbiturates like Luminol, respectively. For his heart problem, nitroglycerin and digitalis were used. For his parkinsonism tremors, belladonna was the primary drug."

On two occasions in 1942, Dr. Schenck said, Dr. Morell used leeches to treat Hitler's borderline high blood pressure, which occasionally ran as high as 180/100. "At the time," Dr. Schenck said, "leeches were still an honored, effective way to lower blood pressure by lowering total blood volume."

His bunker visit to Hitler still "astonishingly vivid" in his mind, Dr. Schenck concluded, "The drugs did not work." Dr. Schenck offered this breakdown of Hitler's treatment by drugs:

For treatment of his persistent colds: "Dr. Morell treated the colds, including cough, rhinitis, and pain, with codeine (for pain), cocaine (to clear the nasal passages), expectorants, quinine, salicylic acid, and sulfonamids. This was standard treatment for the time, but exaggerated in amount to accommodate Hitler's demands."

To restore energy and to invigorate: "Dr. Morell gave Hitler almost daily injections of multivitamins mixed with glucose and caffeine. He said that these injections did not include Pervitin, a methamphetamine. The special Fuhrer pills included vitamin combinations and, I suspect, on some occasions, Pervitin, the use of which I strongly opposed." Dr. Schenck added, "Back in 1942 and 1943, someone who knew me in my capacity as superintendent of nutrition for the armed forces brought me some of the Fuhrer pills. Handing me the brightly colored pill in the gold wrapping, he said, 'Look how well our Fuhrer is being cared for!' I was suspicious, so I had the pill pulverized and sent the contents to a lab under a special code. The results showed that the mixture included Pervitin. At the time, I thought that Hitler was an addict and that Dr. Morell was keeping him addicted. In a roundabout way, I expressed my concern and a directive came down to me from Heinrich Himmler (head of the SS). 'If you persist in this inquiry,' I was told, 'it will be the end of you.' I did not persist, and today, after reading all of Dr. Morell's papers, I no longer believe Hitler was addicted to Pervitin. Apparently, the contents of the Fuhrer pills were variable, and Pervitin was used only occasionally."

In addition, Dr. Schenck said, "Dr. Morell also tried to restore Hitler's energy by using a hematinic containing iron; organ-extract preparations from the kidney, liver, and prostate; phosphoric acid; and the sex hormone progesterone, to help blood synthesis. The use of progesterone, the phosphoric acid, and the organ preparations are clearly invalid today. While they apparently did Hitler no harm, they were given in incredibly large amounts. The amazing thing is that Hilter never suffered an inflammation or infection from all the injections. Clearly, Dr. Morell was very careful with him."

For colitis: According to Dr. Morell, this was Hitler's most persistent complaint. Both Hitler and Dr. Morell believed that the bacteria in Hitler's digestive tract were not in the proper proportion and that this was the cause of the problem. Hitler would have private conversations with Dr. Morell, alternating between questions about his intestinal bacteria and complaints about his cowardly generals. "In truth," Dr. Schenck said, "he probably had an irritable bowel syndrome, and the stress aggravated it beyond his endurance.

"Dr. Morell prescribed anti-gas pills and 'digestivums' to try to get his patient's intestinal bacteria in order. For the painful gut cramps, he used morphine and papaverine. The drugs, oxycodone or morphine (for pain) and papaverine (an anti-spasmodic), were mixed together and injected in one shot. As soon as the injections began to work, Hitler would talk and work for hours, deep into the night. This led to many of his famous 'Table Talks,' in which Hitler would deliver monologues about his genius in every field. Hitler welcomed this exultant feeling of well-being because the pain was very discomforting.

"Long discussions, difficult decisions, strain, disappointment, and excitement would cause his colitis to flare up. Here was a man who felt he had to agonize over decisions such as whether to level Paris or, as a self-styled art expert, preserve its art treasures. He had the most trouble with colitis in 1943 and 1944, when the Russians took the initiative on the Eastern Front. Hitler had wanted to raze Leningrad and Stalingrad, with their hated names, and turn them into man-made lakes. And yet, toward the end of the battle of Stalingrad, a German soldier was dying every seven seconds. Hitler ordered his commanders to stand firm and fight to the last bullet, but 180,000 Germans were captured and marched off to Siberia. Hitler often complained bitterly to Dr. Morell about the perfidy of his generals, and he was sure his gut would feel better if only he could execute the generals who had betrayed him."

Dr. Schenck continued, "For Hitler's constipation, Dr. Morell prescribed standard laxative medications of the time: Calomel, Leo, Mitilax, Relaxol, Rezinius, and Epsom salts. Bismuth salicylate was used for his occasional bouts of diarrhea.

Dr. Schenck offered another aside that indicates the power wielded by Dr. Morell through his relationship with Hitler: "In the fall of 1944, after Dr. Morell had helped Hitler recover from the July, 1944, bomb attempt made on his life by a minority of disillusioned Germany officers (Hitler suffered only minor injury to his skin and ears, bravely faced the pain, and viewed the episode as another indication that he was protected by Providence), the Fuhrer's physician was confronted by two top government doctors—Karl Brandt and Theodor von Hasselbach. For years, they had suspected that Dr. Morell was drugging Hitler, but since Dr. Morell operated in total secrecy, they had no proof. Now they had uncovered evidence that Hitler was using a digestivum called 'Dr. Koster's Anti-Gas Pill.' It was a nostrum left over from World War I, and they felt that no reputable physician would use it for a patient. They accused Dr. Morell of incompetence. It developed, however, that Hitler himself had prescribed the drug over Dr. Morell's objections. Hitler had used the anti-gas preparation during World War I and believed in it. Drs. Brandt and von Hasselbach were outmatched. They were the two top doctors in the German government, and Dr. Morell, with Hitler's support, ordered their firing. This, however, is an isolated example because Hitler did not usually prescribe drugs for himself. He relied upon Dr. Morell's advice. Shortly after this medical confrontation, Dr. Morell had his second stroke.

For the arteriosclerotic heart disease: "Dr. Morell constantly monitored Hitler's blood pressure and cardiac status, but he had few medications to alleviate the disease. He used Strophanthin, a digitalis-like drug, to increase the force of contraction of the heart muscle. He also prescribed pentylenetetrazol, which then was considered a 'cardiacum' (cardiac stimulant), but which we now know is not true and therefore irrational therapy. He gave Hitler nitroglycerin to be used for 'pressure on his chest,' though Dr. Morell did not say that Hitler ever suffered true angina. Iodine was used to try to treat the narrowing of his arteries. By the very end, Hitler's heart disease had progressed to a point where he might have died of acute heart failure at any time."

For the Parkinson's disease: "Dr. Morell used the standard medication, belladonna drops, to quiet the tremors, and he also used a testosterone derivative, which was irrational. Interestingly, Hitler's tremors stopped for about two months after the assassination attempt on his life in July 1944, but they started again in September, 1944, after a violent argument with *Reichmarschall* Hermann Goering, and increased in severity until his suicide. I believe that at the end the parkinsonism was affecting his mind, too."

For anxiety and sleeplessness: "Dr. Morell used eight different drugs to try to calm Hitler down and allow him to get sleep. They were Brom-nervazit, Luminal, Phanodorm, Profundol, Quadro-nox, schlafmittel, scopolamine, and Tempidorn. Most contained barbiturates (phenobarbital, cyclobarbital, barbital, talbutal, secobarbital) or the now obsolete sedatives bromisoval, cabromal, and phenazone. Scopolamine is still used as an anticholinergic drug, and it also has sedative properties. A few preparations also contained analgesics like phenacetin. None seemed to work to Hitler's satisfaction. Hitler had turned night into day by working until 5 a.m., fitfully sleeping only until 11 a.m., arising, showering, and holding his first military conference at noon, adjourning for lunch at 2:30, meeting again with his generals at 5, working until midnight, and then hosting parties and receptions into the early morning. (His wedding to Eva Braun took place at 3 a.m.) He was always greatly fatigued from loss of sleep, but Dr. Morell could not find a medication that would allow him to get enough sleep to awake refreshed."

Dr. Schenck said that one of his purposes in writing a book about the Morell papers was to obtain comments from other physicians about Hitler's medical condition and care. The first physician to comment was Donald R. Bennett, MD, PhD, an AMA expert on pharmacology and associate director of AMA's Division of Drugs and Technology. In reviewing Hitler's pharmacological treatment, as outlined by Dr. Schenck, Dr. Bennett commented, "The use of narcotics—morphine or oxycodone—to treat the abdominal cramps may have induced or at least aggravated Hitler's constipation. This is a classic pattern that is seen among narcotic addicts. The drug causes constipation, and they often need a laxative to move their bowels.

"The eight sedatives used for anxiety and sleeplessness are way too many," Dr. Bennett said. "The number of dosages is not that remarkable, but the use of this many different sedatives probably means that none was giving adequate relief. The drugs used by Dr. Morell on Hitler are comparable to today's barbiturates and benzodiazepines like Librium and Valium. Dr. Morell used the strongest anti-anxiety and sedative-hypnotic drugs available. Today, a patient like Hitler would be worked up for a differential diagnosis of sleeplessness. This type of sleeplessness might be due to snoring or sleep apnea, anxiety, depression, or schizophrenia.

"My guess is that Hitler had severe depression," Dr. Bennett said, "although some physicians might feel that his insomnia, paranoia, and refusal to take off his clothes for a medical examination might suggest a schizophrenic-like personality or psychotic disorder. In any event the Germans did not have then, as we do now, the major classes of anti-depressant and anti-psychotic drugs. Therefore, a psychiatric evaluation of Hitler based simply on the drugs he took in the early 1940s would not characterize him as having a depressive disorder or being psychotic, even if he was. He likely was a hypochondriac in regard to his personal living habits—he was a lot like some of today's fanatics who overdo in using vitamins or over-the-counter drugs—but there is no pharmacological evidence that he had a psychotic disorder. Also, it's evident that Hitler was either carefully monitored by Dr. Morell or lucky, because he could have had a number of serious adverse interactions from taking all these different drugs.

"The heart condition was undoubtedly aggravated by the multiple stresses he endured," Dr. Bennett added. "Of the people who developed parkinsonism in Hitler's period, many could be traced to post-encephalitic parkinsonism from the flu epidemic of 1918–1919. But, then again, Hitler's case may simply have been of unknown origin. It would not have been caused by the war, but that would have been aggravated by the stress."

Dr. Bennett concluded, "The stress of losing the war almost certainly severely aggravated all his imagined and real diseases. Today's values tell us that losing a spouse is 100 on the stress scale and losing a job is 70. Well, think what it must have done to Hitler to lose the world! The pharmacology doesn't tell us that he was psychotic, because today's anti-psychotic drugs were not available, but knowing the punishment he in-flicted tells us that probably he had at least some kind of a personality disorder."

Dr. Schenck's book about the relationship between Hitler and Dr. Morell also covers the dictator's fears of being poisoned, his conversations with Dr. Morell, his vegetarian diet, Dr. Morell's supervision of the medical care of Mussolini, and Dr. Morell's later, unsuccessful attempts to find Hitler a new physician.

Martin Bormann was in charge of procuring food for Hitler, and Dr. Morell was in charge of preparing it. Hitler trusted both men completely.

Dr. Schenck described Hitler's typical meals: "For breakfast, he ate very sparingly—crisp Swedish bread, with perhaps a little jam, and herbal tea. For lunch he would have raspberry juice sprinkled with flax seeds, a tomato with a little rice, and apricot or spinach pudding; for dinner, orange juice with flax seeds, oat soup (porridge), crispy bread, perhaps with butter, and occasionally an egg yolk on bread. It was a strict vegetarian diet, with few deviations. Occasionally, Hitler would include barley or cucumber soup, potatoes, and fresh cheese with herbs. His professional dieticians, under Dr. Morell's command, always served it up the same: juice or soup, vegetable or potato, pudding for dessert."

Dr. Schenck said that Dr. Morell unsuccessfully tried to persuade Hitler to include red meat in his diet. "Apparently, Hitler always leaned toward a fanatical diet, and after the suicide death of his niece (and love object) Geli Raubal (in 1931), he renounced meat forever. I do not know what the connection might possibly have been. When Dr. Morell used leeches to treat Hitler's high blood pressure, the dictator was fascinated by the sight of his own blood. He told his physician, 'Since you love red meat, I shall prepare you a pudding of my own blood!' Dr. Schenck added that Hitler's diet was perfectly healthy and did not contribute to his need for injections.

"Hitler and Dr. Morell had many private conversations," Dr. Schenck said, "but Hitler never discussed anything of a personal or political nature. He would complain about his generals because he believed that their stupidity was causing his stomach cramps, but he never talked about his private thoughts. Adolf Hitler never had a friend."

He said that there were no medical influences on Hitler other than Dr. Morell because both Hitler and Dr. Morell wanted it that way. Toward the end, Dr. Schenck said, the ailing Dr. Morell was desperately searching for a physician to replace him. "He had a professor in Frankfurt in mind,"

Dr. Schenck said, "but this physician died in late 1944. Dr. Morell would stay until the bitter end."

"Beware of him in whom the urge to punish is strong."

—Friedrich Nietzsche

"No one shall escape his punishment."

—Adolf Hitler

Nietzsche, the greatest German philosopher, went mad in 1889, the year Adolf Hitler was born.

Was Adolf Hitler insane?

Unsatisfying as the answer was, Dr. Schenck was emphatic: "No!"

The physician said, "There is nothing in the Morell papers to indicate that he was treating an insane patient. Furthermore, after Hitler had committed suicide and right before I left the bunker, I had a lengthy conversation with Ambassador Walter Hewel. He was the liaison between the Reich's Foreign Minister, Joachim von Ribbentrop, and the Fuhrer's headquarters, and he was probably Hitler's closest confidant.

"I told Hewel that in my opinion Hitler was a very sick man, at least in the last few months. Hewel contradicted me, saying, 'Hitler was never mentally sick. Never, not even right before his suicide.'

"Hewel knew Hitler very well. For many years he escorted Hitler; he was a guest at the Fuhrer's dining table, and he saw him daily. He told me, 'Even though Hitler may have lost his judgment about what was going on around him and refused to see the growing opposition, he was not mentally sick.'

" 'Until the last moment, Hitler was convinced that the Americans and the Russians would quarrel over Germany. For Hitler, a war between the two Allied powers was almost a reality. Even when Russian soldiers surrounded the Reich Chancellory, Hitler was still waiting for the news that the Americans and the Russians were shooting at each other right above his bunker. He thought that this would save him.

" 'He refused to see the ruins around him. They meant nothing compared with a victory over Bolshevism and the Jewry. Goebbels agreed with Hitler's vision and reinforced him in it. Bormann, as always, stood next to him, smiling. However, Goering and Himmler had their doubts. Goering would laugh aloud at this scenario; Himmler would gnaw his lips.

" 'Hitler was erratic, passionate, uncontrolled, and unable to listen to advice because he was convinced he was chosen by Providence. Those around Hitler studied him very closely and learned how to use his overreactivity to their advantage. He was induced to act without realizing that he was being manipulated. He believed that he was acting on his own.' "

Dr. Schenck said that Hewel also told him, "During the war years, Hitler changed considerably, compared with previous years. Glory and sovereignty gradually left him and wickedness and wildness came more and more to the fore. Mistrust grew. Hitler's suspicions that he was being betrayed grew stronger and stronger, almost like a craze. He was haunted by the thought that the plans Providence had given him would fail because of the betrayal and stupidity of his aides, and yet he did not know to change the situation. At the same time, he began to lose contact with people, because human beings meant less and less to him. Because of this mistrust, the number of faithful people surrounding him became less and less. The German nation and the German people did not mean much to Hitler, except for the soldiers, whom he would personally decorate because they reminded him of himself."

Ambassador Hewel, faithful to Hitler's memory to the end, became one of Hitler's last victims, Dr. Schenck said. "Hewel had only recently been married," Dr. Schenck said, "but Hitler made him promise that he would commit suicide to avoid interrogation by the Russians. Hitler gave him the last distinction conferred by the Third Reich—a cyanide capsule. Hewel showed it to me only hours before we left the bunker to attempt our escape. Later I learned that, when the Russians entered the bunker, Hewel followed his beloved Fuhrer by swallowing the capsule and shooting himself at the same time. A young Russian officer asked, 'Why? It was not necessary. The war is over.' "

And with it the strange saga of Adolf Hitler, who rose from his days as a young man in Vienna, where he wandered the streets a homeless beggar, surviving only by the sale of postcards he painted, through the days when he dodged the draft of the Austrian military, through a furtive trip to England to visit his half-brother, to the days when he gave himself the title *Oberster Gerichsterr,* "Supreme Law Lord." Adolf Hitler literally put himself above the law, and by November, 1942, he commanded an empire that stretched from the Pyrenees Mountains in the West to the Caucasus Mountains in the East. He was the overlord of 15 nations. And his SS troops were taking Jewish prisoners off to death camps whose entry arches bore the ironic words: *"Arbeit macht frei."* ("Work makes men free.")

Dr. Schenck concluded, "Hitler was not insane. He had a political obsession that led him to attempt insane things. The German people followed him because, like Hitler, they believed that they were surrounded by dangerous enemies. Most German people had never been out of

Germany, and they knew little of the outside world. Perhaps, in the television era, Hitler would not have lasted."

But what kind of Providence offers up visions like the nightmare inflicted by Hitler?

The physician had a ready answer: "Stalin in Russia, Franco in Spain, Mussolini in Italy, Idi Amin in Uganda, Alexander the Great, Julius Caesar, Genghis Khan, Napoleon. . . . If we have learned anything from history it is that we have not learned anything. And political leaders can not be explained medically or psychologically."

Did he and the German people know of the Holocaust?

"Well," the physician began, "of course, we knew that there were camps to which the Jews were being sent, and we knew that they would not be coming back from the camps in Poland."

He hesitated, and added, "I had something to do with the nutrition of the camps and I artificially inflated the requirements, so that the inmates would have enough to eat. I defied orders to try to get more food and, if I had been discovered, I would have been in danger."

Dr. Schenck was growing weary. "The Jews probably knew what their fate would be, but the women and children were the real victims. It is a great guilt that will have to be borne by the German people."

The interpreter pointedly interrupted, "This is all you are ever going to hear from a German of Dr. Schenck's generation."

The interview was concluded. Dr. Schenck noted, "Like Hitler's leeches, you have bled me dry."

The physician dug out an old news clip. In a rare interview, Dr. Morell had, while convalescing in a German hospital in May, 1945, told a correspondent from the *New York Times,* "Hitler had the most complicated nature I have ever encountered. I was never able to explain Hitler's personality to my own satisfaction." Dr. Schenck added that he too is not satisfied. Then, smiling across the language barrier, he offered farewell gifts: a box of the finest German chocolates and a recording of his daughter-in-law performing a cello concert.

On this, the second day in Aachen, the fog had lifted and the weather had brightened. Dr. Schenck was anxious to pack and rejoin his wife in Austria. A taxi was outside for his guests.

Ernst Gunther Schenck, Hitler's last living physician, escorted his guests to the door and stepped out into the waiting sunlight.□

Howard Hughes

I used to fantasize about what it would be like to interview the late
Howard Hughes, the eccentric billionaire who inspired so many rumors.

Once, in 1972, while covering an earthquake in Nicaragua, I
arrived in the capital city, Managua, only hours after he had vacated his
rooftop suite at the Inter-Continental Hotel. Later, while covering the
laetrile story in Tijuana, Mexico, I made the acquaintance of a Canadian
character, Andrew McNaughton, who not only was the brains behind
the laetrile operation but who also personally knew both Fidel Castro,
for whom he had worked as an agent against Batista, and Hughes, with
whom he had negotiated some Canadian mining rights. McNaughton's
father had been the commander of the Canadian armed forces and the
son enjoyed privileged entrees around the world. McNaughton said he
might be able to arrange an interview with Hughes, but, alas, the elusive
tycoon died in 1976 before the attempt could be made.

Instead, I found myself trying to cover Hughes' autopsy. Officials at
Houston's Methodist Hospital had steadfastly refused all requests for
interviews, issuing only brief communiques on a topic that intrigued the
world. My case was made for me by an old friend, James R. Hickox,
executive director of the Harris County (Houston) Medical Society. A
story outlining how the hospital had observed medical ethics and
preserved Hughes' passion for privacy would be a public and professional
service, Hickox argued to Methodist President Ted Bowen. Jim also told
the skeptical Bowen, "I believe that the 6,000 physicians in Harris
County will support such a story, and I know that Dennis will report it
with accuracy and sensitivity."

I'm sure that Jim had never polled his 6,000 members on this
matter, but I am grateful that he stuck his neck out for me.

The interview was granted, and pathologist Jack Titus, MD, shared
his official findings. The pressures on Dr. Titus were so intense that he
once jokingly told a colleague, "Sure, I'll tell you what we found. We
opened his chest and it was stuffed with $10,000 bills!" Seriously,
though, Dr. Titus says he has discussed this famous case only with me
and that "my wife knows no more."

For which I thank one of my favorite medical execs, Jim Hickox.

AFTER HIDING OUT for a quarter century to protect his privacy, Howard
Hughes finally returned home to Houston.

And the billionaire recluse probably would have approved of the professional manner and confidentiality with which his medical records and autopsy results were safeguarded by the physicians and staff of Houston's Methodist Hospital.

"Our goal from the start," said Jack L. Titus, MD, the man who performed Hughes' autopsy, "was to keep with traditional medical ethics and assure complete confidentiality. We were determined not to be swayed by the fame of the patient, nor the great interest of the public."

Henry D. McIntosh, MD, chief of the medical service at Methodist, which is affiliated with the Baylor College of Medicine, noted, "Howard Hughes had sought privacy and a life style of secrecy while living; in death, he deserves no less."

In supervising a low-key handling of the details of the death of Hughes, the hospital's staff encouraged press coverage that was generally restrained and professional. Press reports were extensive in their largely pre-written coverage of Hughes' Houston boyhood and flamboyant and eccentric career, but the medical reportage was subdued.

Said Larry Mathis, a Methodist Hospital vice president: "Press coverage was professional and was not sensationalized."

In appraising the hospital's performance, Methodist President Ted Bowen said, "Our major regret is that the patient had died enroute from Acapulco and we were unable to attempt to help him."

During a group interview with *American Medical News,* the four Houstonians stressed:

Hughes, 70, died before his plane reached Houston. Some early press reports had indicated that Hughes was comatose but alive when he arrived.

There was no indication Hughes was in a diabetic coma, as some press reports noted.

Cause of death as determined by an autopsy participated in or observed by eight physicians was "chronic interstitial nephritis with papillary necrosis."

(In a separate statement, the Harris County medical examiner, Joseph A. Jachimczyk, MD, who observed the autopsy, said there was no evidence of foul play. Hughes' toxicological tests were negative, Dr. Jachimczyk said, except for the presence of codeine, "which undoubtedly was used as a therapeutic measure. There's no question the man was in pain."

(Dr. Jachimczyk reported that Hughes was emaciated and shrunken, the body weighing 90 pounds and looking much like a "terminal cancer patient," but that he had no major anatomical abnormalities other than the ravages of chronic renal failure. Hughes had a moustache, goatee, and long hair, Dr. Jachimczyk said, but his appearance was not grotesque.)

Close cooperation between Methodist Hospital officials and the office of the medical examiner of Harris County, Tex., was crucial to protecting the privacy of Hughes' autopsy results. The examiner, Dr. Jachimczyk, said that although Hughes probably would have wished to avoid an autopsy, the situation obviously required one. Had permission not been granted by the next-of-kin, he said, his office would have had to step in and take responsibility for the case. In such an event, he said, the autopsy would have fallen into the public domain and detailed results "would have been available to anyone willing to pay the $15 fee."

Although hospital personnel have reportedly been offered as much as $500,000 to provide a photo of Hughes, the matter is totally out of the question. None was taken of Hughes' outward appearance.

It was 8:30 a.m. April 5 when Dr. McIntosh received a call from the Miami-based Hughes Medical Institute. Would Methodist Hospital please prepare immediately to provide care for the critically ill Howard Hughes?

Methodist is one of 12 U.S. institutions receiving support from the Hughes medical foundation and its selection implies the high regard in which it is held.

By noon, the hospital had assembled a team—Dr. McIntosh, a cardiologist, the chief medical resident, two nurses, several medical specialists, several administrative people, and an emergency care ambulance. Hospital employes, meanwhile, prepared for the imminent arrival of a prominent patient referred to as "J. T. Conover."

Methodist Hospital frequently treats prominent patients, Bowen noted. He added that, "Our top people are experienced in such matters. This experience helped us maintain Hughes' confidentiality."

The craft carrying Hughes touched down at about 2 p.m., but the patient had died at 1:27 p.m., said the two physicians and one aide accompanying the flight.

The team assembled by Dr. McIntosh was not to be able to use its skills to help Hughes.

Dr. McIntosh recalled that he had been told by the Miami center that Hughes was in a diabetic coma. But he warned his team to "make diabetic coma the last condition we suspect, lest we overlook something else."

Hughes' body was taken to the Methodist autopsy suite, where Dr. Titus, chief of the hospital's pathology department, recalled, "we needed to resolve some procedural issues."

Since neither of the physicians accompanying Hughes was licensed in Texas, the state law required that the death be reported through the office of the Harris County medical examiner, Dr. Jachimczyk. An autopsy seemed desirable, but could not be performed without the permission of next of kin. And the next of kin, Houston's Mrs. F. R. Lummis Sr., Hughes' aunt, was not immediately available. The matter was deferred overnight.

Mathis, meanwhile, issued three brief news releases on April 5, noting only the early morning call requesting care; a statement that, "Today at 1:27 p.m. enroute from Acapulco to Houston by air, Mr. Howard R. Hughes expired. Mr. Hughes was enroute to the Methodist Hospital for medical treatment;" and a subsequent announcement that, "Officials of the Methodist Hospital have consulted with Dr. Joseph Jachimcyzk, chief medical examiner, and Dr. Ethel Erickson, deputy medical examiner. Additional information will not be available until consultations with attending physicians are completed sometime tomorrow."

The next morning, permission to perform the autopsy was granted by William R. Lummis, on behalf of his mother, Mrs. Lummis. The autopsy, Dr. Titus noted, was accomplished between 1:30 and 3:10 that afternoon.

Assisting Dr. Titus were two of Methodist's senior pathologists. Also attending were Dr. McIntosh; Drs. Jachimczyk and Erickson of the medical examiner's office; and the two physicians who had flown from Acapulco with Hughes, Wilbur S. Thain, Logan, Utah, and Lawrence Chaffin, Los Angeles.

During his time at Methodist Hospital and during his previous experience at the Mayo Clinic, Dr. Titus had performed autopsies on prominent people. Nevertheless, he admitted to taking extra precautions in connection with the autopsy of Hughes.

Dr. Titus told *AMN* that he and his two colleagues "had a thorough discussion outlining procedures," and then conducted a "complete, routine autopsy, just like the other 400–500 we'll do this year."

Routine, he said, "except for the extraordinary care we took to positively identify the patient." Dr. Titus and colleagues secured formal written statements identifying Hughes from Drs. Thain and Chaffin and the aide who accompanied Hughes, John M. Holmes Jr. Fingerprints were obtained with the aid of the medical examiner's expert; and a full dental chart was taken with the aid of an oral surgeon.

Although Dr. Titus had not yet written his final autopsy report— which will not be released—he said it would probably not differ from the initial gross finding of death by chronic renal disease.

"We paid attention to every detail in developing our provisional anatomical findings," Dr. Titus said. "We made every effort not to overlook anything."

And so the findings were presented to the press that afternoon at 4 p.m. by Bowen and Drs. McIntosh and Jachimczyk. The finding of death due to renal failure was characterized by Dr. Jachimczyk as "an extraordinary man—an ordinary death."

During the press conference, Hughes' body was taken from the autopsy suite to a Houston funeral home. The press conference was orderly and uneventful, Mathis recalls, and ended in about 25 minutes as reporters left to file stories.

The statement released at that April 6 press conference was the last official press release issued by the hospital, the Methodist spokesman stressed.

On April 10, Dr. Titus attended the annual seminar of the Houston Society of Clinical Pathologists and politely refused all requests from his colleagues for additional information. "My wife knows no more," he said.

"Press interest in the case is abating," Bowen said, although he noted that "there have been some outrageous offers for a photo, that kind of thing."

In explaining Methodist's handling of the case, Dr. Titus leafed through the "Code of Cooperation" developed by the Harris County Medical Society to facilitate relations between the medical profession, news media, and hospitals. He then read its section from the American Medical Association's *Principles of Medical Ethics* on protecting patient confidences:

"A physician may not reveal the confidences entrusted to him in the course of medical attendance, or the deficiencies he may observe in the character of patients, unless he is required to do so by law or unless it becomes necessary in order to protect the welfare of the individual or of the community."

By honoring this code, Methodist Hospital and its staff were able to assure Howard Hughes' privacy even in death.□

Howard Hughes was pronounced dead on a plane enroute from Acapulco to Houston. The physician who signed the death certificate was Wilbur Thain, MD, chief of the group of Mormon physicians who alternated caring for Hughes.

For three years, I had been corresponding with Dr. Thain, seeking to persuade him to tell his story of Hughes' medical history. The physician felt that the pending legal battles over Hughes' estate precluded him from talking.

By summer, 1979, I had pretty much forgotten about the idea. While doing a story at the Mayo Clinic in Minnesota, I made a routine call to the office to check for messages. There were four, three of small consequence and a fourth obscurely scrawled down by a temporary secretary. It read: "Call Dr. Thain in Utah."

Howard Hughes' physician had changed his mind, and I was on the next plane to Salt Lake City for a remarkable interview.

ASPIRIN KILLED Howard Hughes, says his physician, Wilbur Thain, MD.

In the only interview he has ever granted to discuss his remarkable patient, Dr. Thain, 54, a Logan, Utah, family physician who specializes in working with retarded children, hypothesized for *American Medical News* Hughes' death three years ago as follows:

"He had become very dehydrated. He was concentrating his urine. He was taking large doses of (an over-the-counter analgesic), up to 20 to 30 tablets a day. The combination of the dehydration and the massive dose of acetylsalicylic acid triggered the renal papillary necrosis that caused his sudden death. The combination of dehydration and aspirin, a fatal combination that only recently has been reported in the medical literature, particularly in studies of Australian arthritic patients, would explain why Hughes had no evidence of renal involvement only five weeks before he died—he had a negative urine—and why his BUN (blood urea nitrogen) was only slightly elevated—creatinine at 1.6—the day before he died. It was previously supposed that the phenacetin in his codeine medication destroyed the kidneys, but the literature does not support such rapid onset by phenacetin alone. The (acetylsalicylic acid) dehydration combination would have proven fatal even if Hughes had never used a single tablet of codeine.

"It was the (aspirin) that killed him."

Hughes, an American original whose passion for privacy created both a public legend and a private enigma, was, in many ways, no less a stranger to his physician.

"I knew him very well," Dr. Thain said. "I should say I was very well acquainted with him. No one knew him well. But, personally, I liked the man very much. This was a man who had a lot of emotion, a lot of feelings for people.

"As a patient, he was totally impossible. Totally. I never saw an x-ray of him until after his death. He wouldn't allow it. But I had a choice of whether to walk away from the man or to do what I could for him under the circumstances. I am not known for walking away from patients. I am proud of what I tried to do for Howard Hughes."

Dr. Thain started to work as a secretary-courier for Hughes in 1948 when he was 23 and a medical student at the U. of Southern California, Los Angeles. He supervised Hughes' medical care during the last three years of the industrialist's life, and he treated him on the flight from Acapulco, Mexico, to Houston's Methodist Hospital, a flight on which Hughes died on April 5, 1976. Dr. Thain pronounced Hughes dead at 1:27 p.m.

In a four-hour interview last month, Dr. Thain said he had decided to discuss Hughes as a man and as a patient because "I want to get this off my chest. I have told these things only to my wife—and my attorney.

There has been so much false information published about Hughes, so much emphasis on his dying as an emaciated old man supposedly bombed out on drugs, that I want to discuss it as I remember him."

Dr. Thain has spent much of the past year-and-a-half in court. First, he was exonerated of charges brought by the federal Drug Enforcement Administration that he illegally had been the sole supplier of drugs to Hughes during the last 20 months of Hughes' life. Last fall, a federal court jury found that Dr. Thain's prescription of codeine for Hughes was therapeutically justified. Then, he was charged along with other Hughes' physicians and aides as being part of a conspiracy to reduce Hughes to a "supplicating dependency." That lawsuit was filed by the Hughes' heirs who have taken over the late billionaire's Summa Corp. Dr. Thain and the aides have counter-sued Summa for breach of contract. That litigation is pending. "It may not be resolved in my lifetime," the physician says.

Beyond the legal fights, he feels he has been misrepresented by the media, most recently in *Empire*, a book written by two *Philadelphia Inquirer* reporters that charges Dr. Thain with being callously indifferent to Hughes' medical needs. The book, in fact, speculates that Dr. Thain might have injected a comatose Hughes with codeine and, thus, caused his death.

Being booked as a common criminal for allegedly illegally supplying Hughes with codeine was a shocking event for Dr. Thain. A Mormon father of four, he is prominent in Utah because of his large family practice, his pioneering work with retarded children, and his close ties to the Hughes organization, not only as the chief of Hughes' four physicians but as the brother-in-law of Bill Gay, retired president of Summa Corp. Speaking slowly and deliberately, with soft voice but hard meaning, the Utah physician makes his points:

"I did not allow Hughes to become addicted to codeine; on the contrary, I cut his dosage from 40 grains a day to five at the time of his death.

"I worked for Hughes from 1948 until my graduation from medical school in 1952. At that time, I declined a job with the Hughes organization and went into private practice. I did not see Hughes again until 1973 in London.

"In 1972, at the request of Bill Gay, I agreed to help Drs. Norman Crane and Homer Clark care for Hughes. I joined Hughes in Vancouver, B.C., but he did not choose to see me at that time. When I saw him the following year in London, I learned for the first time that he was taking up to 40 grains of codeine a day. I told him that in no way was this medically justified and that a therapeutic dosage would be no more than 6 to 12 grains a day.

"He said he would cut back, but, first, he wanted to get through having his fractured hip pinned. Over the next three years, I gradually weaned him off the high doses of codeine. Understand, now, that this man had plenty of reason to be on pain medication. I supplied him with codeine during the last three years of his life and I believe it served a legitimate medical purpose. Hughes had arthritis, he had severe neuritic pain in the neck, shoulders, arms, and chest—the postmortem x-rays revealed his compressed vertebrae fractures and clearly show why he was in pain—and he had the worst teeth you've ever seen. He had been badly beaten up and badly burned in two plane crashes, particularly the one in 1946. His skin was extremely sensitive.

"People cannot in a true sense because addicted to codeine. It is a mild drug. It is metabolized extremely rapidly. As patients develop tolerances for codeine, more and more is required to get the same pain relief, but there is no such thing as a withdrawal symptom. Howard Hughes was not addicted to codeine, but he was taking too much for his own good. The phenacetin in codeine was not doing his kidneys any good, and the codeine was also causing his severe constipation. Toward the end of his life, as he cut back on codeine, his constipation problem cleared up. One reason we were glad to have him on the analgesic was that it enabled him to cut back on the codeine.

"Everything possible was done to help Hughes in his final hours, contrary to the implications in the book *Empire* and elsewhere.

"*Empire* says that Jack Real, an aviator friend of Hughes, called me in Logan, Utah, two days before Hughes' death and told me, 'I don't want to play doctor, but your patient is dying.' I reportedly told Real to mind his own business, since I had a party to go to in the Bahamas. Well, the first word I had that Hughes was in trouble was a phone call I got from Dr. Crane at about 9 p.m. on the night of April 4. I was in Miami at the time. I was scheduled back to regular rotation with Hughes on April 11 and I was prepared to leave the morning of April 5 for a business trip to Ecuador to look at some business properties for Summa. Since I was going to be in Miami, I went to a Saturday night (April 3) charity ball in the Bahamas benefitting a center for retarded children. The night of April 4, I had dinner in my hotel and went back to the room, where I received the call from Dr. Crane saying that Hughes was suddenly very ill and that maybe I should change my plans and fly to Acapulco, rather than Ecuador. I changed my plans and booked the first flight the next morning to Acapulco. Then, at about midnight Real called and said that Hughes had suddenly become very critical and it looked as if he were going to die. It was a shock and a surprise. I had been called to see Hughes in mid-March because he was not eating and drinking, but he put me off and put me off and, finally, fell to sleep without seeing me. But he ate and drank more the day I was there than he had in the previous two days, and I looked in on him as he slept and although he had lost a little weight he didn't look a lot worse than before. I did not hear anything about his being critically ill until that Sunday night, April 4. Real arranged for a plane and I left Miami at 3:30 a.m., arriving in Acapulco at 8 a.m. April 5.

"*Empire* says that the first thing I did was spend two hours shredding papers in Hughes' rooftop suite at the Acapulco Princess. This is absolutely false. I did not shred one thing. I had no papers to shred. Any record of medical or other discussions I had with Hughes I kept in my logs, which I would record after leaving his suite. I walked into Hughes' bedroom with my medical bag, and other than a trip to the bathroom, spent the next four hours with Hughes. We were delayed for two hours, trying to find a non-leaking oxygen tent and a new aircraft. We finally had to convert the aircraft on which I had flown in to fly Hughes to Houston. We left at 11:30 a.m., after the Mexican physician who had seen Hughes advised against trying to take him to a local medical center.

"*Empire* says I gave Hughes an intravenous shot that might have been codeine, although he was in a coma. When I walked into Hughes' bedroom he was unconscious and having multiple seizures. He looked like he was about to die. He was not conscious at all from the time I got there until the time he died. He had lapsed into a coma shortly before Real called me the night of April 4 so he must have been unconscious somewhere from 12 to 16 hours, certainly less than 24 hours. I gave him a shot. I gave him two intravenous shots of Solu-Cortef. We were afraid he might die from cerebral edema. We thought we were dealing with a stroke. I did not inject Hughes with codeine. I never personally gave Hughes a shot of codeine. The autopsy report was mixed, with the first version reporting only therapeutic levels of codeine and a subsequent version reporting up to eight grains. Codeine is liver detoxified and kidney excreted, and since the autopsy found that Hughes' kidneys were shot, it's likely he injected himself with codeine before the coma and was unable to detoxify it normally during 24–48 hours before his death. He was only getting five grains of codeine a day before his death. The codeine did not kill him.

"At no time did the writers of *Empire* try to get in touch with me. There was a short period of time when my phone was unlisted but I could always be reached at the university. It may have been that I would have declined to talk to them, but at least they could have made the effort and said, 'Dr. Thain refuses to comment.' But the press just did not follow up with honest reporting.

"Hughes was not psychotic at any time in his life.

"He was severely neurotic, yes. He was an extreme obsessive-compulsive personality from childhood and he became more so as he got older. He was eccentric and reclusive, secretive to an extreme degree, but he was not psychotic. Howard Hughes may have had some fanciful ideas, but he was not out of touch with reality. He did not have hallucinations or fantasies. He was rational until the day he died.

"Hughes was an impossible patient.

"That's a masterpiece of understatement. He wanted doctors around, but he didn't want to see them unless he absolutely had to. He would allow no x-rays, no blood tests, no physical exams, no referrals. He totally understood his situation and he chose to live the way he lived. Rather than listen to a doctor, he would fall asleep or say he couldn't hear.

"Howard Hughes could have lived any way, anywhere in the world with anybody or anything that he wanted. He chose these things this way because he wanted to.

"When I saw Hughes in the spring of 1973 in London, it was the first time in 21 years. He really hadn't changed that much. He was just older and grayer.

"Let me backtrack for awhile. When I worked for Hughes in medical school, I mostly talked to him on the phone. That's how he liked to do business. But the last two years of medical school, I saw him once a week. I remember him as a tall, skinny man. He was 43 then, always wore a hat. Had a moustache. He was pretty normal then. He had his girls and his flying and his moviemaking.

Even then, he was secretive, a little eccentric. Ate erratically, worked odd hours. He would work two, three nights in a row.

A day staff could not keep up with him, and so Bill Gay, who had just been hired and who was married to my sister, Mary, set up a round-the-clock operations office. Bill hired a lot of young men to staff the operations office. I was one of those part-time staffers.

I worked three nights a week, from 7 p.m. til 7 a.m. the next day. Some nights were busy, others I just studied, though never, it seems, when I had a test the next day. Hughes was a difficult, demanding employer. He was a perfectionist and expected a high degree of perfection from himself and his employes. I remember him as being brilliant, aggressive, eccentric.

"Hughes at this time was very active, very effective. The only thing that would have set him apart from most other 43-year-olds was his secretiveness and the way he shunned crowds. He'd been badly beaten up in his plane crash of 1946, and that's when he started taking pain medication. It was prescribed by Dr. Verne Mason who, along with Dr. Lawrence Chaffin, cared for Hughes after the crash. Hughes almost died. Hughes also had some hearing loss, partially due to his work around aircraft. That's why he liked to use the telephone; he had an amplifier.

Anyway, when I graduated from medical school, I was offered a business job with the Hughes organization. I declined, and Hughes, I understand from Bill Gay, was quite upset. But I wanted to practice medicine. I didn't see Hughes again for 21 years, although Bill Gay kept me informally informed about him.

"Anyway, here I am in May, 1973, seeing Hughes again. We were supplementing his diet with vitamins, and he wanted to know everything about them. That was typical. He wanted to know everything. So I discussed Vitamin B-1 and thiamine with him.

"Hughes looked the same but a lot older. He was 67 then. He had grown a beard, his hair was longer, he had lost a little weight. Was down to about 130. He remembered who I was and discussed where we had met before and all that. He was very alert, very well informed, knew what was going on. You only saw Hughes when he wanted to see you. This day, he wanted to know about the vitamins. His toenails and fingernails were pretty long, he had a bad case of onychomycosis (a disease causing thickening and brittleness of the nails of the fingers and toes) and it hurt like hell to trim them.

"He had hip surgery in London in August, 1973. At that time I was informed about his codeine usage, but he said we'd do something about it after the operation. Hughes went in for hip surgery Sunday afternoon and he was done by Dr. Walter Robinson that night. Dr. Robinson did a beautiful job, the hip healed beautifully. Dr. Robinson didn't want him to, but Hughes signed out that Tuesday and arranged for an ambulance to take him back to the hotel.

"By his own choice, Howard Hughes never walked again. Once, with help, he walked from the bedroom to the bathroom. But only once. That was the beginning of the end for him. We tried everything. The aides got him a walker, a wheelchair. I told him we'd even get him a cute little physical therapist. He said, 'No, Wilbur, I'm too old for that.'

"I never had the chance to pry the top off his head to see what motivated his decisions like this. He just made up his mind he would not walk again, that, somehow, he would be happier if he didn't walk. He would never get his teeth fixed, either: Worst damn mouth I ever saw. When they operated on his hip, the surgeons were afraid that his teeth were so loose that one would fall into his lung and kill him. Hughes' approach was to promise you anything, and then never do it. He was always like that. He was going to get his teeth fixed as soon as he took care of this and that; he would try to walk again as soon as he resumed flying. He had flown a plane again that spring of 1973 and it was one of his best decisions. But he never flew again. And he never walked again. I got so frustrated that I almost quit.

"Two medical things that bothered him from time to time and that he wanted help for were recurrent paroxysmal tachycardia—his heart beat would get up to 200, 240 but would usually respond to carotid pressure—and severe constipation—he had severe hemorrhoids and a rectal prolapse that had to be reduced and he wanted somebody around all the time to take care of this. Dr. Crane used to do it, until Hughes left the country.

"I've often wondered what I might have done differently to persuade Hughes to get the care he needed. He would not accept referrals. He would not see a dentist. He would not see any other physicians. The only outside physician he saw was the British surgical team he had to see and he ran from that as soon as he could. When I saw him in London, I noticed that he had a benign tumor on his head. I thought I might be able to remove it while he slept, but it was firm to the scalp and would have required a plastic surgeon to do a flap rotation to properly close it. He wouldn't go to the hospital, of course.

"He exercised the right all of us have, and that is to choose our destiny. He chose not to have the care he needed.

"Hughes was a real person, with real human feelings.

"This is the sad thing about all the reporting on Hughes, portraying him as a robot. This man had real feelings.

"One of my first assignments for him when I was a medical student occurred when one of his drivers, Ben Carlisle, ran a car into his own daughter. Hughes called me at 2 a.m. and turned the town upside down getting the finest physicians and the finest care for the little girl.

"My wife-to-be Ruth used to get angry because Hughes would always interrupt our dates with some request. Once we had Saturday night tickets to see 'Annie, Get Your Gun' at the Greek Theater. A special occasion. Hughes wanted me, instead, to go pick up Ralph Damon, the president of Hughes' airline, TWA. I missed the play, but later that week I got box seats, the best in the house, to see 'Annie.' He never made any outrageous requests of me and he always compensated for the unusual demands he made of people.

"When I got married after my junior year of medical school, Hughes tried to call me during the ceremony. We were married at my folks' home in California, and Hughes talked to Bill Gay at the house. I figured he wanted to talk me out of the marriage or something, tell me I was stupid. 'How much are we paying Wilbur?' he asked Bill Gay, who told him the amount, $100 a week, great money in those days for part-time work. 'Well, you can't support a family on that,' he said. 'We're giving him $125 a week now.'

"The reason I closed my practice in 1975 and signed a contract with Hughes was because of the medical projects he wanted me to direct. I would have been sort of a buffer between Hughes and his medical institute. He was proud of the institute, but he wanted it to do great things. He always talked about having the institute accomplish something that would do as much for people as did the discovery of penicillin. That's how he put it, he wanted another penicillin. He didn't want research in cancer or heart disease—he thought too much money was already being spent on them. But something in genetics, metabolic diseases like diabetes. And he wanted to set up a Nobel Prize-type of thing. He didn't want the same thing as the Nobel Prize, but something similar to reward and inspire medical research.

"The last year of his life, we would talk about the medical projects and about his earlier life. Hughes talked one day for a long time about his parents, whom he loved very much, and how his father had discovered the rock-bit oil drill. He talked about his flying trip around the world and his movies and his girls. The last conversation I ever had with him he told me how much he had loved Jean Peters and how much he still loved her.

"I strongly encouraged Hughes to leave the Bahamas for Acapulco because in the past everytime he moved it had been an activating influence. If it hadn't been for the kidney failure, Hughes might have lasted for quite some time longer. He was always talking about things he would be doing five, six, ten years down the road."

Dr. Thain has been talking slowly, reflectively. Does he have any regrets? The answer comes tumbling out.

"Sure, sure, I wish I could have treated him the way I wanted. Get him in a hospital, do the proper workup. Fix his teeth, that would have been number one. Then, get him walking. Reduce his pain. I wish I could have treated him just like I would treat any patient in a county hospital who comes in with a broken hip and bad teeth and rundown health."

The outburst is over. Dr. Thain again speaks softly. "Was Hughes happy? Perhaps, at one time. I would not have traded places with him. Was it repulsive to care for him? No, you do what you can. I suppose many patients are repulsive if you look at it in a certain way. Was Hughes pathetic? There was pathos in the man, in all of us, because he had so much more to give. He chose his own destiny but he could have chosen a better option.

"When you never look at yourself, as Hughes never did, I suppose you're not too concerned about your appearance. I never discussed Hughes' appearance with him. He would sponge bathe his body and hair. At the end, he was shrunken, wasted, under 100 pounds, but he was still imposing that tremendous will of his upon things right up until the end. When his kidneys failed in Acapulco, a major medical center—like Houston—was the only hope. But knowing Howard Hughes, he probably would have refused to be placed on a dialysis machine. 'I don't want to be kept alive by machines,' he always said.

"I prefer to remember him the way he was and for the things he did. He gave so much and created so much, and I'm not just talking about designing Jane Russell's bra, if, indeed, he did design it. His supreme love was flying, and he gave so much to aviation. Aviation was his religion. Anyone who doubts his ability should stop sometime at the Smithsonian Institute. He always said he was going to fly again, and then he would walk. People accused him of watching the same movie time after time, but he loved moviemaking. He watched old movies not just for content, but for techniques. He was always going to make another movie. And he revived Las Vegas at a time when it was about to be sucked under.

"He always made his business decisions at the last possible moment—even when I worked for him as a medical student—and I suppose you could second-guess a lot of them. But we shall never see his like again.

"He had a total understanding of his predicament, and there was nothing else he would have done. Knowing what I and my family have been through in the past few years, I don't know what I would do if I had to make over again that 1972 decision to join Hughes. Howard Hughes? A very, very interesting man. Brilliant, irascible, eccentric, human. I don't regret for a moment knowing him, working for him, caring for him. Only the nonsense that followed I regret. But hindsight's always 20–20.

"This I know. He had no one else, and I could not have walked away from him."□

Elvis Presley

It is hard to overestimate the media magic carried in the words, "Elvis Presley." Anything about Elvis is big news.

By late summer, 1979, the news was that Elvis had been a "medical drug addict" and that his drug-induced death had been covered up by the medical profession. These were the charges advanced by ABC-TV on its "documentary" program "20/20." Thrown into the public spotlight was Memphis medical examiner Jerry T. Francisco, MD, who in 1977 had ruled that the King died of heart disease and heart disease alone. Also, by 1979, Elvis' personal physician, George C. Nichopoulos, MD, had been charged with overprescribing drugs for the late singer.

For coroners like Dr. Francisco, controversy is an occupational hazard. It can happen at any time in any place. If a famous person suddenly drops dead or is involved when someone else suddenly drops dead, the coroner in that city is going to be thrust into the public spotlight. Some coroners relish the role; others deplore it.

Dr. Francisco is in the middle. Immediately after Elvis died in August, 1977, Dr. Francisco attributed the death to heart disease, with drugs being neither a primary nor contributing cause. However, the medical examiner did painstakingly point out that Presley's autopsy showed traces of 11 different drugs. The "evidence" upon which ABC-TV would two years later base its exclusive report was actually divulged at the time of death by the coroner who alone has the official responsibility to determine a cause of death.

The controversy surfaced two years later because of a dispute between doctors. Nine physicians participated in the Presley autopsy, one of the most thorough ever conducted by Memphis' Baptist Hospital. By orders of the Presley estate, the autopsy remains sealed, but, apparently, some of the physicians disagreed with Dr. Francisco's interpretation of the factual findings and opted for a death by polypharmacy, or drug overdose. The implication is that this line of reasoning is contained in the sealed autopsy. The news media pounced on the story.

Dr. Francisco, however, the man who alone had the ultimate responsibility to look at the totality of the record and pronounce a cause of death, remained unruffled. To clarify his finding, he sat down with me and provided this factual and reasoned explanation of a circumstance that the media did not want to accept:

Sure, Elvis was abusing prescription drugs, and this didn't help him, but it doesn't mean that the drugs killed him. Millions of Americans, including some of those in Elvis' entourage, abuse drugs at a much higher level and are still living. Ironically, some of Elvis' friends who said drugs killed the singer also admitted that their own drug habits dwarfed his.

Dr. Francisco probably could have sidestepped the controversy merely by listing drugs as a "contributing cause" of death. But, as he explains, "Medical examiners do not deal in speculations. We deal in science. I have my own reputation to protect without worrying about somebody's else's reputation . . . I feel very comfortable with my decision."

"Autopsy—Inspection and dissection of a body after death, as for determination of the cause of death; postmortem examination."

IT IS ART, as well as science, the autopsy. There are findings and there are interpretations.

Jerry T. Francisco, MD, a board-certified specialist in forensic pathology, has been analyzing autopsies for 23 years, and he takes a historical view.

"The autopsy dates from the British coroner system," Dr. Francisco patiently explains. "William the Conqueror brought it to Britain back in 1066. In the early days of Britain, the only purpose of the coroner was to distinguish for the Norman king the death of Saxons from the death of Normans. If Saxon, nothing more need be done. If Norman, the king would extract a tribute from the villagers where he died. The British coroners have evolved to our current system of medical examiners. . . ."

For Dr. Francisco, medical examiner of Memphis, Tenn. (Shelby County), since 1961, the "Norman" in this case is Elvis Aaron Presley, but as tribute some people seem to want Dr. Francisco's head.

It has been two years since Elvis collapsed and died at age 42 in his Memphis mansion, and his memory lives on to make money for countless entrepreneurs.

Within hours of Presley's death, it was Dr. Francisco who told a press conference that death was due to "cardiac arrhythmia of undetermined cause." Two months later, he concluded his investigation by describing the death as "HCVD associated with ASHD," hypertensive cardiovascular disease associated with atherosclerotic heart disease.

At that time, he acknowledged to a press conference that autopsy toxicological studies indicated the presence of up to 11 drugs in the singer's blood, but stated that, "Elvis Presley died of heart disease and prescription drugs found in his blood were not a contributing factor. . . . Had these drugs not been there, he still would have died."

Last month, when Elvis' personal physician, George Nichopoulos, MD, was charged by the Tennessee Board of Health with improperly prescribing 5,300 pills for Presley in the seven months before his death, and when ABC-TV charged on its "20/20" news broadcast that Elvis was a "medical drug addict" and that his drug-induced death had been "covered up," Dr. Francisco held a third press conference. Presley died of a weak heart not a drug overdose, the medical examiner repeated.

The combination of the charges against Dr. Nichopoulos and the allegations of cover-up against Dr. Francisco have had their effect. Although everyone wants to "let the man rest in peace," a change in public attitude seems to be setting in. Bartenders know it. Cabdrivers know it. Real estate agents know it. *Everything points to drugs.*

But does it, really?

Because of the exceptional interest in Presley and the everyday issues posed to medical examiners, Dr. Francisco gave the only interview he has ever granted to discuss the Presley autopsy to *American Medical News.* His views are these:

Presley died of heart failure and heart failure alone. "This is based on the totality of the medical record—Elvis' medical history, the detailed autopsy, including the toxiocological findings, and the circumstantial evidence at the death scene."

Drugs were present, but neither caused nor contributed to death. "There is no proof that the level of drugs found in his blood would cause death."

Restrictive Tennessee laws regarding medicolegal cases preclude an open discussion of the case. "In Shelby County, an autopsy can only be ordered by the county district attorney, although the county medical examiner can recommend one. The DA can order an autopsy only if he suspects a homicide or foul play. None was suspected in Presley's death. Had not the family requested a private autopsy, it is unlikely there would have been one at all."

The crux of the current controversy is that Dr. Francisco's medicolegal finding is based partially on a private autopsy protected by confidentiality statutes. Dr. Francisco offers here his reasoning for a finding of heart failure, but disbelievers claim the suppressed autopsy argues for death by drugs, or "polypharmacy."

To many, the cause of death is irrelevant. Nothing can bring Elvis back. But a principle is involved. In many ways, Dr. Francisco's dilemma is common to all medical examiners bound by a law as pro-privacy and anti-autopsy as the one in Tennessee

For a medical examiner, it is Catch-22. Dr. Francisco is in many ways a victim of circumstances. First, the Presley family, for reasons all their own, ordered a private autopsy through the singer's attending physician, Dr. Nichopoulos. (A rumor that would later surface claims that the late Vernon Presley feared his son had been poisoned and that he was actually relieved to find only prescription drugs in the body.)

Since the singer's death was sudden and the medically unattended body was found dead, the death was a medical examiner's case. By statute, the medical examiner, Dr. Francisco, would have to pinpoint a cause of death—only one cause—but the crucial evidence to that determination, the autopsy, was entirely out of his control.

That is the law—then and now.

The bare outline of Presley's death is summarized in Dr. Francisco's "Report of Investigation by County Medical Examiner," a single-page public document that entrepreneurs have, astoundingly, hawked by the thousands to fanatical fans of the entertainer.

Presley was found dead in the bathroom of his Memphis mansion by a female companion, Ginger Alden. It was 2 p.m. on Aug. 16, 1977. At 3:30 p.m., he was pronounced dead by Dr. Nichopoulos, who, with the family's consent, requested an autopsy. The Memphis Police Dept. was notified at 3:30 p.m., and promptly began its investigation. Dr. Francisco was attending an educational seminar at the time of death, but his office was notified by 4 p.m. At the request of the family, the body was taken to Memphis' Baptist Hospital for autopsy. Dr. Nichopoulos' report to medical investigators of conditions for which Presley was under treatment stated "hypertensive cardiovascular disease/colon problems."

At 5:30 p.m., some 30 people gathered under tight security in a room at Baptist Hospital to conduct the "most meticulous autopsy this hospital has ever done. I doubt if a single hair on Presley's body was lost." There were 10 physicians participating in the procedure, including eight Baptist Hospital pathologists under the direction of E. Eric Muirhead, MD, plus Drs. Nichopoulos and Francisco.

Both Dr. Francisco and spokesmen for Baptist say that relations between the hospital and medical examiner's office have always been smooth. The hospital and Dr. Francisco's office are within a block of each other in Memphis' medical center.

"The hospital contacted me," Dr. Francisco said, "and we agreed that because of the crowd forming outside Baptist and the danger in trying to bring the body across the street to my labs, the autopsy would be performed at Baptist. Furthermore, I do not see how that without bending the law I could have taken control of the autopsy and/or requested the district attorney to take control of the autopsy. There was no suspicion of foul play.

"I decided that I would instead, participate in the Baptist autopsy, make sure that it was performed correctly, and use the autopsy findings as part of my record in determining the cause of death and completing the medical examiner's report."

The autopsy was concluded within three hours. "The pressure for some sort of statement to the press was incredible," Dr. Francisco said, "and the autopsy team decided that it was my role to be the spokesman. With their knowledge, I said that based upon the results of the gross autopsy, the death was due to 'cardiac arrhythymia of undetermined cause.' "

Explanations from this point on become blurred.

Officially, only Dr. Francisco is empowered by law to sign a medical examiner's report and a death certificate.

In October 1977, Dr. Francisco listed death as natural due to hypertensive cardiovascular disease. Contributing cause was coronary artery disease. He signed the death certificate (under Tennessee law, a death certificate is a private document for 50 years and then it becomes a public record).

At that time, Dr. Francisco held a press conference to explain his determination of cause of death. The detailed toxicological reports, he said, detected as many as 11 prescription drugs in Presley's blood, but these were not related to the cause of death. A weak heart—period—killed the singer, the forensic pathologist concluded.

Officially, that should have been the end of it. But the doubts persisted. Two years ago, the *Memphis Commercial Appeal* published portions of a contraband copy of a report of one of five laboratories involved in the autopsy. "Near toxic levels of drugs reported in Presley's blood," said the headline.

Last month, ABC-TV apparently obtained the lab report. The network's documentary charging a "cover-up" of a drug-induced death consisted of five elements:

The drug levels reported two years ago by the Memphis newspaper were again reported; the laboratory in question, Bio-Science of Van Nuys, Calif., states that it always stands behind its findings, although it specifically refused to discuss the Presley case; various Presley intimates told stories of how the singer abused drugs; a former Baptist hospital pathology resident, Noel Florendo, MD, who was present at the autopsy, stated that the gross autopsy did not in his opinion indicate severe heart disease; and two "expert witnesses" concluded from toxicology data alone that the drugs in Presley's blood had proven fatal.

A sixth element that gave the show added impact was the accusation of Presley's physician, Dr. Nichopoulos, with indiscriminate prescribing of pills in the seven months before the singer's death.

Both the newspaper story and the television show strongly implied that the autopsy team at Baptist Hospital did not agree with the findings of the medical examiner, but was by law precluded from explaining why.

Unraveling the story is somewhat like Plato's description of interpreting the shadows on the wall of a cave.

On the one hand, Dr. Francisco discussed at length—and for the first time anywhere—his findings for heart failure.

On the other, Baptist Hospital says it is bound by law to respect the privacy of the autopsy. The drug labs used as consultants by Baptist—Bio-Science and its two sub-contractors, the forensic toxiocology lab in the Orange County (Calif.) coroner's office and the Center for Human Toxicology Studies in Salt Lake City, Utah; the lab at Memphis' Methodist Hospital; and the forensic toxicology lab at Memphis' U. of Tennessee Center for Health Sciences—are bound by consultant-client privacy agreements.

Only the executors of the Presley estate, essentially his ex-wife Priscilla Presley, can release the autopsy for discussion. Attorneys for the estate say this is not going to happen. Meanwhile, ABC-TV has filed suit to open the autopsy to public scrutiny. The Tennessee Board of Medical Examiners, which on Nov. 7 will hear the charges brought against Dr. Nichopoulos by the state board of health, could seek a court order to see the autopsy. Many say, "Everything is going to come out in the open."

So be it, says Dr. Francisco. The 46-year-old pathologist is the only medical examiner Shelby County has ever had since the state abolished the old coroner system and in 1961 approved a post-mortem examination law. For 18 years he has been the Shelby County medical examiner; for the past nine years, he has also served as the Tennessee chief medical examiner, a salaried position.

His roots are as deep in Tennessee as those of Elvis: born in Huntingdon, Tenn., medical school at the U. of Tennessee Center for Health Sciences, Memphis, and internship and residency at the City of Memphis Hospitals.

"I am not involved, and never have been involved in a cover-up," Dr. Francisco said. "I have my own reputation to protect without worrying about somebody else's reputation."

Wherever Elvis is involved, motives are suspect, but even Dr. Francisco's doubters say it is unlikely "he would cover up for his mother." Some imply, however, that he is mistaken about his finding of a fatal heart attack.

"OK," the forensic pathologist says. "Let's look at the entire record, the totality of the record upon which I base my decision.

"First, there was cardiac hypertrophy. The heart was enlarged to double its normal size. There was severe coronary artery disease. The arteries were 60% clogged. In reviewing his (Presley's) medical records, I found a pattern of abnormal electrocardiogram readings.

"Second, he had a history of high blood pressure, as much as $^{16}\%_{110}$. He also was treated over the years for diabetes, depression, insomnia, overweight.

"Third, the circumstantial evidence. This was a sudden death. His body was found in a flexed position in the bathroom. There was a pressure point upon the side of his head. Had he died of drugs, the body would have first gone into a coma and it would have most likely been found in a comfortable, reclining position. Had he suffocated by falling into the bathroom carpeting, the pressure marks would have been on the nose and chin.

"The evidence of cardiovascular disease found in the detailed autopsy, the medical and family history disclosed in the medical charts—his mother died at 42, too—and the circumstantial evidence all point to a heart attack.

(Speculations abound as to what might have triggered the fatal attack, but Dr. Francisco says, "We do not know. It could have been many things. Medical examiners do not deal in speculations." One speculation is that an anxious Presley, worried about the concert tour he was to begin the day he died, was fasting to get down his weight. The fasting, combined with a history of constipation, might have led to "straining at stool" and stress on the heart. A valid basis for such a hypothesis, Dr. Francisco said, can be found in the medical literature.)

"As for the drugs, there were four drugs found in significant or therapeutic concentrations (expressed as micrograms per 100 milliliters of blood); Ethinamate, or Valmid, 100 micrograms; methaqualone, or Quaalude, 600; codeine, 100; and unspecified barbiturates, 800. Four drugs were found in trace levels; chlorpheneramine, an antihistamine often used to control hay fever; Demerl; Valium; and morphine, which may have metabolized from the codeine.

"Based on my study of the toxicology reports from the five labs, I believe these eight drugs were present. The Bio-Science report also reported 500–700 micrograms of ethchlorvynol, or Placidyl, and specified three barbiturates—pentobarbital, butabarbital, and phenobarbital—at a level of 1,940 micrograms.

"Even assuming the highest concentrations, it is my opinion, sup-

ported by advice from two forensic pathologists and three forensic tox-
icologists with whom I consulted, that these drugs neither caused death
nor contributed to death.

"He died of heart failure."

The medical examiner's critics are pushing for a finding of a drug-
induced death. Interpreting the toxicologal numbers is complex.

One thing can be said with certainty. There is no possible medical
indication for the number and levels of drugs found in Presley's body. The
AMA Dept. of Drugs says that any patient using these 11 drugs—all
central nervous system depressants—clearly has a drug abuse problem
and is putting his health at risk.

But did this list of drugs kill Elvis Presley?

Probably not, informed sources say. The reason, ironically, is the
tolerance undoubtedly developed by Presley, who for almost two decades
reportedly abused prescription drugs.

Forensic toxicology, like forensic pathology and forensic psychiatry, is
art as well as science. Estimates for lethal doses of prescription drugs can
vary widely, a hundredfold in some cases, even without the factor of
tolerance.

For the five drugs found in significant levels in Presley's blood, the
breakdown would be as follows: Valmid at 100 micrograms is well within
the therapeutic range of 500–1,000, furthermore, it almost never occurs
in lethal concentrations. Quaalude at 600 micrograms is near the
therapeutic range of 500 and below the lethal dose of 2,000 (source for
this and others is the Southwestern Institute of Forensic Sciences Toxicology Laboratory consulted by Dr. Francisco); the barbiturates at either
800 or 1,940 compare with a therapeutic range of 2,500 for slow-acting
agents to 400–870 for the intermediate agents and a lethal range of 7,500
for the slow-acting to 3,000 for the intermediates (two of the barbiturates
identified by Bio-Science are slow-acting and one is intermediate); Placidyl
at 500–700 compares with a therapeutic level of 200 and a lethal level of
10,000.

The principal offending drug appears to be codeine, which at 100
micrograms is 33 times the therapeutic dose of 3 and one-fifth the lethal
dose of 500. A key potential synergistic agent—alcohol—was apparently
seldom used by Presley, and was not in his blood at death.

Theoretically, the high levels of codeine, ethchlorvynol, and barbiturates, all CNS depressants, could interact to induce death.

This was the interpretation advanced on ABC-TV by two physicians,
Cyril Wecht, MD, Pittsburgh, Pa., and Matthew Ellenhorn, MD, Beverly
Hills, Calif. Both physicians—Dr. Wecht is a board-certified pathologist

specializing in forensic pathology and Dr. Ellenhorn an internist specializing in clinical pharmacology—had access only to the toxiocology reports. Both said the drugs Bio-Science reported to be in Presley's body could kill.

In a one-hour special show alleging a medical examiner's cover-up in Tennessee, ABC-TV produced only three professional witnesses: Dr. Wecht, Dr. Ellenhorn, who, ABC says, was paid a fee to render an opinion, Dr. Florendo, who now refuses to discuss the case, saying, "My role in the autopsy, really, was rather limited."

The rest was subjective footage outlining how Presley abused drugs. That abuse—and the tolerance it built up—is, ironically, the factor that leads many to think the drugs did not kill the singer.

One physician-toxicologist said, "If the case went to court with the autopsy findings as outlined by Dr. Francisco, the medical examiner would win hands down. If only one choice can be made, heart failure is that choice."

Fueling the controversy is the unavoidable implication that the Baptist Hospital autopsy team, headed by Dr. Muirhead, opted for polypharmacy. Dr. Francisco said, "I understand why many people are upset about the number of drugs found in the blood. But the medical examiner is neither concerned with lifestyle nor compelled to comment on drug abuse. He is concerned only with cause of death. I accepted the findings of the autopsy—the factual material—but I did not necessarily accept the interpretation of the autopsy—the opinion.

"It is my responsibility to decide the cause of death. I made that decision based upon my education, experience, and ethics. The autopsies I have done are in the thousands, the drug deaths in the hundreds. Sure, anything can happen. The drugs could have killed him. Bananas can cause cancer. That's a little strong, but when you're obligated by law to take the responsibility for making your best judgment, you look at the entire record. You look very carefully.

"I feel very comfortable with my decision."

Dr. Francisco has been through it all before. "When Martin Luther King was killed back in 1968," he said, "I handled the investigation. There were people who refused to believe he'd been shot, although the bullet holes were there to see. Some people refused to believe it was really him. I learned a long time ago that I do not have the ability to convince everybody of everything I do.

"The Presley case proves two things: medical examiners are always going to be in the public spotlight and they are always going to be second-guessed."

For eighteen years, Dr. Francisco has stood for election by the Shelby County Quarterly Court to one-year terms as county medical examiner.

He plans to run again.

He is paid $1 a year.□

"What is it now you want to interview me about?" the physician asks impatiently.

As if George C. Nichopoulos, MD, widely known in Memphis as "Dr. Nick," did not know. He had just been cleared in a criminal trial of overprescribing prescription drugs for his late friend and patient, Elvis Presley. Earlier, he had undergone the same ordeal in a civil hearing.

Dr. Nick does not like to talk to the press. The interview would probably never have happened had it not been for a positive recommendation from Hadley Williams, executive director of the Tennessee Medical Assn. For months, Dr. Nick had neglected to return my calls. "You can at least pick up the phone and call the man," Hadley reasoned with his medical-society member.

And, now, the reluctant physician is about to begin an interview.

Or, is he? At first, the answers come grudgingly, in a soft voice that is hard to follow. Four years after Elvis' death, Dr. Nick is still finding it hard to discuss his patient.

THE PHYSICIAN IS summoned by his patient. The patient sits on a sofa in his dressing room. In minutes, he will take the stage for a concert. Seated next to him is his father.

The physician is asked again if he will turn over the drugs the patient wants. The physician slowly shakes his head.

At this point, Elvis Aaron Presley produces a pistol and wrapping his arm around his father's leg, points the weapon at the leg of the sofa. Can he have the drugs? George Constantine Nichopoulos, MD, again shakes his head.

Presley pulls the trigger, the bullet ricochets off the sofa, careens around the tiny room, and slaps against the physician's chest. Next to his heart. The bullet, however, is spent.

The singer laughs and treats it as a joke. Vernon Presley is silent. Dr. Nichopoulos tells his patient, "Elvis, you're displaying some pretty poor judgment. You know your Daddy just had a heart attack and he can do without this kind of nonsense. And so can I."

The singer's comeuppance is delayed, however. The music strikes up and Elvis is due on stage. His fans are screaming for the King. Smiling, the man who influenced a generation goes out to meet them.

It is 1981, five years later, and Dr. Nick, as he is widely known, is granting a rare interview. On a gray November morning, he has come to his small office at The Doctors' Group building in Memphis, Tenn.

He is on call this weekend, covering for his colleagues in an internal-medicine partnership. He has just resumed the practice of medicine after being acquitted last month on 11 counts of criminally overprescribing addictive drugs to Presley, country-western singer Jerry Lee Lewis, and seven other patients.

In 1980, he had been investigated on basically the same charges by the Tennessee Board of Medical Examiners. At that hearing, the physician was found guilty of overprescribing prescription drugs for Presley and nine others, but innocent of similar charges for 10 others, and blameless of charges of unethical conduct and malpractice on each of the 20 counts.

For two solid years, the life of George C. Nichopoulos has been pure hell. The Elvis Presley tragedy has tarnished the reputation of the singer's physician.

It has done so unfairly, argues one of Dr. Nichopoulos' strongest supporters, the Rev. Nicholas Vieron, pastor of Memphis' Annunciation Greek Orthodox Church. Father Vieron, who attended at least part of every day of Dr. Nichopoulos' five-week trial, has stopped by to cheer up his parishioner.

"This is something so unique in my ministry," Father Vieron said. "I've never encountered someone—as Dr. Nick was—so unjustly indicted for a crime. I dare say that every person who knows Dr. Nick personally would discover he is a compassionate man . . . all his patients, all his colleagues. The reason I believe in him is simple. The word that best describes Dr. Nick is 'compassionate.' I cannot believe that this physician would intentionally do anything wrong.

"There is nothing heroic about my support of him, because I know what kind of a man he is . . . I am simply hurting for someone who is hurting."

Dr. Nichopoulos looks as if he needs all the friends he can get. While letters of support stack his desk and while Father Vieron is voluble in the defense of his parishioner, Dr. Nichopoulos even now—more than four years after Presley's death (on Aug. 16, 1977)—has trouble coming to terms with it. Or talking about it.

The physician's office is crammed with books. On one wall is a needlepoint design of the staff of Aesculapius, done by a grateful para-plegic patient. Above it and almost unnoticed is a small mirror with the likeness of a young Elvis Presley. A patient gave him that, too. A small crack in the class cuts across the singer's face.

Dr. Nichopoulos has a great shock of silver hair, but he is small and shy. He takes a phone call for an orthopedic consult and the voice is firm and strong. But when he returns to the discussion of Elvis and his role in the singer's care, the words come softly—and slowly.

"Elvis was always a difficult patient, whether he was on drugs or not. Sometimes he would act like a little boy, like that night in Asheville, N.C., when he fired the pistol, and you would have to treat him like a little boy.

"That afternoon, he'd been to a dentist's office and he'd seen all these drug samples in a drawer. Now, Elvis knew a lot about drugs. He had his own copy of the *Physician's Desk Reference* and he always said he would have liked to have been a doctor. Well, he got to chatting with the dentist about how this drug was for this and that drug was for that, and asked if he could have some samples. I guess the dentist wanted to impress Elvis, so he said, 'Sure.'

"When I found out, I took the samples away. I told Elvis that there was no way that I was going to be on tour with him to supervise his drug use and allow him to have his own supply. There was no way this batch of drugs could have been of use to him, anyway. Well, he didn't like it, and I guess he wanted to let me know. After the concert, I chewed him out. It wasn't the first time I had to confront him about drugs, and it wasn't the last.

"Did he listen? That's a tough question. I talked to Elvis about drugs and his health for hours, days, weeks, months, years. What he would do would depend upon his moods, pressures, circumstances of the time. Sometimes, he would say, 'Sure, Doc, you're right.' Then a few hours later he'd be up in his plane off for another city. And other drug suppliers.

"Listen, I'll tell you the difference between me and other doctors Elvis saw. The others would say, 'Here's this bottle and this bottle and this bottle.' Elvis could take as many pills as he wanted. I was trying to regulate his drug use.

"He was addicted to prescription drugs when I became his doctor (in 1965), and my hope was to gradually win his trust and wean him off the drugs altogether. I would tell him, 'Now, this envelope has three pills for this, and that one has two pills for that. You take these only and nothing else.' Did he listen?

"Sometimes.

"Oh, I tried every trick in the book. I tried to expose him to every top-notch doctor I knew, to let them advise him. Twice, I had him detoxified. Well, really once and a half. One time he was in the hospital for something else and I figured that as long as I had him in a controlled environment, why not make the best of it? Have you ever played blackjack and insured your bet? Well, that's what I tried to do with Elvis. I tried to have him detoxified, but it didn't take.

"I had some top psychiatrists talk to him. I think Elvis could have been helped by a good one. He was under a lot of pressures and he was a very complex man. But the minute Elvis found out he was talking to psychiatrists, that was the end of that. He refused to talk to one. Elvis and I had a lot of long talks and he would confide in me sometimes about what was bothering him. Sometimes, I think I know what troubled him, but no, I'm not going to discuss it."

Dr.Nichopoulos is wearing a gold tie pin with the letters, "TCB."

"That's for 'Taking Care of Business,' " he says. "Elvis gave all the men 'TCB' pins and all the women 'TLC' pins for 'Tender Loving Care.' Only recently, I've started wearing mine again."

The physician's medical business is in a shambles. The two years with the threat of losing his medical license have taken their toll. As he talks, he nervously drums a fingernail clipper against his desk. He frankly admits to his dilemma.

"Everything I have is mortgaged. My home, my cars (one, a Mercedes, a gift from Presley), my property. My legal bills are $300,000 and I had to mortgage everything to borrow the money from the bank. The notes are due Jan. 1. (His loans of $280,000 from Presley also are being repaid.)

"Being acquitted is great, but the trials have affected my health. My blood pressure is up, and I'm on medication. I have trouble sleeping. Father Vierno thinks that practicing medicine is my salvation, that taking care of patients will get my mind off things. All my patients, all my colleagues have been very supportive. But that's only the people who talk to me.

"When I make hospital rounds, I always wonder what other patients are thinking, what other nurses, other physicians are thinking. It weighs on my mind. A lot of physicians will give you a pat on the back, but when the chips are down, they run for the hills. I guess, in some ways, I can't blame them. They're afraid to get involved. And all they've heard is the bad news.

"Five testified against me in the criminal trial. All they knew was what the prosecution told them. You have to wonder how many more out there believe the same charges.

"Sure, I'm bitter about ABC-TV and its 20/20 program (which, in 1979, charged that drugs killed Presley, that Dr. Nichopoulos had prescribed those drugs, and that there had been a "medical coverup" of the death, which Shelby County Medical Examiner Jerry T. Francisco, MD, ruled was caused by only heart disease).

"It's funny, but when state officials suddenly ordered their audit of prescribing patterns in Tennessee, there was only one physician in all of Memphis who was audited. Me. I think the other cities were added on to make Memphis appear legitimate. Whether it was meant to or not, that sudden investigation sure played into the hands of ABC-TV.

"Now that everything's over and I've been acquitted, some of my friends are urging me to sue ABC. I don't know, I'm still up in the air about what to do. Perhaps, I might, if an attorney would take the case on a contingency basis. If there's one thing I do not need, it's another bill from an attorney.

"Some people tell me I need a vacation. But I wouldn't want to be off somewhere trying to relax and spending all my time worrying about how I'm going to meet my financial responsibilities. 'Go away,' they say. But you can't get away from yourself."

The adverse publicity has deeply hurt Dr. Nichopoulos, 54, a graduate of the Vanderbilt U. School of Medicine. And the media barrage continues, even after his acquittal.

"This morning, some bearded guy from West Germany showed up at my office door with a camera crew and everything. Said that Elvis is very big in Europe and he had to talk with his doctor. Well, I know that Elvis is big in Europe, but it's so hard to get the facts out. So much trash has been said about Elvis."

Communicating the complex story is difficult, Dr. Nichopoulos admits.

"I felt that I did a very poor job during my 1980 trial before the medical board. Had the criminal trial been held first and had I been acquitted, I'm sure the medical board thing would have been forgotten. As it worked out, it was double jeopardy.

"But I just couldn't do a good job before the medical board. It was an open hearing and it was like a circus. All those TV lights, all those cameras clicking—you couldn't hear yourself think.

"I'm sure if I could do it over again, I would be totally cleared. I would make my points much better that I was trying to wean Elvis off drugs, that prescriptions written did not equal prescriptions taken. I would have been much stronger in outlining my treatment strategy. But I was treated fairly. My record keeping was inadequate. It hurt to have my license suspended (for three months) and to be put on probation (for three years). Once, I called one of the medical board officials to ask about some aspect of my probation and he asked me, 'My God, what are those people in Memphis trying to do to you?' Sure, some people were out to get me."

Dr. Nichopoulos continues. "The trouble with keeping records for Elvis was that everybody wanted to see them. We had to keep his medical charts in a locked safe and even then, there were attempts to steal them. Remember, this is a patient who, when hospitalized, had people fighting over his blood samples, his urine bottles, even slides of his fecal matter."

During the hearing, Dr. Nichopoulos was testifying about matters that had taken place three years earlier. "Taking care of Elvis was a day-today thing, and when I was treating him I knew exactly what drugs I had prescribed and what he was scheduled to take. We had a nurse living at Graceland (Elvis' Memphis home) and other people in the entourage who tried to provide 24-hour surveillance of Elvis' drug intake. But the medical board is right. I should have kept better records.

"That's one thing I would do differently today. As for the rest, I'd do it all over again. Elvis needed me.

"Had I turned my back on Presley, walked away from him, it might have been good for me. It would have been bad for Elvis, but it might have been good for me.

"But there was no way. No way I would have turned Elvis down. I cared about him. He was my friend and my patient.

"Once, Father Vieron was urging me to quit going on tour with Elvis. The tours were exhausting. I would get only three hours sleep a night trying to keep up with Elvis. Taking care of him was like trying to take care of a complicated computer. So many parts that could go wrong. Father Vieron said, 'You're sacrificing the church, your family, and your medical practice to be with Elvis. Let him get another doctor for the tours.' I told him, 'If Elvis goes out and gets another doctor, it will mess him up. He needs my help.' Otherwise, he has to go to the Yellow Pages."

The singer's death devastated the physician. "I am still confused about it and trying to regroup my thinking about how it could have happened. I had talked to him the day before he died and he was so full of life, so raring to go on this next tour (scheduled to start the day Presley died), that I just couldn't believe he was dead. I still have trouble accepting it.

"Sure, Elvis had his medical problems—depression, diabetes, hypertension, impacted colon, insomnia—but they were all treatable problems. I didn't think any of them were life-threatening problems. My wife and my son, Dean, were going to go on tour this time. It was to have been their first time on tour with Elvis. In fact, for days my son refused to unpack his suitcase. It was just so hard to picture Elvis dead."

Although Presley's cause of death was never an issue in either the medical board hearing or the trial, the question still concerns him.

"After all," he says, "Elvis was my friend. When I got to Graceland that day, Elvis was being put into an ambulance, and we still hoped he could be saved. I administered cardiopulmonary resuscitation for 45 minutes. I remember praying, 'Breathe, Elvis, breathe for me.'

"I was the man who persuaded Vernon Presley to authorize an autopsy. There was some concern at the time that Elvis might have been poisoned or something. I participated in the autopsy and all we found was evidence of cardiovascular disease. Elvis had a history of hypertension.

The toxicology data, of course, weren't available then. We concluded that death was due to a cardiac arrhythmia of undetermined cause, and that's what we reported.

"Now this is what really hurt. When the final autopsy was released, including the drug findings, Vernon Presley refused to let me have a copy. No, he never blamed me for Elvis' death, but I was deeply hurt that he wouldn't let me as a courtesy see the final autopsy. I was the man who had wanted it in the first place.

"I'm at peace with myself—only two of the drugs in Elvis' blood were prescribed by me—but I'd like to know if the drugs had an effect. I still believe that the primary cause of death was an arrhythmia.

"It could have been triggered by any number of stresses. Elvis had played racquetball only hours before his death and he had been fasting for two days to lose weight. We found evidence of plaques on his coronary arteries, and his heart was enlarged. He was under pressure over the tour that was about to begin, and he might have been arguing with his girlfriend over whether she would accompany him at the start of the tour. Presley was very vulnerable to arguments with his women if he cared about them.

"I'd still like to know about the other nine drugs, for my own peace of mind. I know that he didn't get them from prescriptions I had written. I'll tell you this. You can take at random any 50 patients in intensive care and you'll find they have more prescription drugs in their bodies than what is claimed to have caused Elvis' death. And, don't forget, this is a man who had built his tolerance to drugs for over two decades.

"I found it hard to talk about Elvis' drug problem because, at first, I was worried about Vernon's health (he died a year later of a heart attack) and the other relatives, and because of concern for Lisa Marie (Presley's daughter). You know how cruel kids can be, and I didn't want her to hear her father described as a drug addict. I think I even had trouble telling the medical examiners board about Elvis' problem. When I hired James Neal (the former Watergate prosecutor) to defend me in the criminal trial, Father Vieron told me, 'For God's sake, George, tell him everything this time. Confide in others. Open up.' But it's hard."

(Neal's defense of Dr. Nichopoulos was based on the argument that he was a "Good Samaritan" aiding a desperate patient. The jury agreed. The conundrum of what killed Elvis remain shrouded by a secret autopsy that the courts have ruled only the Presley estate can release.)

Dr. Nichopoulos is still not ready to tell Elvis' complete medical story. "We used to worry," he says, "that he might choke to death. Sometimes, he would wake up while on sleeping pills and try to eat something. That's why we had people watching him around the clock.

"Who knows why he was so dependent upon drugs? You know, there are a lot of people like Elvis out there. Elvis was a firm believer there was a medicine for everything. You know how some people will sneeze and think they need a pill, or get a muscle cramp and want relief, or go to the dentist and need a pain-killer. Others aren't bothered. Elvis was convinced he needed drugs.

"We were trying to break him away, to help him get his life back together. We thought this last tour might do it. Maybe he could put aside his worries, settle down with a woman again.

"Maybe, someday, I'll write my book about Elvis. I guess the thing I remember most about him is Elvis the giver. He was always giving: himself, his songs, his words, his reassurances. You always knew that if Elvis were around, he would give of himself in some way. He would never turn you down. I don't think he had any idea how much he was always giving. And he was raring to go on tour.

"But that tour never left."□

President Reagan

The Washington Office of the American Medical Association enjoys a well-deserved reputation as a powerful lobby, whose influence extends into every nook and cranny of capital life. As a reporter, I have occasionally called upon my Washington colleagues for a favor or two.

They outdid themselves in the aftermath of the shooting of President Reagan.

The President was shot in the early afternoon of Monday, March 30, 1981, and all afternoon I was on the phone talking to Wayne Bradley, director of the AMA's Washington Office, and Paul Donelan, the Association's liaison with the White House. Paul thought that the White House physician, Dr. Dan Ruge, might be able to help us arrange interviews with the medical staff at the George Washington U. Hospital, where security was tight and the press was barred. Wayne thought that Helene von Damm might be able to help us. (Ms. von Damm, an immigrant from Austria, had begun her storybook career back in the early 1960s as a secretary with the American Medical Political Action Committee (AMPAC). The AMPAC experience had helped her land a job with Ronald Reagan and, by now, she was working out of the White House as chief of patronage. She would later be appointed U.S. ambassador to her native Austria and return in triumph to her homeland.) By the end of this day, however, no progress had been made on arranging an interview. Paul and Wayne were still "working on it."

Tuesday morning, I took the 7 o'clock flight from Chicago to Washington National and called Paul from the airport. "Just go to the hospital," he said, "and they'll be expecting you." By noon, while the rest of the press waited in a lecture hall across the street for prepared handouts, I had cleared the thicket of security surrounding the hospital and was sitting in the office of Dennis O'Leary, MD, the GWU dean for clinical affairs and the man who had met the press the night before on behalf of the medical team. Dr. O'Leary granted the AMA the first exclusive interview allowed within the top-security GWU hospital complex. (Dr. O'Leary's adroit performance before the TV cameras would make him an overnight celebrity, and within the next few years he would rapidly become the president of the District of Columbia Medical Society, a prominent spokesman for AMA on medical issues, and the president of the Joint Commission on Accreditation of Hospitals, his current position.)

Meanwhile, later that night, Dr. William Knaus, the co-director of the GWU intensive care unit, met me for dinner to provide additional details about how the medical teams treated the President. Dr. Knaus is a noted medical writer in his own right and he was extending a professional courtesy.

Our weekly newspaper closes on Wednesday night and that morning I filed from the AMA's Washington Office the following report on how the GWU medical team met its Presidential challenge. I never did get a chance to ask Paul and Wayne how they had managed to get me past the Secret Service.

PRESIDENT REAGAN DID NOT KNOW he had been hit. In the first chaotic moments of the assassination attempt in Washington, D.C., the President thought he had been hurt only by the Secret Service agent who wrestled him into the limousine.

The President would later tell William Knaus, MD, co-director of George Washington U.'s intensive care unit, "I told the Secret Service agent, "I think you have cracked my rib." " The Secret Service, Dr. Knaus was told, was rushing the President back to the White House—the nearest "secure" area—when the true extent of the injury became known. The President suddenly coughed up blood. The limousine wheeled about and the race was on for the George Washington Hospital emergency room six blocks from the White House.

In the ER nursing station, there was an ominous ring on a special telephone. It was the white phone, the one on a shelf and out of view and the one connected to the White House. The white phone had last rung a week before President Reagan's inauguration. "They wanted to see if it was working," recalled Dr. Knaus.

"The message," said Dennis S. O'Leary, MD, the GWU dean for clinical affairs, "was less than clairvoyant. We were told, 'The President and his party will be arriving any moment.' There was sufficient urgency in the voice, however, to alert us to be prepared.

"The limousine must have been in our driveway when we received the call. I was at a faculty meeting across the street and rushed to the ER. Our trauma team was already preparing the President for surgery. What followed was a masterpiece of medical care and cooperation at a time of high drama."

In retrospect, said Drs. O'Leary and Knaus, two of the GWU medical team caught up in the drama, the President remained calm, the medical staff remained calm, and, inevitably, the nation remained calm. This tone of remarkable composure was set at the top.

"The President is absolutely remarkable," said Dr. O'Leary. "The man is a physiological marvel. His spirits never flagged and his spirit spread to our medical team."

Added Dr. Knaus: "Why, following the completion of surgery, at about 3:30 a.m. and while he was still intubated, the President scratched a note on a piece of paper. It read, 'On the whole, I would rather be in Philadelphia' (quoting from the famous W. C. Fields line). He wanted to let us know that everything was going to be all right."

As an anxious nation waited in horror during the first hours after the shooting, it was Drs. O'Leary and Knaus and their physician colleagues who were on the spot. Their care of the shooting victims is a proud moment for medicine.

(Press Secretary James Brady was shot in the head, Secret Service agenty Timothy J. McCarthy in the abdomen. The fourth victim, Thomas K. Delehanty, was shot in the neck and taken to the Washington Hospital Center. President Reagan, of course, was shot in the chest, with the bullet lodging in the left lung.)

A day later, Dr. O'Leary sat in his office, on the second floor of the GWU Hospital and recalled the early hours. The Secret Service had commandeered the hospital's executive office for its command post during the President's expected two-week stay. Outside Dr. O'Leary's office, the hospital bristled with security and crackling walkie-talkies. Inside, however, things were quiet and still.

"If the President had to be shot," Dr. O'Leary said, "he certainly was shot in the right place at the right time and treated by the right people. He was at our ER within 10 minutes—at the absolute outside—of the shooting. He was in surgery within 40 minutes. He sailed through the surgery and his vital signs were rock stable throughout. Our trauma team is trained to report to the ER within 60 seconds of an alarm, and that's what they did this time. Even so, the Presidential limousine beat them by 30 seconds or so.

"Our people were working simultaneously on Reagan, Brady, and McCarthy. Their surgeries began immediately." (Reagan's bullet was removed by cardiovascular surgeon Benjamin Aaron, MD; Brady's operation was performed by neurosurgeon Arthur Xobrine, MD, and McCarthy's operation by Neofytos Tsangaras, MD, and thoracic surgeon Stephen Pett, MD. The trauma team was headed by surgeon Joseph Giordano, MD.)

As the surgeries proceeded, the news media began saturation coverage. Already, two rumors were spreading—that the President was in trouble and that Brady was dead.

Dr. O'Leary, who had been in the ER throughout and talked to all the physicians, knew differently. It would be up to him to tell the world.

"We needed a spokesman to face the TV cameras," he recalled. "We sat down and talked with the White House staff. Everyone agreed that the spokesman should be a physician, since there would be medical questions. Furthermore, the physician should be prepared to discuss details on all three shooting victims, and not just the man they might have treated. Finally, it was agreed the physician should represent GWU.

"The choice was really between myself and White House physician Daniel Ruge, MD (a neurosurgeon who scrubbed for Reagan's operation and who was in the hospital with the President throughout his ordeal). I cannot say enough for the professionalism and skill with which Dr. Ruge handled this emergency. As White House physician, he could have taken command and waved us off. But he decided, 'You people are professionals and know what you are doing. I am just going to keep a close eye on things and let you people do your jobs.'

"So it was decided that I would meet the press. The first press conference was scheduled that evening (March 30) right after the President's surgery.

"I looked out onto hundreds of people, each one of whom, it seemed, was carrying a TV camera. It was an awesome sight. This was to be my first press conference. I took a deep breath.

"Two things helped me. First, Presidential counselor Lynn Nofziger is a very calm, composed guy, and he made an opening statement. Second, I had some good news to report. I was determined to let people know that the President was OK, that Brady was going to live, and that we were on top of things.

"The questions came at me in torrents, and from 180 degrees. At times, the questions seemed like so much babble. But I just tried to hang in there, to get out accurate medical information. I was already tired from being in the ER so long, and I think this was a plus. I was simply too tired to get real excited."

Dr. O'Leary's grace under pressure was to make him an overnight celebrity.

That night, he recalled, "I got home about 10 p.m. or so. The phone was ringing off the hook. My parents called from Kansas City and said people they hadn't heard from in 40 years were calling to say how pleased they were with the news I had presented. My three children (from a first marriage) called. My (second) wife is doing her medical residency at GWU and she was scheduled to work the night in the ER. But since she is eight months pregnant and the ER was basically closed for the night, she was let out early. She got home shortly after I did and we started fielding the phone calls."

The next morning, Dr. O'Leary held his second—"and last"—press conference.

"The reporters seemed a little more hostile this time," he said. "I was telling them about the President's great spirits, his joking ('Honey, I forgot to duck,' he told his wife, Nancy), and they seemed to think this was a sign that he was not in complete control of his faculties.

"I told them, 'Absolutely not.' This is simply the way the man is. President Reagan and his wife are remarkably strong people. Throughout this ordeal, they have been calm and helpful. The President is a witty man and this is his way of coping with the situation and helping us cope."

As Dr. O'Leary talked to *American Medical News* (the first exclusive interview granted within the top-security GWU hospital complex), plans were being completed to transfer medical control to the White House. Dr. O'Leary's days as an overnight TV star were about to end. "And none too soon," he said. "It was fun, but enough is enough."

Hours later, after the transfer had been completed, Dr. Knaus delayed his long-awaited sleep long enough to describe for *AMN* the scene in the ICU.

"The amazing thing," he said, "is that this was damn near normal care. Had President Reagan been simply a 70-year-old man out for a walk and had been shot near GWU, he would have received pretty much the same kind of care. Our ER chief, Saul Edelstein, MD, would have been there to meet him. Our trauma chief, Dr. Giordano, would have had his team on the alert. Dr. Aaron would have been on call to remove the bullet. Dr. (Jack) Zimmerman and I would have worked with the surgeon in joint management of his post-op recovery.

"This has been a marvelous story of medical cooperation. There have been no ego clashes. This is because of one man, the White House physician, Dr. Ruge. He could have taken over, insisted that for security reasons the President be moved to Walter Reed (Army Hospital) or Bethesda (Navy Hospital). But, no, he simply said, 'Gentlemen, we have a job to do. Let's get about it.' In a case of this importance, things might have very easily become medically chaotic—the case of the late Shah of Iran comes to mind—but things went like clockwork.

"The President is a great patient. He has cooperated all the way. And since the medical outlook is so positive, all of us on the medical staff are on an incredible emotional high."

President Reagan was wheeled into the hospital ICU at 6 a.m. (March 31), where Dr. Knaus and his team took over. Although the President's condition was stable throughout, there was a critical period, Dr. Knaus says, when his loss of blood had to be carefully monitored.

"Remember, now," Dr. Knaus said, "this is a 70-year-old man. The bullet had entered the lower lobe of his left lung and he was bleeding from the lung. He lost 3,700 ccs of blood. Between the time of his operation and 3:30 a.m., he required transfusion of eight units of packed-cell blood, more than half the body's total supply. At one point, his partial oxygen pressure at 80% ventilator oxygen was only 100—normal might be more like 400 for a younger man. He had to be kept on the ventilator for seven hours. But the surgical team stayed right on top of things and constant blood replacement plus a careful monitoring of his blood gases kept things stable.

"We put the President in the ICU at 6 a.m. Brady had been placed here at 9 p.m. the night before. We have a 16-bed ICU and besides Brady and the President there were 11 other patients, all very sick. The others were so sick, in fact, that they had no idea who their new roommates were.

"We put the President on nasal oxygen, deep-breathing exercises, and mild physiotherapy. Both lungs were collapsed, but after applying positive oxygen pressure, the right lung expanded in the surgical recovery area and the left lung in the ICU.

"The President is a great patient. He is cooperating with the exercises. His toughest moment came when we told him about the seriousness of the injury to Brady (who remains in critical condition).

"He told me, 'You know, I only got shot once. A few weeks ago, I presented the Medal of Honor to a soldier who had been shot four times and still rescued his fellow soldiers from the enemy. I don't see how he could have done it, after being shot four times. I can't imagine doing something like that.' "

Dr. Knaus said Mrs. Reagan "has been asking us a lot of questions, about how long the President will have to be hospitalized, what to expect next, and so on. Now, there are ways to ask questions. You can be patronizing and demanding, or you can be concerned and respectful. Mrs. Reagan is acting just like any wife would when her husband is injured. She treats us as professionals and has been extremely gracious. I cannot say enough about how remarkably poised both the President and his wife have been throughout this whole thing.

"When we made the decision to take the President out of the ICU, I sat down with Dr. Aaron, Dr. Ruge, and the Secret Service. Dr. Ruge asked, "What would you do if he were Ronald Smith?' I said, 'We would move him out of the ICU because he is out of danger and we need the ICU beds for the critically ill.' Dr. Ruge said, 'Let's move him.'

"We have transferred the President to a special suite on the third floor, where he will run the nation for the next two weeks or so. It has taken the Secret Service great effort and great expense to secure this hospital. It would have been easy to have moved the President to a military hospital, but medical decisions have prevailed from the start. The best medical decision is to keep him at GWU."

Dr. Knaus mused, "You know, as we sit here talking, the bed just vacated by President Reagan is being readied for another patient. After Dr. Aaron removed the bullet from the President's lung, he had to turn right around and do major cardiovascular surgery on another patient.

"It's a way of life."□

Pope John Paul II

The good news was that the Pope was going to pull through from his gunshot injuries. The bad news was that I couldn't get his Italian doctor, Emilio Tresalti, MD, to say so.

Also, I was being frustrated in my swing-for-the-fences attempt to gain an audience with the Pope. Working through AMA contacts with the World Medical Assn. (WMA), I had been trying to persuade an Italian board member of WMA to arrange an interview for me with the Pope, whose recovery was now well along. In broken English, the Italian physician told me over the phone: "Ah, I see, you want to see THE POPE. Understand now, that it will be very, very difficult." At that point, the connection went out. Of course, I never got near the Pope.

Rome, the eternal city, deserves a little more *la dolce vita,* but I was over and back—with copy written—within 72 hours. When I turned the file and film into my editor on Wednesday morning, he calmly informed me that as I was flying back, I must have crossed paths with a delegation of five top U.S. physicians who were flying to Rome to consult on the Pope's case. One of the five was Claude Welch, MD, an international expert on abdominal surgery and a prominent member of the AMA.

Dr. Welch would have been a goldmine of information for me, had I known he was coming and had I been able to wait. I might even have been able to wrangle the audience with the Pope. Oh, well, you can't win them all.

SQUINTING AGAINST THE MORNING SUN, Emilio Tresalti, MD, cups his face in his hands and says in a weary voice:

"The Pope kept his promise. I wish that it had not had to be, but the Holy Father told me years ago that if he were ever in medical need, he would come to Gemelli. And so he has."

On Oct. 17, 1978, a day after his election to the papacy, Pope John Paul II suddenly left the Vatican with only a few aides and went to the Gemelli Hospital to visit a sick Polish friend, the Most Rev. Andrzej Maria Deskur.

Dr. Tresalti recalls, "He was very pleased with our care of his sick friend. That is when he told me, 'If I should ever be in need of medical attention, this is where I want to be.' Before the Pope left, he gave a talk to

the many doctors, nurses, and patients who crowded around him. When
he was finished, an aide whispered into his ear. The Pope smiled and told
us, 'He reminded me I ought to bless you. I haven't yet learned how to be
Pope.'

"He is a very special man."

Dr. Tresalti was to be given a chance to redeem the Pope's request
when on May 14, 1981, the two bullets fired by Mehmet Ali Agca severely
wounded the Pontiff while he conducted his weekly general audience for
10,000 worshippers in St. Peter's Square in Rome.

Within minutes, the ambulance that is always standing by at the
Vatican during special ceremonies was racing the two miles for the modern Polyclinico Agostino Gemelli, which sits on a hill high above the
ancient city.

And, within days, Dr. Tresalti, the medical director of Gemelli Hospital, was to become known throughout the world as the hospital
spokesman who daily reported for the waiting millions the slow but
steady recovery of the spiritual leader of 600 million Roman Catholics.

Five days after the shooting, Dr. Tresalti is still speaking cautiously, at
least to the public. He speaks in clear English to *American Medical News*.

"He is improving, yes, but his condition still is unascertained. There
is still the possibility of infection. It is difficult to tell for certain but we
believe he was hit by two bullets. The police are still investigating. The one
bullet caused only a flesh wound above his right elbow. The other, however, pierced the abdomen. It entered below the level of the umbilicus and
passed out near the sacrum. Upon exit, we believe, it struck the Pope's left
index finger. This bullet caused the damage. It tore several small holes in
the small and large intestines.

"The police called me immediately after the shooting and we were
ready for the Pope's arrival. He was talking rapidly, but in Polish. I could
not understand him. Later, it was translated for me. The Pope asked, 'How
could this happen?'

"Within 15–20 minutes of the shooting, our medical team had prepared the Pope for surgery. The operation took 5 hours and 25 minutes,
with the last half hour or so on the arm and hand. Our medical team—
there were three surgeons, headed by Francesco Crucitti, MD, with a
fourth assisting at the end—was very excited, of course. But though this is
a very special patient, what is needed is very normal care. We treat many
gunshot victims at Gemelli. Crimes of passion, we call them.

"We had to do a temporary colostomy and resect the intestines in
two places. The Pope's vital signs remained stable throughout the operation, but we had to replace about half his total blood volume.

"The reaction of our medical team was, how can I say it, extremely correct. It is a very nice feeling to see how correctly everybody reacted. Of course, it is to be expected, but still it is wonderful.

"As for danger to the Pope's life, the immediate danger was the second the bullet entered the body. Call it providence or divine intervention or good luck, but the bullet did not hit any vital organs. It might have hit the pancreas or the aorta. But it did not. The Pope was saved from sudden death. Then, it was up to us. Now, the danger is infection. Of course, we have from the start given him major amounts of antibiotics. And our intensive-care area has an unusual feature—the patients are enclosed in glass to assure sterile conditions. The Pope's visitors talked to him through an intercom. So we have done everything possible to assure that infection does not strike. His laboratory tests have all been normal, except for his temperature, which is slightly elevated. But with any gunshot wound to the abdomen, there is always the possibility of infection, from fecal matter leaking from the intestines into the abdominal cavity. In intensive care, we have monitored the Pope's vital signs for 24 hours a day.

"The Pope will need two more operations. One to repair the colostomy, the other, a minor procedure, to repair his finger. He will be with us a long time. Not less than one month. We cannot say for certain that he is out of danger."

Dr. Tresalti must temporarily break off the interview. He has to preside over a pleasant duty. On May 18, his 61st birthday, the Pope is to be transferred from his private room in the hospital's intensive-care area to a four-room suite in the hospital's regular section. It is another positive sign of the Pope's remarkable recovery, and throughout Rome the news is trumpeted with joy.

Dr. Tresalti recalls that only the day before he sat in the intensive-care area as Pope John Paul II laboriously recorded in a sometimes-trembling voice a short broadcast to be played at St. Peter's Square. There were 15,000 jamming the ancient worshipping ground that noon when the Pope's broadcast was played. In heavily accented Italian, the Pope asked forgiveness for his assailant, good health for the two American women wounded in the shooting, and a chance to dedicate his own sufferings to the world. Dr. Tresalti says, "When the worshippers heard the Pope's voice, they looked up at the window of the Apostolic Palace where he usually appears. The window was closed. But when the worshippers heard the Pope himself speaking in such a strong voice, they wept. And who would not have wept?"

As the Pope is being moved, the lobby of Gemelli Hospital bustles with action. The television crews have set up shop right in the middle of the lobby of this prestigious institution, which is the teaching hospital of the Catholic University of the Sacred Heart. It is Rome's best hospital and, to many informed observers, on a par with the best in Western Europe and the U.S. But security is not a strong point. The Pope is secure but people elsewhere come and go at will. The TV cameras compete with the split-leaf philodendrons as lobby decor. And on the Pope's birthday, there is a steady stream of visitors.

There is little Giovanna, dressed in pigtails and flanked by nuns, who comes to read a get-well note. There is little Carlo, who has brought the Pope a present—an electronic game. Each makes his way to the small room off the lobby, where the Pope's flowers, presents, and get-well messages are being stored. At regular intervals, the TV crews are allowed to film the outpouring of support. A class of handicapped children is brought in to pay their respects. One reads a letter concluding, "We love you, Holy Father." The Pope will be told of the tributes later this evening, after a special Mass is said for him. Meanwhile, the hospital's routine goes on. In one room off the lobby, patients are brought by wheelchair to vote in Rome's referenda on major issues, including a proposal to repeal Italy's liberal abortion law. The Pope supported the repeal proposal, but it will lose 2–1.

By late afternoon, Dr. Tresalti is ready to resume the interview.

"He is in much less pain," the physician reports. "He is making steady improvement. In the first days after the operation, the Pope had sharp, lancing pains in the abdomen and we had to administer sedatives. But, now we are using only very mild pain-killers, if needed at all. The Pope no longer needs the oxygen mask. He cannot yet stand, but he sat up for a half-hour Sunday to record his broadcast. He is still being fed intravenously. His temperature Celsius is . . . oh, all right, it is 100.4 Fahrenheit, but you people need a new system of measurement. This is only a mild temperature elevation and is consistent with the body's healing process.

"Only two hours ago, we transferred the Pope to a regular suite. There are about 30 doctors, nurses, and technicians, who have had access to the Pope's room in intensive care. Before he left, the Holy Father blessed us all and told us to have courage. A few of the nurses cried. Well, at that, a few of the doctors cried, too."

Dr. Tresalti holds firm to his diagnosis—"The Pope's medical condition remains 'guarded.' We cannot yet say he is out of danger." This is at least a departure from his earlier news statements, made in the prevailing Italian medical parlance, that, first, "The situation is critical—the prognosis is reserved," and "The situation remains critical—we can be neither optimistic nor pessimistic."

Dr. Tresalti is an epidemiologist and, in normal times, the *direczione sanitaria* of the hospital. In these special times, however, he has had to field a barrage of medical questions from around the world.

"It is," he says, "how you say, very heavy. It is heavy duty. But I believe we must get the essential information out to the world."

He sits in his bare office in a wing of the hospital far removed from the lobby and the glare of the television cameras.

"How do you handle the hospitalization of a Pope?" he asks. "You know, this is the first time ever a Pope has been in a hospital. There are no rules to go by. Pope Paul VI had a prostate operation, but it was performed in the Vatican. Oxygen and other equipment was brought in to care for Pope John XXIII as he was dying. But, never, has a Pope been brought to a hospital. He is not only a very special personage but he is also a very special person. We are doing our best. We are very happy that so far nothing has gone wrong. But we still have our fears. But, tonight, we will have a special Mass for the Pope and give our thanks."

The next morning, Dr. Tresalti continues his reports on the Pope's recovery. "He is very alert," the physician says. "He is seeing not only the doctors and nurses, but his secretaries and Vatican officials. He has not delegated any major duties. He is still running the Vatican. Last night, he was very tranquil. He is praying daily and is very serene."

Surely, the physician must believe the Pope is out of danger? What does the physician tell his wife?

"Ah," Dr. Tresalti responds, "but you are not my wife. You are a journalist. We are hopeful, that is all that I can say.

"We have more positive developments to report today. The Pope's temperature has dropped to 98.6 degrees. For the first time since the shooting, he has taken oral nourishment—sugared water and weak tea. His laboratory tests are normal. He is doing mild exercise. Yes, you could call this a vast improvement."

By now, six full days after his wounding, the Pope is receiving distinguished visitors in his four-room suite, which contains a portrait of the Black Madonna of Czestochowa, a patron saint of his native Poland. The President of Italy has been a daily visitor. Prime Minister Trudeau of Canada is expected at any moment. An international team of five distinguished physician consultants is expected to confer with the Pope.

(The consultants, Dr. Tresalti said, were agreed to at the request of the Vatican, which for days had been receiving offers of free consultations from doctors throughout the world. Among the distinguished group are two American physicians, Kevin Cahill, MD, New York City, and Claude Welch, MD, of Boston. Dr. Cahill is an expert in infectious diseases of the bowel. Dr. Welch, who has been very prominent in the American Medical Association and its Massachusetts components, is an expert in abdominal operations. In a joint bulletin, the five-physician team of consultants reported, "We are very pleased by the Pope's progress to date, but it is clear that even a patient as remarkably fit as the Pope will require a prolonged recuperation." The physicians praised the Roman anesthesiologist, Corrado Manni, who heads Gemelli's intensive-care unit.)

Meanwhile, Dr. Tresalti must leave for his morning press briefing. A few final questions are permitted. Could it have been prevented? "In America," he says, "you have seen in the shooting of President Reagan what can happen when a leader believes he must meet the people. The Pope is a man of the people. Who would ever think someone would shoot this Pope?" He shrugs.

The final question: He will live, won't he?

"People," Dr. Tresalti says, "have been saying that 'The Pope may die.' Well, that is true."

The Italian physician breaks into a broad grin. "But it is also true that he may live."□

The Shah of Iran

Dr. Ben Kean is a renaissance man—physician, raconteur, boulevardier, sportsman, and patron of the arts. A society doctor with a who's-who clientele on New York's fashionable Park Avenue, he also is an internationally renowned microscopist, parisitologist, and pathologist. He has traveled the world over many times and squired—and married—some of the world's most beautiful women. His first scientific paper, on shark bites, was first published in *JAMA* in 1941.

He was thrust into the public spotlight, however, in a new role—as the personal physician to the late Shah of Iran during the last year of the monarch's life.

I had been pursuing an interview with Dr. Kean for some time, but he kept deferring it, pending a possible congressional investigation into the hospitalization of the Shah in New York and the subsequent seizure of the U.S. Embassy in Tehran. When Congress decided not to pursue its inquiry, Dr. Kean gave me a call. He said he wanted "to make a contribution to history."

DECEMBER, 1979. In one room, there was only the physician and his patient. Anxiously waiting in the other were top officials of the U.S. government. Across the world were the stakes—the American hostages being held by Iran.

The patient was the self-proclaimed Shahanshah ("King of Kings, Light of the Aryans, and Vice Regent of God") Mohammad Reza Pahlavi. Sent to Texas' Lackland Air Force Base to recuperate after his 41-day stay at New York Hospital, the shah was very, very sick. His spleen was enlarged to 1,000 grams, seven times normal, and, more ominously, was enlarging each day. His blood counts were plummeting.

The physician was B. H. Kean, MD, a Manhattan internist who in the past three months had become the shah's personal doctor, confidant, and friend. Dr. Kean was adamant:

"Your spleen has to come out and it has to come out soon. Will you allow us to operate now?"

The shah slowly shook his head.

"They want me out of the country. They think it will help the hostages. It won't, but I am not staying."

Dr. Kean calls the shah's decision at Lackland "the turning point."

"That's probably what helped kill him. Acting under great pressure, the shah sacrificed his life.

"At this point, there was no other country in the world that would let him in. No place except Panama. For the shah to agree to go with a major illness and with the need for a major operation to a strange country of limited medical facilities was a sacrifice.

"I insisted, 'It has to come out.' He said, 'Today?' I said, 'No, but soon.' He asked, 'Can it be done in Panama?' I told him, 'It can be done in Mali (the poorest country in Africa).' This had become a running joke between us. I had months ago told him we could—if absolutely necessary—assemble a medical team and do the operation any place in the world. The shah was very tired. He told me:

" 'I want to get out. They want me out. Let me tell you what I want to do and tell me if I am crazy. I believe in Allah. I know I am going to die. I hope my country will survive. Put me back on chlorambucil (a mild anticancer drug prescribed for the shah for five years by French physicians). It worked before.

" 'I don't want to spend Christmas in a hospital. I want to be with my family. (The shah, a strong family man, observed Christmas because "my holidays are determined by my children's vacations," and they all attended Western schools.)

" 'If this does not work, then you can take my spleen out.' "

Dr. Kean was distressed. He knew the shah needed not chlorambucil, but a splenectomy (which in his weakened condition carried a 15% chance of death). "The shah knew it, too. When his spleen rapidly enlarged again, he knew that this was not the original cancer, that it was a new ballgame. But he had made up his mind."

Dr. Kean left his patient and entered the other room. Among the 20 people in the room were Lloyd Cutler, chief of the Carter Administration's delegation; Hamilton Jordan, White House chief of staff; attorneys for the shah and the State Dept.; and seven physicians (a State Dept. MD, five Air Force MDs, and Hibbard Williams, MD, chief of medicine at New York Hospital and Dr. Kean's colleague throughout the shah's ordeal). All of the physicians who had examined the shah had agreed: He has a big spleen. It has to come out.

"But now, I told the group: 'We all agree that the shah's spleen should be taken out now. But it's not going to be taken out now. The shah wants to leave.' "

Some 19 months later, sitting in his spacious office at New York's Cornell U. Medical School, Dr. Kean, 68, stops his narrative and stares out the window. Then, his words come with a hard edge.

"They asked me, 'How soon can he leave?' I replied, 'In half an hour.'

"There is only one word for the mood of the President's men. Glee. I was very, very sad. I did not have the big picture, I guess. I was working for my patient. Minutes later, President Carter called the shah. Placing the shah at Lackland was the first time the U.S. government had provided anything for him. This telephone call was the first time Carter had spoken to the shah since he was admitted to New York Hospital. The President thanked the shah for leaving the country. What did the shah say?

"Under the circumstances, he was very gracious. He thanked the President for allowing his hospitalization. The shah was realistic. He knew he had to go. But he was disappointed and I was disappointed.

"From that point on, it was all downhill."

For 19 months, Dr. Kean has maintained silence on the complete medical story of his famous patient. He thought that either a proposed Congressional investigation or depositions from his libel lawsuit against *Science* magazine would provide the answers. But the former never happened and the latter was settled out of court.

In an exclusive six-hour interview with *American Medical News*, Dr. Kean traced the shah's medical pilgrimage from Cuernavaca, Mexico, where the illness worsened and the shah agreed to full disclosure and treatment, to Cairo, Egypt, where 10 months later he died. The physician, who was the Carter Administration's sole source of information about the shah's medical condition, contends:

For political reasons, the shah for five years kept his cancer a secret, thus probably shortening and possibly sacrificing his life. Some oncology experts think that had the shah been treated by splenectomy and intensive chemotherapy in 1974, when his lymphatic lymphoma was first observed by French physicians, he might have been cured. Others believe it is a six- to eight-year disease and the shah had almost his full span. Dr. Kean thinks "the shah hoped to hold on long enough to turn the throne over to his son, as his father had done for him."

The back-of-the-hand treatment accorded the shah by the U.S. government tormented his final months and probably hastened his death. Disappointment and sadness were the shah's prevailing emotions in those final 10 months. There were few joyful moments.

In September and October, 1979, Mexican MDs mistakenly were treating the monarch for malaria. Dr. Kean accurately diagnosed the shah in Mexico and found him to have obstructive jaundice, requiring hospitalization and surgery. The two leading possibilities for the obstruction were gallstones blocking the bile duct or cancer of the pancreas. One or the other would be confirmed within 24 to 48 hours of hospitalization, Dr. Kean told the State Dept. The words he used were the need for "prompt" hospitalization and medical care, "preferably" in the U.S. Because State Dept. depositions corroborate this account, the published reports saying President Carter thought the monarch was "at the point of death" and could be treated "only in New York City" must represent either misinformation or misinterpretation at levels above that of the State Dept. physician to whom Dr. Kean made his reports. The existing medical facts were compelling reasons for admitting the shah for treatment; any exaggeration of those facts was simultaneously pointless and political.

Allegations in *Science* magazine and elsewhere that Dr. Kean was "a paid minion" of Rockefeller interests and that he performed a "flawed and superficial diagnosis" and lied to get the shah into the United States are, in Dr. Kean's words "pretty villainous stuff." Dr. Kean says, and it is now generally acknowledged, that he never met, spoke to, or corresponded with David Rockefeller until meeting him in the corridor of New York Hospital one month after the shah was admitted. In a settlement of Dr. Kean's libel lawsuit, *Science* acknowledged that Dr. Kean's care of the shah included "thorough diagnosis," a "prudent recommendation (for admission to a major teaching hospital)," and followed "accepted medical and diagnostic procedures and the ethics of his profession." To Dr. Kean, this meant that *Science,* "while not telling the complete medical story, has recognized the propriety of my conduct, as judged by those who were in a position to make an informed judgment." Dr. Kean says he remains bitter about what he calls the magazine's "disinterest and unwillingness to publish the truth, even when the medical facts were made available." To *Science,* it also meant, "We stand by our original statement that the shah could have been treated in Mexico and that President Carter got bad advice from somebody over the urgency of admitting the shah." The settlement was based on affidavits provided by Dr. Kean's medical colleagues and U.S. government officials.

The seizure of the U.S. embassy "was not caused by the admission of the shah to a U.S. hospital. The shah knew this, I knew it, and so do many others, including State Dept. officials. What caused the takeover was the meeting (Zbigniew) Brzezinski had with Iranian leaders (Mehdi) Bazargan and (Ibrahim) Yazdi, (MD). Three days before the seizure, Brzezinski held a press conference and reported the progress he had made with the Iranian leaders. The ayatollah (Ruhollah Khomeini) was threatened by the prospects of a reasonable government run by reasonable men. He wanted to solidify his power. And you know what happened to Bazargan and Dr. Yazdi (they were ousted from their government posts)."

State Dept. efforts to have the shah examined by two Iranian physicians trained in the U.S. were refused by the shah.

The "most distressing things in this whole affair are the press allegations that doctors would lie to get the shah into the country and the sad events in Panama. The Panamanians turned away (internationally famed surgeon) Michael DeBakey when he came to take the shah's spleen out, calling him an itinerant surgeon.' " Gen. Omar Torrijos, the Panamanian strongman, betrayed one promise in moving the shah from the island's Gorgas Hospital, a U.S. military facility, to Paitilla Hospital which the general controlled. The U.S. betrayed a second when it reneged on an earlier promise that if the shah were not able to have his operation at Gorgas, he could return to Houston. Cutler told Drs. Kean and DeBakey, "It cannot be done."

As the shah's condition worsened and his splenectomy became imperative, Iranian officials arrived in Panama to try to arrange the arrest of their exiled leader. The shah felt he would be arrested on a Monday. Although it might have been only a house arrest—the shah never would have gone to prison—he feared he would lose his independence. He said he was afraid he would become a trapped pawn in a bargaining game— either he pays to get out or the Iranians pay to take him out. Gen. Torrijos, he believed, had already broken faith by ordering him from Gorgas Hospital and he was not going to risk another sell-out. On Sunday, March 23, only hours before he would have been arrested, the shah left.

The people who come out the best in this whole story are Egyptian President Anwar Sadat and Dr. DeBakey. "Compared to U.S. officials, Sadat was a towering figure of compassion and courage. Dr. DeBakey was noble in every way."

This, then, is Dr. Kean's story of the shah's medical odyssey, a journey that would shake the world.

Dr. Kean was in Washington, D.C., discussing his proposed diarrhea-control project in Haiti before the Pan-American Health Organization when the call came on Sept. 27, 1979.

The caller was Joseph V. Reed, a high-ranking officer in the business empire of David Rockefeller. Reed and his family had for 20 years been Dr. Kean's patients. Most recently, they had referred to him the shah's public relations aide, Robert Armao, a former Rockefeller aide who had incurred a case of Mexican turista.

Dr. Kean lives two lives. He practices general internal medicine on Manhattan's Park Avenue. However, in his Cornell Medical School office and lab, he is widely known as one of the world's leading authorities on tropical diseases.

Culminating 20 years of research, he co-discovered the cause of Mexican turista. His textbook, "Tropical Medicine and Parasitology—Classic Investigations," is the basic work. As a consultant for the Ford Foundation and others, he has traveled the world checking on health conditions among U.S. workers. One of his first research papers—on shark bites—was published in 1941 in the *Journal of the AMA*.

Reed told Dr. Kean that he was calling about the medical needs of "Peter Smith." The physician's response was immediate—"What, not again?" Reed replied, "No, this is a different Peter Smith."

Dr. Kean explains: "A few years ago, I was called to Sweden as a consultant to treat a distinguished Swedish banking tycoon who during a Florida vacation had picked up a rare lung infection. It was a peculiar strain of pneumonia, somewhat akin to the Legionnaire's disease. When I arrived in Stockholm, the man had a high fever and was near death.

"Now, this man was very wealthy. He owned the auto company whose limousine picked me up at the airport, he owned several banks we passed along the way, and he owned the hospital where he was staying. I told the Swedish medical authorities, 'This man cannot be treated according to the status of his real identity. He must be treated as an ordinary patient, as a "Peter Smith," if he is to survive. He needs not the coddling of private care, but the all-out team effort of the best public hospital.' They listened to my advice and the patient recovered.

"Now, Reed was telling me, 'We have a new Peter Smith. He is in Mexico and he is suffering from malaria and jaundice. Will you fly down and examine him?'

"I said, 'Of course. As soon as possible.' Immediately, I knew it was the shah."

Press reports had speculated about the shah's Mexican stay. Malaria is always a possibility in Mexico, but is seldom accompanied by jaundice. Since the shah had recently been in Iran and North Africa, Dr. Kean thought that he had malaria and hepatitis, which would explain the jaundice. Because Dr. Kean is an authority on malaria, he was not surprised that Reed called him.

Before leaving for Mexico, Dr. Kean wanted to check with New York Hospital to see if the shah would be welcome. Dr. David Thompson, director of the hospital, was out, so he checked with Theodore Cooper, MD, dean of the sister Cornell Medical College.

"I told Dr. Cooper, 'I do not have to tell you, a distinguished surgeon, what the possibilities are when a 60-year-old patient has malaria and jaundice. If he only has malaria, that can easily be cured in Mexico. But if the jaundice is due to obstructive causes, the differential diagnosis is undoubtedly gallstones or cancer of the head of the pancreas. Will the shah of Iran be welcome as a patient at New York Hospital?'

"Dr. Cooper said, 'I cannot speak for the hospital, but it is not likely to turn away any sick patient seeking admission. I will be interested in hearing what you find.'

"So, even before getting on a plane, I had discussed this matter with hospital officials and I suspected that the shah either had cancer or gallstones."

"I arrived in Cuernavaca on Sept. 29 and was met by Armao's aides, who immediately took me to see the shah. He was in bed, but he was not bedridden."

Dr. Kean had met the shah before—in 1949, when he examined the shah at New York Hospital for tropical diseases, and later while working in Iran for the Ford Foundation and on research projects.

"But he did not recognize me. He simply said, 'Thanks for coming. I am very sick. I hope you can help me.'

"I simply looked, listened, palpated. He was very, very sick—deeply jaundiced and a weight loss of 30 pounds. But he was gracious, afebrile, and coherent. For many weeks now, he had been under the care of two Mexican physicians, who were treating him for malaria. Everyone in his entourage had accepted the Mexican MD's conclusion that he had malaria.

"My gut hunch was that the shah had neither malaria nor hepatitis. His jaundice was too deep and too persistent for either disease. That meant it must be obstructive jaundice, due to gallstones or pancreatic cancer.

That night, Dr. Kean met with the two Mexican physicians, who catered to vacationing tourists. They told him that for weeks they had been treating the shah for malaria with chloroquine. They said they had cured it once, but then it had recurred. He asked for their slides of the malaria species, but they didn't have any slides of the first case.

"Well, to an old malaria hand like me, the rule is, 'No slides, no diagnosis.' " He asked if they had reported the disease to Mexican health authorities, since malaria is a reportable illness in Mexico, and they hadn't. They did have slides on the current case of malaria.

"So for two hours we sat over the microscope and examined what the Mexican physicians swore were malaria parasites. I said, 'No, what you see are not malaria, but normal blood platelets and precipitated stain. There is no malaria, but I do see signs of anemia.'

"The next morning, I met again with the shah and did another thorough exam—rectal exam, lymph nodes, spleen, a check of his drugs for possible causes of toxic hepatitis. At the time, I was not aware that the shah's French physicians had for five months been treating his cancer with MOPP chemotherapy (a combination of nitrogen mustard, oncovin, procarbazine, and prednisone). Since, as I would later learn, he had just completed a regimen of the drugs, both his neck nodes and spleen had shrunk to normal limits.

"I told the shah, 'You do not have malaria, and you probably never did. I think you have obstructive jaundice and we need to find out what is causing it.'

"I did not ask him if he had cancer and he did not volunteer the information." Dr. Kean suggested sending two blood samples to the Social Security Hospital and the Children's Hospital, both in Mexico City, and taking a third sample back to New York City.

"I was pretty much down on the lab facilities in Cuernavaca, but I knew the two Mexico City hospitals had excellent pathology labs. After all, I had been working with Mexican physicians for 20 years.

"The shah was very noncommittal. He was very polite, but very reserved and cautious. He told me that his French physicians had prescribed cortisone for his hepatitis and that he had taken a dose this very morning.

"I told him that I was very opposed to the cortisone. Although hepatitis was still a possibility (one of the shah's security guards had the disease), it had not been confirmed and, in any case, cortisone is no longer the drug of choice. The shah had told me he had had hepatitis as a child and this argued against his having it now.

"I was very upset. I said, 'You require much more sophisticated care than you are now receiving. I urge you to call your French physicians and forget the cortisone until you have a firm diagnosis.'

"I told him my 'Peter Smith' story and said, 'You need to change your name to Peter Smith.' The shah said, 'Ah, but do not forget. I am a Moslem. I cannot change my name.' At the time, I thought it was a pretty good joke.

"It was clear that the shah was calling his own medical shots and that he trusted his French physicians.

"He was very firm. There would be no blood tests. I said, 'Well, then I urge you to call back your French doctors or seek the best possible medical care in Mexico. You need better care than you are now receiving. He thanked me and I left.

"On the plane ride back, I was very depressed and very puzzled. I was upset at the shah's apparent inability to get proper medical attention. But I also knew that after my departure he would be seeking new medical advice. He was intelligent enough to realize that the malaria should not have happened a second time while he was taking an anti-malaria medication. And, of course, in hindsight, although he initially accepted the diagnosis of malaria, he was probably also concerned that it might be something related to the cancer.

"But I thought of myself simply as a consultant. I thought that my advice was either not needed or not welcome. I did not expect to hear from him again.

"Two weeks later, I received a phone call from Armao. His tone was very urgent. 'Some new facts about the shah's illness have emerged,' he said. 'He has had cancer for five years, and he wants you to return to help treat him. His French physicians will tell you everything when you get here.'

"Before leaving for Mexico, I received a call from Eben Dustin, MD, the State Dept.'s medical officer. He said, 'I understand the shah has cancer and you are going to examine him. Please call me when you return.' On Oct. 18, I was met at Cuernavaca by Georges Flandrin, MD, one of the shah's French physicians.

"He handed me a 35-page report summarizing the shah's five-year treatment for cancer. The secret was out, at least to me. I could appreciate why the shah's other French physician, Jean Bernard, MD, was kept in the background. As the head of Paris' Institute for Research on Leukemia, Hospital St. Louis, Dr. Bernard is known throughout the world as an expert on leukemia and lymphoma. To say 'Bernard' is to say 'leukemia,' or its related disease 'lymphoma.'

"Dr. Flandrin was almost apologetic about the care the shah had received. You see, the shah had never permitted Drs. Bernard and Flandrin to make a definitive diagnosis. He had a deathly fear not of his illness but of public exposure of his illness. So, in May, 1974, when he found his spleen enlarged, he would not permit the French physicians to do the tests necessary to make a diagnosis beyond the general 'chronic lympho-proliferative disease.'

"Without a biopsy, the French physicians could only theorize that he had Waldenstrom's macroglobulinemia, which is sometimes associated with chronic lymphocytic leukemia. It would turn out, however, that the shah had a related disease, lymphatic lymphoma. Had Dr. Bernard insisted on removing the swollen spleen, the shah simply would have found a new physician. He was put on chlorambucil and he did remarkably well under this mild drug until he arrived in the Bahamas in March, 1979.

"At that time, the shah developed hard nodes in his neck. Again, the French physicians were not allowed to do a biopsy and, instead, aspirated the node. They thought they were still treating the original cancer and prescribed MOPP chemotherapy. Subsequent tests would show that the shah had developed histiocytic lymphosarcoma, representing either a second cancer or a transformation of the original lymphoma. Clearly, his case was worsening.

"When the shah became ill in Mexico, Dr. Flandrin and everyone else accepted the Mexican MDs' diagnosis that he had simply picked up malaria. But when I returned the second time, there was no longer any doubt.

"The atmosphere had changed completely. The shah's appearance was stunningly worse. Any fourth-year medical student could tell he needed to be in a hospital.

"Clearly, he had obstructive jaundice. The odds favored gallstones, since his fever, chills, and abdominal distress suggested an infection of the biliary tract. Also, he had a history of indigestion.

"Besides the probable obstruction—he now had been deeply jaundiced for six to eight weeks—he was emaciated and suffering from hard tumor nodes in the neck and a swollen spleen, signs that his cancer was worsening, and he had severe anemia and very low white blood counts. Dr. Flandrin was disturbed that his chemotherapy was not working, that the nodes had returned to the neck and that the spleen was again swollen to three times normal.

Dr. Kean had a long talk with the shah. "He told me, 'You must understand that for reasons of state I could not before tell you the nature of my illness. I appreciate your concern.'

"I said, 'You must be hospitalized so that we can make the correct diagnosis. Almost certainly, you will need an operation. This is a very complicated case and you have multiple life-threatening illnesses. No one doctor can handle your case. You need a medical team—a diagnostician, surgeon, oncologist, infectious-disease specialist, and supportive house-staff. You need a teaching hospital.'

"The shah said, 'Where can it be done?' Well, I started with Mali and we worked our way up. Slowly, I rattled off the countries with adequate facilities—North Africa, Britain, Switzerland, Brazil, Argentina. He just sat there and shook his head. 'I am not welcome.' I said that most properly he should return to France, whose physicians had been treating him all along. 'I am not welcome.' It all came down to the U.S. or Mexico.

"The shah was a proud man and he was quietly bitter that his former ally of 37 years would not offer him a haven. His questions to me were always, 'If I were to come to the U.S., where should I go?'

"I mentioned Houston, Los Angeles, Palo Alto, San Francisco, Chicago, Boston, and, of course, New York. The shah's medical and security advisers had checked out the best medical facilities in Mexico City and there were three reasons why he preferred the U.S. to Mexico: security (the shah feared assassination and Mexican facilities are notably lax), language barriers (only the top Mexican medical officials speak English and few of the shah's advisers spoke Spanish), quality (there is no way the best Mexican facilities can match the best American).

"I knew that negotiations were under way to have the shah admitted to the U.S. But our agreement was simply this. I would return to the U.S. and assemble a team to treat him here, if possible, or I would return to Mexico City and assemble a team there. Dr. Flandrin had withdrawn as chief of the case, although he would stay to the end. I was now the shah's physician. In my own mind, I was convinced he had gallstones and I was already formulating plans for New York Hospital's Bjorn Thorbjarnarson, MD, a world expert, to remove them. I knew the precise diagnosis would be made within 24 to 48 hours of admission to any quality hospital.

"My aim was to relieve his obstruction. A man can remain jaundiced for only so long. Whether he had gallstones or a worsening cancer was clearly secondary to getting him hospitalized and treated. I decided to stay out of any negotiations to get him admitted to the U.S., unless the government asked my opinion. The shah and the State Dept. would have to decide whether I would treat him in the U.S. or in Mexico. There were no other choices."

The shah gave Dr. Kean permission to discuss his full medical picture with the U.S. government.

That night, Dr. Kean called Dr. Dustin of the State Dept. and asked if the report to the State Dept. might be sent to the President? Dr. Dustin said yes.

"I said, 'Then, since I was once a physician in the military, I will make this report with all the accuracy and earnestness that I would give if I were reporting directly to the President.' He said, 'That is very good.'

"In great detail, I described for Dr. Dustin the multiple illnesses of the shah, his need for treatment by a medical team, and the need for prompt care, preferably in a teaching hospital. At no time, did I mention the U.S. or New York City. I said the shah had obstructive jaundice and would almost certainly require surgery. I said he was anemic and had low blood counts and would require tranfusions. I said he had nodes in the neck and a swollen spleen and would require either chemotherapy or radiation, or both. I said it was a complicated case and it would require sophisticated care.

"He asked, 'How much time do we have?' I replied, 'Days we have, weeks maybe. We do not have months.'

"Then, he asked, 'Where is the best place to treat him?' I told him I would prefer my team at New York Hospital, but several other U.S. facilities were perfectly qualified. He asked, 'Can you treat him in Mexico?' I said, 'Yes, but not as easily and quickly.'

"I then asked, 'Dr. Dustin, do you want to come to Mexico and examine the shah? Do you want to send a physician to obtain a second opinion? Do you want our Mexican ambassador to choose a Mexican physician? Do you want to pick up the phone and call Drs. Bernard and Flandrin in Paris? Do you require confirmation of what I have just told you?'

"He responded, 'We'll get confirmation, but we do not need it.'

"I said, 'A second opinion is not needed because everything is so elementary and obvious that if anyone says other than what I am telling you, forget it. This diagnosis will be confirmed within 24 hours of his hospital admission.'

"Dr. Dustin asked me to repeat my diagnosis. I did and he listened carefully to every word. What I am saying was submitted as a State Dept. deposition during my libel lawsuit against *Science* magazine. I think that Dr. Dustin is a superior physician and I am confident that what I told him was reported exactly that way to his immediate superior at the State Dept. However, there may be 5, 10, 20 people between Dr. Dustin and what was told to President Carter.

"Any statement that the shah was at 'the point of death' and 'could be treated only in New York City' is obviously ridiculous. Who could say such a thing? Who could believe it? It flies against common sense. Now, I am not going to speculate about what somebody said somebody said, but if President Carter believed the shah either had to come to New York or die within days, somebody misinformed him or somebody misinterpreted some pretty straightforward medical information.

"Medically, a second opinion was pointless. Politically, they probably should have called a medical conference.

"Dr. Dustin thanked me and we concluded the conversation without my knowledge of where the shah would be treated. I hoped it would be New York, for obvious reasons. But had it been Houston, I would not have considered it a personal rejection. I was not as keen on Mexico for the reasons already discussed. Plus, I knew that if the shah had pancreatic cancer, it would require a Whipple operation, which is an enormously difficult six- to eight-hour procedure. And once the shah was installed in a Mexican hospital as the personal guest of the Mexican president, there would be no removing him to the U.S." Three days later, on Oct. 22, the shah was admitted to New York Hospital to the same two rooms that he held in 1949.

"On Oct. 22, the shah was admitted and within 24 hours his gall-stones were removed. Two days later, he turned 60. Nine days later, the Iranians seized the U.S. embassy.

"During the shah's surgery, a lymph node was removed from his neck and biopsied. He now had histiocytic lymphosarcoma, a more serious cancer. Our oncology experts rated it as Stage III or IV, but said the potential for cure exists. It was projected that he might require 18 months of intensive chemotherapy. This diagnosis meant, in effect, that back in March in the Bahamas, Drs. Bernard and Flandrin had been treating either the wrong cancer or the wrong stage. By then, the shah's neck nodes were already evidence of the more serious cancer. Without the biopsy, the French MDs could not be sure.

"Shortly after the gallbladder operation, x-rays showed that a single gallstone had been left behind and was blocking the shah's bile duct. Despite the best of precautions and precision surgery, this sometimes happens. A second operation through diseased tissue would have been very dangerous, so we called on Dr. H. Joachim Burhenne of the U. of British Columbia in Vancouver to perform a stone-crushing technique he had perfected to remove the stone without risk of an operation. During the five weeks it took to prepare for this intricate maneuver, we treated the shah with radiation for his neck tumors. Because the spleen was only moderately swollen and because of the additional risk, we decided to postpone his splenectomy.

"Dr. Burhenne successfully removed the retained stone, and after 42 days, the shah seemed to be in good shape. His jaundice was gone, the neck nodes were gone, the spleen was down, his blood counts were better, and he was no longer anemic.

"I believed then and I strongly believe now that the embassy seizure was related not to our care of the shah but to a power play by the ayatollah."

The State Dept. tried to have the shah's medical condition corroborated by two Iranian physicians who had been trained in the U.S. and who were to have reported their findings to Khomeini.

"I put the question to my patient and he said, 'Under no conditions.' Then, the suggestion was that I fully discuss my findings with the Iranians. Again, the shah refused.

"Finally, the State Dept. asked if I would discuss the shah's case with State Dept. officials. I said only on federal grounds. They suggested the U.S. facility at the United Nations. I presume the intention was to let the Iranian MDs listen to the discussion, but days later I was told that the effort was being scratched.

"It was time for the shah to leave the hospital. Had he been a normal patient, I would have sent him to Connecticut to recuperate. But security was paramount in everyone's mind and the State Dept. decided to send him to a military base in Texas. This decision represented the first thing the U.S. government had provided for their former ally.

"When it was agreed that the shah would leave the U.S. for Panama, I made two requests of the Carter delegation headed by Lloyd Cutler.

"Since I had spent part of my military years training at Gorgas Hospital, a U.S. facility, I knew that it alone in Panama was qualified to provide quality medical care. Since the shah would very soon need to have his spleen removed, I told the government officials:

" 'I will recommend that he have it done in Panama only if it can be done at Gorgas Hospital with the assistance of the U.S. government. This means I want to know you will give me everything I need, even if it means flying in a B-52 with medical equipment. If this is not possible, then I want assurances that I can bring the shah back to the U.S. for medical care at Houston or elsewhere.'

"Cutler looked me in the eye and said, 'You've got it!'

"The promises were never to be redeemed. Nevertheless, the shah was off to Panama. There was nowhere else to go.

"In Panama, things got really disastrous. While hospitalized in New York, the shah's liver biopsy was negative and there was no evidence of lymphoma in a small axillary node. Chest x-rays, bone scans, sonograms, and lymphangiograms were all negative. But cancer cells have a life cycle of their own and, beginning at Lackland Air Force Base, the shah's cancer was coming back with a vengeance.

"By the time he reached Panama, it was mandatory that his swollen spleen be removed. I had made it very clear to the medical staff at Gorgas Hospital that the operation could be done only at Gorgas. I had talked to two surgeons at New York Hospital about possibly doing the operation, but both were noncommittal.

"The shah came down with an infection and I was shocked to learn that he was hospitalized not at Gorgas but at Gen. Torrijos' hospital, Paitilla. The U.S. did not object. I confronted the Panamanian physicians and reminded them of the promise that the shah's operation was to be done at Gorgas.

"Gen. Torrijos' surgeon is Carlos Garcia, MD. He said, 'We don't care what you were promised. This is an order.' I said, "I dare you to tell this to the shah.' He said, 'Take me to him. This is an order from the general.' Dr. Garcia proceeded to spit out the ultimatum to the shah. It was Paitilla or nowhere. The shah just listened. I was disgusted.

"I needed a new solution. I needed a surgeon so big that no one would dare buck him. I needed a man of international acclaim. I needed Michael DeBakey. I called him at midnight from Panama and within a hour he said he would perform the splenectomy.

"But when Dr. DeBakey and I arrived in Panama, it was disgraceful. No one met our plane, no one directed us to our accommodations, and when we arrived at Paitilla, we were denied entrance. Only by resorting to counter-threats was I able to straighten things out. The shah's advisers and I demanded to see the general. He reversed his order and we were allowed to enter the hospital. But Dr. Garcia now insisted that the splenectomy could only be performed by Panamanian surgeons. Dr. DeBakey was described as 'an itinerant surgeon,' though they later said they would permit him in the operating room as 'an observer.'

"This is where Dr. DeBakey's great gifts as a diplomat came into play. He put the best face on things and, since the shah was still battling an infection, agreed that surgery could be postponed. He returned to Houston.

"The Panama card was played out. I decided to play the Houston card, which now had a double meaning since Dr. DeBakey, of course, is in Houston. I called Cutler. He said, 'It cannot be done.'

"Cutler was merely following orders and President Carter had to weigh the worth of a promise given in Texas against what he thought to be in the best interests of the Americans. I can understand their perspective.

"But the shah believed that what Gen. Torrijo's henchmen did is despicable. The shah was again in touch with his old friend Anwar Sadat. The Iranians were in Panama seeking an arrest order. The shah would have been arrested on Monday. He believed that Gen. Torrijos would either make him or the Iranians pay.

"The shah left for Egypt on March 23. "Sadat and Dr. DeBakey were to be the heroes in this tragedy.

"On March 28, Dr. DeBakey arrived and removed the shah's spleen. The night of the operation, Sadat came to the hospital and met the entire medical staff. As we moved through the reception line, I told the Egyptian president, 'When the history of the twentieth century is written, there will be two towering figures—Churchill and Sadat.' Sadat merely nodded. The shah still had his sense of humor. When he recovered from the operation and I told him of my remark and Sadat's reaction, he said, 'Ah, but such an odd pair. Remember, Churchill once imprisoned Sadat!"

"The operation went beautifully. That night, however, was terrible. The medical team—American, Egyptian, French—was in the pathology lab. The focus was the shah's cancerous spleen, grotesquely swollen to 20 times normal. It was one foot long, literally the size of a football. But I was drawn to the liver tissues that had also been removed. The liver was speckled with white. Malignancy. The cancer had hit the liver. The shah would soon die.

"The next morning, I told the shah's wife Empress Farah Diba, and his sister, Princess Ashraf, to cut back on the chemotherapy, to let the shah spend his remaining months in as much comfort as possible. I told them, 'He might live to see another Christmas.' Then, I paid final respects to my patient, sparing him the bad news, and left.

"Before, the shah and his family had always—with the exception of the Lackland decision—followed my medical advice. They knew it was a distillate of the best information I could get.

"This time, however, the family could not accept the inevitability of a fatal illness. The MDs increased the chemotherapy, the weakened shah became infected, sepis developed while he was immunosuppressed, and he was struck by a massive hemorrhage.

"On July 27, 1980, he died. In the spirit of Islam, Sadat buried him with full honors. Finally, the shah had found a resting place."

One year later, Dr. Kean sits in his medical school office and snuffs out a cigar. His only mementos from the shah are an autographed book and a gold-and-silver Persepolis horse. And the memories.

"The tragedy is that a man who should have had the best and easiest medical care had, in many respects, the worst. President Reagan, the Pope, they were shot down in the streets and taken to the emergency room as ordinary patients. Their outcomes might not have been as successful had there been time to search for the 'best' chest surgeon, the 'best' abdominal surgeon. They got the best care because they were treated as 'Peter Smiths.' The shah did not have this luxury.

"Was he a sympathetic character? He became my friend. Today, I believe that most Americans think he should have been granted U.S. asylum as soon as he left Iran. As it is, the U.S. did more than other countries. Britain, France, Switzerland are all former allies of the shah and all have a history of granting political asylum. They turned their backs on the shah and that has not been widely reported.

"The shah was very disappointed with Jimmy Carter's policy toward Iran, which he thought was naive and stupid, and he was baffled that the American people would let their President persist in such folly. But he understood human frailties. He was gracious to the end.

"Any physician will tell you that just having one desperately ill patient is a full-time job. When you add to this a background of international intrigue and tension and, then, the extraordinary situation of the hostages, and intensive press coverage, you have a unique situation. I was not trained in medical school to deal with something like this.

"Would I do it again, answer that call to treat Peter Smith? Of course. If you are a physician, you really do not have a choice." □

Muhammad Ali

Muhammad Ali is one of the most-recognizable faces in the world. That is why millions of Americans were saddened to see the ex-boxing champion being interviewed on TV during the 1984 Summer Olympic Games.

The man who used "to float like a butterfly, sting like a bee" in the boxing ring could barely talk, his face frozen into passive immobility. Some thought it was an act; others attributed it to his "weariness of celebrity." The doctors who watched, however, saw it for what it was: Ali suffers from parkinsonism, a disease that, in his case, was brought on by blows to the head from boxing.

The ex-champ was admitted to a New York hospital in September, 1984, provoking a media blitz and Ali's melodramatic announcement that if it were "Allah's will, I am ready to die." The facts were to be much more Earthbound.

On a hunch, I picked up the phone and began to call around to Ali's old doctors. As I suspected, it turned out that Ali's "pugilistic parkinsonism" was first diagnosed in 1982—two years before the press circus in New York—and the advice to the patient then was the same as it is today:

Take your medicine, as directed by a doctor.

If Ali will follow doctor's orders, he can lead a normal life with none of the unfortunate symptoms of untreated parkinsonism; if not, his condition will worsen.

The champion's sad deterioration, as shown on TV to millions of viewers, helped prompt a new move to ban boxing, a move that, in part, was reinforced by this story and by the continuing campaign against the "sport" by the editor of the *The Journal of the AMA*, George Lundberg, MD. In December, 1984, two months after this story appeared, the AMA House of Delegates called for legislation to ban boxing.

And I got a call from the Pharmaceutical Manufacturers Assn., which was about to hold a conference on treatment compliance with physician-ordered medication. Patients who won't take their medicine as directed are a major medical problem. Would Ali, they asked, be willing to appear as keynote speaker?

It was a terrific idea. Millions of blacks suffer from high blood pressure and to effectively control the condition they need only to take their medicine. Ali is one man who could penetrate them, perhaps, through TV advertisements.

The champ, however, was unavailable for comment, reportedly on his way to a Muslim meeting in the Sudan.

I still think it's a terrific idea.

FORMER BOXING CHAMPION MUHAMMAD ALI was diagnosed in 1983— one full year before his current hospitalization—as having Parkinson's syndrome, or parkinsonism, and though it is being reported here for the first time, the key to the successful management of his medical condition remains now as it was then: Taking the medication prescribed for him.

The standard treatment for parkinsonism is the drug, L-dopa, which delivers to the portion of the brain that controls voluntary movements the amount of dopamine essential for such control. The fact that Ali appeared in New York to be responding well to L-dopa indicates that his parkinsonism can be controlled and he can again walk and talk without the disease's characteristic rigidity and slurring.

The first physician to diagnose the condition was Dennis Cope, MD, of Los Angeles, who was unsuccessful in persuading Ali to do as he was told. His new physician, Stanley Fahn, MD, of New York City, says he is confident that the man who in his prime was unbeatable in the ring will be able to stay on top of parkinsonism (named after a 19th-century English physician) and lead a normal life.

Although an autopsy would be required for a definitive diagnosis, both Drs. Cope and Fahn contend that Ali's medical troubles are caused by "pugilistic parkinsonism," caused by repetitive trauma to the head from boxing blows.

Dr. Cope, an internist at the U. of California at Los Angeles (UCLA) School of Medicine, directs the internal medicine residency program there and is a subspecialist in endocrinology. Ali first was referred to him in 1980 by the fighter's Chicago physician, Charles Williams Sr., MD, in the wake of Ali's surprisingly lack-luster performance against heavyweight champion Larry Holmes. Ali not only lost the Las Vegas fight badly, but he also appeared barely able to defend himself. Ali, who previously had passed a stringent battery of medical tests at the Mayo Clinic, Rochester, Minn., looked so bad that ringside physician Donald Romeo, MD, said he never again would let Ali fight in Nevada.

Dr. Williams, however, suspected that Ali, in his passion to lose weight to be light on his feet, had overmedicated himself on thyroid pills. Upon examination, Dr. Cope confirmed this diagnosis and held a post-fight press conference with Ali to explain the situation to the press.

In an exclusive interview last month, Dr. Cope told *AMN:*

'Thyroid pills had been prescribed to help Ali lose weight, but he simply overdid it. He told me, 'I'm a big man, so I thought I could take a big dose, and I took twice what was recommended.' Ali, in effect, took three times the normal replacement prescription. At the time he fought Holmes, he was probably suffering from hyperthyroidism and extreme fatigue. Whether or not he would have been able to beat Holmes is another question. Ali was then 38 years old. In 1980, Ali was tested by a neurologist and we found no evidence of any brain damage. He previously had been tested by the Mayo Clinic, and within a few months of our tests he was also given a battery of neurological tests at the Neurological Institute of New York U. There were no signs of neurological damage then."

After the Holmes fight in 1980, Ali would be hospitalized three times at UCLA in connection with the emergence of his parkinsonism.

Reading from Ali's hospital chart, Dr. Cope continued: "In August, 1982, Ali was hospitalized at UCLA for the very early signs of parkinsonism. I consulted with a neurologist and neurological surgeon, and we found evidence of very minimal neurological dysfunction. The brain scans appeared to relate it to blows to the head from boxing.

"By October, 1983, Ali's symptoms were worsening and he checked back into UCLA. At that time, we diagnosed his condition as parkinsonism. I explained to him that he had the mild form of the Parkinson's syndrome and not the degenerative form of the disease. I told him that it appeared to be due to the blows he had taken as a boxer. I put him on L-dopa—Sinemet—and explained to him how important it is that he regularly take the medication every day.

"By October, 1983, he was displaying immobile facial appearance and expression, a difficulty in speaking without slurring his words, and a stiffness in his gait. He also had hand tremors, which probably had begun a few months before he was hospitalized.

"I told him, 'It will not be difficult for you to control this condition, but you have to do your part and follow through. You have to take the medication.' Now, he is a very cooperative patient, and he said, 'I'm going to do it.' I replied, 'Fine, because the real key to your recovery is taking the medication we prescribe.'

"Well, as the next year wore on, I would talk to him from time to time and I always had the feeling that the medication was not being taken properly. For one thing, Ali is a Muslim minister and he doesn't like taking any form of drugs. For another, it just wasn't an important detail to him. He refused to build it into his lifestyle, and there was no one around him to make him do it. The big problem is that he travels so much and he's never in one place.

"The last time I saw him was earlier this year and his symptoms were not improving—a sign that he was not properly using the L-dopa. He was otherwise in excellent health, his blood pressure was normal, and his medical outlook was great—if he would only listen. I told him that if he didn't pay attention, he would begin to walk more stiffly and have more trouble talking."

Apparently, Ali did not listen. On Sept. 5, 1984, he abruptly left London and checked into New York City's Columbia-Presbyterian Hospital.

His physician there is Dr. Fahn, a neurologist who specializes in movement disorders and Parkinson's disease and syndrome.

Dr. Fahn told *AMN:* "It's ironic, but back in August during the Olympics I happened to see Ali being interviewed on TV. I took one look and I said to myself, 'This man may have parkinsonism.' He had the classic symptoms—frozen face, difficulty speaking, stiff movements. But I never thought that I would treat him."

Ali was referred to Dr. Fahn by Martin Ecker, MD, a radiologist who is a business partner and friend of Ali's. Toward the end of the summer, Dr. Ecker had become concerned about Ali's deteriorating symptoms. When the former champion reached Columbia-Presbyterian, he came quickly to his point:

"They think it's parkinsonism," the former boxer said. "Well, do I have it or do I not have it?"

Ali arrived late on the night of Sept. 5, and after a clinical examination Sept. 6, Dr. Fahn was equally straightforward:

"Yes, you do, and here's what we're going to do about it."

Ali responded, "Well, I guess I'll have to live with it."

"The clinical diagnosis was very straightforward. But we weren't sure about the cause," the neurologist told *AMN.* "I suspected blows from boxing, but ordered a series of neurological tests. Ali had not been taking the L-dopa prescribed for him at UCLA because apparently he was not convinced that he needed it. I put him back on L-dopa, and then he left for Europe on a business trip."

On Sept. 18, Ali came back to Columbia-Presbyterian and, this time, the press was waiting for him. Ali's theretofore unreported medical condition, already one year old, was about to become a public property, and the nation was about to get a crash course in parkinsonism.

On Sept. 19, Ali met the press, with Dr. Fahn standing on the sidelines. The boxer gave an accurate description of his medical condition, but many reporters picked up on only one quote:

"I've had a full life," Ali said, "and even if I have cancer of the heart, I have no regrets. I'm ready to meet my maker; I'm ready to go to Allah."

Dr. Fahn said, "Reporting that statement was unfortunate. It was a noble thought, but Ali's predicament was nowhere near that serious. To clarify his situation, I decided to hold my own press conference the next day."

On Sept. 20, Dr. Fahn told reporters:

"Muhammad Ali's neurological evaluation is still in progress, but we have learned the following:

"Ali has some mild symptoms of Parkinson's syndrome, or parkinsonism. We have detrmined that it is highly unlikely that he has the more serious Parkinson's disease, which is degenerative and progressive.

"There are many possible causes for parkinsonism—injuries to the head, adverse reactions to drugs, infections such as encephalitis, and vascular insufficiency. In Ali's case, we think that the leading cause is blows to the head from boxing.

"With standard medication, he can lead a normal life. He shows no signs of dementia, and he definitely is not 'punch drunk.' His life is absolutely not in danger and his condition is not contagious."

Later, Dr. Fahn explained to *AMN:* "It seems to me that repetitive trauma to the head from boxing is a very reasonable explanation as the cause of Ali's parkinsonism. It is our leading diagnosis and likely to remain our leading diagnosis, though we would need an autopsy to ascertain 'pugilistic parkinsonism.'

"But, no, he does not have multiple sclerosis, he does not have any other central nervous system lesion, and, in general, his condition is a lot less serious than the press was reporting.

"Ali's mind is very sharp. He is very calm and very accepting of what has happened. He told me, 'As a boxer, I knew the risks. I'm ready to accept Allah's will. I think that I am much more fortunate than most boxers."

Dr. Fahn continued, "He accepts the fact that his condition is probably due to all the punishment he took as a boxer, but he's not depressed about it. He says that he's accepted the need to take his medication, but time will tell."

Although Dr. Fahn did not want to be drawn into the growing controversy over whether or not boxing should be banned, he said, "I'm not a fan (of boxing), I think it causes injury, and I'm not happy with it." He continued, "Although there are several cases in the literature of 'pugilistic parkinsonism,' this is not a common condition among boxers. And, of course, the overwhelming majority of patients with either Parkinson's disease or parkinsonism have cases totally unrelated to boxing. The etiology is often unknown."

Dr. Fahn, who has been sent the records of Ali's three earlier UCLA hospitalizations for parkinsonism—which at the champion's request never before were made public said—"The key now is to find the optimal medication for Ali's condition and see that he learns to live with it.

"There is art as well as science to prescribing for parkinsonism patients. Right now, I'm using Sinemet (L-dopa) in conjunction with Symmetrel (to enhance the effect). The results have been encouraging. Ali's symptoms appear to be melting away."

Dr. Fahn offered a clue as to Ali's character:

"On Sept. 20, I briefly took him off medication, because I wanted to do some sleep studies. I knew that Jesse Jackson was coming to town to see my patient, but I asked Ali, 'Please, just let Jesse come alone to your room. Skip the press conference. Without the medication, you're not going to be your best and, besides, you need your rest.' Well, he said he would, and then, I had to leave the hospital. That night on TV, I watched Ali and Jesse meet the press.

"Well, I can't blame him for what he did. He took his medication anyway and put on a great show for the press. He's a very smart man. He knew that people were thinking that he was in terrible shape, and he wanted to show them that he is fine. It was the right thing to do. It ruined the sleep study, but we've since repeated it. Meeting the press was the best thing Ali could have done. He knew how good he looked and he wanted to go down and show off one more time—to prove that his doom is not at hand."

The next morning, Ali left for a Muslim conference in the Sudan, though he had promised his neurologist that he would return within a week for the results of his additional tests and possible fine-tuning of his medication and dosage.

Dr. Fahn added, "Well, we'll see what happens. I'm not going to hold my breath. I know what happened after his UCLA stays. But, so far, he's been an ideal patient. Parkinsonism is no threat to his health and life, and he's seen that he and everybody around him wants what's best. He has this entourage around him, and they were always in his hospital room trying to be helpful. Finally, I said, 'Look, he needs a nap. Please leave him alone.' Well, they all seemed relieved, as if that were what they wanted to hear.

"It's certainly added a little spice to my life. It disrupted things for awhile, but everything is working out," the neurologist concluded. "He's the most famous patient I have ever treated, and everyone on our medical team wants to help him. We all admire him for who he is and what he's done. It's very gratifying to see him responding so well to medicine and to be able to rule out other medical conditions, including hypoglycemia, which some people [had] feared he had.

"He's quite a smart guy, he looks good, he has a very alert mind, he's very friendly, he jokes with the staff, he never complains, and he's been very cooperative.

"In short, he's been a very good sport. Now, if we can just get him to keep taking his medicine and maybe lose a few pounds. . . ."

Ali for once was not talking—at least not until he returned from the Sudan.

When he does, Dr. Fahn said, "I will be looking to determine the optimal medicine to regulate the parkinsonism. That, and trying to help him sleep better. Our studies show that he has many awakenings during the night. If he will exercise more, slow down his lifestyle a little, lose a little weight, and take his medicine, his outlook is superb. I think that we can prevent the condition from progressing."

Dr. Fahn's advice, of course, also could apply to millions of people who have serious medical conditions other than parkinsonism and to millions of others who are healthy but have unhealthy lifestyles.

Muhammad Ali, a self-proclaimed (and widely recognized) legend worldwide, now could become a medical role model for millions.

If he would use common sense and follow his physician's advice, the boxer who could beat every man in the world also could beat his medical problem.□

The Reverend Jim Jones

The 1978 mass suicide in Guyana commanded by the Rev. Jim Jones, leader of the "Peoples Temple," wrote a new chapter in cultist horror.

There can be no satisfactory explanation, but in this exclusive interview, Jones' physician and friend, Carlton Goodlett, MD, offers the theory that a frenzied Jones, suffering from a tropical lung infection that may well have spread to his brain, snapped into a paranoid psychosis.

As Dr. Goodlett concludes, "If I ever come back to life, it will be as a plumber. As a physician, I've seen too much."

ONE MAN WHO MIGHT HAVE PREVENTED THE CARNAGE in Guyana is Carlton Goodlett, MD, for the past seven years the physician and close friend of People Temple leader, the late Rev. Jim Jones. But Dr. Goodlett's patient wouldn't listen.

"He should have been in a hospital," Dr. Goodlett told *AMN*. "Last August, I got an urgent call from Jim, who told me he was sick. He said he was putting our friendship on the line, that if I valued the friendship I would come to treat him.

"Well, I flew to Guyana, and found that he had a lung infection, probably from some tropical fungus. I told him he had to go to a hospital for a good workup. He said he thought he had cancer, but he didn't have the time for the hospital right then. I told him, 'You put our friendship on the line to get me down here. Now, I'm putting the friendship on the line to get you in the hospital. Either you get your ass in the hospital or you find another doctor.'

"He promised me he would go, but he never did. A month after I visited him, he had lost 30 pounds and was spending most of his time in bed. The camp physician, Dr. Lawrence Schacht, was worried about him and wrote to me. Again, I insisted to Jones that he enter a hospital for tests. He said he would, but first he had this visit from Congressman Ryan. Jones never made it."

In a two-hour telephone interview, Dr.Goodlett, the dean of physicians in San Francisco's black ghetto, traced his friendship with Jones and views on why the tragedy happened. Dr. Goodlett, a 1944 graduate of Meharry Medical College, has been a family physician in San Francisco since 1945. The physician said he "is disappointed that Jones chose to die rather than fight for his cause," that he "senselessly took his followers with him;" but maintained that "Jim Jones died a friend of the black man." Racism is the culprit, the MD said.

Dr. Goodlett said, "No question about it, the man broke. He broke psychologically and he broke physically—you can never divide the two— and what happened is a tragedy, but you can never take away what Jim Jones did for the black man.

"He had a great compassion for the rejects of society. He fed them and he clothed them and he housed them and he gave them medical care. You know, there are a lot of people still living in this country who are success stories because of what Jim Jones did for them. Not all his followers are dead.

"Right up until his final act, he was an upstanding man who was trying to do a lot of good. The publicity now is all negative: that Jones was a monster and a homosexual and bisexual and all that crap. Well, that's all hindsight. Right up until the end he appeared to be a stable, tough-minded man. Anybody who tells you otherwise is lying."

Jones "never took care of himself and he was always overextended," Dr. Goodlett said. "He was often ill and fatigued.

"I treated him only intermittently over the past seven years. He had diabetes and we controlled that by diet. When I saw him in Guyana, he had a fever of 103°. I knew he had some lung pathology, but without bronchoscopic tests and a hospital workup, I couldn't diagnose him. Jones seemed to think he had cancer or some terminal disease, but we found no evidence of cancer. He could have been successfully treated.

"Psychologically, he had his paranoid moments, but he was stable, too. He gave every appearance of continuing his struggle right to the end. I never thought of him as a man who would kill himself, who would give his enemies the chance to see him dead. I never dreamed he would do what he did, and neither did anyone else.

"I told him he had to go to a hospital, and we discussed either New York, Moscow, or Cuba. But when I learned that there was a good hospital in Georgetown (Guyana), I told him, 'You know, Jim, it will be an an embarrassment to Guyana if you follow the advice of the Soviet Embassy and fly 10,000 miles to Moscow when you can be treated right in your own back yard.' He agreed.

"If my patients in San Francisco don't follow my orders, they are told to find another physician. Well, Jim Jones was not your typical patient, and he was a long way from me. When I learned a month later that he still hadn't gone in for the tests and had lost 30 pounds, I tried again. By now his fever was up to 105°. I'm sure a secondary infection had set in that probably would have proven fatal. He said he would go to the hospital as soon as Rep. Ryan left.

"The autopsy performed on Jones in Guyana showed a lung infection. I told them to go back and study the tissues to see if there were a tumor or abscess of the brain or meningitis or encephalitis. I think it's quite possible that he had a brain infection. Certainly, that would help account for his bizarre behavior at the end. I'm sure the Guyanese authorities still have Jones' body tissues and can do the microscopic work to determine exactly what his medical problems were. To my knowledge he was not a drug addict, although he did take pain-killers.

"I think he thought his dream was dying, and when Congressman Ryan came down, he snapped. I had told him that this was not the time to see Ryan, that he should be in the hospital recuperating and waiting until he was well before he agreed to see Ryan. But, then, he didn't always listen to me.

"You know, 75% of the people in Guyana were black. Hell, at least 150 of them were my patients."

Dr. Goodlett, among other things, is also a publisher. He owns nine San Francisco Bay-area newspapers that espouse black and liberal causes.

The physician said, "Sure, it's a tragedy. But what is really stirring the media up is that you had 900 people commit suicide in the same place at the same time. That's the whole hue and cry and horror over Jim Jones. Well, every day in this country, you have more than 900 black people who die because of racism, who die because of the effects of the system. They're dying from alcoholism and drug addiction and poor medical care. The black masses in America are worse off today than at any time since Reconstruction.

"Jones broke, and I'm disappointed that he decided to die for the cause rather than live for it. But he died a friend. I'm sure the deaths were part suicide and part murder. Jones shot himself, he was saying, 'I'm for real, I'm going to kill myself.' He was also paranoically self-centered, and believed that the others had to play follow the leader. If they wouldn't take the poison, they would be force-fed.

"The doctor who mixed the poison potion, Dr. Schacht, was a protege of myself and Jones. When I first met him, he was a confused drug addict who had come to the temple and who talked about becoming a doctor. We got him straightened out and placed at Guadalajara for two years. Then, we used my political connections and Jones' and got him enrolled at the U. of California, Irvine, medical school, where he did fine. After three months of his internship, he left for Guyana to be with Jones.

"What about the Hippocratic Oath when he prepared the poison? His loyalty to Jones was stronger than his loyalty to Hippocrates.

"Jones had his vices, no doubt about it. I can see him doing a lot of those terrible things. When you run a cult and everyone calls you 'Dad' and 'Father,' you set your own code and your own morals. I was never a member of the temple, and he never pulled any of that crazy stuff with me. I never would have sat still for it for a minute.

"I treated Jones, and I treated his wife and family. And I saw them socially. They were my friends. I heard reports about disciplinary abuses within the temple, but that wasn't my business.

"Jones never discussed this mass suicide exercise with me. I wouldn't have stood for it. But then I couldn't have changed his mind. I couldn't get him to go to the hospital. It was always manana, manana. When he thought he was dying and his dream was dying, the only way out was a revolutionary suicide. And execution. A little of both.

"It was a tragic loss. The man down the street, a butcher, lost his wife and seven children in Guyana. Before I left for Guyana, he asked me to check up on his family to give them hugs and kisses. They all looked healthy and happy to me and I told him so. Well, today that man's about to lose his mind.

"I don't think it was just Jim Jones who did it. It was the system, too. Jones believed in reincarnation. I don't, but if I did, I would want to come back as a plumber. As a physician, I've seen too much."□

Adolf Hitler: Still alive, but "at the lowest level of existence." AP

Ernst Gunther Schenck, MD, has spent half a lifetime searching for secrets to Hitler's behavior.

Photos (unless otherwise credited) by Dennis L. Breo.

Wilbur Thain, MD, describes his patient Howard Hughes as "brilliant, irascible, eccentric, human."

Elvis Presley, 1975. AP

George Nichopoulos, MD, still finds it difficult to discuss his celebrity patient, Elvis Presley.

Muhammad Ali is joined by Jesse Jackson in a 1984 press conference outside the hospital. UPI.

Emilio Tresalti, MD, medical director of Gemelli Hospital, Rome.

The Shah of Iran and his wife, the Empress Farah Diba, in Mexico, 1979. UPI.

B. H. Kean, MD, reflects on the months he spent treating the Shah.

2. *Medicine and the Media*

DOCTORS, BY AND LARGE, don't trust the press, and reporters, by and large, don't trust doctors, at least when a controversial story is at stake.

Often, the news media have not reported accurately and fully the complexity of many medical issues. Much of this is medicine's fault because too often physicians and their medical societies have not identified themselves as having something to say.

There are reasons for this, of course. Many doctors have a story about how their remarks were "taken out of context" by a reporter. Many reporters have a story about how doctors deliberately "misled" them or talked down to them or, worse, refused to talk to them at all.

Also, doctors, unlike journalists, make their livings practicing medicine, not journalism, and their time is in short supply. Upon their return from Moscow after the nuclear-reactor explosion at Chernobyl, the UCLA bone-marrow transplant team was besieged with requests for interviews. One doctor observed, "If I talked to every reporter who calls, I'd never have time to brush my teeth." Certainly, it's easier to have one superficial press conference, take a few questions, and let things go at that.

However, it is the public who suffers from this standoff between medicine and media, as people have to pick through contradictory claims to try to get at what is really going on.

As the Special Assignments Editor of *American Medical News*, I have had a privileged entree to doctors in the news. Over the years, I have found that many medical controversies are incompletely reported because of the mutual mistrust of medicine and the media. Now, it is true that a reporter for the AMA does not lightly assault the reputations of doctors in the news, but, over the years, I have found that the enforced reflex of looking for both sides of the story, of trying to find the truth in the middle, usually leads to not only a more accurate story, but also to a more interesting story.

One of my most striking examples (not included in this anthology) is the 1977 case of Camarillo (Calif.) State Hospital. The Ventura County, Calif., district attorney had found 100 cases of "suspicious deaths" and he convened an extraordinary open grand jury. TV cameras recorded the lurid charges. It was made to appear that mental-health professionals were murdering their patients, that Camarillo was "Cuckoo's Nest" on a major scale. TV stations and major publications called Camarillo a "snake's pit."

When all was said and done, however, it turned out that Camarillo simply represented the grim situation that one can expect when an under-funded and overstaffed facility is overcrowded with the hard core of society's mentally ill. Of the five cases (of the original 100) the Ventura County grand jury found actionable, all were subsequently dismissed. The eight health professionals charged, including three physicians, were all cleared. They were working against enormous odds to try to help their patients, it was determined.

They will never forget, however, being treated as common criminals and being presented to the world in that light by the media. The big losers were those who had friends and relatives being treated at the facility. Camarillo, for years one of this country's major mental-health treatment centers (the pioneering work on schizophrenia was done here), was being presented as a graveyard.

Had the Camarillo officials, mental health professionals, and mem-bers of the local medical society spoken out earlier—as they subsequently did to me—the media might have picked up in a story that was played for its narrow sensationalism the saving truth:

Mental hospitals everywhere exist to ease life for the rest of us, and were they all emptied tomorrow, a clamor to build new ones would be raised by their true clients—parents, police, judges.

The scenario of false accusation against a medical professional, the stonewalling by a stricken medical facility, the baying of the (press and police) hounds, and the subsequent determination that the malpractice was media, not medical, would be replayed three years later in the case of the "Death Angel" of Las Vegas, a story that does appear in this book.

This pattern has happened many times in the past and it will happen many more times in the future. It's easier for journalists to work the wrong side of the street and it's easier for medical people to avoid getting involved to clarify the situation.

The media can often make medical controversies. Richard Kunnes, MD, the man who gained lasting fame—and notoriety—by disrupting a 1969 AMA convention and calling the organization "the American Murder Assn." told me in 1978:

"I had decided to say I was burning my AMA membership card because I knew the media would go for it (actually it was his Blue Cross card, he confided; he did not belong to the AMA)."

Dr. Kunnes continued, "The AMA was really a favorite target of the media in those days . . . the media loved the radical physicians. It was the media that egged me on to demonstrate again at the AMA meeting. After our press conference (held by the counter-culture physicians who called themselves the "Medical Committee on Human Right"), several reporters came up to me and said, 'God, this is terrific. Why don't you do more like it. We'll give you all the coverage you need.' "

Dr. Kunnes, of course, was but one of many media creations (Spiro Agnew would later address that same AMA convention). But had flustered AMA officials not appeared so baffled, bewildered, and, ultimately, angered by Dr. Kunnes' radical rhetoric and had they responsibly replied *to the press* about his charges rather than thrown up a wall of security (a few angry delegates even threw ashtrays at the young physicians), the media might not have been able to make such a theatrical spectacle of things. But, then, that was the 1960s.

More recently, the news media appeared for awhile to be infatuated with the claims for laetrile, an apricot-pit concoction that supporters claim can cure cancer. There are many complex problems in medicine for which there are no easy—if any—solutions, and, certainly, cancer is near the top of the list. It is no surprise that many people—and for awhile many state legislatures—decided to put to flight the conventional medical wisdom and legalize the worthless laetrile.

The issue to the media, however, is not only whether or not people should have the freedom of choice to use laetrile, but also whether or not there are violations of important scientific and legal principles:

Scientifically, the principle is that the medical value of a drug or procedure should be determined in the lab or the operating room and not in the press and the legislature; and, legally, the principle is that the rights of sick minors, like three-year-old Chad Green, who was removed from Mass General chemotherapy in favor of Tijuana laetrile to treat his leukemia, should not be abridged by misguided adults. The sad fact is that medicine believes—then and now—that it has a viable form of treatment for the illness that killed Chad Green. These stories, too, are important issues for the press.

Medical controversies are invariably complex and the public deserves nothing less than medicine and media working together toward a joint goal of balanced reporting.

Examples abound.

When Hinckley was acquitted, it was easy to make fun of the psychiatrists who helped sway the jury. It was harder to accurately portray the conundrum in which psychiatry finds itself with the insanity defense.

When nurse Jani Adams, the alleged "Death Angel" of Las Vegas, was indicted for murder, it was easy to speculate about the ghoulish charges. It was harder to take a look at the actual medical record of the death in question and to realize that the police and press of a provincial town were trying to make policy on complicated ethical questions, and, in the process, were callously accusing an innocent woman.

When the clamor grew for an autopsy of Mary Jo Kopechne, who drowned at Chappaquiddick after apparently being in a car driven by Sen. Edward Kennedy, it was easy to criticize the medical examiner who failed to secure it. It was harder to look at the holes in the Massachusetts' medical examiner system that made the slip-up not only possible, but virtually certain.

Similarly, it was easy for the media to accuse the Memphis medical examiner of a cover-up in the autopsy of Elvis Presley, who, some reporters had decided, must have died from all the drugs prescribed for the late singer by his personal physician. It was harder to report the actual facts of the Presley autopsy—including all the drugs found in his blood—and the actual care rendered to Presley by his personal physician—including the drugs that were prescribed. The real stories are often too complicated to fit into a 30-second spot on the network news or into a slanted "documentary."

When the coroner of Los Angeles, Thomas Noguchi, MD, spoke out about the drug-induced deaths of celebrities like John Belushi and Natalie Wood, it was easy to condemn his apparent play for publicity. It was harder to accept the creed of forensic pathology: "The living must learn from the dead."

And, when surgeons Bill DeVries (who implanted the first artificial heart into a human, Barney Clark) and Leonard Bailey (who implanted the first baboon heart into an infant, Baby Fae) boldly acted to try to save failing lives, it was easy to report on the apparent "medical miracles." It was harder to go beyond the headlines and report on the science that had enabled the surgeons to take their leap into faith and report on the extremely difficult clinical challenges that still confront their experiments (doctors never use the word, "breakthrough," since every apparent breakthrough by one physician has usually been preceded by decades of painstaking work by hundreds of peers).

It is time for a new relationship between medicine and the media. While the media must be on guard against self-serving statements, it must also seek out informed medical opinion behind current headlines. While medicine must be on guard against sensation-seeking distortions, it must actively interject itself into the media's reporting of medical issues.

Medicine and the media must help each other to tell it like it is.

The Laetrile Gang

The laetrile gang was an odd collection: John Birchers, entrepreneurs, both American and Mexican; a mad scientist; desperate patients and their families; and, primarily, the man behind the movement—Canadian Andrew McNaughton.

McNaughton, a man of many lives, has been a tycoon, gun-smuggler, and manufacturer of laetrile, the apricot-pit substance that supporters claim can cure cancer. He is one of the most colorful personalities I have ever met and he personally escorted me through the laetrile clinics in Tijuana.

The "Apricot Mafia" make big profits off the hopes of terminal cancer patients, who might as well be putting their trust in popsickle sticks. McNaughton says he believes in laetrile, but, then, he also believes in reincarnation.

One of the saddest cases of this fraud involves Chad Green, the three-year-old Massachusetts boy who became a fugitive from justice when his parents decided to treat his leukemia not with chemotherapy from Massachusetts General Hospital but with laetrile from Tijuana. The child's parents said that the fateful decision was the will of God, but the patient, little Chad, never got to cast his vote. Within six months of the flight to Mexico, laetrile's most famous patient was dead.

Andrew McNaughton

THE WOMAN FROM Chicago had a question. "What did you say your involvement with laetrile is? Are you an attorney?"

Rocking gently back and forth in his chair, the neatly bearded, professorial-looking man laid it out:

"My name is Andrew McNaughton, president of the McNaughton Foundation, which, for the past 21 years, has been producing laetrile in eight factories around the world. The McNaughton Foundation sponsored the request to have laetrile legalized by the U.S. Food and Drug Administration.

"In fact, the FDA still refers to the application for laetrile, as Amygdalin-MF. Amygdalin is the chemical name for laetrile and MF stands for McNaughton Foundation."

It is high noon in Tijuana, Mexico, on this spring day in 1977, and McNaughton, 60, is conducting his weekly class for new cancer patients at the two Tijuana clinics that dispense laetrile, the banned and unproven apricot-pit derivative supporters say is effective against cancer.

The 40 or so people overflow the room. Most have been diagnosed in the U.S. as having advanced cancer. Tijuana is the last stop, and laetrile seems the last chance.

The patients have only begun to use laetrile. They want to know how they can be assured of its continued supply when they return to the States.

McNaughton has the answers:

"None of you are professional smugglers," he said, "and I don't think you should start now.

'The best way is to have your name added to the Oklahoma class-action decision allowing the importation of laetrile for personal use. You must have your name on the court order, get a prescription for laetrile from Dr. Soto (medical director of the Clinica Cydel), and show the border guards a sales invoice and pay the 5% duty.

"The next best way is to join the Committee for Freedom of Choice in Cancer Therapy, Inc. It has members, including physicians, around the country, and they can tell you where to find laetrile. It only costs $15 to join and, for that, you get the committee's publication, *The Choice,* which will keep you informed of anti-cancer activities.

"Or you can arrange for C&R, a distribution firm, to buy laetrile for you here in Tijauna and ship it to you.

"Let's review it now. First, ..."

McNaughton goes on for two hours, fielding questions from the patients.

Andrew McNaughton is the main man behind laetrile, and he is buoyed by the unprecedented resurgence in the past few months of the so called cancer drug.

For 25 years, organized medicine—including the American Medical Association, the American Cancer Society, and the National Cancer Institute—has said laetrile is worthless in the treatment of cancer.

In April, 1953, the Cancer Commission of the California Medical Assn. collected information on 44 cancer patients treated with laetrile. "All the patients," the commission reported, "either have active diseases or are dead of their disease, with one exception. Of those alive with disease, no patient has been found with objective evidence of control of cancer under treatment with laetrile alone.

"Nine patients dying from cancer after treatment with laetrile have been autopsied, and histological studies done for the commission by five different pathologists have shown no evidence of any chemotherapeutic effect.

"In two independent studies by experienced research workers, laetrile has been completely ineffective when used in large doses on cancer in laboratory animals, in lesions which are readily influenced by useful chemotherapy."

Yet, decades later, in great part due to the persistence of McNaughton, the laetrile issue is alive and well.

In May, 1976, Alaska legalized the prescription of laetrile by physicians. At the very time McNaughton is holding his class, three other states—Arizona, Indiana, and Nevada—are considering legalizing its manufacture and sale.

In California, a state senate subcommittee approved a proposal to legalize the substance.

Laetrile is being featured in several national magazines. A recent series of broadcasts by a Chicago television station accounts for several new patients in Tijuana.

Across the border in San Diego, four members of the Committee for Freedom of Choice in Cancer Therapy, Inc. (CFCCT) are on trial for allegedly smuggling laetrile into the U.S. from Tijuana.

Two dates are essential to an understanding of the laetrile phenomenon.

The first is 1956, when McNaughton, a Canadian adventurer-entrepreneur, met Ernst Krebs Jr., a biochemist who in 1949 patented laetrile.

The second is 1972, when John Richardson, MD, was arrested in Albany, Calif., for using the drug. Dr. Richardson is a prominent member of the John Birch Society, and several society members sprang to his defense.

In 1956, McNaughton was an arms merchant who had supplied weapons to both Israel and Cuba. He also had just incorporated the McNaughton Foundation, which was seeking projects "on the outer limits of scientific knowledge."

McNaughton said he listened to Krebs for 2½ hours in a Miami Beach drugstore, and "found laetrile to be an entrancing problem."

McNaughton said his foundation's advisory board considered the laetrile theory to be "pretty far out, but why not give it a try?"

Factories have been built to manufacture the substance in Canada, West Germany, Italy, Switzerland, Monaco, and Sausalito, Calif. The two newest ones in Tijuana capitalize on laetrile's sudden popularity.

Along the way, McNaughton has dealt with various foreign governments, Howard Hughes, and has been caught up in three stock swindles in as many countries.

Laetrile, however, languished until 1972 when political liberal McNaughton inadvertently became involved with the ultra right-wing John Birch Society.

Dr. Richardson's friends first formed only a defense organization, but the Birch Society found in laetrile an irresistible issue: Freedom of Choice against Big Government on a matter of life or death.

The Birch organization was galvanized into action, as freedom of choice committees sprang up across the country. Legislative compaigns to legalize laetrile are under way in at least 19 states. Teaching clinics are being held to instruct physicians in using laetrile.

The U.S. government charges that a smuggling network run by committee members is illegally bringing millions of dollars worth of laetrile to the U.S.

Last May, a federal court indictment in San Diego charged Mc-Naughton, eight Americans, seven Mexicans, and three Mexican firms with 171 counts of smuggling involving 20 separate operations.

On Jan. 18, four of those Americans went to trial—Dr. Richardson, 53; his business manager, Ralph Bowman, 48; Robert W. Bradford, 45, of Menlo Park, Calif., a former Stanford U. engineer who is now the president of CFCCT; and Frank Salaman, 51, a California yacht broker and CFCCT vice president.

The indictment noted that during the period 1973–75 deposits in Dr. Richardson's bank account totaled $2.5 million, and that Bradford received $1.2 million for 700 shipments of laetrile. One of the Mexican nationals indicted, Ernesto Contreras, MD, allegedly deposited $2 million to his account in San Ysidro, Calif., just across the Tijuana border.

Bradford was arrested Dec. 20, 1975, carrying in his Cadillac 3,900 three-gram vials of laetrile and a Browning automatic revolver. Bradford and Salaman allegedly have been distributing the laetrile under the name, "B & S Distributors."

The trial of two other indicted Americans, Donald Hanson, 46, and Donna Schuster, 44, doing business as Shaklee Distributors, has been split off and will be held later in Minneapolis.

The trial of three others, McNaughton; Guido Orlandi Sr., 64, president of the Food Science Laboratory, Burlington, Vt., and Frank Spolnik, 61, a Hammond, Ind., gas station operator and part-time health food distributor, is scheduled in San Diego after the current trial is concluded.

The seven Mexican nationals are fugitives.

During the three-month trial, Federal District Judge William Enright has ruled that laetrile efficacy is not an issue, nor are the defendants' tax records. The issue, Judge Enright has contended, is whether smuggling occurred.

Asst. U.S. Atty. Herbert Hoffmann has charged that the defendants used American and Mexican "mules" (couriers) to make laetrile "drops" across the border and then distribute it across the country by mail, parcel post, air freight, and private courier. Customs agents and alleged smug-gling couriers who have turned state's evidence have testified to the orga-nized nature of the alleged operation.

The defendants have countered that although they have handled laetrile in this country, they have had nothing to do with bringing it across the border. Furthermore, they charge, the trial is "an outrageous abuse of federal power" and that they are the "victims of a conspiracy."

Although its leaders are limited by the trial, the CFCCT movement continues at full-strength.

Bradford was formerly with the Stanford U. Linear Accelerator Facil-ity; Salaman's family has owned a yacht brokerage for three generations. The two met years ago at a gathering where Bradford introduced an American Way film by John Wayne, and have been good friends ever since. Following their successful defense of Dr. Richardson on the charge of illegally using laetrile, Bradford and Salaman formed the CFCCT in Los Altos in the San Francisco Bay area.

In court, Bradford and Salaman were dressed in identical navy-blue suits, as were Dr. Richardson, a former Marine platoon sergeant who still looks the part, and Bowman. All wore the Birch pin.

Other Birch Society members associated with the CFCCT include Mike Culbert and Maureen Salaman, wife of Frank, who are co-editors of *The Choice;* George Kell, a Modesto, Calif., attorney who is legal adviser to the committee; and Rep. Larry MacDonald, MD, a Georgia con-gressman who has admitted prescribing laetrile and who is the commit-tee's legislative adviser.

Ernst Krebs Jr., the committee's scientific adviser, is not a member of the John Birch Society, although his views are compatible with those of the society.

McNaughton, in Tijuana, has built the two new laetrile-manufactur-ing firms, plants that can be expected to serve as prototypes if he is allowed to move the operation to the U.S. Both firms are affiliated with laetrile clinics.

The Clinica Cydel was built by McNaughton in 1975 as a showcase for the "holistic approach to the metabolic therapy of cancer with Vitamin B-17" (when California and federal officials cracked down on laetrile as a drug, Krebs reclassified it as Vitamin B-17).

McNaughton says Clinica Cydel was built to meet FDA specifications and with the support of the Mexican government.

The clinic is off the Ensenada toll road, a few miles from the Amer-ican border. A few yards down a dusty road is the Cyto Pharma de Mexico, currently the world's largest manufacturer of laetrile.

Both Clinica Cydel and Cyto Pharma are sponsored by the Mc-

Naughton Foundation and owned by the eight Del Rio brothers, a Tijuana family whose firms manufacture everything from fire extinguishers to leather coats and jewelry. Jorge Del Rio, the leading brother, was indicted by the U.S., as were brothers Gustavo and Sergio and the Cyto Pharma concern.

Medical director of Clinica Cydel is Mario Soto, MD, a former Mexico City oncologist.

A few miles away at Tijuana's ocean beachfront is the Del Mar Clinic and Hospital of Ernesto Contreras, MD, the Mexican Army pathologist whom McNaughton introduced to laetrile in 1963. Dr. Contreras has since become the most prominent laetrile doctor, having treated thousands of American patients.

To ease any competition to Dr. Contreras brought by the new Clinica Cydel and its Cyto Pharma, McNaughton has built a new laetrile-manufacturing firm for Dr. Contreras. Due to a dispute with the local health authorities, it is currently shut down. Dr. Contrearas' laetrile firm, Kemsa, was cited in the indictment. (The third Mexican firm charged in the indictment is C&R Distributors, run by another defendant, Rudy Alvarez-Hota, a friend of the Del Rios.)

Dr. Soto greeted visitors at Clinica Cydel with, "Good news. Good news. We have 10 new patients from Chicago who have come down since the television show."

Dr. Soto describes himself as an "oncologist conventional, radiotherapist conventional." It was his studies with laetrile at Mexico City that led to Mexico's legalization of the drug. In the past, he had been a registered investigator for the National Cancer Institute, but this had nothing to do with his use of laetrile, according to an NCI spokesman.

Dr. Soto is regarded suspiciously by laetrile hardliners, because he mixes orthodox treatment with laetrile. Although such combination therapy is counter to Cydel's claim of "specializing in nontoxic therapies," Dr. Soto says he is getting excellent results.

"Since opening Cydel," he said, "we have treated 770 patients. All are advanced cases, and 99% are from the U.S." Laetrile is only a control, not a cure, he stresses, "but we are pleased with the progress."

Dr. Soto is proud of the modern facility, with its 20 outpatient suites, nuclear medicine and chemical labs, and offices for seven other physicians. He talks excitedly about laetrile studies to start in Israel.

Suddenly, swirling through the clinic lobby are five of the Del Rio brothers. The brothers are expensively dressed, sleek and smooth.

Bradford, although acknowledging that "we're strapped right now by the time and expense of the trial," says that, "I don't look upon my job as committee president as a millstone. I think it's a great chance to unite people to accomplish something we all believe in. It's a high."

Salaman, still upset over allegations about an "Apricot Mafia," notes that, "Much of the story of science is a history of entrenched error. The AMA is a prime candidate for the world-is-flat society. Think how foolish all those 'on-O-cologists' will feel if they find out that cancer can be controlled by a simple vitamin, even if we don't know how it works."

Both Bradford and Salaman say that even if the committee's freedom-of-choice mission is met by legalization of laetrile, there may be merit in continuing it for the purpose of furthering "metabolic therapy" and "mind-body studies."

The next day, while waiting for Dr. Contreras, McNaughton reminisces about his unusual background.

"I set out to become a Jesuit seminarian," he recalls, "But I discovered girls along the way. . . ."

McNaughton is the son of the late Gen. A. G. L. McNaughton, commander of the Canadian Armed Forces in World War II. A distinguished soldier-scientist-statesman, Gen. McNaughton was a former president of the Security Council of the United Nations and of the National Research Council of Canada.

His son, Andrew, became the chief test pilot in the Royal Canadian Air Force (at one time holding licenses to fly 77 different types of aircraft). After the war, young McNaughton, who had studied electrical engineering, business administration, and mining and geology, quickly made a fortune by converting cheaply obtained war surplus items into useful products for other nations. He gave it all up "when I realized I was working so that my servants could lounge around the pool all day."

The McNaughton name was an entree to top military and scientific councils, and Andrew helped provide arms for the emerging nation of Israel ("The Canadian government sanctioned it, but if I'd been caught, they would have disowned me; in my opinion, Israel should have conquered the Amazon Basin then and built up that area. With their industry, think what it would be today!")

McNaughton continued his arms sales ("at one time, I was on a first-name basis with most of the dictators in Central and South America"), throughout the '50s, when he simultaneously formed his foundation and got caught up in the Cuban civil war.

In his office at Clinica Cydel, McNaughton still has a letter authorizing him to buy arms on behalf of the Castro underground. He says he was also authorized to provide arms to Cuban dictator Fulgencio Batista, often arranging for the purchases to be hijacked by Castro supporters.

The double-agent stretch included some deals with Haiti's "Papa Doc" Duvalier. He fled to Florida and sweated out the last six months of the Castro takeover, returning as an honored comrade to share in the 10-day victory spree of the liberators ("a marvelous time," recalls McNaughton, who is an honorary citizen of Cuba).

Today, at 60, McNaughton is wiry and energetic, appearing at least a decade younger than he is. "My father was an unorthodox man operating in orthodox society," McNaughton says. "I am an unorthodox man operating in unorthodox societies."

Asked if he ever feared for his life, McNaughton notes, "No, dying doesn't scare me. I believe in reincarnation and have lived many lives before."

Dr. Contreras' sprawling Del Mar clinic and outpatient living units take up a block across from the Tijuana bullring. The 47-bed Del Mar hospital and the laetrile-producing Kemsa Lab are a few blocks away.

A genial, smiling man, Dr. Contreras goes through the familiar litany:

"Laetrile is not a 'cure,' but it does lessen the pain and, in some cases, prolong life. Undeniably, the use of laetrile increases the well-being of the patient, the quality of his life—and of his death. Patients say they have less pain, better appetite, better well-being, better performance. This is unquestionable."

Dr. Contreras is preparing a research paper suggesting that patients with inoperable lung cancer, who normally would be expected to live only 3–6 months, are surviving 20–24 months with laetrile.

McNaughton's "every Wednesday" talk to the new patients takes place at Clinica Cydel, but patients from Dr. Contreras' Del Mar Clinic also attend.

"Laetrile is not a magic bullet," McNaughton tells the patients. "It is a crown jewel among other dietary and enzymatic jewels that, cumulatively, can be helpful in the control of cancer."

One patient at the back of the room wants to know why "Scientists never seem to get cancer? Are they, perhaps, keeping laetrile for themselves?" McNaughton hastens to assure the group that scientists, too, die of cancer.

McNaughton takes those patients who want to come on a tour of the Cyto Pharma. Young Mexicans methodically grind California-grown apricot seeds into the mash that is converted, by a simple solvent extraction process, into laetrile. About two-thirds of the Tijuana laetrile is liquid, distributed in three-gram amber vials. The rest are yellow, 500-milligram pills, except for some 100-mg pills being made for a sickle-cell anemia project.

In one room of the factory is the old machine McNaughton used to produce laetrile in Sausalito. It is about the size of a coffee urn. McNaughton figures he used to manufacture laetrile for 15 cents per 500-mg tablet. The Mexicans, he figures, do it for 30 cents and sell it in Mexico for 70 cents, with U.S. costs at about $1.10.

Similarly, the three-gram vials cost the Mexicans $3, sell in Mexico for $7 and in the U.S. for $9–10. With proper use of the apricot-pit byproducts, laetrile "could be made for nothing," McNaughton says.

In five years, he observes, laetrile, or amygdalin, may not be used at all, since it can easily be supplanted by other cyanogenic glucosides that are more efficient. He is also working on a synthetic laetrile, looking ahead to a day when the natural supply of the drug will be exhausted by a nation using it regularly.

"I am a seller of dreams," McNaughton says.

His current dream is to set up a laetrile teaching clinic in Nevada that will emphasize the "holistic approach of metabolic therapy." He is also pursuing with a major U.S. insurer the possibility of clinical trials of laetrile's use as a cancer preventive. Encouraged by laetrile support in California, his ultimate goal is to establish a "mind-body study center" in the San Francisco Bay Area.

In the preface to the McNaughton Foundation's "Physician's Handbook of Vitamin B-17 Therapy," he writes: "From contact with more than 5,000 cancer patients over the past 15 years, it is apparent that for many of them cancer was a form of socially acceptable suicide.

"For best results under Vitamin B-17 therapy, the patient must cooperate mentally and physically, positively and actively in his treatment.

"More often than not: Quitters die, fighters live."

Attitude is all to McNaughton, and all is possible.

The uphill drive to Clinica Cydel from the San Diego border goes through the hillside shacks of the Mexican poor. "This all will be torn down and rebuilt into a grand, new gateway to Mexico," McNaughton says.

If McNaughton is a dreamer, the scientific father of laetrile, Ernst Krebs Jr., is a diehard Prussian dogmatist.

Krebs' father, Ernst T. Krebs Sr., MD, San Francisco, discovered laetrile as a byproduct of trying to improve the flavor of bootleg whisky ("just like Pasteur made his discoveries while working on wine for the French government," says Krebs Jr.).

The younger Krebs, a biochemist, reported in 1952 that he was able to "make the empirical apricot formula safe for parenteral administration to humans."

Krebs reportedly named his new drug laetrile "because this apricot kernel preparation was '*lae*vorotatory' (left-handed) to polarized light, and because amygdalin was chemically a 'mandeloni*trile*' ".

The biological rationale for laetrile is provided in "The Trophoblast Theory of Cancer" by the Scotish zoologist and embryologist, John Beard (1857–1924). In a recent booklet published by the McNaughton Foundation, Beard's theory is "restated in a modified form in modern terms."

This is it:

"Cancer represents primarily trophoblastic tissue derived either from an aberrant germ cell or from a somatic cell whose normally repressed 'asexual generation' genes are abnormally reactivated ('derepressed'). The variety of tumors, other than teratomas, may be due to a parallel chance depression of some genes of somatic ('sexual generation') characters. This would be a defensive reaction against intramural parasitization by trophoblast and would result in the differentiation and hyperplasia of normally present more primitive somatic cells."

Chemically, laetrile supporters now say, each Vitamin B-17 molecule has two units of glucose, one unit of benzaldehyde, and one of cyanide. They say the benzaldehyde and cyanide, both poisons, are harmlessly locked chemically and are prevented from harming normal cells because of the presence of the enzyme "rhodanese," which they say is absent from cancer cells.

Their conclusion: "Only cancer . . . cells contain the enzyme beta glucosidase which unlocks the poison inside the Vitamin B-17 cell, freeing it to kill off the cancer cells."

To Krebs Jr., the theory is "as obvious as the geometric principle that the 'straightest distance between two points is a straight line.' ".

"Just take a 9×12 sheet of paper," Dr. Krebs said (the degree is honorary from American Christian College in Tulsa, Okla. He reportedly studied medicine for three years at Philadelphia's Hahnemann Medical College), "and work it out. You'll see that it could be no other way."

According to the Beardsian, or "unitarian" theory Krebs subscribes to, the production of cancer cells is normal to the human life cycle. Previously, though, the theory goes, mankind's immunity came from eating the 1,200 or so plants that have evolved with man over the centuries and that provided amygdalin.

Krebs Jr. termed laetrile a drug when he first patented it. Subsequently, under heat from California and federal authorities to ban its use as a drug, he reclassified it was Vitamin B-17 (says McNaughton, "There was an opening for Vitamin B-16, but I guess he just liked the sound of 'B-17' better").

It is to a vitamin that laetrile's supporters, including physicians, now rally, contending the substance is useful for cancer as an adjunct to "metabolic therapy," involving other vitamins, notably Vitamin C, enzymes, rest, and exercise.

Several critics have disputed the claim that laetrile (amygdalin) has the properties of a vitamin. Several investigators have said there is no substantial evidence that any vitamin prevents the development of, or has a beneficial effect in the treatment of neoplasms.

McNaughton refers to Dr. Krebs as "our beloved guru," but The Founder is a little testy today. For one thing, he will not allow his photo to be taken.

Recent magazine articles, he noted, have concentrated too much on his penchant for mod clothes and accessories, despite his portly build, and not upon his scientific views and those of his supporters.

Lunch is served in the formal dining room of the Krebs family's San Francisco mansion. Laetrile-encrusted ice cream is the dessert. Dr. Krebs, like McNaughton, believes laetrile should be eaten every day as a cancer preventive, but allows that he seldom gets around to it, "simply due to plain human cussedness. I also smoke, although I know I shouldn't."

Dr. Krebs' tie sports the "male chauvinist pig" logo and his views of Germanic pride and superiority, racism, and women are, in many ways, as traditional as his mansion. It is an affront to him that the drug he named is now produced in Mexico. "When you want a top chemist," he said, "you look in Germany or Russia, not El Salvador or Mexico. You've seen Mexico."

Himself divorced, Dr. Krebs is engrossed in a book about the sanctity of the family and the "instinctual human need to find joy in the family."

The mood is fairly buoyant, as CFCCT official Mike Culbert and McNaughton trade notes on the promising laetrile legislative picture. From time to time, Dr. Krebs will interrupt with monologues that are neither listened to nor answered. Krebs contends he has never made a penny from laetrile.

McNaughton also contends that profit is not a motive in his crusade for laetrile.

In a letter to Nevada legislative authorities, McNaughton said, "I would like to emphasize once again that neither the McNaughton Foundation nor I personally have ever made any profit from the manufacture or use of laetrile in the 21 years during which we have been sponsoring the development of this material. In fact, we are primarily responsible for putting laetrile in the public domain, and the various laetrile patents which we have obtained have been similarly handled and are also in the public domain."

Others think McNaughton's patents to process laetrile can corner the emerging market.

McNaughton, the mystic champion of laetrile, believes the substance will eventually be taken over by the major American pharmaceutical firms. They'll buy amygdalin from established chemical firms and re-package it under their brand names, he says.

If so, it will mark the end of an era. McNaughton has managed to maintain his romanticism through some unusual dealings.

There was the 1972 stock swindle in New Jersey, when McNaughton was accused by the U.S. Securities Exchange Commission of engaging in "schemes to defraud the public by making untrue statements about laetrile."

The company was Biozymes International Ltd., set up to manufac-ture and distribute laetrile, and it has often been alleged that, under someone else's name, a major shareholder in Biozymes was "Bayonne Joe" Zicarelli, a one-time gunrunner for the Dominican Republic and a man identified in U.S. Senate testimony as a New Jersey mobster.

Zicarelli is in New Jersey State Prison on six counts of conspiracy to bribe public officials in connection with gambling.

McNaughton recalls Zicarelli as "a wonderful guy" whose sister he treated with laetrile. He also recalls Bayonne Joe's gift of $130,000 to the McNaughton Foundation (which currently operates out of a California box office).

The Zicarelli gift was "entirely proper," McNaughton said, "and I think it was wonderful of him."

Another time, McNaughton thought his fondest dreams would come true when he was approached by top representatives of Howard Hughes. McNaughton and his wife, Jacqueline, were whisked to Las Vegas and given VIP treatment.

McNaughton said he hoped Hughes might be interested in some of the McNaughton Foundation's health projects, particularly laetrile. It turned out, he said, that Hughes' aides wanted to test for oil and other minerals on land Hughes owned but hadn't developed. They needed contacts, and McNaughton introduced them to the top securities people in Canada.

The Pan American Mines case followed, in which $5 million van-ished. McNaughton, in effect, the group's sponsor to the Canadian finan-cial community, has appealed his conviction for fraud. (The sentence was recently reduced to one day in jail and a $10,000 fine, and McNaughton believes it will never be imposed because, he alleges, the prosecutor suppressed evidence that would have cleared him.)

On both these cases and a third in San Remo, Italy, McNaughton alleges that the real issue "is laetrile and people are out to get us." He asserts that, today, laetrile is absolutely free of any criminal links. ("That's why we're not too excited about going into Arizona," he says, "what with all the recent unfavorable publicity there.").

McNaughton was recently determined by the San Diego District Court to be so lacking in private funds as to need a court-appointed defender—should he ever go to trial.

He drives an old Toyota and says his "true spiritual home" is a one-room cottage by the ocean in California's Marin County. The outpost was willed to him by a Polaroid heir and sits on five acres. He shares the land with a Zen Buddhist group who act as forest rangers in exchange for living on the land.

In the meantime, he makes do with a two-room office at Clinica Cydel, space in the turret of Krebs' mansion, and an oceanside villa in Baja Malibu.

McNaughton is upset by media accounts picturing the villa as sumptuous. McNaughton has just sold it for $29,000, and says he will soon take up residence in a trailer.

McNaughton said that if he could have one wish, it would be to be appointed to an FDA or NCI or AMA committee to thoroughly investigate "alternative approaches to cancer treatment." For his part, he is convinced that mind-body studies and metabolic approaches, tied into a program of prevention, are the key.

"I'm sure Dr. Richardson has made his million from laetrile," McNaughton said. "And Bradford, who has burned his Stanford bridges behind him, may stay in it for the money. That's compatible with their free-enterprise principles. Salaman is a different case. He doesn't need the money, and I think he'll get out when the freedom of choice issue is upheld. (McNaughton figures Bradford and Salaman have grossed "maybe $300,000" from laetrile sales; the prosecution charges $642,000).

"A lot of committee members may want to make a financial killing from laetrile, but once it's legal the drug houses will take it over, and they have no need for laymen. Their only value now is as distributors.

McNaughton says that in previous incarnations, "I lived a long and productive life as an innovative builder of bridges and ferries in ancient China; then, I was a bull-jumper in Crete and studied philosophy in Egypt until I was killed in a volcanic eruption; next, I was the chief of the emperor's guards near what is New Delhi, India, until I betrayed my trust and was killed for seducing one of the temple dancers; and, most recently, I was a Scottish physician who emigrated to Boston in the 1700s and outraged the medical establishment with some of my ideas."

He continued, "In a way, my current activities with laetrile are an extension of those days as a Boston physician."

Throughout his lives, McNaughton said, his romantic interest has been his late second wife Jacqueline, who, also, has played different roles.

"In my next life, we will be leading a religious revival, and it appears that it will be a bit dreary.

"I may just prolong this life another 30 years or so. I'm not looking forward to leading a revival in religion."□

Chad Green

HE LOOKS GOOD, real good. That is the first thing you notice about Chad Green, age three.

Racing down the sidewalk, he looks like a clothing ad: tall for his age, long ash-blond hair, dark brown eyes, and a mischievous smile.

He is 3,000 miles from home and his winter coat—the one with the fur-lined hood—is wrapped snugly around him against the unseasonably cool breezes blowing in from the Pacific Ocean across the grounds of the Clinica Del Mar in Tijuana, Mexico.

Chad is no pre-schooler out for a romp. He is, bib overalls and all, a fugitive from justice.

In late January, 1979, his father, Gerald Green, 28, and his mother, Diana Green, 25, took him from his grandparents' home in Scituate, Mass., where the family had been living, and fled to Tijuana.

"We had to do it, to make sure that he gets the medical treatment he needs," says Gerald.

Chad, rosy cheeks notwithstanding, suffers from acute lymphocytic leukemia, and it is his parents' decision that he be treated in dusty Tijuana at the laetrile clinic of Ernesto Contreras Rodriquez, MD. Because their son was denied laetrile and other forms of "metabolic therapy" in the United States, the Greens have turned their back on Boston's prestigious Massachusetts General Hospital.

The flight to Tijuana caps a one-year legal fight pitting the Greens against Mass General and John B. Truman, MD, chief of the hospital's Pediatric Hematology Unit.

Interviewed in Tijuana, the Greens said their son, whose disease is now in remission, "will continue to receive dual treatment. He is getting the same chemotherapy, exactly the same as he got at Mass General, combined with metabolic therapy, including laetrile, a high-nutrition diet, massive doses of Vitamins A and C and enzymes.

"He needs the metabolic therapy to counter the side-effects of the chemotherapy, and we're going to make sure he gets it, either here, or back in Massachusetts, when we win our case."

Chad's physician, Dr. Truman, an assistant professor of pediatrics at

Harvard, fears that if the boy's chemotherapy is either discontinued or improperly administered, a "relapse will almost certainly occur," and that the so-called metabolic approach will result in "toxic buildups of cyanide (from the laetrile) and Vitamin A," not to mention pain and discomfort from the enzyme enemas.

Caught in the middle of this landmark legal fight, Chad can find nothing better to do this January morning than fidget with a game of Parcheesi and overturn a coffee table when his parents refuse to play with him. He races about and mugs for the camera. By now, being photographed is old-hat. The media have descended on Tijuana to see the Greens, coming from nearby San Diego and from as far away as Boston.

"What do we do with our time?" says Gerald. "Well, we talk to reporters."

Wife Diana adds, "I only put up with it because it might help somebody else."

Diana says, "We thought Chad had the flu back in the summer of 1977 when we took him to the hospital in Omaha, Neb. (Gerald was working in Hastings, Neb., as a welder.) Diana, a petite, dark-haired woman, looks at her husband as she continues.

"Chad was only 20 months old and the doctors gave him a shot of penicillin. We thought everything was cleared up." "No such luck," says Gerald, a wiry six-footer with sandy hair and twinkling blue eyes. "The next day he had a fever of 106. The medical center diagnosed it as acute lymphocytic leukemia."

Diana and Gerald Green, both high school graduates and devout Baptists, had their doubts about chemotherapy from the start. "The only one who could save Chad," says Diana, "was God. That's what we thought, and we also thought that if we let him go right then, we knew that he'd be in glory with God."

But the Greens went ahead with the initial four-week regimen of chemotherapy: daily prednisone pills and weekly vincristine shots. The chemotherapy, painful as it can be to a child, worked. Chad was found to be in remission.

But he was now due to begin irradiation of his brain to prevent fatal leukemic meningitis. Diana balked at this, and decided to return to Massachusetts, where Gerald's father and stepmother had in Scituate a white-frame house that Chad still considered "home."

Scituate was only a half-hour from Boston, and the Greens had learned that Mass General's chemotherapy program did not include cranial radiation.

"I told them," Dr. Truman said, "that Chad, indeed, could be treated against leukemic meningitis without radiation." That first visit, Dr.

Truman recalled, was Oct. 14, 1977. "I told them that Chad's overall chance of survival, now that he was in remission, was probably somewhat better than 50-50. He was in the most favorable age group (from one year to eight or nine), and he also had the ·most favorable form of acute lymphocytic leukemia (involving the 'null cell' lymphocyte)."

Dr. Truman laid out for the Greens what had to be done to guard against leukemic meningitis: a series of six weekly injections, directly into the spinal fluid, of methotrexate, while Chad continued taking at home, in the form of pills, 6-mercaptopurine, a drug that he had begun before leaving Omaha. Dr. Truman also urged the use of a fifth drug, asparaginase, to consolidate the remissions induced by prednisone and vincristine.

Once the spinal injections are completed, Dr. Truman told them, and if Chad remains in remission, the worst will be behind him. For the next six months, he will take 6-mercaptopurine pills daily and methotrexate pills twice a week. Once a month, he will return to the hospital for a checkup and a shot of vincristine. One week a month, he will take prednisone.

He will continue, Dr. Truman told the parents, on a less-intensive maintenance chemotherapy schedule for two or three years—until he is four or five years old.

Childhood leukemia is no longer a death sentence, but the Greens never believed it.

"He told us Chad's chances were 50-50," Gerald said, "but we did our own investigating. Nobody ever expected us to read all the data and call all the people, but we did. We found that the survival rate for acute lymphocytic leukemia is only 3%."

Diana adds, "Only 3%, and yet Chad was living a life of terror because of the chemotherapy. He couldn't eat, he couldn't sleep, he was constipated to the point of screaming, he would wake up shouting in the middle of the night."

The Greens had found what they believed to be an answer: a special diet they termed "nutritional therapy." The diet avoided meat, white sugar, white-flour products, preservatives, artificial colorings and flavorings, and consisted largely of fresh fruits and vegetables, fish, cheese, goat's milk, and distilled water, plus vitamin and mineral supplements.

"The diet helped protect Chad from the toxic effects of the chemotherapy," Diana said.

Dr. Truman warned the parents that only chemotherapy can kill the leukemic cells and that—if discontinued—Chad's leukemia would inevitably recur within one to six months and shortly therafter take his life.

The Greens refused the asparaginase medication, but Dr. Truman believed they were successfully continuing the rest of the chemotherapy.

Some disturbing indications in Chad's blood samples, however, alarmed Dr. Truman in February, 1978, and Diana soon confirmed his fear: Chad, she had decided, would be better off with only the nutritional therapy. He had been off all chemotherapy since November, 1977, she told the startled physician.

Chad went into relapse, and Dr. Truman went into court to protect the child's health. For the past year, Chad's chemotherapy has been continued at the order of Plymouth County (Mass.) Superior Court Judge Guy Volterra, who on several occasions has had to employ policemen to transport the child to Mass General. Shortly after Chad's chemotherapy resumed by court order last winter, the disease was back in remission.

His parents, in the meantime, had found a new hope: laetrile.

"It was at the April, 1978, regional meeting of the National Health Federation (a pro-laetrile organization)," Diana said, "when we first found out about laetrile." Diana and Gerald soon were supplementing Chad's nutritional therapy with laetrile, Vitamins A and C, and enzymes.

Dr. Truman, who was now noting high levels of cyanide and Vitamin A in Chad's blood and urine, was back in court for an order forbidding the couple to administer laetrile. Testimony indicated that laetrile was causing chronic cyanide poisoning in the child.

This latest court decision, handed down by Judge Volterra last month, forced the Greens into flight.

"I think we're heading into a Spartanistic-type society," says Gerald, "when the state tells you what you can and cannot feed your child. We're staying here in Tijuana until the Supreme Court decides in our favor."

The couple remain defiant.

"Dr. Truman, bah," says Diana. "What does he know about nutrition? I mean, the man eats graham crackers for breakfast. I've seen him do it more than once. He's fine as far as he goes. But he and all those other doctors, it just seems like they don't want to know. I tried to get Dr. Truman interested in metabolic therapy. I gave him books to read and had him invited without charge to conferences, but he never would listen. Why wouldn't he listen?"

Gerald has an answer. "He's just a cog in a big machine," Gerald said. "Dr. Truman is all caught up in the thing with Mass General and the AMA and all the other doctors. Cancer treatment, you know, is a $40-billion-a-year industry. If you start using metablic therapy in place of chemotherapy, you start cutting some of those profits."

The Greens say they will continue Chad's chemotherapy. "Exactly the same schedule as laid out by Mass General," says Diana. "But we're going to include the metabolic therapy, too, to protect him against the side-effects."

Gerald says, "If we had enough money, we would have taken Chad to Hans Nieper in Hanover, West Germany. Nobody would have found us there."

Diana is still thinking about what Dr. Truman doesn't know. "I mean," she says, "people are dying because of this kind of ignorance. Dr. Contreras thinks that chemotherapy is the best way to put cancer in remission—he testified at our trial, you know—but he believes you need the laetrile and metabolic therapy to stay healthy. I mean what does Dr. Truman know about diet. Graham crackers for breakfast, brother!"

The upstairs waiting room is jammed with patients from the United States, and they laugh heartily at Diana's outburst.

Chad races down the stairs, but is swept up by Dr. Contreras, the affable, moustachioed church organist who has built a lucrative family business by combining conventional cancer therapy with the contraband laetrile. His son, Ernesto Jr., is supervising Chad's case.

And how is Chad doing? Spreading wide his hands, the Mexican physician says, "So far, so good." Chad, he claims, remains in remission, and his medical tests, completed the day before, show no abnormal amounts of either cyanide or Vitamin A. How is it the Mass General doctors found differently?

"It is hard to tell," Dr. Contreras says. "How long will Chad remain in remission? "We never know. We never know," he says.

Chad's records from Mass General are being sent to Tijuana, he adds.

Chad is becoming a little unruly, but Dr. Contreras placates him by putting around his neck a stethoscope. Chad pretends to take his own heartbeat.

"Well, we are busy," Dr. Contreras reminds. "We do have some patients to see." He is off.

Back in the fall of 1977, Dr. Truman had thought Chad's chances of survival were "substantial."

"Of the majority of children who—like Chad—achieve remission, some 80–90% are still ostensibly disease-free after one year of chemotherapy. After three years, 60–70% are still without signs of leukemia, and after five years, 50–60% are still alive and apparently well," he said.

"Because the therapy itself is only 10 years old, there is yet no way of knowing how long these children will remain well, but there are children alive today who went through this treatment 10 years ago. In fact, relapses after five years are exceptionally infrequent. If relapse is going to occur, it usually occurs within the first one to three years. Of course, the only way we'd be able to tell if a two-year-old child had been cured of leukemia is if at the age of 72 he expires for some other reason."

Dr. Truman now puts Chad's' chances at "somewhere between zero and 50%. That relapse last winter did not help. And who knows what kind of chemotherapy he will receive in Mexico or what kind of toxicity from cyanide and Vitamin A may build up?"

Chad is off to see the people from a San Diego television station.

"He looks good, doesn't he?" Gerald asks. "I think now that he'll live to be 90. I'm 90% sure of that, and we're trying to do everything we can to increase his chances about that.

"We've been lucky. Some people have given us their Tijuana apartment rent-free and a lot of people have donated money. We're making it. I've checked the Mexican labor laws, and I can't work here as a welder because I'm an alien, but that barbed-wire fence across the border has got some pretty big holes in it. I may just slip across now and then to make some money working on the other side. Things like this either bind you together or tear you apart, and Diana and I have never been closer.

"This is really a clinic of love."

Diana adds, "We're getting more for our money here, too. The chemotherapy costs less, and the Mexican doctors are more observant. And we get a bonus: the laetrile and nutritional therapy. We had to come 3,000 miles just to continue exactly the same treatment Chad had back home. We'll get back, you just wait and see. Even though I think they're all glad to be rid of us."

Chad's chances? Diana ponders before submitting to yet another interview:

"Let's face it. It's up to God."□

FEW BORDER CROSSINGS OFFER the contrast one encounters driving south from San Diego, Calif., into Tijuana, Mexico.

The sleek engineering of Interstate 5 gives way to the dusty roads, and washed-out signs of the Tijuana hillside. Though harsh, this observation, like a slap in the face, cannot be ignored.

Driving west along the barbed-wire international border fence fronting the Ensenada toll road, one comes face to face with the hillside shanties of the Mexican poor. It is a short ride up and down a hill to the Pacific Ocean and the grounds of the Centro Medico Del Mar directed by Ernesto Contreras Rodriquez, MD.

It is to this clinic where seven months ago Diana and Gerald Green brought their son, Chad, for what they hoped would be a life-saving treatment of laetrile and "metabolic therapy."

Chad, a blond, brown-eyed charmer of impish disposition who will be four this December was in the news again late last month, July 1979.

First, his mother was quoted in the press as saying Chad was "cured," a fact ascertained by "signs from God." next, both Drs. Contreras Sr. and Jr. were quoted as expressing "concern" that the youngster apparently is no longer being administered by his parents the chemotherapy the Mexican clinic has been providing Chad in addition to laetrile and metabolic therapy.

This morning, Chad is blithely ignoring the controversy. Dr. Contreras is in conference and his door is closed. Chad momentarily makes do by playing with his miniature cars and terrorizing secretaries. Shortly, he raps loudly on the physician's door and whispers, "Dr. Contreras, Dr. Contreras." Diana Green, 25, admonishes her son "to wait your turn."

Chad begins the makings of a major tantrum only to be confronted by father Gerald, 28, who advises, "What's this noise all about. Nobody wants to hear it." Chad falls quickly quiet. "There is something about a father's voice," sighs Diana, "that gets the job done better than I."

For seven months, the Greens have been in Tijuana so Chad can have the treatment of their choice. That treatment, the Greens were telling reporters earlier this year, "is chemotherapy—exactly the same chemotherapy schedule he was receiving at Mass General—supplemented by laetrile and metabolic therapy to ward off the toxic effects of chemotherapy." This was the story until last month's contradictory headlines. The Greens and Dr. Contreras now request that interviews be conducted only when parents and physician are all present.

And so it is this morning. Chad, his parents, and Dr. Contreras gather in the physician's spacious, well-appointed office. Affable and personable, Dr. Contreras practices well the art of medicine. His patients are almost entirely Americans—one never finds Mexican cancer patients at the laetrile clinics—but the decor is decidedly Mexican. Looking out one side of his office, one sees the Tijuana bullring; out the other, the Catholic church of which the physician is "a member, let's say an active member," and benefactor.

"In the strictest medical sense," Dr. Contreras says, "we cannot say that Chad is cured. We can say that he is in complete remission and he is in excellent health."

Gerald Green adds, "His bone marrow test taken last week shows 100% normal lymphocytes. And his blood tests are normal." Gerald, who has become "the family herbologist," attributes some of this to the "vitamins, herbs, and minerals we have used to help Chad.

"We're giving him Vitamin A, Vitamin C, minerals, and combinations of 20–25 different herbs. Natural medications. Do you know that the Indians used these medicines for hundreds of years and some people say that Indian medicine is superior to Western medicine?"

Diana adds to her husband's comment, "We feel that the laetrile and vitamins and minerals are as much a valuable medication as the chemotherapy."

Gerald says, "There's one rule we follow with this little guy—we always give him more, not less metabolic therapy."

The chemotherapy?

"Exactly the same as he got at Mass General," Diana says impatiently. "Just what Dr. (John) Truman was giving him before we left." Dr. Contreras adds, "We used the same chemotherapy schedule developed by Dr. Truman. Actually, it is not Dr. Truman's schedule, it is the standard chemotherapy for this form of leukemia." Gerald Green says, "The herbs and vitamins have helped Chad fight off the poisons of chemotherapy. They help cleanse the intestinal tract."

Then, those press reports about Chad being off chemotherapy and the Mexican physicians concerned about a relapse must be fabrication?

Diana Green, like her husband a high school graduate and devout Baptist, is not one to lightly take liberties with the truth.

"Well," she says, "we're tapering him off the chemotherapy. Slowly. Most of it is taken orally, and I started a few months ago to cut back the dosages. First, I would cut the pills in half, then in quarters. We told Dr. Contreras we were doing this back in, oh, March or April. We didn't want him to be alrmed by any changes in Chad's test."

How does the physician feel about this?

"Well," Dr. Contreras says, "in the strictest medical sense, I am not as secure as I would be if Chad were on the recommended dosages. But we are keeping a close watch on Chad and if we notice any changes in his blood or bone marrow, the parents assure me they will reinstate the full dosages."

The Greens agree.

At this point, Chad interrupts to ask in the whispery voice he reserves only for the physician, "Dr. Contreras, Dr. Contreras, can I play with your car?" The physician adds to Chad's collection of toy cars a hefty model of a Rolls-Royce and Chad is soon happily stretched out on the carpet putting his newly acquired Rolls Royce through its paces.

Why does Mrs. Green think Chad is "cured"?

Diana says, "It's not like I told the reporters I saw a burning bush or something. I just know that the Lord Jesus Christ is the same today as he has been to me in the past. I have been with Him through too many bad times not to express my joy when victory comes. I believe the Lord has provided for Chad's healing. It is a matter of faith. Because of my faith and belief in the Lord Jesus, I believe Chad to be cured."

Dr. Contreras, who plays the organ and sings in his nearby church and teaches a special class for cancer patients, has been known to say that neither physicians nor laetrile cure, but rather that healing belongs to the Lord.

"We have two sides here," says the physician who has built a lucrative family business by combining conventional cancer therapy with the contraband laetrile. "We have the medical and we have the spirtual. In the strictest medical sense, we cannot yet call this a cure. It will be years before we can say that.

"It is my philosophy to combine faith with treatment. I cannot go against her beliefs. Mrs. Green's faith tells her that Chad is cured. I, too, hope that proves to be the case."

Faith, yes, but how important is the chemotherapy and how much is still being given?

"Well," Diana Green says, "I've been slicing the pills into little slivers lately." How little? "Actually, Chad's chemotherapy right now is almost nonexistent." How little is he given? "Actually, he is not being given any."

And how does the physician feel about the youngster's complete removal from chemotherapy, an action that when first done by the Greens back in Massachusetts resulted in Chad's falling into a relapse? The next relapse, doctors warn, might be fatal.

"It is a risk, yes," Dr. Contreras says. "But we feel it is a slight risk. And we are monitoring Chad closely."

But why would a mother run a needless risk—no matter how slight it is perceived—with her son's life?

"Let's just say," Diana Green concludes, "that we have faith in a higher power. He tells us there is no risk."

Dr. Contreras says that his hematologist is severely upset by the dropping of chemotherapy, "but he has agreed to keep a close eye on how Chad progresses." Gerald Green notes that, "The toxic effects of chemotherapy can kill you, too. That's something the American Cancer Society and the American Medical Association never tell you. I've been doing a lot of reading. Do you know that the AMA was founded by a hemeopathic, I mean homeopathic physician who then turned around and outlawed homeopathic medicine in favor of allopathic medicine. How can you work for an outfit like that?"

There is a crash. Chad has dropped the physician's model Rolls-Royce against a cabinet. He is becoming rambunctious again. Running into an adjoining office, he returns with a cotton swab and begins to prepare his father's arm for an imaginary IV. "Chad, Chad," Dr. Contreras says, "and now you want to play doctor?"

The interview is over. Chad refuses to let Dr. Contreras hold him for a final photo. His father sweeps him aloft, but Chad resolutely turns his back to the camera.

Dr. Contreras has the solution." Chad, Chad," he says, "play with my moustache." Chad pivots and pulls on the physician's moustache.

Physician and youngster both smile broadly.□

CHAD GREEN, the young leukemia patient who in the past nine months became the center of the laetrile controversy, died Oct. 12, 1979.

Chad, who would have been four this December died less than two months after his mother, Diana Green, acknowledged in an interview with *American Medical News* that she had completely cut off the child's chemotherapy.

Two years ago, physicians at Massachusetts General Hospital outlined a chemotherapy program for Chad and put his survival chances at "better than 50-50." When they found Chad to be in relapse because his parents, Diana and Gerald Green, were not giving him the prescribed chemotherapy, a court order was obtained to continue the recommended treatment. The Greens, meantime, discovered laetrile, and Mass General physicians discovered high levels of Vitamin A and cyanide—from the laetrile—in Chad's blood. Another court order was obtained to forbid the laetrile.

At this point, the Greens took Chad and fled to the laetrile clinics in Tijuana. Diana Green told *AMN* she gradually tapered Chad off the chemotherapy the Mexican physicians wanted to continue—along with the laetrile they administered. She was putting her faith, Diana Green said, not in chemotherapy but in laetrile, vitamins, minerals, various herbs, and "faith in a higher power. He tells us there is no risk."□

Of Crimes and Coroners

Jeffrey MacDonald

Few of my stories have attracted as much interest as did this interview with Jeffrey MacDonald, MD, the former Green Beret captain who was convicted of brutally murdering his pregnant wife and two small daughters. Or, I should say, few stories have so often prompted the questions: "What is he really like? Do you think he did it?"

This interview, conducted in a federal prison in Texas, is one of the last ever allowed by Dr. MacDonald, who hoped to turn it into a plea for a new trial. The interview took place just as the book about MacDonald's case (*Fatal Vision* by Joe McGinniss) was shooting to the top of the best-seller lists. One year later, there would be a smash TV mini-series.

Dr. MacDonald is a magnetic man and, within the confines of a small interviewing room off the reception room of Bastrop (Tex.) Federal Prison, he put on a powerful performance. Later, listening to the tapes, even my wife, Suzanne, found him to sound charming and reasonable.

The tip-off came when my questions turned questioning. The ex-doctor (his licenses have been lifted) turned from smiles to scowls, from persuasion to complaints.

By then we were in the prison yard, where his shifting mood and sudden glowers made possible some terrific photos. "This will be the last interview," he protested. "All you journalists are alike—sleazeball artists."

On this day, in 1983, some 13 years after the murders, Dr. MacDonald still finds it easier to complain loud and bitterly about the Army, the courts, and the press than to quietly reflect upon what happened on Feb. 17, 1970 in the early hours of that North Carolina morning.

CENTRAL TEXAS, A LAND OF SUNSHINE, is shrouded in early-morning fog as visiting hours begin at the Federal Correctional Institute in Bastrop, outside Austin.

One signs a few forms, is led through a few security doors, and suddenly, there he is, dressed in prison khakis and running shoes, fit and tanned, bouncing and smiling, the All-American enigma:

Jeffrey MacDonald, MD.

In high school, in blue-collar Patchogue, L.I., he was the quarterback of the football team, the king of the senior prom, voted both "most popular" and "most likely to succeed." In college, at Princeton and at the Northwestern U. Medical School, he was an outstanding student. In his medical career, he interned at Manhattan's Columbia Presbyterian Medical Center, served as a Green Beret captain at Ft. Bragg, N.C., and developed into an outstanding emergency room physician and administrator at St. Mary's Hospital in Long Beach, Calif.

In Bastrop, Texas, he is federal inmate 164-67-034, the convicted killer of his pregnant wife, Colette, and their two young daughters, Kimberly, 5, and Kristen, 2½.

The murders took place 13 years ago in the early hours of a dark and dank North Carolina morning. To this day, four years after his conviction by a jury that sat for six weeks and required only 6½ hours to return its verdict—a Green Beret on the jury walked in, head down, crying—and 10 months after the U.S. Supreme Court declined without comment to hear his final appeal, Dr. MacDonald steadfastly maintains he is an innocent victim of a mismanaged Army investigation and a justice system run amuck. Certainly, though, he has had his day in court.

With the financial support of friends and the earnings from his medical practice, he has hired teams of attorneys and investigators to plead his case in one of the most publicized criminal prosecutions in American history, a 13-year odyssey that four times reached the U.S. Supreme Court.

The physician (he retains his medical license only in North Carolina and it soon will be lifted there) has served less than three years in prison. He avoided trial on procedural grounds for nine years, and, after his 1979 conviction, was granted a 19-month reprieve on procedural grounds.

Dr. MacDonald contends that drug-crazed hippies, chanting, "Acid is groovy, kill the pigs," murdered his family, left him lying unconscious in the hallway of his small apartment at 544 Castle Drive in the sprawling Ft. Bragg military complex, and left as a grim reminder of their murderous intrusion the words, "Kill the pigs!" written in blood in letters eight inches high on the headboard of the bed in the master bedroom.

Dr. MacDonald's version of events is contradicted not only by his jury conviction but also by an appellate court ruling that found the trial "error-free" and "ample warrant" for guilt. Now, author Joe McGinniss, in a best-selling book, *Fatal Vision*, has devoted 663 pages to building a case, developed in wave after wave of physical evidence and character and psychiatric testimony, that the physician did it.

The book, and the media attention it has generated, have put Dr.

MacDonald back into the notorious glare of the public spotlight. Author McGinnis advances the theory that the former Green Beret physician was pushed to the breaking point by a combination of pathological narcissism and amphetamine-triggered psychosis. Still, the question remains—the question that McGinniss is asked on every talk show:

How could he?

After the death of his family, Dr. MacDonald once offered this reminiscence about his wife:

"Colette . . . was to me soft and feminine and beautiful, big brown eyes, very intelligent, quiet sense of humor, not very aggressive, but a magnificent woman. I still see her as the epitome of womanhood."

Dr. McDonald begins the interview with a wry smile. "How am I doing? Pretty good, under the circumstances. I feel terribly soiled by all of this. People are buying Joe's trash. There's nothing being said about the decent things I did, the papers I wrote on emergency medicine, the lives I saved, the hundreds of hours of volunteer medical work I've done.

"There's a terrible contradiction here—decent, normal people don't slaughter their families. I know what happened that night. I know who I am—a decent person—and it doesn't matter what Joe says. I didn't murder my family."

Drawing from some of the extensive psychiatric testimony, McGinniss portrays Dr. MacDonald as a man who psychologically coped by repressing his rage at the need to consistently achieve and perform, who denied his true feelings, and who allowed his anger to surface only in peripheral, unrelated areas. Thus, the theory goes, the physician denied the brutal murders he committed and allowed his anguish to surface only by railing at the Army, the prosecution, and the press.

In 1979, U.S. prosecutor Jim Blackburn, the father of three children, took a simple position: "If we prove he did it, we don't have to concern ourselves with whether or not he's the kind of person who could have done it." He proved it.

During the 1975 indictment hearing, Dr. MacDonald's character witnesses were cross-examined with only one question:

"Were you there at 544 Castle Drive on the morning of the murders?" The answer was no, and the witnesses were dismissed.

Robert Sadoff, MD, a psychiatrist who examined Dr. MacDonald in 1970, 1975, and 1979, says he would say in 1983 what he said before:

"Dr. MacDonald's personality is not consistent with the type of personality likely to commit this crime. I think that it is very unlikely that he could have done this. I base this statement today, not only upon my previous examination of him, but upon his total actions and behaviors over the 13 years since the murders." Defense attorney Bernard Segal adds, "If he had a psychotic personality, he would have left a trail a mile wide in the last 13 years."

A prosecution psychologist, Hirsch Lazaar Silverman, PhD, disagrees:

"This man is a pathological narcissist," Dr. Silverman told *AMN*. "We are all insecure, but he is excessively so, and his personality is such that under certain pressures he would revert to violence. His thinking is very compartmentalized, not logical and natural, and he represses his true feelings.

"During the 1979 trial, I noticed a total absence of deep emotional response. This is the kind of man who could commit asocial acts with impunity. He has repressed his true feelings, his fear of women and his latent homosexuality, with an expansive egotism—sports cars, boats, oceanfront condo. I'm not into jewelry, but he wore some of the best male jewelry I've ever seen and he dressed impeccably. He liked to flaunt his body and he also liked to flaunt things more socially acceptable—his possessions, his medical accomplishments, his sophistication.

"I watched him at the trial and I was struck that when they showed autopsy slides of his wife and children, he simply swiveled around in his chair and turned his back. He showed no guilt, no remorse, no tears, no feelings, no reaction at all. It was as if he were saying, 'This is not part of me; they did not exist.' I also think that the murders may have been premeditated—he did not want the responsibility of marriage and family holding him down.

"Frankly, I am certain of my diagnosis—irrevocably, unremittingly certain. I examined him very carefully and very scientifically.

"I liked him very much, though. He is very likeable. Had it not been for what he did, I might have wanted him for a friend.

"And finally, he is very much the kind of man who will always live on, who will always say, 'Nothing will get me down.' "

In 1979, shortly before his trial, Dr. MacDonald suggested to McGinniss that he might want to write a book about the case, a suggestion that the physician previously had made to other writers. He says he figured a book "would clear my name once and for all."

It is now ironic that under the terms of their agreement, one of every three royalty dollars McGinniss earns will go to the man who says he is being "soiled"—Dr. MacDonald. Or, more accurately, to his new attorney, Brian O'Neill, Santa Monica, Calif., and to his new investigator, Ray Shedlick, Raleigh, N.C. O'Neill says he plans to file for a new trial "by the end of this year, based upon new evidence we have supporting Jeff's innocence."

The motion for a new trial will be Dr. MacDonald's last roll of the dice. He was convicted in 1979; freed in 1980 after 51 weeks in prison when an appellate court ruled his right to a speedy trial had been infringed; returned to prison on April 1, 1982, when the U.S. Supreme Court ruled, 6–3, that his constitutional right to a speedy trial had not been violated. He has been in prison ever since. In 1982, the U.S. Court of Appeals rejected his argument that he had been denied a fair trial, and in January, 1983, the U.S. Supreme Court refused to reconsider the motion.

The earlier legal history includes the Army's formal charging of Dr. MacDonald with the murders in 1970; dismissal of the charges after a four-month Article 32 military investigatory hearing; and the 1971 re-opening of the case by the Army's Criminal Investigation Division and the U.S. Dept. of Justice, both responding, in part, to the intense pressure brought by Dr. MacDonald's father-in-law, Freddie Kassab, who at first believed in the physician's innocence but who came to believe so fervently in his guilt that he vowed, "If the courts of this country won't administer justice, I will."

In 1975, a three-count murder indictment was handed down by a federal grand jury in Raleigh, N.C.; but it was dismissed in 1976 by an appellate court on the basis that Dr. MacDonald had been denied his right to a speedy trial. Two decisions by the U.S. Supreme Court finally cleared the way for trial—a ruling in 1978 that Dr. MacDonald's speedy-trial claims could not be appealed before trial and a ruling in 1979 that the earlier military hearing did not constitute double jeopardy. His trial for the murder of his wife and children began on July 16, 1979, in Raleigh, N.C., before U.S. District Court Judge Franklin T. DuPree Jr.

The complicated case involves a cast of thousands—the Army alone interviewed 6,000 people who knew about Dr. MacDonald—but barring a new trial, its legal chapters are closed. Up until 1983, Dr. MacDonald had employed attorney Segal, from Philadelphia and San Francisco, and investigator Ted Gundersen, Los Angeles, to develop his claim that a band of drug-addled intruders committed the killings. In recent months, he has employed attorney O'Neill and investigator Shedlick, a former New York City policeman now working in Raleigh, N.C., to "rebuild a new case from the ground up."

His only hope for freedom rests upon the motion for a new trial, a motion that first will be heard by Judge DuPree in North Carolina ("The odds are 99% against me," Dr. MacDonald says) and then by the U.S. Circuit Court of Appeals, ("I think we have a 60–40 chance here," Shedlick says) and, perhaps, a final appeal to the U.S. Supreme Court.

This day, time weighs heavily upon the former Green Beret. He has been imprisoned now for 18 consecutive months, the last 12 at Bastrop, an isolated outpost that is hundreds of miles from his friends and supporters in Southern California.

He says the book has had a devastating effect upon his reputation. Author McGinniss portrays Dr. MacDonald as a narcissistic womanizer who, tiring of the responsibility of marrage and family, snapped one night into a psychotic rage and brutally slaughtered his family, a deed that perhaps, McGinniss theorizes, was abetted by the consumption of three to five amphetamines (Eskatrol Spansules, since taken off the market) per day during the previous month. Dr. MacDonald might have used the drugs both to lose weight and to remain alert during his moonlighting ER jobs off-post, McGinnis theorizes.

If McGinniss' assumption about the dosages is correct, drug experts say that an amphetamine-triggered psychosis causing assaultiveness and violence is possible.

Dr. MacDonald is 39 now, and his blond hair is turning silver, but running and pumping iron have kept him remarkably fit. A man of magnetic energy, he dominates the tiny interviewing room with a voice that alternately rises and falls and hands that alternately stab the air and stroke his muscular biceps. Occasionally, he will lightly run his fingers through his hair.

For four hours, he will hold forth on two broad topics of conversation: the book's insult to his reputation and the new investigation he thinks will clear him. He speaks in sweeping statements. The book is "asinine," "ludicrous," "terrible," "vicious," and a "fantastic scenario." The investigation is "dramatic," "impressive," "magnificent," "powerful," and an "iron-clad case that will convince everyone in the criminal justice system of my innocence." He says he is sorry he cannot be more specific.

"The book," Dr. MacDonald begins, "is an absolutely vicious personal attack. It is a novel masquerading as non-fiction. Joe and I had an agreement to do the book, but he has left entirely out of it my defense. Any evidence that argues for my innocence, any character testimony that supports my decency and normalcy have been edited out. He has totally broken our agreement about 'fair representation.'

"Joe is hardly qualified to make psychiatric diagnoses, and his theory about 'pathological narcissism'—which I guess he bases on the fact that I have mirrors on the wall of my California condo—is bizarre, unsupported, and unsupportable.

"His theory about amphetamine abuse is even more bizarre. The facts are simple—over a period of several weeks in the winter of 1970, I had a total of three to five single diet pills while working out with a Ft. Bragg boxing team and running a weight-loss program for fat men in the Army. I have never abused drugs at any time in any form. The note I wrote to my attorney (Segal), the note upon which Joe bases this bizarre theory, says that it is possible, mind you, possible, that I might have had a single diet pill during the day preceding the murders.

"Joe think's he's invulnerable now, because the Supreme Court ruled against me. But he's wrong. I'm going to sue to stop the paperback and the movie and—I want you to understand this—I hope that the hardcover does not sell a single copy. And I'm going to sue him. Joe will pay.

"This psychological theorizing is all crap. It's like Psych 101 to say that a man who is a Green Beret and believes in physical fitness must be macho and narcissistic. But to make a quantum jump from that to my snapping into a psychotic rage is terribly unfair. All of the psychiatric testimony was barred at trial, secondary to prosecution motions, but the bulk of it held that I was not horribly evil, but a decent and normal person. Joe's theory that I have a 'boundless repressed rage against women' is simply trash. He didn't even take the time to talk to the women I've known and dated since the terrible tragedy of losing my family.

"I'm no playboy. I confess to liking the pleasures of the flesh and I like beautiful women, but most of my time was spent on my work.

"I'm angry, yes, I'm very angry. My sense of impotence grows larger and larger. How do I fight anymore? I'm out of money. All the earnings from my medical practice are gone. I'm maybe $200,000 in debt. The boat is sold, the sports car is sold, and the condo is leased because I cannot find a buyer. I'm locked in a prison thousands of miles from my friends and attorney—I've only seen Brian twice since I've been here—and it's been a terrible harassment ever since they tranferred me from Terminal Island (a prison near Los Angeles). Now there's a bad book out about me and some sleazeball who's globbed onto this story to make a buck is going on every TV show in America—he did 29 in four days last week—and saying that I did not have a good marriage, that (his voice rising in disbelief) I AM A HOMOSEXUAL. The book says 'latent homosexual,' but in his interviews Joe is deaccentuating the 'latent.'

"And, even worse, the other journalists, the press, people who in the past have been fair with me, appear to be taking Joe's trash to heart.

"My frustration builds and builds and builds.

"Look, it's easy to take potshots. This cheap, sleazy book has very carefully orchestrated an evil view of me. The news media are buying it. Some of the reviews are outrageous. But that's just journalists stroking each other. I'm surprised that some investigative reporter has not globbed onto how shabby this book really is. But I'll get through it. People do what they have to do.

"I guess I just never took the time to properly grieve. I was too busy having to fight off the government and trying to rebuild my life. I threw myself into my work.

"I don't wear my heart on my sleeve. That's not the way I was raised. My father never once told me, 'I love you,' Now, I know he did love me, but he was not a verbal man. If I got straight 'As' or scored a touchdown, I was never put on a pedestal. He would just say, 'Good job.' I was never that verbal, either, though I tried to be more demonstrative and loving with my children. If they were alive today, I would make a big effort to be very demonstrative and loving.

"After the murders, I always thought I was not quite OK—I mean I was alive and my family was dead—until Randi (Lee Markwith, MacDonald's former fiancee) came into my life. This is 1982, now, and she had a wonderful way of making me confront painful things. We could talk and talk. The verbal freedom was completely new to me. She made me aware of how afraid I was to confront the past. One night, she said, 'Jeff, you seem down. Let's talk. We're getting serious about each other. Do you want children?'

"It was like a light bulb switched on in my head. Here was this wonderful, neat person who I was falling in love with, and I looked at her and I said, yes, yes, I want children again. She made me realize that I was a decent guy, that I was OK, that what happened 12 years ago didn't matter. I had to get over my guilt that my family was dead and that I was still alive. I felt very happy.

"The government killed it. I was returned to prison and the pressures killed the romance. No, Randi won't talk to you. She's what, 21 now, and she has her own life to live.

"I cope by compartmentalizing. I took months to complete a paper on emergency medicine. Now I'm working on my new legal motion. My mornings and evenings are free. Mid-afternoons, I work in the prison yard—put chalk stripes on the baseball diamond and pick up cigaret butts.

"I'll wake up next morning at 3 or so and have to figure out what's eating at me the most—the book, the interviews, the legal case. I've developed some exercises and deep breathing to quiet myself down.

"What keeps me going are the good people around me—family, friends, my attorneys. My new investigator, Ray Shedlick, is magnificent, and he is going to be a lifesaver.

"I was not guilty in 1970, I was not guilty in 1979, and I am not guilty today. The jury did not hear all the evidence. I'll get by. I'm not guilty."

Dr. MacDonald was convicted in 1979 on the basis of a web of circumstantial evidence, including:

Autopsy reports showed a massive fracture in the skull of Kimberly; more than 30 stab wounds in the chest and back of Kristen; and massive injuries to Colette that included a skull fracture, fractures of both arms—apparently as she tried to fend off the attack—and dozens of stab wounds by both knife and icepick. All in all four murder weapons—two knives, an icepick, and a club—were determined to be part of the MacDonald household.

Dr. MacDonald, a physically fit Green Beret and an athlete, suffered a bump on the head, two slight cuts from a knife, some fingernail scratches, and a puncture wound between two ribs that was one centimeter deep, enough to cause the partial collapse of a lung. His testimony stated that he was unable to defend his family against the three or four armed intruders because he could not get his hands out of his pajama top, which somehow had become twisted around his arms.

The intruders who the physician contends ran berserk through the apartment left no physical evidence. Dr. MacDonald's blood was found in only two places—in front of the bathroom mirror (where the prosecution contended he inflicted the chest wound on himself) and in front of the bathroom sink, where the prosecution contended he disposed of surgical gloves used to write "kill the pigs!" on the headboard.

Blood from his children and wife was found throughout the master and children's bedrooms, where fibers from Dr. MacDonald's pajamas were found, along with his bloody footprint etched in the blood of his wife.

Now, his response begins softly: "It's very embarrassing. Everyone wants to know how it is that a Green Beret never landed a blow. I'll have to live with it the rest of my life—the burden that I was not man enough to defend my wife and daughters."

His voice rises sharply:

"I know what happened that night, and I did not murder my family.

"There is testimony that when I was brought to the emergency room, I was hysterical and highly upset, and that when I regained consciousness my first words were: 'How are my kids?' Isn't that what you would expect from someone who's been through what I suffered that night?

"I'm not denying that I was convicted, but the jury never heard all the facts. We were zero for 24 on major motions, and the judge never allowed character testimony or seven critical witnesses who could have testified that they knew about the intruders."

He was convicted, he asserts, "because my story did not exactly match up with the physical evidence. My story is not 100% supported by the evidence, but to make a quantum jump to murder is terribly unfair.

"We're talking about things that happened in a matter of seconds and I was in a daze. There is lost evidence, hidden evidence, incredibly sloppy investigations, non-investigations of critical leads, and command decisions not to investigate the real suspects described by myself (a woman in a floppy hat holding a candle dripping blood, and three men). We have evidence now—I cannot go into detail, but it involves fibers and blood stains and forensics—that will bring out the truth."

Dr. MacDonald has his backers.

Says new attorney O'Neill: "I believe he is innocent and our motion for a new trial is based on real new evidence. We have a chance." Old attorney Segal calls the 1979 conviction a "monumental tragedy," adding, "These have to be very, very painful times to Jeff now, and it is a tribute to his character, courage, and decency that he still keeps his sanity. I'm still a consultant on the case—we parted because I didn't have the time to build a new case from the ground up—but the new evidence shouts out to free Dr. MacDonald."

New investigator Shedlick says he has a "smoking pistol" in new forensic evidence and in testimony by new witnesses. "We can't tell you who they are because we don't want the government to get to them before trial and intimidate them, as happened before." He adds: "The record shows that at the very least he did not receive a fair trial and that at the very most he is innocent. I believe he'll get a new trial and if it were held today, he'd be a free man tomorrow."

Steven Shea, MD, Dr. MacDonald's business partner in running the ER in Southern California, says, "The man I have known for the past 12 years could not have committed these crimes, and I was at the trial in 1979."

Dudley Warner, who grew up with Dr. MacDonald in Patchogue and proudly watched him go to an Ivy League College and earn a medical degree, says, "I've known him for 30 years—I was at Ft. Bragg within hours of the murders—and I believe in his innocence 100%. I say that as a family man with children of my own. As a young man, I used to always want to double-date with Jeff and Colette, so my dates could see what a good marriage is like."

> "There are some things that one remembers even though they may never have happened. These are things I remember which may never have happened, but as I recall them so they take place."
> —From *Old Times*, a play by Harold Pinter

During a two-hour interview, author McGinniss has been trying to explain the most baffling question:

If he did it, how could he?

McGinniss shakes his head. "Maybe the Pinter quote says it best. I saw the play last night, and it stuck with me.

"Sure, it's easier to think these kinds of things are done by spirits in the night than by the All-American Boy. I liked Jeff. When I first met him, I thought he was very charming, almost seductive, sort of reminiscent of some politicians I've met, people who are very nice to you because they think you can help them. There's no doubt but that Jeff can be a great guy and he's saved lives and he's done wonderful things and a lot of people like him very much.

"But he's not in prison because he took diet pills or is narcissistic. He's in prison because a jury convicted him of killing his family.

"After I sat through the trial in 1979, I was 100% convinced he was guilty. Still, I had been living with Jeff and his family and friends throughout the trial and I had become close to them and I wanted to believe that he was innocent. Maybe I missed something, I told myself. During the next four years, I tried to reawaken some doubts about his guilt. I could not.

"This is a very depressing story. My wife says that working on it caused me to lose the one thing she thought I would never lose-my sense of humor. Yet it's funny—Jeff was always up, always sunny. I used to wonder, 'Where's the sadness, where's the sense of loss?' When I began work on the book with Jeff, we were friends. But it's only when you sit down at the typewriter that you discover what you really believe.

"Who can say why he did it? His sister once said that in their family if you didn't achieve, you were half-dead. Maybe he resented all those years of having to live on stilts, of never being able to walk on level ground. Oh, he'll go on protesting his innocence and if he were innocent that would be an even bigger story—he would be an all-time victim—but, believe me, it isn't there.

"You know, Jeff got along great with a certain type of woman, usually much younger and dependent. He often said he would prefer a 'jury of waitresses.' The waitresses all loved him."

Meanwhile, back in Bastrop prison, Dr. MacDonald is winding down. After four hours of vigorous argumentation and conversation— "I'm talked out"—he whips out his watch and takes his pulse:

"It's 60. Usually, I stay between 52 and 56, but I'm a little upset."

A final question: "Do you ever consider busting out and running for freedom?"

"That question is beneath me," Dr. MacDonald says. "No, wait, I'll answer it. No, I'll never run. Never. To do so would give the people bent on keeping me guilty something to seize on.

"I'm not guilty. Somewhere on this planet in this universe, the truth has to count for something. I will never be ground into the dust. I will keep fighting."

The interview is over.

The former golden boy breaks into a wide grin and the smile lights up the room. The final plea:

"Now, be fair."□

John Hinckley

When John Hinckley was acquitted in 1982 of the attempted assassination of President Ronald Reagan, a shooting that occurred in broad daylight before news photographers and cameramen, millions of Americans were outraged. A firestorm of criticism rained down upon psychiatry and upon psychiatrists.

I tracked down the psychiatrists who had interviewed Hinckley and who had testified at this trial. There was only one question:

Was Hinckley insane?

The experts I talked to argue, "Yes;" of course, there were also those who argued, "No," both to the media and during the trial.

The real dilemma, however, confronted Melvin Sabshin, MD, medical director of the American Psychiatric Assn., which is based in Washington, D.C. For psychiatry, it was a no-win situation, but Dr. Sabshin uses the unpopular verdict to make the main point:

Regardless of the insanity defense, the finding of guilty or not guilty is a moral decision that can only be made by a jury.

PSYCHIATRIST DAVID BEAR, MD, was prepared for a faker, but what he found upon meeting John W. Hinckley Jr. was a "miserably unhappy man."

"He was flabby, pallid, shy, and his emotions were as flat as a pancake. As I talked to him over the course of a year, that is what helped convince me that he was severely mentally ill—his flat emotions.

"The fakers are florid. That's easy enough to fake. If you say that a voice told you to shoot the President, that's hard to dispute.

"But when you think like a child, as Hinckley does, and when your emotions are dead, that can be documented, and that's a strong sign of mental illness. John Hinckley, in my opinion, was psychotic with severe schizophrenia when he shot the President."

Dr. Bear and the two other psychiatrists who testified for the defense in the recently concluded Hinckley trial, Thomas C. Goldman, MD, and William T. Carpenter Jr., MD, talked with *American Medical News* about their controversial patient.

In testimony that took weeks on the witness stand and that comprised thousands of transcript pages in the official record, the three psychiatrists said under oath that Hinckley had been suffering from severe schizophrenia on that fateful day of March 30, 1981. Their independent appraisals of his illness were based upon a combined total of 120 separate interviews over one year. Hinckley's mental illness, they testified, constituted a substantial impairment on the two crucial issues; his emotions, thinking, and behavior on that day; and his ability to appreciate the wrongfulness of his conduct.

The testimony of the three psychiatrists was influential in the subsequent jury decision finding Hinckley "not guilty by reason of insanity." To Drs. Bear and Goldman, the verdict was "correct," under existing law, and they leave to society the Solomonic task of deciding if the verdict were "just." Dr. Carpenter declined to comment on the jury decision.

The executive director of the American Psychiatric Assn., Melvin Sabshin, MD, points out that the basic issue in an insanity case depends upon a *moral decision by a jury,* and that this responsibility cannot be removed from the jurors and placed upon psychiatric experts (see related story).

In the federal court criminal trial, the prosecution carried the burden of proving to the jury that Hinckley was *sane.* That burden was not met, partly because the three defense psychiatrists—who evaluated Hinckley independently—testified that the defendant was schizophrenic. While schizophrenia does not necessarily equal insanity—which is purely a legal, not medical term—the jurors, in Dr. Goldman's words, "clearly got the picture that this was a man with a severe disturbance."

Dr. Bear, 39, interviewed Hinckley for 35 hours during a one-year period before the trial. Like Drs. Carpenter and Goldman, he had access to Hinckley's previous psychiatric records and to physical exams conducted after the arrest, including the controversial CT (computed axial tomography) scan of Hinckley's brain that Dr. Bear requested and then successfully fought to have introduced as evidence.

A Harvard graduate, Dr. Bear, a research psychiatrist, did his residency at Boston's Massachusetts General Hospital, and is board-certified in psychiatry and neurology. The Hinckley trial was his first appearance as an expert witness.

"We had access to a tremendous amount of John's writings over the past six or seven years," he says "and I was tremendously struck by what he called the 'two obsessions of my life—my writings and my love for (actress) Jody Foster.'

"He was tremendously moved by the movie, 'Taxi Driver,' which he first saw in 1976, and in his writings there were references again and again to two themes—Hinckley as a defective male, a hopeless outsider, and Jody as an innocent victim.

"Hinckley saw himself as Travis Bickel, the main character in 'Taxi Driver,' and he thought of Jody Foster as Iris the prostitute. In Hinckley's view, he and Jody were both in jeopardy, both prisoners of society. He would write about how Jody was being 'brutalized at Yale on that dung-heap of a campus' and about how he—a great musician and a great man—was being unfairly kept down by society. Once, he compared himself to the 'Elephant Man' (from another film), as a chronic misfit. His thoughts and his writings were very childlike. He said again and again that he had no sexual thoughts about Jody—this was a man who had been friendless for seven years—that she was simply a fellow victim like himself and he thought that by saving her he would also save himself.

"Psychiatrists often refer to the 4As of schizophrenia, and Hinckley had all four symptoms:

"He had a *flat affect*. His emotions were as flat as a pancake. He thought like a child, but unlike a child, who may go from laughter to anger to tears in five minutes, Hinckley displayed absolutely no emotion at all. Here was a man in a federal prison for committing a 'historic deed,' and he showed no emotion.

"He was pathologically shy. In 35 visits, he never once looked me in the eye. He was very uninteresting, not socially engaging at all, and it was easy to see why he had been friendless for seven years.

"He had *autistic retreat* into himself. He lived in a fantasy world of primitive thoughts and feelings.

"He had *pathological ambivalence,* thinking of himself as simultaneous aggressor and victim. When John Lennon, Hinckley's idol, was slain, Hinckley grieved for Lennon, but he also modeled himself after Lennon's murderer, Mark David Chapman. Similarly, when Hinckley flew across country with handcuffs in his suitcase intending to 'rescue' Jody Foster, he also wrote the FBI a note saying, 'Save this girl.' In his mind, he played both sides of the street.

"He had *association disorders*. This is typical of the 'split' between a schizophrenic's thoughts and emotions and in his thought sequences. Schizophrenics will say things like, 'You have a gray tie, my father had a gray tie, you're a lot like my father.' Hinckley would remark on how he and Travis Bickel had certain letters of their names in common, and how this meant they shared a joint destiny."

The Boston psychiatrist says he was struck with the impression that "Hinckley had negative, not positive, symptoms of schizophrenia. To my mind, this was a strong argument that he was not trying to fake it. You know, there has never been in literature or films an accurate portrayal of schizophrenia, from Shakespeare down through the production of 'Equus.' That's because a lot of schizophrenics are, like Hinckley, very uninteresting people.

"The popular portrayals have been of the florid types—voices telling them what to do, rays shooting through their bodies, ideas beamed into their heads—but the flat types are more common. Many schizophrenics actually live very quietly. They are more likely to be immobilized and paralyzed than to be raving lunatics. Literature has always overplayed the schizophrenic.

"Most, like Hinckley, are very withdrawn. Inside, Hinckley was very turbulent. Outside, his emotions were stalemated. Flat. Had Hinckley said, 'God told me to shoot the President,' I would have thought he was faking. But on the stage of Hinckley's mind, President Reagan was only a bit player. Jody Foster was the overriding luminescent reality. All Hinckley wanted to do was make a connection with Jody."

Dr. Bear offers the theory of how Hinckley "broke the logjam of his emotions" in the months before the shooting. In retrospect, the psychiatrist notes, Hinckley's previous medical care underestimated and, perhaps, aggravated his pathology.

"In December, 1980, John Lennon was killed. Not only was Lennon Hinckley's idol, but the death of the singer also became the death of Hinckley's dream that he, too, was a great musician.

"Also, that fall, he was rebuffed by Jody Foster. This was the death of the dream that she would save him. Interestingly, the prosecution psychiatrists caught Hinckley in a lie—he told them he had actually talked to Jody and later admitted he had not.

"To my mind, this is consistent with Hinckley's illness. After flying across the country 10 times to see Jody, often with handcuffs in his suitcase, after going to all that effort and coming up empty, he felt pretty pathetic. So, he lied.

"The two physicians who had previously treated Hinckley put him on Valium for depression. Ironically, as Hinckley's illness worsened toward psychosis, the Valium, by calming down his anxiety, may have allowed the inner rage to surface. Before, the anxiety and depression had blunted the inner turbulence.

"In the months before the shooting, Hinckley was cut off from his parents, and to a man who had been friendless for seven years, this removed the last links with reality. He lived in a world of sensory restriction—motel rooms with the shades drawn. Even the method by which he was treated by one psychiatrist—biofeedback—intensified this sense of sensory restriction. Right before the shooting, he took a long bus ride and went days with little sleep.

"By March 30, 1981, he needed hospitalization and anti-psychotic medication. Then, he could have been treated with intensive psychotherapy and group counseling to try to help him overcome to some degree his marked emotional retardation. He didn't go to a hospital. He went to the Washington Hilton to meet the President."

Dr. Bear cites the importance of the CT scan admitted into evidence as proof of the shrinking of Hinckley's brain.

"I feel very strongly about the importance of that test," he says. "Before I argued for its submission into evidence, I spent hours on the phone talking with experts around the country, and I reviewed the medical literature. By itself, a CT scan is not a diagnosis of schizophrenia, but combined with my clinical impressions, it was a powerful diagnostic tool.

"To the naked eye, the CT picture of Hinckley's brain appeared dramatically shrunken. The brain, of course, shrinks with age, but Hinckley is 26. On the computer picture there are deep black rivers of indentation cutting into the lacy white network of Hinckley's brain. These indentations are folds that are abnormally large and that are part of the brain's shrinkage. A normal 26-year-old has folds in his brain, but they are not detectable. Hinckley's are very apparent, and they do not represent reversible degeneration because two scans taken a year apart showed the same pattern.

"It looks as if a worm has eaten away at his brain. Hinckley himself wrote, 'Sometimes, I feel that maggots are eating away at my brain.' In my opinion, if you thought that there was a 50-50 probability of a patient being schizophrenic, the presence of this type of shrinkage would raise the odds to better than 90%. One of three severe schizophrenics has this type of brain shrinkage. Among normal people and those with mild personality disorders, the rate is less than 3%.

"Charles Whitman, the 'Texas Tower' mass murderer of 1967, turned out to have a brain tumor. He was killed during his capture, but had he survived, neurosurgery would have been more appropriate than punishment. There were no CT scans then, but today, he might have been diagnosed before the outburst."

Hinckley's shrunken brain, the MD says, "might have been present at birth from a virus, hormones, or genetics, or it might have been caused later by a specific degenerative disease. We don't know what caused it."

To Dr. Bear, Hinckley was a "pseudoneurotic schizophrenic." He notes:

"Hinckley presented as a neurotic with anxieties and aimlessness, but his real problem was schizophrenia. I was very struck by his childlike nature. He is 26, but he looks 17. He talked of his crime as a child might fantasize abut Hans Solo killing Darth Vader (from the film "Star Wars").

He thought the movie 'Taxi Driver,' was made exclusively for him. He saw himself as a misfit, a loser, an outsider.

"Hinckley thought of his father and older brother as making demands that he couldn't meet. By contrast, his mother and sister were very nurturing. They didn't demand anything from him. He saw himself as an innocent victim of society.

"When asked, Hinckley will say he 'loves his father,' but he hated authority, the authority that he saw keeping himself down. He was being kept down as a musician and he was being kept away from Jody.

"Unfortunately, President Reagan was a projection figure for the authority he hated."

Drs. Goldman and Carpenter declined to discuss their testimony about Hinckley, but both indicated their opinions that he suffered from severe schizophrenia.

Dr. Goldman calls it "schizotypal personality disorder, regressing under stress to psychosis."

A graduate of Harvard with internship at the U. of Chicago and residency at Bronx (N.Y.) Municipal Hospital Center, Dr. Goldman, 40, practices private psychiatry in Washington and has been doing forensic psychiatric work for 10 years.

He stresses: "The psychiatrist appears in court as a clinician. The jurors want to hear what he has to say as a physician, and the ground rules are that the psychiatrist is to testify as though he were evaluating the patient's case for his family.

"Our testimony reflects our unbiased understanding of the patient's condition. Many times, I have been asked by the defense to evaluate a client for an insanity defense and I have advised them against it because I have found the defendant to not be severely ill enough to sustain an insanity defense. On the other hand, many times I have been asked by the prosecution to evaluate a defendant for whom they anticipate an insanity defense and I have advised them that, yes, this person is really very sick, the insanity defense is justified.

"So we take the oath seriously. We are not 'hired guns.'

"Based on the evidence presented, the Hinckley verdict was a correct verdict. It's up to society to decide if it were just. But I strongly believe that psychiatric testimony is relevant to the criminal justice system.

"I tried to be as plain as possible in my testimony, but clearly, some of the jurors were confused and blocked out some of what they were hearing (five jurors said as much to a Senate panel that held hearings after the verdict).

"In many ways, we psychiatrists are trying to understand the most complex phenomenon of all—human behavior. Obviously, we do not know everything.

"But just because we do not know everything does not mean that we do not know anything.

"Hinckley's mental disorder was chronic and progressive and severe. It was closer to schizophrenia than any other definable form of mental illness. I characterized it as a schizotypal personality disorder, with regression under stress to psychosis. This is the nomenclature of the *Diagnostic and Statistical Manual III (DSM III)*. In *DSM II,* it would have been called simple schizophrenia.

"I tried to make my testimony as non-technical as possible, but the adversary system often works against this. But everybody, prosecution and defense, agreed that Hinckley was definitely abnormal in some very profound ways—the way he lived and the way he thought.

"Clearly, the jurors got the picture of a man with a severe mental disturbance."

Dr. Carpenter, 45, is a graduate of the Bowman Gray School of Medicine of Wake Forest College, Winston-Salem, N.C., and did his residency at North Carolina Baptist Hospital, Winston-Salem, and Strong Memorial Hospital at the U. of Rochester, N.Y. He is board-certified in psychiatry and neurology. The Hinckley trial was his first criminal court appearance.

The Catonsville, Md., psychiatrist said that psychiatric diagnoses are complicated "by a lack of animal models—as are common in many other medical specialties—and by a lack of confirmatory tissue tests—we don't do biopsies of the brain—but that the reliability of a schizophrenia diagnosis is extremely high."

Dr. Carpenter, who runs the Maryland Psychiatric Research Hospital, says, "Schizophrenia is the same all over the world, and the agreement rate on diagnosis under *DSM III* field trials runs as high as 80% to 90%.

"It's unfortunate that some of the jargon might have confused the jury, but medical nomenclature is meant to serve the interest of medical science, not a public debate. As psychiatry has broadened and deepened its understanding of mental illness, diagnostic labeling has changed. This is the same thing that has happened in oncology, as physicians have increased their understanding of cancer, and in cardiology, as physicians have increased their understanding of heart disease.

"But the basic understanding of schizophrenia was known at the turn of the century. Diagnosis is based upon a constellation of features and of functional deficits, but a core feature that holds in cases throughout the world is the flat affect, or the burnt-out or blunted emotions. This is a key feature and a highly documented finding among schizophrenics."

In his court testimony, Dr. Carpenter said that Hinckley displayed a very flat affect and that he suffers from "process schizophrenia." This disease, he said, "is marked by a very severe and very grave course. There are episodes of improvements and worsenings, but core deficits in psychic functioning are never fully recovered. Process schizophrenia cannot be prevented and it cannot be cured, although we do have effective treatments for some aspects.

"We can diminish the effects of short-term outbursts, but we cannot compensate for the long-term deficits. That is why schizophrenia represents a greater economic loss to the country than does cancer. Schizophrenia strikes early and it stays forever.

"I won't second-guess the jury, but I believe that a system of blameworthiness should remain a part of our judicial system. As an inmate of a mental institution, Hinckley is as far removed—and will probably stay as long removed—from society as if he were in prison. This is being lost on some people. Remember, Sirhan Sirhan, who was found guilty of killing Robert F. Kennedy in 1968, has been recommended for parole. (Parole was denied, however.) The man who tried to assassinate President Teddy Roosevelt was found insane, but was never released from a mental institution.

"Prison is no more a guarantee against future release than is commitment to a mental institution. John Hinckley is likely to be removed from society for a long, long time. A lock-up for mental illness is as effective for society as a lock-up for criminal guilt."

All three defense psychiatrists expressed sympathy for the difficulties of John Hopper, MD, the Evergreen, Colo., psychiatrist who had been treating Hinckley before the shooting. "This type of personality puts obstacles in way of understanding," Dr. Goldman says. "Hinckley may not have allowed previous doctors to get his full picture," Dr. Carpenter says. "Hindsight is wonderful," Dr. Bear says. "We did retrospective evaluations."

Dr. Bear concludes: "The attacks on psychiatry are a bum rap. If you look through the entire transcript, you will find much psychiatric testimony that is very logical and very powerful and very lucid. Psychiatry is not all smoke. And we take that oath very seriously. I deeply resent any implication that my opinion could be 'bought.'

"I think that psychiatry can help John Hinckley. I think that right before the shooting, he was ready to 'spill the beans' if only someone had been able to get to him.

"Sure, he likes seeing himself in the newspapers and he has elements of grandiosity and narcissism, but that is consistent with his illness. Like a child, he thinks that he is at the center of things. But to argue as the prosecution psychiatrists did that he is merely narcissistic and neurotic is to miss the profound nature of his thought disorders.

"The prosecution psychiatric report is 'preposterous.' To Hinckley, the entire crime was making a connection to Jody. Hinckley always said,

'If only I can find one person who cares.' The President and the others were paper dolls.

"How much can Hinckley be helped? How long does it take to walk to Krakow? The answer is: 'Let me see how fast you walk.'

"I think that Hinckley can be helped, though never restored to a full range of normal emotions. The violence could have been prevented, though, if he had been reached in time.

"John Hinckley may be a narcissistic child, but I know this:

"He is a miserably unhappy man."□

INSANITY IS A LEGAL, not medical term. Jurors, not psychiatrists, must decide if a particular form of mental illness constitutes insanity on the given day that a crime is committed. Defendants found not guilty by reason of insanity and committed to a mental institution usually are locked up longer and commit fewer future crimes than do defendants found guilty and sentenced to prison. The diagnostic reliability of psychiatry on chronic mental illness is as high as in any part of medicine, except for infectious and toxic diseases.

With these four declarative sentences, Melvin Sabshin, MD, executive director of the American Psychiatric Assn., outlined his profession's response to the "firestorm of criticism" that has rained upon medicine after the unpopular verdict in the John W. Hinckley Jr. case.

To Dr. Sabshin, the criticism was hardly a surprise. The APA offices in Washington, D.C., had weathered an even more tumultuous reaction in the days immediately following the March 30, 1981, shooting. For him, the dilemma for psychiatry has been "no-win" from the start.

"Had Hinckley been found guilty," he says, "people would still have said, 'Thank God, the jurors did not listen to the psychiatrists who testified that he was severely disturbed.' "

What is surprising, however, Dr. Sabshin emphasized in an interview with *American Medical News,* is this:

"The public is dead wrong about the perception that psychiatry has a very low rate of diagnostic reliability. Clinical evidence of disease outcome criteria clearly show that the reliability of diagnosis of chronic psychiatric disease is as high as in any part of medicine, except for infectious and toxic diseases. The recent field trials of the *Diagnostic and Statistical Manual III* are demonstrating this high rate of reliability around the world."

The public outcry over the Hinckley verdict already has produced Senate hearings in which five of the Hinckley jurors told the senators that they were "confused" by the expert psychiatric testimony. It has produced major newspaper columns in which the writers have termed psychiatry a "bogus" science and a field that "cannot have experts because it does not have expertise." The controversy is sure to continue because immediately after Hinckley was found not guilty by reason of insanity in his criminal trial, three lawsuits seeking $72 million in damages were filed against him as civil cases.

Psychiatry's conundrum in the Hinckley criminal case was due to a fact that has been lost in the subsequent uproar: The psychiatric witnesses testified only on Hinckley's mental illness—severe schizophrenia, as argued by the defense, and less severe personality disorders, as argued by the prosecution. The psychiatrists argued medical diagnoses, not sanity or insanity. Since the prevailing trial instructions put the burden on the government to *prove that Hinckley was sane,* however, and since the jurors had *only two choices*—guilty or not guilty by reason of insanity— the effect to the jurors of all the testimony—defense and prosectuion— was that of a man who clearly had a mental problem.

The moral conclusion that his problem, under this set of trial circumstances, constituted insanity was made by the jurors. The psychiatric testimony that Hinckley was schizophrenic in no way had to mean that he was *insane.* If the insanity defense is allowed in the civil cases and if they come to trial, the shoe will be on the other foot—Hinckley will have to *prove that he is insane.*

Dr. Sabshin comes quickly to his points:

"First, psychiatry shares the concern of the public over the Hinckley trial, the process of justice, and the decision. The shooting of a president and members of his staff gives me great pain personally, and I'm sure it saddens all psychiatrists, as well as all Americans. But when we come to the point where it is not the defendant that is on trial, but rather medicine—through psychiatry—that is on trial, then it is time to step back and make a cool appraisal of the real issues.

"Americans, of course, are terrified by the notion that a man might murder and get away with it. This concern, of course, is greatly intensified when the intended victim is the President of the United States. But one overriding fact has been lost in the impassioned public outcry:

"A man found not guilty by reason of insanity is just as effectively removed from society and locked up as is a man found guilty. In fact, statistics show that those assailants found not guilty, but insane, actually spend more time locked up than do those convicted of the crime. They also are found to be far less likely to commit another crime."

Having made his point that Hinckley "did not get away with anything," Dr. Sabshin emphasizes that psychiatry must not be made the scapegoat for an unpopular decision that must be made not by psychiatrists but only by the judicial system and the society it represents.

"Long before there were psychiatrists," Dr. Sabshin points out, "there was an 'insanity defense.' Whether there should be an insanity defense and what standards should be used to determine an insanity defense are issues for society to decide. Just as other citizens do, psychiatrists disagree on these issues.

"The American Psychiatric Assn. is deeply concerned about the determination of what should be the appropriate legal tests of insanity in a criminal trial, as well as who should bear the burden of proof—the defense or the prosecution. As is the case with medical knowledge in general, it should be remembered that psychiatric knowledge cannot be expected to meet demands for *absolute certainty*.

"Inevitably, psychiatrists will be asked to testify on the insanity defense in criminal trials. Psychiatrists are not in the courtroom to decide the ultimate issue of guilt or innocence, but only to provide expert testimony to help jurors make that determination. The final moral decision—guilty or not guilty—always has and always will be a jury decision, regardless of the insanity defense.

"The fact that psychiatrists disgaree on the insanity defense is neither novel nor surprising. Experts often disagree in criminal and civil trials. Other physicians may disagree on the interpretation of x-rays, engineers on structural issues, economists on market issues. While such disagreement may be disquieting, it only reflects the fact that professional and scientific judgments have *not reached closure*. It does not mean that the testimony is not helpful or relevant to jurors trying to resolve difficult issues.

"The scientific disagreements in an insanity case are intensified by two legal factors—the psychiatrists are testifying on the basis of *retrospective* inquiries into the patient's condition and they are testifying under the rules of the *adversary* system.

"Finally, the 'yes or no' nature of the verdict in an insanity case do not allow for the *harmonizing* of reasonable professional opinions, as often happens in a non-criminal trial setting."

Dr. Sabshin reiterates his main message:

"Since disagreements in medical conclusions may have an impact on these important moral decisions by jurors, it is often made to seem as if the psychiatrists are responsible for the moral judgment themselves, rather than for the presentation of medical testimony.

"This is an unfortunate perception, because it removes responsibility for the jury decision from the jurors and erroneously places it upon the experts."

The APA official said that some people view psychiatry as "a threat to the moral fiber of our nation."

"Unfortunately, there is a small cadre of people who make a living by attacking psychiatry. There are psychiatrists who have said for years that there is no such thing as 'psychiatric illness.' They don't let the evidence get in their way.

"Ironically, psychiatry is attacked from both ends of the political spectrum. Liberals charge that we are too conservative and restrict civil rights by committing the mentally ill to institutions; conservatives charge that we are too liberal and sabotage justice by allowing the mentally ill to escape punishment. Sometimes, both extremes attack us on the same television program.

"I cringed when the Hinckley trial began, because I knew that regardless of the outcome, psychiatry would get a black eye. But despite its imperfections, the adversarial system of justice is the best we can devise, and psychiatrists must learn to cope with it for the public good. There will always be a role for expert psychiatric testimony in our criminal-justice system.

"In the Hinckley trial, the issue was insanity. Three psychiatrists testified that Hinckley had severe schizophrenia, and that is a diagnosis for which the reliability is 80-plus % accurate. But it is possible to be schizophrenic and not insane.

"The Hinckley trial had a melange of expert psychiatric witnesses—MDs who are experts in researching schizophrenia, and MDs who are expert in treating schizophrenia, MDs who are expert in arguing for and against the insanity defense. All argued from their unique perspective.

"The dilemma faced by Dr. (John) Hopper, who treated Hinckley before the crime, was especially poignant. In retrospect, he underestimated Hinckley's pathology. But many psychiatrists are criticized for over-esti-mating a patient's pathology. Where do we draw the line?

"The public only hears of psychiatry's errors. Thousands of times a year, psychiatrists will correctly choose to keep thousands of patients out of mental hospitals and help them remain independent. Psychiatrists have to take risks. Do we want to take zero risks and put every questionable patient in a mental hospital? Where would we find the facilities and the funds? The type of dilemma that faced Dr. Hopper faces psychiatrists every day. These are tough decisions.

"The media barrage over the Hinckley verdict has been extraordinary, but now it is time for cooler heads to prevail. We need rational, sober long-term analysis to find the best methods by which psychiatry can serve patients and justice.

"Many people are arguing for a legal system that will put the burden on proving the 'insanity' side of the equation, or for a system that will allow a verdict of 'guilty, but insane.'

"To my mind, these are very cogent arguments."□

"Death Angel"

Occasionally, journalists and journalism can make a difference. The usual way is to expose corruption, fraud, or murder. The unusual way is to expose stories falsely alleging corruption, fraud, or murder. This story does it the unusual way.

Jani Adams, a former teacher of English who gravitated into intensive-care nursing, was accused of ghoulish charges:

That she not only had killed people on her intensive-care ward, but that she timed the deaths to rig bets on when the unfortunate patients would die. Since Jani worked at Las Vegas' Sunrise Hospital, only minutes from the Vegas strip, the charges made headlines around the world. Her accuser was the *Las Vegas Review-Journal,* which made the charges in big, bright-blue headlines. The newspaper called her "Death Angel" and said that police reports backed up its lurid charges. The DA indicted her on one count of murder. The paper stood to win a Pulitzer Prize, it was being said.

In 1980, the entire Sunrise Hospital, a member of the Humana Chain, had circled the wagons and were in a siege mentality, paralyzed by the charges that are the most serious that can be made in the health-care field. I persuaded the 5-foot-98-pound nurse to consent to an interview. She agreed, on condition that it take place in the small house she shared with boyfriend Bernard Deters (a health technician who also had originally been charged) and her collection of prized Persian cats, who intermittently attacked my tape recorder.

Jani not only denied the allegations, but authorized the hospital to discuss the charges against her. Then, with the invaluable help of Sunrise PR chief, Rena Ruby, I was able to persuade the hospital's medical staff to open the chart on the one patient whose death had drawn the murder indictment.

This man, it soon became clear, had died from natural causes and despite heroic nursing care by Jani Adams and her nursing colleagues. At one time or another, seven different doctors wrote into the record that the man's condition was hopeless, an outgrowth of complications from a 7½-hour surgery performed to stop massive gastrointestinal bleeding that was aggravated by cirrhosis of the liver brought on by alcoholism and by a 20-year peptic ulcer. For six weeks, the hospital medical record showed, medicine and Jani Adams had given the patient everything there was to offer (at a cost of $90,000), but he simply could not be saved.

This story, outlining the actual medical record of the death upon which Jani Adam's indictment for murder was solely based, was subsequently reprinted in Las Vegas' *other* newspaper—and elsewhere. Within weeks of its appearance, the indictment against the so-called "Death Angel" was quashed.

Somewhere in my files I have a nice handwritten note from Jani Adams, thanking me for taking a different look at her story.

"DEATH ANGEL," THE NEWS MEDIA have named her, and, today, they are out in force. Elbowing for position, the TV cameramen crowd the end of the carpeted corridor in the Clark County, Nev., Courthouse.

Promptly at 9 a.m. on April 4, 1980, she walks down the corridor and into the bright television lights. The cameramen are allowed to follow her into the courtroom, where District Judge Michael Wendell begins:

"I presume the defendant can read and write and understand the charges against her. You are charged with a felony, the murder of a Mr. Vincent Fraser on March 3, 1980. How do you wish to plead?"

Jani Adams, RN, 32, at 5 feet tall and 98 pounds, a tiny, terrified figure, rises and replies in a loud, clear voice:

"Not guilty."

The arraignment is over, and Judge Wendell sets June 22 for the trial of the intensive-care nurse, on charges that she cut back vital oxygen and killed the patient she claims to have helped keep alive for six weeks.

The TV cameras follow her as she walks out of the court and across the street to the offices of Las Vegas attorney Gary Logan. Looking straight ahead, she clings to the arm of the man she lives with, respiratory technician, Bernard Deters, 39.

Some believe Jani Adams is a victim of the Las Vegas press and prosecutors.

J. Daniel Wilkes, MD, a pathologist and trustee at Sunrise Hospital, where the crime allegedly took place, says:

"Our investigation, based on talking with those involved, shows absolutely no suggestion of any wrongdoing on the part of any Sunrise employes. Jani Adams is found not only to be innocent but to be a highly conscientious and competent nurse. What we have here is a case of media malpractice and a political indictment handed down to protect a newspaper and the district attorney from civil suit."

It is a bizarre case, and for three weeks now has attracted international publicity. Ever since March 13, when the Las Vegas *Review-Journal* in a copyrighted story on page 1 in bright blue ink announced:

"Vegas police probe Sunrise 'death bets.' "

The newspaper told a grisly tale: that Las Vegas police and the district attorney's office were investigating up to six suspicious deaths in the intensive-care ward of the city's Sunrise Hospital, and that, "according to reliable sources, certain staff members of the hospital's graveyard shift were making bets on what time a patient in the unit would die."

The story added, "Sources said a Sunrise nurse—like an oddsmaker at a booking establishment—has taken bets from other staff members on what time a patient in that ward will die . . . Authorities believe that in some cases the patients, clinging to their lives, have been 'put to sleep' with the help of a Sunrise staffer."

The lurid charges were brought to the attention of David Brandsness, executive director of Sunrise Hospital, at 10:30 the morning of March 13. The paper would be on the street by noon, Brandsness was told.

The stunned administrator promptly suspended the seven employes being investigated, including Adams and Deters. All had been working the night shift (11 p.m. to 7 a.m.) in a 10-bed surgical respiratory intensive-care unit that is part of Sunrise's football field-size 70-bed ICU that commands the hospital's entire second floor.

Brandsness could only tell reporters, "The charges are the most serious that can be made in the health care field."

The seven employees were given no reason when suspended on the morning of March 13. They would find out when the *Review-Journal* hit the street.

Adams and Deters recall it well. Sitting in her attorney's office, her eyes red from crying, her hands clenched to whiteness, her feet locked behind her and pushing against the floor, Adams begins for *American Medical News* the only interview she has allowed:

"I'm scared. Sure, I'm scared to death. I'm a Catholic. I believe that only God can take life. We tried so hard to keep Mr. Fraser alive. We did our best. We did everything we could, but he was such a sick man. He just died. Now, to be charged with murder, I guess I'm just numb, in a state of shock."

Deters breaks in, "Right after the story broke, the police contacted us. They call it an investigation. I call it an interrogation. They were saying things to Jani like, 'Do you know you can go to the gas chamber? Do you know that Nevada believes in the death penalty for murder?' We couldn't believe it."

Adams had nothing in her background to prepare her for the Las Vegas police. A former English teacher at Clemson U. in North Carolina, she holds master's degrees in English from Washington State U. and in costume design from Kansas State U. A former licensed practical nurse, she earned her RN from Pima (Ariz.) Community College in 1976 and became an intensive-care specialist. For the past two years, she has been at Sunrise Hospital, where the medical staff unequivocally call her "an exemplary nurse." Says a former chief of staff, "If there were one nurse I would want with me in intensive care, it is Jani Adams. No one fights harder to keep a patient alive."

Jani Adams knows you don't win them all. Her father died of a heart attack, her mother of cancer. Pointing to Deters, she says, "That's my whole life now. Bernard and nursing."

She says, "It was terrible, simply terrible. There was no physical abuse, but the police pushed me around mentally, accusing me of this and that. I didn't know what to think."

Deters did. "We needed an attorney," he said. "We knew for something like this we needed the best. Well, you can't just go through the Yellow Pages. My first choice was F. Lee Bailey, but I was in such a state of shock that although it was only noon in Las Vegas I thought it was 2 p.m. I figured it must be 5 p.m. in Boston and Bailey would have left the office. I figured it was local time—only 2 p.m.—in San Francisco, so we called Melvin Belli. That's how it happened."

Jani adds, "We didn't even know Gary (Logan), then. But he's been working with Mr. Belli for years. Everybody asks, 'How can I afford Melvin Belli?' Well, I can't, but he agreed to take the case. I am determined to make the best legal fight, and if it takes the rest of my life, I'll pay Mr. Belli back."

Belli's involvement in the case intensified the media publicity. Newspapers picked up the "death angel" tagline and for weeks speculated on the case. By April 2, however, law enforcement investigators had backed off the betting allegations. They and Clark County District Atty. Bob Miller selected two cases to take to the jury—the deaths of Fraser, 52, and Marian Bartlett, an 85-year-old woman.

In two sessions, the grand jury heard 21 witnesses, most of whom are medical professionals at Sunrise Hospital. Belli, the 72-year-old attorney who himself is a media favorite as the "King of Torts," was talking countersuit, and everything hung on the grand jury action. In one prominent story, *Newsweek* magazine terms the case, "Malpractice—medical or media?" The stakes were growing.

On April 2, Miller told a packed press conference that the grand jury had returned an indictment for open murder against Adams in the death of Vincent Fraser. She had tampered with the patient's oxygen support, he said. There were no charges in the death of Marian Bartlett, he said. The open murder indictment, Miller explained, could be prosecuted as first- or second-degree murder or as voluntary or involuntary manslaughter. The person who triggered the initial investigation, he said, was another Sunrise nurse, Barbara Farro, RN, who reported "suspicious actions" to police officials.

Adams was released on $15,000 bond, and arraigned for murder two days later. "Death angel" had become her second name.

The grand jury testimony runs 400 pages and is unknown to Adams, Deters, her attorneys (they will have it in time to prepare for the trial), and Sunrise Hospital staff. What is known, however, is that the case rests on the death of one man, Vincent Fraser.

Las Vegas' *Valley Times* interviewed the widow, Bertha Fraser, and quotes her as saying, "After we moved to Las Vegas several years ago, Vincent started to develop a hernia. Nothing serious, but it gave him a pot belly. He went into Sunrise in January (1980) to have surgery on the hernia. Until then, he was in perfect health. He died 40 days later with what authorities called liver problems."

Mrs. Fraser is preparing a wrongful-death suit against the hospital.

Appalled at this description of the patient, Ms. Adams directed her attorneys to allow Sunrise Hospital officials to comment for *AMN* only on Fraser's medical history, which will be central to her trial.

Fraser spent seven weeks in intensive care as a Class I (all-out attention) patient. His medical records are a half-foot thick. A physician-representative of the Sunrise medical staff sat down with *AMN* and reviewed the physicians' progress notes on Fraser.

Simply put, the records show Fraser had chronic cirrhosis of the liver from prolonged alcoholism and a 20-year peptic ulcer. Following two episodes only weeks apart of massive upper gastrointestinal bleeding, he required $7\frac{1}{2}$ hours of major surgery to prevent the internal bleeding.

He had a stormy post-operative course, including the draining of fecal matter from his abdomen and massive infection, and weeks before his death five physicians noted in the charts that his condition was "terminal."

On Jan. 8, 1980, said a Sunrise medical staff spokesman, "A Sunrise general surgeon admitted Fraser to the hospital. The patient had an upper GI bleed from a 20-year peptic ulcer. His medical record indicated cirrhosis of the liver from alcoholism so severe as to have required two previous surgical shunts—the Levine shunt and the Warren-distal spleenorenal shunt. The GI bleed was complicated by the cirrhotic liver. Fraser responded to transfusions and in about a week was discharged on the standard peptic-ulcer regimen.

"However, on Jan. 22, 1980, he was readmitted after vomiting bright red blood. His hemoglobin was 4.7, compared to the normal 14–16. He was given six pints of blood, but continued to bleed.

"On Jan. 23, he agreed to having a Sunrise thoracic surgeon perform radical surgery:

"A portocaval shunt, gastrostomy, pyloroplasty, spleenectomy, and ligation of the short gastric arteries. This major surgery required 7½ hours, and his post-operative course was stormy. From the time of his second admission, he was constantly in intensive care.

"After surgery, he developed low blood pressure (treated with Dopaine), required a tracheotomy, developed gram negative sepsis, was continually on a ventilator, and developed heart failure (treated with digoxin and diuretics).

"His condition gradually stabilized somewhat, but he continued to need transfusions, IVs, hyperalimentation. On Feb. 3, he became hypoxic and went into shock. He developed a right-side pleural effusion. On Feb. 4, he developed kidney failure with his blood urea nitrogen greatly elevated. By Feb. 7, the gross wound infection from the surgery caused shock. He had intestinal fistulas and fecal matter was draining from the abdomen. There was respiratory and renal dysfunction; the white cells were elevated. He was treated with antibiotics for the bacterial growth from the surgical wound and for his fever.

"By Feb. 16, things were terrible: Continued sepsis, fever, heart failure, multiple draining fistula from the abdomen, retroperineal abscess, positive blood cultures for pathological organisms.

"On Feb. 18, he went into septic shock from intra-abdominal abscesses. The admitting physician's progress notes on Feb. 18 say, 'Prognosis terrible, but surgery indicated to drain the sepsis.' The same physician's Feb. 19 note reads, 'Survived the Operation!! Significantly improved!!' There were two exclamation marks. It seemed a miracle. Fraser remained in respiratory intensive care. By Feb. 20, he had developed left lower-lobe pneumonia, his BUN was 76, compared to the normal 18, and things were worsening.

"By Feb. 25, the patient's condition was rapidly deteriorating. He was in shock and all major organs were failing—heart, lung, liver, kidney. Admitting physician's notes read: 'Doubt survival.' This is the first of five physician notes in the record indicating the patient would die of natural causes. An internist wrote in the chart that dialysis was not recommended because the patient was not 'salvageable.'

"On Feb. 27, one thoracic surgeon wrote in the record: 'Terminal status.' The next day, the thoracic surgeon who performed the surgery wrote in the chart: 'Very difficult to see how we can salvage him—will talk to family.'

"Mrs. Fraser was told on Feb. 28 of the likelihood of her husband's death, and that same day on her own made arrangements with a Florida funeral home. At about 11 p.m. on March 2, hours before Vincent Fraser died, Mrs. Fraser told the medical staff, 'I simply cannot take it anymore. I am going to leave.' Now, this is a woman who does not have a phone and whenever we had to contact her we would have to send a police car by to pick her up and take her to a phone. She is an ill woman, heart disease and hypertension. We explained the options to her—she could wait until her husband died, she could come back later, or she could sign the mortuary release form before leaving. She chose to sign the form. A few hours after she left, at 4:20 a.m., Vincent Fraser died of septic shock."

The Sunrise physician-spokesman concludes, "This was an agonizing, horrible death. During the last three days of Vincent Fraser's life, our nurses say that every time he was touched he would scream in pain. Our intensive-care nurses are pretty hardened people, and they say this was one of the worst deaths they've ever seen. Some said, 'I don't see how we can take much more.' But the charts show everything was done for Vincent Fraser right until he expired.

"What happened here was a patient with a 20-year history of peptic ulcer complicated by chronic cirrhosis of the liver—the presence of two previous surgical shunts is presumptive evidence of severe alcoholism—had two massive GI bleeds within two weeks. Surgery was recommended, and the patient's tissues were not good enough to withstand the surgery. The draining fistula led to infection and the infection to shock and death.

"Anybody who saw this man die knows it was agonizing, but he was given everything medicine has to offer for six weeks. It just wasn't enough."

Vincent Fraser is dead, but the issues live on.

The indictment charges Adams (no charges were placed against the other six hospital workers, including respiratory technician Deters) with murdering Fraser by modifying his oxygen supply.

Jani Adams categorically denies the charge. "I fought for this patient's life for six weeks," she said, "and I fought for it right up until the end. I do not believe in mercy killings."

Says Deter, "Some nurse heard somebody say, 'I bet he doesn't make it until 4 a.m. and, sure enough, he dies at about 4 a.m. Big deal, that's just the way it was. He was dying and we knew he was dying and we knew he would die sometime that morning."

T. K. Christiansen, MD, who performed Fraser's surgery and who signed the death certificate (sepsis), calls Adams, "a highly qualified nurse with whom I've worked many times. I have no hesitation about recommending her." Dr. Christiansen adds, "I know of no clinical evidence that supports an allegation that this patient died of anything but natural causes."

DA Miller says only, "In Nevada, we do not indict on hearsay. We indict on evidence, and it will be presented during the trial."

The primary witness, Barbara Farro, RN, refused to discuss the case, though adding, "I would love to explain what I saw and heard but this is not the time." Her husband, casino dealer John Farro, supports this view and now keeps their phone off the hook.

"Look man," Farro told *AMN* after persistent inquiries, "My wife saw something unprofessional, she was bothered by it, she talked to me about it, I referred her to George Franklin, who I know and who used to be the DA, and he referred her to the DA. Had she told Sunrise, the hospital would have had to report it to the police. So, we saved them that trouble. The police investigated and they turned it over to the grand jury. The grand jury indicted. Now, these are ordinary people. They must have found something. That's it. My wife and I just got married. We don't want to be hassled. Come back after the trial, and she'll talk to you."

The day Adams was indicted for murder, Farro returned to work at Sunrise after taking a brief leave of absence to get away from reporters. A one-year Sunrise employe, she was last March working her required one-month on the night shift (in a unit adjacent to but not part of the unit where Fraser was treated) when she allegedly observed the events that led to Adam's indictment.

Intensive-care nursing supervisor Shirley Wakefield, RN, says flatly, "I don't think it could have happened. The system is too sophisticated and there are too many people caring for the critically ill. For Jani to have turned off the oxygen would have required the collusion and conspiracy of everyone on the unit, and I don't think that is the case. Jani is the charge nurse, someone else actually cared for Fraser under doctor's orders. That person would have had to be indicted, too."

Sunrise officials note that Jani Adams, like many ICU nurses, is aggressive and can be curt, even abrasive. "I suppose," said one physician, "she has developed a type of black humor, gallows humor, as a defense mechanism against what she sees every day, but nobody works harder to keep patients alive. Maybe she said something and somebody mis-construed the meaning."

In the meantime, the 666-bed, 2,000-employe proprietary hospital tries to carry on business as usual. Says Brandsness, "This was a good hospital yesterday, it is a good hospital today, and it will be a good hospital tomorrow."

Dr. Wilkes says, "The only betting done in the ICU is after a grateful patient leaves behind a fruit bowl for the nursing staff. Employes put their names in the bowl, and the lucky winner gets to keep the bowl. That's how the betting rumor started."

The larger issue to American medicine posed by the "death angel" case is this:

Caring for the critically ill. Who shall live and who shall be allowed to die? How much can be spent in extraordinary but futile efforts to prolong the life of the terminally ill? (Fraser's bill: $90,000.)

Dr. Christiansen says, "My patients are always kept in the ICU as Class I. I never go to Class II (a lesser form of medical heroics to sustain the terminally ill). I see no evidence in this case that anything but Class I intensive care was carried out. Maybe the police are setting new law."

Concludes Dr. Wilkes:

"Sure, these are complex issues, and medicine must resolve them. We can't have some policemen and the press doing it for us."□

Chappaquiddick

Some men make history; some men miss their chance.

Probably the most famous autopsy never performed is the one that might have been done on Mary Jo Kopechne after she drowned in a tidal pond under a bridge on the island of Chappaquiddick. Her companion that fateful evening, of course, was Sen. Edward Kennedy, then and now a powerful political figure. The man who might have done the autopsy is Donald R. Mills, MD, associate medical examiner of Dukes County, Mass.

Dr. Mills, a mild-mannered family physician, told me that he had more important things on his mind that day—delivering a baby. In July, 1969, he had never thought twice about ordering an autopsy. After all, the girl looked "as drowned as any person I have ever seen."

Ten years later, on the eve of Sen. Kennedy's entry into the 1980 Presidential race, Dr. Mills consented to an interview and retraced for me his steps from his office-home in Edgartown, Mass., on across the ferry to Chappaquiddick's one main paved road, and off that main road down the packed-dirt road leading to the historic bridge.

He recalls, "Of course, there should have been an autopsy. But at the time, the people in the DA's office and the people in Boston were in no big hurry to come down to Chappaquiddick and help me out."

THE NEWSPAPERS REPORTED IT: "Some time after midnight on the morning of July 19, 1969, a car driven by Sen. Edward M. Kennedy plunged off a bridge into a tidal pond on the island of Chappaquiddick, carrying a young woman companion to her death by drowning."

Ten hours later that same morning, Donald R. Mills, MD, associate medical examiner of Dukes County, Mass., crossed by ferry from Edgartown to Chappaquiddick, stepped into a waiting hearse, was driven a few miles to the waiting body of Mary Jo Kopechne, and stepped out into history.

Dr. Mills was caught in the center of a swirling controversy, a controversy that continues a decade later.

At the center of the continuing controversy is the fact that an autopsy was never performed on Mary Jo Kopechne. And at the center of that fact is a physician, Dr. Mills, who failed to secure an autopsy.

Dr. Mills is the first to admit that neither by inclination nor imposition of will is he the stuff of which legends are made. He is, rather, a gentle country doctor who 10 years ago found himself "thrown into a situation way over my head. I went by the book, but the book didn't cover this kind of thing."

It could happen again at any time in any part of this country to any other medical examiner. That is why American Medical News *went back to visit Dr. Mills and retrace his steps of 10 years ago in Edgartown and Chappaquiddick.*

He is 73 now, and has lived for 44 years in Edgartown.

After being graduated in 1934 from the Yale U. School of Medicine, he "was of no mind to go back to Rhode Island where I had grown up, so I decided to become a general practitioner in Edgartown." He bought in 1935 a combination home-medical office on North Summer Street (there is no need for street numbers in Edgartown, population 1,500), and has been there ever since.

He went to war in 1942 and returned four years later to marry his wife of 33 years, Esther. He still practices medicine four days a week, and sums up his life: "I am happily married to a wonderful woman, the father of two wonderful children, and have lived a quiet and professionally satisfying life on Martha's Vineyard."

His home has a lived-in look. Letitia, the family Labrador dog, greets you at the door. Inside, three cats, all former strays, assault you. Dr. Mills recalls that his mother "wanted me to become a musician, but music never held my interest like medicine." He plays the pipe-organ at church and the grand piano at home. Decorative flugel horns hang from the walls. Mrs. Mills is quick to point out her husband's real pride and joy, though: elaborate rugs on the floor and walls woven by Dr. Mills, often in the early-morning hours as he puffs on his ever-present pipe.

One rug-hanging shows the island of Chappaquiddick. Marked in red thread is the bridge over Poucha Pond, where Sen. Kennedy's car took its fatal plunge. In the next room, his administrative office, Dr. Mills points out his favorite piece of art:

The original drawing of a newspaper cartoon showing former Dukes County District Attorney Edmund Dinis astride a horse and carrying an empty coffin labeled "no autopsy." The captain reads, "Bounty hunter."

Looking back a decade, Dr. Mills says, "Of course there should have been an autopsy, if only to have avoided the hue and cry that arose within a few hours of the tragedy. Had this occurred almost anywhere else, it would have been handled quite differently. There was—and still is—no higher echelon to whom I could appeal for advice, assistance, or even criticism. Other than the district attorney's office, which is 20 miles away.

"District attorney Dinis and his office abandoned me completely from the start. The case was all mine. Nobody else wanted to get involved."

Dr. Mills makes it clear that "never at any time did I oppose the performance of an autopsy on this girl's body." It was just that the physician knew only a little more about an autopsy than he did about Sen. Kennedy, whom he has never seen.

The physician had never performed an autopsy, except "oh, maybe, once or twice when I was in medical school. I am not a pathologist, let alone a forensic pathologist. I cannot do a meaningful autopsy. Neither can anyone else on this island. There are no pathologists on Martha's Vineyard. Boston pathologists, he adds, are "highly unenthusiastic about coming down here for autopsies."

In 1969, Dr. Mills recalls, there were openings for six medical examiners on Martha's Vineyard and there were only five physicians on the entire island. To Dr. Mills, the position as associate medical examiner was strictly part-time.

He was first appointed Dukes County associate medical examiner in 1954, and in the 15 years before the Chappaquiddick incident had ordered "maybe one autopsy every other year. My entire medicolegal caseload was only 8 to 10 cases a year. Almost all of these were handled without an autopsy. An autopsy has never been ordered for a drowning death, either by myself or the other medical examiner."

Dr. Mills says, "I am no medicolegal expert, but my conscience is completely clear. I did the best I could under the circumstances, considering what I knew at any given time."

The physician says he was convinced the "case was clearly an accidental drowning," but that "after examining the body I became aware that the Kennedy family might be involved in this. Although I saw no medical reason for an autopsy, I recognized the importance of the Kennedy name and was keenly aware that this case must be reported to the district attorney's office at once, emphasizing the fact that this dead girl might be a Kennedy employe.

"I instructed the undertaker to remove the body and hold it unembalmed until I had contacted the district attorney. I returned to my office in Edgartown and immediately notified the state police to contact the DA's office, to give him full particulars of the case including the possible Kennedy connection, and to request a ruling."

The DA's office, Dr. Mills was later to learn, had hours before been well aware of the death and the connection, including the fact that Sen. Edward Kennedy was both owner and driver of the black sedan dredged up from the tidal pond. But the third-hand word filtered back to the physician was that, "If I were satisfied that the girl had drowned, that was it, there was no need for an autopsy."

The idea for an autopsy actually died in that great void of incomplete and unclear telephone calls between Dr. Mills and the DA's office. Dr. Mills said he was desperate at the time and convinced that, "The DA wanted nothing to do with this case. Dinis never came near Chappaquiddick. I took this as their decision that no autopsy was needed."

The DA's office would later change its mind and Dr. Mills would later come in for some dramatic criticism, but that is another part of the story.

The death of Mary Jo Kopechne put the country doctor briefly into the national spotlight, and the experience was not altogether disagreeable. "I wouldn't trade it for a million dollars," Dr. Mills says, "but I wouldn't give you a nickel to go through it again."

The bridge is a short ride from Dr. Mills' house. The Chappaquiddick ferry holds but three cars at a time and is, he notes, "one of the most expensive rides in the world—$1.25 one-way for less than three minutes." The ferry from Edgartown to Chappaquiddick is called the "On Time."

There are no stores, no gas stations, no commerce of any kind on the island. There is but one paved road—two-lane Chappaquiddick Road or Main Road—that runs from the ferry landing for five miles into the interior of the fan-shaped island. There are several dirt roads, branching off from the main road. Dr. Mills takes Chappy Road to the small cottage where the cookout was held the night of July 18, 1969, then turns the car around and drives about one-half mile to the intersection where Sen. Kennedy says he made his wrong turn.

It is a peculiar intersection, the physician notes. Approaching it, a traffic sign indicates the sharp turn to the left to follow the main road to the ferry back to Edgartown. Straight ahead and spinning off from the paved road is a private dirt road marked "no trespassing," and called Cemetery Rd. If one takes a hard right off the curve of the paved road, he is on Dyke Road leading to Dyke Bridge and the ocean bridges beyond.

Approaching the intersection, the physician notes, "You cannot even see Dyke Road unless you are looking for it, especially at night. The curve of the paved road is deeply banked and the entrance to Dyke Road is obscured."

Asked how the senator might have made the mistake, Dr. Mills says, "Well, I'm a pretty gullible guy. I think he might have thought it was the way to the ferry. Well, but then, you got me. Dyke Road does ride like a washboard and the paved road is smooth. You'd have to know you were on a different road."

(The ruling by Justice James A. Boyle after the inquest into the death of Mary Jo Kopechne noted that earlier on July 18, "Kennedy had been driven over Chappaquiddick Road three times and over Dyke Road and Dyke Bridge twice." Kopechne had been driven over Chappaquiddick Road five times and over Dyke Road and Dyke Bridge twice." The judge concluded, "I infer a reasonable and probable explanation of the totality of the facts is that Kennedy and Kopechne did not intend to return to Edgartown at that time; that Kennedy did not intend to drive to the ferry slip and his turn onto Dyke Road was intentional . . . I therefore find that Edward M. Kennedy operated his motor vehicle negligently on a way or in a place in which the public have a right of access and that such operation appears to have contributed to the death of Mary Jo Kopechne.")

Dr. Mills drives at 20 mph down Dyke Road—the same speed Sen. Kennedy testified he was driving. The road is hard-packed sand and the physician's small car vibrates with the bumps. It is 7/10 of a mile to the bridge.

Toward the water, the trees and bushes that have been crowding the road disappear and there are two cottages. The lights in one—the Malm cottage—"were on at the time of the accident," the physician says. After passing the Malm house, the road comes into an open area. Plainly a change is coming; the sea is ahead. The Dyke Bridge is about 600 feet— two football fields—ahead. The wooden bridge is 27 degrees to the left of the road.

"Dyke Bridge has been here 75 years," Dr. Mills said, "and there had never been an accident. There's no reason to cross it except to fish and go to the beaches. A regular car is immobilized by heavy sand as soon as it crosses the bridge."

Dyke Bridge has long been known to natives, the physician said, as the end of the line. The area today is wind-swept, desolate, and lonely. Not so 10 years ago, Dr. Mills recalls when he got the important call from Island Communications.

"My office opened officially that day at 9 a.m. when my secretary arrived. She said, 'Doctor, don't be surprised if you get a call to go over to Chappy. I heard on the street that there is a car in the water at Dyke Bridge, and they think there may be a body in it.'

This was a dismal thought, because not only did I have a heavy patient-load that day but two hours before my office opened I had examined a multiparous woman in labor. I sent her to the hospital seven miles away, and phoned in routine orders. She was still on my mind. No sooner had my secretary finished talking, than the phone call from Island Communications told me I was needed in my official capacity at Chappy. At the ferry, I ran into the undertaker, and he and his assistant drove me in their hearse to the bridge. We arrived July 19 at 9:30 a.m.

"The scene was slightly spooky. There were more than a dozen people—official, semi-official, and casual observers. There was a wrecker-towing car on the side of the road with the sign, 'You wreck 'em, we fetch 'em!' An unidentified girl had been retrieved from the submerged car by a skin diver hired by the police.

"In a town as small as Edgartown, everybody knows everybody else, and a policeman said, 'It's a girl, Doc. We've got her in the cruiser.' I looked in the back of a police cruiser car and saw a body wrapped in a blue blanket and lying in a carrying litter. I had the police place the body on the ground in front of the cruiser, so I could make my examination.

"The body was that of a very attractive, well-developed girl in her 20s, blonde, with upswept hair and a lovely clean complexion. I estimated her height at 5'3", weight 115–120 pounds. She was fully dressed in a white shirtwaist, bra, dark slacks, sandals, and panties. Her clothes were all in order, fully buttoned and in place."

To Dr. Mills, the girls' entire appearance "reflected quality, refinement, and good breeding. She looked like a pretty girl who might wake up at any minute and head for a party. But she was the most drowned person I had ever seen. Anybody could have seen she had drowned."

Dr. Mills said he made his finding of drowning on four counts—"The history of having been removed from the submerged vehicle; the fact of complete rigor mortis, evidence of prolonged submersion following her death; the presentation of the classical picture of drowning, blood-tinged froth about the nose, the mouth and nose filled with water, and upon percussion of the chest finding water welling out of the mouth and nose and succusion sounds in the throat; and lack of evidence of any other cause as manifested by marks or bruises."

Dr. Mills' findings, accomplished in a physical exam requiring only 5–10 minutes and involving only the unbuttoning of the blouse, were to be challenged later in a petition for exhumation and autopsy. An editorial in *Massachusetts Physician* would note, "We have long heard that old maids' husbands are always well-behaved, and on the same principle, the pathology of those who do not make postmortem examinations is often confident and definite."

But on the morning of July 19, 1969, Dr. Mills was just thinking about getting back to his office. He asked if anybody had any leads as to who this girl was. An onlooker said "she might be a secretary in the Kennedy family." At this point, Dr. Mills said, "the case took on new dimensions."

Knowing that autopsies were never done on drowning deaths in Martha's Vineyard and the pathologists in Boston were "highly un-enthusiastic" about coming to the remote Martha's Vineyard to perform an autopsy, Dr. Mills normally never would have considered an autopsy.

But this political connection, he decided, "might indicate the advisability of an autopsy otherwise not required."

The physician told the undertaker to hold the body unembalmed for further instructions and asked the state police to obtain a ruling from the DA—Edmund Dinis—on whether an autopsy should be performed.

Third-hand, the word came back. A state policeman called Dr. Mills to say that another state police officer attached to the district attorney's office had been contacted and determined that " 'If I was satisfied that the girl had drowned, that was it, and he saw no need for an autopsy.' The state policeman said the DA was not available but that the state police officer attached to the DA advised that I obtain a blood sample for alcohol content."

Dr. Mills was greatly relieved. It was now about 11 a.m. and he had a medical practice to get back to. "I told the undertaker to obtain the blood sample, turn it over to the state police, embalm the body, and turn it over to the girl's family, once identification had been completed. I would be through with the case once the death certificate had been signed."

Dr. Mills' mind was on the baby he had to deliver, "otherwise I probably would have gone to the funeral home and made a more leisurely examination of the body. I went to the hospital, made hurried rounds, delivered a baby during the noon hour, and returned home satisfied that I had handled a busy and complicated Saturday morning both completely and effectively."

When Dr. Mills returned to his home-office at 2 p.m., he still had no idea who the girl was. He also thought that she alone had been in the car.

His first call came from the *Chicago Tribune*. A reporter wanted to know how he had treated Sen. Kennedy. The next was from Brockton, Mass. Dr. Mills had patients in his waiting room, but the phone kept ringing and ringing. How had he treated Sen. Kennedy and who was the girl and what had happened?

Seeing that her husband was besieged, Mrs. Mills decided to walk to the Edgartown police station a block away and find out what was going on.

After she left, a representative of the Edgartown funeral home came by with a young man who introduced himself as a "Kennedy representative and said that he was authorized to take charge of the body, which was to be flown to Pennsylvania that afternoon."

Relieved for the second time that day, Dr. Mills signed the certificate, "cause of death—asphyxiation by submersion; manner of death—submerged automobile." For the first time, he learned that the girl's name was Mary Jo Kopechne and, yes, she had worked for the Kennedys.

Meanwhile, Mrs. Mills was finding out at the police station that Sen. Kennedy had been the driver of the car. Reporters, too, had learned this, and when Mrs. Mills returned home, "I had to fight my way through the crowd."

The reporters had beaten Mrs. Mills to her own door, but, unbeknownst to them at the time, their real prey was gone. The Kennedy representative had already left for the funeral home with a signed death certificate.

When Dr. Mills was told by his wife that Sen. Kennedy had been the driver, he felt "increasingly thankful that I had reported the case as fully as possible to the district attorney's office. It was only much later that I learned the DA had all this information hours before I did."

In 63 years, Dr. Mills had never been subjected to anything like the assault of journalists unleashed upon him.

"I fought off the television people who set up camp in my front yard. On my own radio, I heard my voice in phone conversations taped without my knowledge. My office, my yard, even my kitchen swarmed with reporters. They mingled with patients in my waiting room. They tied up my telephones.

I was 63 years old then, and that's not the prime of life, not by a long shot. By the end of the day, I was at my wit's end. There was nothing left upstairs. I just couldn't think.

The assault continued for the next three days. Dr. Mills said, "I was horrified at the intimate questions I had to parry, but parry them I did. My own ethical sensibilities made me extremely loathe to release medical information on Mary Jo Kopechne, especially the details of my examination.

"I was getting myself increasingly in trouble with the press, the public, and the medical profession. All suspected me of complicity; some said I was bought off. I did the best I could for the press, but followed my ethical training.

"Desperately, I called the Massachusetts Medical Society ethics chairman and asked for help. He rather gruffly told me to read the society's bylaws, which proved to be of no help at all—just a bunch of pages of ethical generalities."

Dr. Mills said he did not think "I would have to face this barrage alone. I anticipated support from the DA's office. How wrong I was. Dead silence for days. Their only comment was a brief press release saying that the DA's office was not involved—it was a motor vehicle case covered by the local police department.

"Incredibly, I was not able to speak directly to DA Edmund Dinis until Tuesday afternoon, a full three days after the accident. He was friendly but a bit shaken as we talked Tuesday, July 22, on the phone—Dinis never did come near Chappaquiddick. We agreed that on purely medicolegal grounds there had been no indication for an autopsy. We agreed that my examination and the blood sample suggested by state policeman Lt. George Killen, the Da's liason man, were enough. The blood test found a blood alcohol level of 0.09—a fair amount of drinking for someone her size, but not drunkenness; 5% carbon dioxide—within normal limits; no barbiturates; and no organic basis.

"At this time, I thought that Dinis and I had common assailants and were being equally harassed. I found out differently a few days later when I gave an interview to CBS-TV and said that the decision not to perform an autopsy had been jointly shared by the medical examiner and the DA. While I was watching myself on TV, I got a second call from Dinis.

"He started to scream at me over the phone, about what a liar I was and how incompetent and worse. When he launched into a personal attack, my wife picked up the extension phone and screamed right back to him.

"The next thing I knew, the DA had picked up the growing clamor for exhumation and autopsy. Ironically, he could have ordered an autopsy anytime within 24 hours of the discovery of the body. I had been told that the body was to be flown to Pennsylvania Saturday afternoon, the 19th, but it never left Massachusetts until noon on the 20th. Dinis never said a word, and then weeks later he turned around and decided to petition for an autopsy."

For the next six months, Dr. Mills would be caught up in legal proceedings brought by DA Dinis, who, as one local newspaper columnist reported in a 1970 "political obituary" on the erstwhile candidate, "held his hand a fraction too long in investigating the tragic death of Mary Jo Kopechne."

First, Dinis petitioned in Luzerne County, Pa., for exhumation and autopsy of the body. The parents, Donald and Gwen Kopechne, opposed the autopsy, contending: "They (Massachusetts officials) had their chance at an autopsy and didn't do it. An autopsy now would be like a second funeral."

The petition transcript runs 278 pages, but Judge Bernard C. Brominski ruled the petitioners failed to make a case to justify a "violation of the sepulchre." The body of Mary Jo Kopechne would remain untouched in an unmarked grave on a mountain slope in Larksville, Pa. Mrs. Kopechne later told *McCalls Magazine,* "Right after I was told about Mary Jo's death, I wanted an autopsy because I thought this was done as a matter of routine, and because the phone calls and letters my husband and I were getting were full of disturbing stories."

Then, Dinis obtained approval for an inquest in the court of Edgartown Judge James A. Boyle. The inquest transcript runs 736 pages. Judge Boyle concluded that Sen. Kennedy "intended to turn on Dyke road, probably knew of the hazard that lay ahead of him on Dyke Road, but for some reason not apparent from the testimony, failed to exercise due care as he approached the bridge. . . . If Kennedy knew of this hazard, his operation of the vehicle constituted criminal conduct."

Despite the strong words, the judge never filed charges, saying Kennedy "has already suffered more than anything that can be done in this courtroom." The only charge against the senator was the one to which he pleaded guilty—leaving the scene of an accident.

One year after Dinis' efforts on the Chappaquiddick case, he was defeated for reelection as district attorney.

Dr. Mills says he harbors no grudge toward Dinis, though he does treasure his anti-Dinis cartoon. Of the Kopechnes, Dr. Mills recalls the sorrowful words of the mother, Gwen Kopechne, who said during the petition for an autopsy:

"I don't want my little girl's body dug up. She'd never seen a doctor in her life except for a little sinus drip a month ago."

Dr. Mills says he has never revealed before what Mrs. Kopechne told him during the petition hearing: "As a medical examiner," she said, "you may be interested in this. My daughter had just completed a menstrual period three days before her death."

Dr. Mills says he expects the phone calls from reporters to start up again, now that Sen. Kennedy is running for president. But there will be no more interviews, he says. He has his rug-hooking, his music, his family, and his medical practice to keep him going.

He remains convinced that the death was an accidental drowning, that according to the letter of the Massachusetts law an autopsy was not necessary, and that under similar conditions he would do everything exactly the same.

"But let's face it," he said. "If I had known then what I do know, I would have called a pathologist in Boston and said, 'Get me out from under this.'" At the time, I was glad to sign the death certificate and be done with things. I didn't want to tangle with the Kennedys.

"Where was the case botched? It was the holes in our medical examiner system, holes that are still there. We need a chief medical examiner for the state, someone to whom the beleaguered medical examiner can turn. We have proposed legislation to create such a post, but it is still pending."

The position of associate medical examiner in Dukes County, Mass., has been open since Dr. Mills resigned in 1975. He is now urging his new associate, a 32-year-old physician, to consider the part-time job.

"It's not much for pay," Dr. Mills says. "I got $25 for the Kopechne case, plus ferry expenses.

"But you never know when you're going to get an interesting case."□

Headliners

Allan Bakke

Throughout his entire "reverse-bias" lawsuit against the medical school that would not admit him, Allan Bakke remained tight-lipped. He simply would *not* talk to the press about the case that shook a nation.

So I did the next best thing. I talked to the chairman of the admissions committee at the U. of California, Davis, that refused to admit him. He says he would do it again, but, at the same time, he wishes Bakke (now Dr. Bakke) well.

CHARLES LOWREY, MD, chairman of the admissions committee at the U. of California-Davis that turned down Allan Bakke, says he would do it again.

"Sure," says Dr. Lowrey, "I'd do it again in a minute. On the other hand, I don't feel very badly that Bakke, now 38, will by court order be starting school here this month (September, 1978)."

In having to decide between solidly qualified candidates like Bakke and minority applicants, Dr. Lowrey says, "the admissions committee was caught between the devil and the deep blue sea.

"I feel a lot of compassion for someone like Bakke, who is obviously qualified to go to medical school. I think of maybe having one of my own children caught in the same situation. But, at the same time, I believe strongly in programs to recruit minority physicians. How are we ever going to make amends to our minorities for the long and bitter bias against them unless we start somewhere?"

Dr. Lowrey feels Bakke happened to be the wrong man at the wrong time applying to the wrong place—and, most importantly, at the wrong age. He cites two factors that he says worked against Bakke's admission:

"First, he was too old. Although we don't have an age limit, we do, because of the scarcity of physicians, like to get qualified applicants as young as possible to assure maximum duration of practice. We don't use age as a cutoff, but tend to look a lot harder at anyone past age 28 or 30.

"Second, as a graduate engineer, Bakke already had a profession. Plus a master's degree. Why not give a chance to the qualified black or chicano who has never before had an opportunity to be a professional?"

Dr. Lowrey says, "We thought of our minority recruitment program in terms of a 'goal' rather than a 'quota,' but we did reserve 16 places each year for applicants from minority groups, basically blacks and chicanos. In this part of California, at least, we don't think of orientals as a minority."

It was this "slotting" of admissions spaces for minority applicants, Dr. Lowrey says, that enabled Bakke to sue successfully. It is likely, the physician adds, that without this "easy target," Bakke would neither have been admitted to medical school on his merits nor been able to win a reverse-bias complaint.

"I think he decided to sue us," Dr. Lowrey says, "because he thought that's where he had the best chance of success. You know Bakke applied to 13 medical schools, including eight of the nine in California (all but Loma Linda U., which is denominational), and was not admitted to any. In fact, he never made the 'alternate list' at any, including Davis. Stanford, I know, anticipated a suit from him.

"When he applied for the 1973 school year, Bakke's ranking by committee interviewers was 468 of a possible 500. No one with a score of 468 or lower was either admitted or put on the alternate list, under our regular admissions program (applicants to the special admissions program for minorities were handled separately and had dramatically lower scores). To fill our class of 84 regular admittees, we sent out about 150 letters of acceptance. And about 20 applicants were put on the alternate list. All of these people had scores higher than Bakke's."

After his first rejection, "Bakke struck up a considerable correspondence with Peter Storandt, who had been appointed by the dean to work with the admissions committee," Dr. Lowrey said. "Storandt was obviously sympathetic to Bakke's case and offered advice on possible legal strategy." (A fact confirmed in the Supreme Court opinion; Storandt, an administrator previously from Wayne State U., is now with Oberlin College in Ohio.)

"Bakke then wrote me a letter saying that he strongly disagreed with our special admissions program. He had previously written to the dean of admissions back in 1970—when he was 30—asking how an applicant of 30 might be received. He was told then that there is no age cutoff but that we do look harder at applicants 30 and older.

"When Bakke then applied for the 1974 school year, I was one of his six admissions committee interviewers. I rate him at 86, the lowest of his evaluations (Bakke was rated at 549 of a possible 600 in his '74 application)."

How would Dr. Lowrey have rated a 25-year-old Bakke? "I might have given him a 92 or a 93 and the other interviewers correspondingly higher. I think the second time around he came much closer to being admitted and had he been younger this might have tipped the scales in his favor.

"Frankly, though, when I interview an applicant for medical school, I'm looking for that spark of brilliance, of inventiveness, of original thought that indicates tremendous potential. Bakke did not strike me that way.

"However, I will be the first to admit that a 45-minute interview is not a foolproof method to assess a person's potential.

"And we spent about a third of the time discussing our special program. Bakke felt strongly that admission to medical school should not be discriminating in any way. He was not sympathetic in any way to our efforts to train minority physicians. I found his attitude limited. He had no alternate plan to attract more minority MDs."

For the 1974 school year, Dr. Lowrey notes, Bakke again was neither admitted to Davis nor put on the alternate list. "This was on the basis of his scores compared to the other applicants to the regular program" he says. "Bakke was also neither admitted nor put on the alternate list at the other schools to which he applied."

Bakke, of course, sued for admission and the rest is legal history. "I expected his suit," Dr. Lowrey says. "He was a Marine, wasn't he?"

Although it is generally conceded that Bakke was better qualified than applicants admitted under the special program, the disparity is striking, Dr. Lowrey says.

For 1973, Bakke's qualifications measured against the special admittees were as follows: scientific grade point average (SGPA), 3.44 (2.62 for the special admittees); overall grade point average (OGPA) 3.51 (2.88 special admittees); Medical College Admissions Test percentiles on verbal, 96 (46 special admittees); quantitative, 94 (24 special admittees); science, 97 (35 special admittees); and general information, 72 (33 special admittees). For 1974, the comparisons of Bakke-against-special admittees were SGPA (3.44 to 2.42), OGPA (3.51 to 2.62), MCAT verbal (96 to 34), quantitative (94 to 30), science (97 to 37), and general information (72 to 18).

During the same years, Bakke's scores were also higher in every category than the average for regular admittees. However, his total benchmark scores of 468 and 549 (based on interviewers' evaluations that took into account grades, MCAT scores, letters of recommendation, extracurricular activities, and other biographical data, did not, according to Dr. Lowrey, give him the numbers needed for admission to the regular program.

Given his age handicap, Dr. Lowrey says, Bakke was lucky to have had the strict Davis slotting system to shoot at legally. "As far as I'm concerned," Dr. Lowrey says, "programs such as the one at Harvard, which the Supreme Court cited, are just like ours. It's just a matter of semantics. But the setting-aside of specific spaces enabled Bakke to win."

The Davis faculty "was divided from the start (1971—Davis was founded in 1968) on the special program," Dr. Lowrey says, "although it had strong majorities both times it came up for a faculty vote. But not everyone wanted the program to work, and I'm sure that many are happy that the Supreme Court has thrown it out."

Dr. Lowrey has two hopes for the future: "I hope we can maintain our momentum on minority recruitment, and I hope that Allan Bakke is accepted like any other student this fall."

It appears likely. Davis, a sleepy town of 30,000 outside Sacramento, may be at the center of a medical education controversy, but on campus life proceeds as usual. The medical school only months ago relocated from its makeshift, warehouse-like building to a new science arts building. The school operates year-round and this summer one student is wrapping up her first year with flying colors. Rita Clancy, who successfully sued for admission last fall in a case parallel to Bakke's, is taking her final exams. She, like Bakke, refuses interviews, but a fellow student observes, "Oh, you mean the famous Rita Clancy. She must be doing OK. She's starting her second year this fall."

School officials say they are prepared for the expected crush of publicity Sept. 25 when Bakke arrives for his first day of class. "The press will be allowed to photograph Bakke (and Clancy) only during the 100 yards or so it takes to walk from the car to the lecture hall," says one official. "Classroom time is for the students. They have a right to pursue their educations without interruptions."

Dr. Lowrey, meanwhile, has found a solution to the admissions conundrum. "I chaired the admissions committee from 1971–76," he says, "and enough is enough. I took a sabbatical last year to write a book (on pediatrics) and now I'm out of administrative work altogether. My time is spent in helping patients and teaching students (at the Sacramento Medical Center with which the school is affiliated). I find this much more satisfying."

Nattily dressed and striding briskly, he arrives with a broad smile at his office in a trailer that temporarily houses the medical center's pediatric clinic. Under his arm he carries the morning edition of the *San Francisco*

Chronicle. "Bakke will start medical studies Sept. 25" reads the headline. Says the man who would have had it otherwise:
    "Good for him!"□

Surrogate Mother

The "surrogate mother," a new term in the language and a new alternative for infertile couples, was brought into the world by an unlikely candidate—attorney Noel Keane, an Irish-Catholic with two sons born into the world the usual way.

The birth of surrogate mothers was midwived by the news media, particularly *People Magazine* and the "Phil Donahue Show," and it subsequently provoked a storm of ethical, legal, and medical questions.

In the beginning, however, as this story shows, the main characters were simply acting the old-fashioned way—from the heart.

"Childless husband with infertile wife wants female donor for test-tube baby. Caucasian background, indicate fee and age. All answers confidential. Make response to . . ."

ON FEB. 4, 1977, THE ABOVE AD ran in the *Eastern Echo,* student newspaper at the U. of Michigan's Ann Arbor campus. It subsequently was published in college newspapers in Detroit and Ypsilanti, Mich. Detroit's two metropolitan dailies turned it down. The man who placed the ad, Dearborn, Mich., attorney Noel Keane, recalls that, "I had never handled an adoption before and knew absolutely nothing about artificial insemination.

"But Al and Betty desperately wanted a baby and had given up on ever being able to adopt one. They had come up with this idea of finding a 'surrogate mother' who would agree to be artificially impregnated with Al's sperm and then give the baby to them for adoption. But they had no idea how to go about it.

"Betty is a friend of my brother-in-law's sister, and the sister told her, 'Why don't you look up Noel Keane? He's a friend of ours and he's an attorney.' So Al and Betty came to me looking for help. It sounded pretty weird, but I discovered that a California man had arranged in 1975 for a surrogate to be impregnated with his sperm. He then adopted the child. He found the woman by placing an ad. So we placed an ad. I still have the payment voucher somewhere in my files."

One year later, Keane is a national figure, at the center of a growing controversy over "surrogate motherhood." But it required an assist from

Sue, 24. Last fall, Sue held a baby shower for her best friend, Debbie, 25. On hand were Debbie's husband George, 28, and assorted friends and relatives.

The baby was due in January. Debbie took all the gifts but Sue got all the attention. Sue, you see, was pregnant. She had been artificially inseminated that past April by Debbie, who with the aid of instructions from the *Reader's Digest Family Health Guide* injected George's sperm into Sue (the guide intended to tell its readers what to expect during artificial insemination, not how to do it). "I hit the bullseye on my first attempt," Debbie proudly recalls.

Sue and Debbie had become friends at the mortgage and realty company where both worked. A prime topic of conversation was Debbie's frustration at being able neither to get pregnant nor to make much headway in adopting a newborn. Then, in January, 1977, Debbie's dream of carrying her own child ended forever. After six years of recurrent pelvic infections, she required a hysterectomy.

"I took Debbie to the hospital for the hysterectomy," Sue recalls, "and I could see how broken up she was. I don't know exactly why the thought hit me but one day at work it just struck me: 'I can give her the baby she wants.'

"I told Debbie and George and they said, 'No, no, there are too many complications.' But after a few weeks, we decided to go ahead with the idea."

Shortly after her artificial insemination, Sue moved in with Debbie and George. In June, 1977, her pregnancy was confirmed. It was an unusual *menage a trois* (household of three, that is; Sue and George say they are not now and never have been lovers), and the strain of keeping their secret had begun to tell.

It seemed a Godsend that August when Noel Keane went on a Detroit radio show with Al and Betty to plead for a surrogate mother.

"Right after we placed the ad," Keane says, "I asked Juvenile Court Judge James Lincoln (now retired) for an out-of-court opinion about surrogate mothering. He said that a surrogate mother could not be paid, except for nominal expenses. Suddenly, our supply of surrogates dried up. Al and Betty were distraught and we decided to make an appeal on the radio."

Says Sue, "I couldn't believe it when I heard on the radio that another couple was trying to do what we had already done but were afraid to tell anybody about. Debbie and George and I decided to call Mr. Keane. It was a call-in show but our call never got through that night. We left a message, though, for Mr. Keane: 'Call us. We've already done it.' "

Keane says, "It was the first thing I did the next morning."

Sue and Debbie and George decided to go public with their unique situation. They retained Keane to handle the adoption they planned, and they talked to the media. Their summer appearance on the Phil Donahue syndicated TV show made surrogate motherhood a national issue.

Letters poured in from infertile couples (one of every six couples, some studies indicate, are unable to have children) who were frustrated with adoption procedures, and who saw parenthood-by-proxy as an exciting prospect.

Today, it is even more so. The reason is busily crawling about Keane's carpeted office in the fashionable Park Lane Towers in Dearborn, Mich. Elizabeth Ann, a beautiful blue-eyed blonde, was born to Sue on Jan. 26, 1978, weighing 6 pounds, 10½ ounces.

Shortly after her birth, Elizabeth Ann appeared with Sue and her adoptive parents-to-be, Debbie and George, for a second time on the Donahue show. This time the letters came to Keane in a blizzard.

"They run about 10% supportive of what Sue and Debbie and George have done," says Keane, "and about 90% asking for help in doing the same thing."

Keane's mail indicates two things: there are many couples who are excited about the possibilities of surrogate motherhood, and they have no idea what to do next.

Keane, for his part, has gone to court seeking a legal opinion to allow fees to be paid surrogate mothers, provided the state regulates such transactions.

Although his mail includes a few letters from women volunteering as "donors," it is clear that without a fee, demand will outstrip supply.

"Of course," Keane says, "there's always the black market. That's why the state should come in and regulate things."

Keane says the publicity given his TV appearances helped locate surrogates for Al and Betty, whose baby-to-be was born this April, and for a third couple, John and Joan, whose surrogate gave birth this July. In all three cases, the adopting couple artificially inseminated the donor. Michigan physicians, Keane said, "wouldn't touch the situation because of the malpractice threat."

The Michigan attorney is seeking donors for two other clients, a professional couple from South Carolina and a single man from California.

In the meantime, he weighs some of the dilemmas raised by surrogate motherhood. What is the liability of the contracting couple if the surrogate mother suffers medical complications? Probably none, Keane says, since she volunteered to have the baby. If the surrogate mother decides to keep the child? Keane says the court would probably support her claim, and the father could be responsible for child support.

Already, a backlash is under way. Some letter writers point out that adoption is meant to help homeless children, not to assuage the egos of childless couples. Women do not have an inalienable right to children, others point out. Most who have written to Keane, however, remark on how beautiful Elizabeth Ann is, how special she is, and how wonderful it is that Sue would give such a gift to her friend. And that it might be wonderful if they could have the same done for them.

"I never thought of her as my child," says Sue, an intense, shy, thin woman. "I always thought of her as their child. Debbie and I always knew it was going to be a girl. George wanted a boy, but we told him it was going to be a girl."

Debbie, stout and dominant, fidgets. "George, are you watching her," she asks as Elizabeth Ann crawls toward Keane's window. "Tell the doctors to be more open about this kind of thing," she says. "George's family physician wouldn't help us, but he referred us to another doctor (a Michigan osteopath). Well, this doctor was on vacation. We had done a lot of studying and knew that this was Sue's fertile period. We decided not to wait. We did the insemination ourselves.

"When the doctor got back from vacation, he retired. We went to his partner, who was terribly busy because now he had the whole practice to himself. When we told him our story, he wouldn't believe us. He just didn't believe we could possibly artificially inseminate Sue on the first attempt. We decided to get a new doctor.

"Our new doctor (Keith Curtis, MD, 45, a Dearborn, Mich., ob-gyn specialist) was just fine, but then the hospital sometimes wouldn't let me in to visit the baby. Seems like I had the wrong kind of germs or something. Now, the state department of social services is sitting on the adoption papers, taking a lot longer than what seems necessary."

(Dr. Curtis recalls that he was a little taken aback when the trio first approached him in the late summer of 1977. A former family physician, he had just finished an ob-gyn residency and was only in his second month of specialty practice.

("I decided not to judge, not to try to psych them out," Dr. Curtis said. "I told them my only concern was to deliver a healthy baby, and that's exactly what we accomplished, by caesarean section, last January.

("I told the hospital that this was obviously an unusual case and that the staff should use common sense in trying to keep the group of three happy, since it was apparent that Debbie would become the child's mother. It was an ordinary clinical case, but an extraordinary social situation.")

Debbie is impatient, but positively glows when she picks up Elizabeth Ann. "We'll tell Elizabeth Ann someday that she is adopted," Debbie says. "It will be up to Sue to say that she is the mother," adds George.

Sue recalls her pregnancy "as a neat experience, but I'm not ready for marriage and motherhood. Maybe someday."

Father George says that most of his friends and co-workers have taken things in stride. There is one exception, though: his father.

"Dad can't believe that there's not something going on between me and Sue," he says. "He asked me, 'Son, did you have intercourse with Sue?' I explained to him how we accomplished artificial insemination, that Sue is still a virgin, that her hymen is intact. We're eyeball-to-eyeball and he said, 'Son, I don't believe you.' That makes me feel bad, but there's nothing we can do about it."

Attorney Keane admits to being sometimes puzzled by the closeness of the three. A psychiatrist, Phillip Parker, MD, has talked to Sue, Debbie, and George, but refuses to discuss them. "Generally, though," Dr. Parker says, "situations like this have a lot of potential problems. The biological mother is apt to feel a sense of loss and the emotions of the adoptive couple toward the donor can range from affection and gratitude to anger and resentment."

Debbie and Sue foresee no problems.

"When we went on the Donahue Show," says Sue, "that was the first time Debbie and I had ever been on an airplane. Since then, we've been to New York and Los Angeles. Many of the people we know are more curious about where we've been, whether or not we've met any celebrities, than what we've done."

Would Debbie have done the same for Sue? "Probably not," says Debbie, "because she's not a relative." George interjects. "But we'd help her find a surrogate." Attorney Keane, 39, was raised by Irish Catholic parents and is the father of two young sons. He says that if he and his wife had not been able to have a family, "I would never have thought of a surrogate on my own, but now that I know about it, I'd do it in a minute." Keane's wife Kathy has a reservation, though: "I'm not so sure how I'd feel, knowing that another woman was carrying his baby," she says.

Sue, Debbie, and George are all Catholic. "The Church tells us that what we did is a sin," George says. "But it's our sin and it won't be held against the baby. We can live with that." Elizabeth Ann was baptized in their church, George said, and no questions about her parentage were asked.

Elizabeth Ann, six months old, is getting restless. The interview is at an end.

"You know, if I had it to do over again," says Sue, "I'm not so sure I would go public. I went on TV because we thought it might help other people and because it might help a little financially. I can live on $5 a day, but the extra money helps."

Sue, Debbie, and George now have a Detroit agent and there is talk of a book, of a TV show, of a movie. Keane will be in New York next week talking to a book agent. Sue will be in Philadelphia to appear on the Mike Douglas Show. The Detroit agent is talking about a trend, a movement, that 15–20 years from now there will be professional child-bearers and professional child-raisers.

"Everybody thought I wouldn't be able to give the baby up," says Sue. "My parents were both alcoholics and my mother died young. Last November, my father was dying of cancer. I didn't want to tell him, but I figured I had to. He said that I'd want to keep the baby. Both of my younger brothers thought the same thing. But Debbie was the first real friend I ever had and I wanted to give her a gift she couldn't have.

"You know, I'll probably lose my job. I'm an excellent worker, but they're giving me trouble at the bank about missing work for these TV shows. I start work at midnight and work through the night processing checks.

"Processing checks, now that doesn't really affect anyone. By having a child, I've affected a lot of lives."□

Grenada

I was lucky. I got to the island of Grenada in 1980, before the big Cuban buildup and before the invasion of U.S. Marines.

My host was Charles Modica, the Jay Gatsby of the Caribbean and the man who put together (for profit) the pieces of the St. Georges U. Medical School. Later, in the fall of 1983, when the Marines landed to rescue the American medical students who were studying on the "nutmeg island" for the MD degree that had been denied them stateside, Modica would provide me eyewitness accounts of the invasion and the self-preservation plans of the plucky medical school.

A personal note: In 1980, I had been warned about LIAT Airlines, the fleet providing Leeward Islands Air Transport. Cynics referred to it as "Luggage left in another terminal." Sure enough, flying from New York JFK to Barbados, I was forced to choose between checking my garment bags with clothes and my suitcase with camera and tape recorder. I put the tools of the trade under my seat and checked the clothes. The carrier from JFK to Barbados was British West Indies and the airline assured me that LIAT would safely deliver the bag from Barbados to Grenada.

Wrong. Even as I cleared customs in Grenada with nothing more than an AMA business card (I had forgotten my passport and the Cuban-trained, machine-gun-armed Grenadian guards at the airport surely would not have allowed me into the country had Modica not been there to assure them that I was OK), I knew that I was in trouble. As I stared for hours at the crude airport slogans proclaiming the Grenadian "Revo" (for revolution), the bitter truth sank in:

My clothes had been lost.

Subsequently, for night after night at the elegant Secret Harbour Hotel, I came down to a formal dinner dressed in the only clothes I had—madras walking shorts and a Hawaiian T-shirt (the suit I wore on the plane was reserved for formal news interviews during the day). The St. Georges U. faculty members vaguely introduced me as, "The gentleman from the AMA."

Finally, the day before I was scheduled to leave the island, chancellor Modica used his not-inconsiderable influence to persuade LIAT to open its downtown lost luggage center. This came on the third consecutive day of an important island holiday and was accomplished only after bitter protests. Immediately, I spotted my tan garment bag, with its navy blazer, tan slacks, club tie, and summer seersucker suit. That evening, my last at one of the world's most unusual medical schools, I proudly dressed in coat and tie and for dinner made a grand entrance.

IT'S NOT OFTEN THAT a medical school provokes a military invasion and an international incident, but then, St. George's U. School of Medicine on the tiny Caribbean island of Grenada always has been unusual.

The medical school's colorful seven-year history recorded its most bizarre chapter late in October when its students were forced to quit studying for their mid-term exams by the sight of U.S. Marines parachuting onto campus and the sound of mortar fire competing for control of a nearby military airport.

This is the story of how the school came about and how it happened to become the scene of the 11th U.S. Marine invasion in history.

> "The name of the game is survival. That's what I have to think about. If we're forced to leave Grenada by the government, we move to St. Vincent. That's our insurance policy. They would welcome us with open arms."
> —Charles R. Modica, Chancellor,
> St. George's U. School of Medicine

Modica, who became the chancellor of his own medical school at age 29, made these remarks to me in 1980. To be sure, the St. George's U. School of Medicine is not really a university (the medical college is the only school) and Modica is not a physician ("I'm a doctor of jurisprudence"), but until late last month, the former failed foreign medical school student had maintained a golden touch in running what many observers consider the best foreign school open to Americans, the English-speaking St. George's.

It all could have ended in the early dawn of Oct. 25, 1983, when

1,900 U.S. Marines, 300 Army Rangers, and a multinational Caribbean strike force from Antigua, Barbados, Dominica, Jamaica, St. Lucia, and St. Vincent stormed the tiny island of Granada by amphibious assault ship, helicopter, and parachutes for the unlikeliest of purposes:

To rescue 585 American medical students.

(At press time, all students and faculty had been evacuated safely. Six American G.I.s, however, and 30 Cuban troops had been killed in the fighting.)

(The invasion of Grenada followed by two days the bombing in Lebanon of the U.S. Marine and French troops headquarters buildings in Beirut. Many observers speculated that one of President Reagan's motives in invading Grenada was to respond to the Lebanon bombing and to avert another possible U.S. hostage crisis. Defense Secretary Caspar Weinberger confirmed that the strike force had captured 600 armed Cuban construction workers and had assured safe passage out of the island for 30 Soviet military advisers.)

(Meanwhile, Sally Shelton, the former U.S. ambassador to Grenada, Barbados, and eight other Caribbean islands, told *AMN* that Peter Bourne, MD, son of St. George's vice chancellor, Geoffrey Bourne, PhD, had told her that on at least two occasions the Reagan Administration had approached medical school officials in an attempt to have them issue a statement that they feared for the students' safety. The St. George's officials had declined to make such a statement, the younger Dr. Bourne said, adding that in the school's opinion, the real risk to the students would be a military invasion.)

For Modica, the American students, and their parents—one-quarter of whom are physicians—the military invasion was the worst of all possible scenarios and ended a tense week of negotiations between the medical school, the Marxist-leaning Grenadian troops who on Oct. 19 had overthrown the government of Maurice Bishop, himself an avowed supporter of Cuba and the Soviet Union, and the governments of the United States and the Caribbean nations.

Modica had made clear throughout the week that no military intervention was necessary to ensure the safety of the students and faculty in Grenada. "The last thing we want is a military invasion," he said.

Modica, the students, who were halfway through their first semester, and their parents had hoped for a preservation of law and order by the new revolutionary government or, barring that, at least an orderly relocation of the medical school to a new Caribbean island, but revelations that Bishop and members of his cabinet had been executed in cold blood—apparently at the orders of foreign communist advisers—prompted President Reagan to strike against what he termed a "brutal group of leftist thugs."

The U.S. intervention against Grenada, which is one of the tiniest independent nations in the world, marked only the 11th time U.S. Marines have invaded a country to preserve law and order or rescue Americans. It also may have marked the end in Grenada of what up until now has been an improbable success story.

Modica has a lot in common with the 585 students, all of whom were rejected by U.S. medical schools. The chancellor, now 35, was himself rejected by American medical schools and he was repulsed by the sight of blood during the one year he spent at a foreign school (in Oviedo, Spain). But the son of a wealthy New York subdivision builder decided to become an expert on the workings of foreign medical schools that cater to Americans. First, he wrote a book (now in its seventh edition) on how rejected Americans best can pursue the MD overseas. Then, he skillfully put together the pieces of St. George's, which in 1981 awarded its first degrees and which has established itself as one of the best of a highly controversial breed of off-shore schools.

On the surface, the idea is outrageous. Grenada, one of the leeward islands in the eastern Caribbean, measures only 10 miles across and 20 miles long, about half of the physical size of Chicago. Its population is 110,000 and before Modica came to town, the principal export was not medical students but nutmeg. There are few native professionals from which to recruit a medical school faculty, and there are virtually no clinical facilities.

Undaunted, Modica created an unlikely scenario. First, he recruited a stream of "visiting professors" from American medical schools as faculty. He then arranged for "clinical externships" in American hospitals to solve the clinical training problem. He stripped a medical education operation down to the bare minimum—teaching. St. George's provides neither patient care nor research.

Part crusader, part entrepreneur, and all savvy, Modica has become the Pied Piper for what otherwise would be an impossible dream: earning a medical degree for highly intelligent, highly motivated, and, often, highly affluent young men and women who have been rejected by American schools.

In a prophetic development, Modica chartered the school as a profit-making operation in 1976. ("It's proprietary because under international law a proprietary corporation, if nationalized, must receive fair value in return. If a government takes over a non-profit corporation, say the Red Cross, it doesn't have to pay for it if it continues the chartered purpose. Also, a proprietary institution can be insured.")

In January, 1977, he opened the doors to the first wave of Americans.

Modica's backers (he refuses to name them) had put up $10 million, and he spent $5.5 million to open the Grenada school. The 11 backers include his father and eight physicians. The charter class included sons of nine of the 11. The vast majority of students are from New York and New Jersey.

Modica's Game Plan for the school was to "scramble and stay one step ahead of things. We knew it would be tough, but we thought we could pull it off."

He enrolled 200 students that first semester, hoping that half would stick it out. He refused to let the students see the school before enrolling, "because I was afraid they might back out. However, once there, I told them that if anyone wanted to leave after 10 days, his tuition would be refunded." There were 15 who left the small island immediately, but two years later, when clinical rotations started, 98 were still around. Modica had won his gamble. Of those 98 pioneers, an astounding one-third achieved transfer to an American medical school and the rest, many of whom had scored high on the medical school qualifying exam, were successfully placed in the "externships" in American hospitals.

Modica's founding principle had been simple: "I knew from the start it had to be an English-speaking school." Despite his Berlitz course in Spanish, the chancellor-to-be had encountered trouble with the language in Oviedo and he wanted to spare his students the aggravation. "What was the use of setting up another school where Americans would have to fight with a foreign language?

"Oh, we looked around. We had decided on the Caribbean. Puerto Rico we rejected because of the accreditation problems (as an American territory, Puerto Rico falls under the aegis of the Liaison Committee on Medical Education). In Jamaica, the U. of West Indies found a hundred reasons why the country didn't need another medical school.

"It all came down to Grenada."

At 29, Modica was probably the youngest chancellor of a medical school anywhere in the world, and certainly, he was one of the few non-MDs. Despite his fondness for the title, he hired as the man in command on Grenada Dr. Bourne, 73, the former director of the Yerkes Regional Primate Research Center in Atlanta, former chairman of anatomy at Atlanta's Emory U. Medical School, and former chairman of anatomy at the U. of London. The island school was to have a heavy-weight administrator.

Modica's one remaining problem was having his faculty and students cope with the vagaries of LIAT Airlines. The chancellor solved this problem by buying (for $250,000) a six-seater airplane that ferries visiting professors, students, and others to and from Grenada, Barbados, the nearest large island, and St. Vincent, the neighboring island where St. Geroge's students are "introduced" to clinical rotations. Modica, a licensed pilot, will in a pinch climb into the cockpit himself.

Until last month, it all worked so well that St. George's (named after the island's capital city) Medical School accounted for one-fourth of the Grenadian gross national product and employed 150 natives.

The "Isle of Spice," as it is known, has but one main road, and to reach the medical school on the island's southwest coast, one must drive from the small airport for an hour on a tortuously winding road through the hilly topography of rain forest. The road is cluttered with strolling Grenadians, dogs, cats, and a few cows. Banana trees and palm trees and other rain forest vegetation crowd the narrow roadway.

When Maurice Bishop proclaimed his "Glorious People's Revolution" in 1979 (it was known to the locals simply as "the Revo"), the airport bristled with security and clumsily scrawled signs celebrating the socialist takeover. On Oct. 25, 1983, the airport became the scene of mortar fire between U.S. Marines and defending Grenadian and Cuban troops. The other major battleground was the medical school's True Blue campus, which abuts a giant airstrip where Grenadians and their Cuban advisers are building what they call a bigger airport to promote tourism and what the U.S. calls a bigger airport to promote revolution.

The capital city of St. George's is located on one of the Caribbean's best harbors and the medical school is only miles away in two locations— the beachfront Grand Anse (great cove) campus and the inland True Blue campus (site of an Expo '69, then abandoned).

The favored Grand Anse location is a converted hotel, with a small office for the vice chancellor (Dr. Bourne) and his secretarial staff, a 600-seat dome amphitheater (which sometimes doubles at night as the scene of local political rallies), an open-air cafeteria on the waterfront, air-conditioned dorms for 150 second-year students (many students live off-campus), and recreational facilities (sailing, snorkeling).

The only lab is an air-conditioned facility for anatomy and neuroanatomy, with a refrigerated room for cadavers. Modica struck a deal with Guyana to obtain cadavers from that country in exchange for scholarships to St. George's. "The economics work in our favor," he says. "Previously, I was paying $3,000 to get cadavers from the U.S."

The True Blue campus 2½ miles away includes a converted motel (no air conditioning) that serves as a dorm for 150 first-year students, a cafeteria, bookstore, 150-seat lecture hall, and small administrative offices. The library includes minimal audiovisual equipment. One building houses the newly built labs for histology, microbiology, and pathology.

(A 1980 preliminary report by the U.S. General Accounting Office observed, "Physical facilities at the two sites in Grenada are reasonably good and both the facilities and equipment are modern. However, laboratory facilities, notably in biochemistry, physiology and pharmacology, still need to be developed and equipment and supplies for such laboratories need to be acquired.")

At $6,000 tuition per student, St. George's U. has had the cash flow to improve its equipment and facilities, but the U.S. invasion turned the two campuses into a military holding area.

The suddenness of the strike ended a tense week for Modica, the students, and the school's "parent network." Modica, a master strategist, was caught off-guard by the invasion, and parents and students contacted by *AMN* said they actively had recommended against an invasion. For St. Georges' U. School of Medicine, this was the week that was:

Wednesday, Oct. 19—A 16-member military council seizes power after killing Prime Minister Bishop, three of his cabinet members, and two union leaders. The new military rulers say Bishop and the others were killed in an unfortunate mob melee. A 24-hour curfew is imposed, and Grenada's 1,200 troops are authorized to shoot on sight.

Thursday, Oct. 20—Caribbean politicians express shock at the killings and contradict the version of events put out by the Grenadian government. Prime Minister Eugenia Charles of Dominica calls the killings "cold-blooded executions." Prime Minister Edward Seaga of Jamaica calls the members of Grenada's ruling council "Cuban-trained Army generals and other Marxist idealogues." Sentiment builds among other Caribbean nations to begin an economic boycott of Grenada and possibly launch a military invasion. The United States is asked to help, and plans begin for military intervention.

Friday, Oct. 21—The phones are ringing off the hook in Long Island, N.Y., where Modica maintains his office for the "Foreign Medical School Service Corporation."

Arthur Mazzola, the school's public affairs director, observes that things may look grim long-term, "but last night the students had a beer party on the beach. They can't be that concerned."

Calls to Grenada are erratic, but *AMN* gets through to Gary Solin, the school's bursar. He says things are quiet and that "this whole thing was nothing but a 10-minute incident downtown. Vice chancellor Bourne and I met today with Gen. Hudson Austin (the new military commander) and we're planning to resume classes Monday when the curfew lifts."

Saturday, Oct. 22—Modica tells *AMN* that his work behind the scenes has helped bring about a substantive action—the new Grenadian government has agreed to allow two American envoys from the U.S. Embassy in Barbados to come in and check on the safety of the American medical students. "My first concern," Modica says, "is the students' safety. They're the ones who pay my salary. We're playing this thing hour by hour, but the next few days should be critical."

That night, a call slips through the jammed Grenadian lines and Nelly Bourne, wife of the vice chancellor, says "things are perfectly safe and secure here. Will you please pass the word? The authorities are bending over backwards to help. Yesterday, we needed some water on campus, something that needed to be taken care of in a day or two. Within 10 minutes, two fire trucks pulled up."

A freshman student, Mike Pope, Richmond, Va., is a neighbor of the Bournes. Since the Bournes' phone has not been working, he has been carrying messages to them. He adds: "Frankly, most of us are concerned about our studies. We're halfway through our semester and mid-terms had been scheduled for next week until this broke out. I spoke with my parents today and the question of my leaving never even came up. We're OK."

Meanwhile, the U.S. announces that as a security precaution it is diverting to Grenada a 10-ship task force that had been headed for duty off Lebanon. Radio Free Grenada announces that an invasion is imminent.

Sunday, Oct. 23—At a jam-packed room at New York's Kennedy Airport, Modica meets with 500 members of the "Parents Network of St. George's U. Medical School." He tells them that U.S. envoys are talking to their sons and daughters and offering safe passage home, and that he is going to make available one-week furloughs for those students who want to take a breather. "We can simply extend the semester for a week," Modica says.

He adds that classes are scheduled to resume on Monday, that the Grenada airport is scheduled to reopen, and that he hopes those students who wish to leave can do it voluntarily on LIAT.

Alvin Buxbaum, president of the parents' group, tells *AMN*, "We gave Charlie a vote of confidence. In fact, the original purpose of the meeting was to make plans for a testimonial dinner for him. We think he's doing all he can and that things will work out. We're going to send a telegram to President Reagan asking him not to take any precipitous actions that may endanger the students."

Fred Jacobs, MD, the only physician member of the board, adds, "I have a lot of confidence in Mr. Modica—he's always come through before—but I don't think that the parents are aware of everything that's going on. Basically, Modica said, 'Trust me.' Now, I do trust him, but this thing isn't over yet."

Dr. Jacobs adds: "I talk regularly to my daughter, Stephanie, on the short-wave radio and she is not terribly impressed with the information she is being given by the school. I don't want to impugn the school's motives, but there are some hidden agendas here, and the school's interest is not necessarily the students'. The school has a vested interest in staying in Grenada.

"Two nights ago, when Stephanie heard rumors of an invasion, she was very concerned. Now, the students have invasion parties all the time—the bars put up signs, 'Welcome, Marines—Bring your money'—but she thought that this time they might not be joking. But the other Caribbean nations probably only have five soldiers between them, so I don't see how they can invade, unless the U.S. helps. I hope there's no need for that."

Monday, Oct. 24—At 2 a.m., an *AMN* reporter is contacted by Dr. Bourne, who has just returned from meetings with the U.S. diplomats and the Grenadian ruling council. "Tomorrow, we resume classes, and the airport should be open in a day or two. Some students say they want to leave for a week, but I estimate the number as less than 10%. Very, very few will withdraw from school. I think we can work it out so that you can come down here and talk to the students and see for yourself how safe and secure they are. The State Dept. has issued a routine advisory against travel here, but it should be no problem."

Modica says he should know within the week whether the school will remain in Grenada. "With enough notice, I can relocate everything to St. Vincent within three or four days," he adds. "There are two factions down there, and we want to see if the new rulers have control or if the Bishop faction will launch a counter-revolution. The next 24 hours should be critical. We don't want to do anything to unnecessarily antagonize the Grenadian rulers. If the students have to evacuate, we want it to be done voluntarily or for the school to charter a plane. The last thing we want is a military invasion."

George Ablin, MD, a Bakersfield, Calif., neurosurgeon, says that his son, "Kip," is "remarkably extemporaneous and discerning, and I'm sure that he'll get us a message in a bottle if things go wrong. But in Grenada the word is only going one-way. The students are only being told what the government and the school want them to know."

J. Shermer Garrison III, MD, Portsmouth, Va., says that his son, Jason, and his daughter-in-law "appear to be pretty secure. They live off-campus, and while things aren't luxurious, he's there to get an education. I'm an old Navy man and I don't think that anything bad is going to happen to our children while the U.S. Navy is cruising off-shore." His wife, Anna, adds, "Well, I'm a mother and I'm concerned, but we're not hysterical. My son and daughter-in-law are pretty strong people."

Frank Gatti, MD, a Manhattan family physician, says: "Well, we're hoping for the best. Marcella is a pretty resourceful girl, but it's a 1½-hour drive over a mountain to get to that airport, and I've told her not to attempt it unless the government escorts her or she goes in a big group. I know a lot of children—I guess I shouldn't call them children, they're young men and women, but they're all somebody's children—want to stay down there and complete their school work—Marcalla is in her fourth semester and we don't want her work to go for naught—so I sure hope this thing quiets down."

Meanwhile, at the AMA headquarters in Chicago, several callers are demanding to know what the AMA is doing to assure the students' safety. The calls are referred to Modica's office in Long Island, N.Y.

Tuesday, Oct. 25—The United States and the six-nation Caribbean force strike and secure Grenada's two airports and the two medical school campuses. A hastily formed Grenada Work Group in the U.S. State Dept. says all students are safe and that their evacuation is imminent.

Miriam Jacobs, wife of the parents' network Dr. Jacobs, angrily tells *AMN:* "The medical campus is under mortar fire. This is sure one hell of a way to get a medical education. I sure hope that the people who make medical policy—like the AMA—can become more sensitive to the problems of the students who want a medical education today." The parents' network chairman, Buxbaum, says: "I'm very upset. We asked them not to invade, but they did anyway. I sure hope that the medical establishment will make provisions to see that these students don't lose their credits."

Wednesday, Oct. 26—The United States begins evacuation. The first plane is scheduled to arrive at the Charleston (S.C.) Air Force Base at 5:30 p.m. EST.

And Modica, the man in the eye of a hurricane, is off again to meet the network news people. At least, he could report the students were safe.□

Barney Clark and Baby Fae

Is the artificial heart worth it? Is the Baby Fae transplant worth it?

These tough questions have provoked a storm of controversy.

My bias is with the surgeons who have dared—William DeVries, MD, with the artificial heart, and Leonard Bailey, MD, with the baboon heart, or xenograft.

It is easy to doubt and criticize, but I have often thought what a great story it would be to let the surgeons, the medical men in the trenches, turn the tables and second-guess the ethicists.

It is the surgeon who daily sees the hopeless patients and who must endure the helpless feeling of having nothing to offer.

Ultimately, this is what led Bill DeVries to implant a plastic-and-aluminum heart in Barney Clark and this is what led Leonard Bailey to transplant a walnut-sized baboon heart into the chest of an infant who would become known to the world as Baby Fae.

Barney Clark died after 112 days, Baby Fae after 20. Their memories, however, live on, and, clearly, their surgeons will dare to try again.

THE SLOW RECUPERATION of Barney Clark, DDS, the man with a plastic heart, has been an ordeal not only for the 62-year-old dentist but also for his medical team at the U. of Utah Medical Center.

Physicians and patient alike, however, agree on the main point—the historic operation was worth it.

In a videotaped interview released to reporters March 2, 1983, Dr. Clark was asked by his surgeon, William C. DeVries, MD, "What would you advise the next potential recipient of an artificial heart?" The famous patient replied, "Well, I would tell them that it's worth it if the alternative is they either die or they have it done. . . . All in all, it has been a pleasure to be able to help people, and then, you people have learned something."

Despite Dr. Clark's optimistic approval, however, his physicians describe a roller-coastal clinical recovery that still is not resolved fully.

Ironically, Dr. Clark's artificial heart has performed almost flawlessly, with the single exception of a broken mitral valve that occurred last December. His main problems since the implant have been weak lungs, weak kidneys, and an organic brain syndrome that at one point left him virtually comatose. The key to his future recovery appears to be more his brain and mental intactness than his artificial heart and normal cardiac output.

The stakes are high because not only is Dr. Clark dependent upon the artificial heart, but also the artificial heart program is dependent upon Dr. Clark's recovery.

To Chase N. Peterson, MD, vice president for health sciences at the U. of Utah and the man who met the news media on behalf of the medical team, the returns are already in:

"Dr. Clark," he says, "has already proven a favorable risk-benefit ratio for the implantation of an artificial heart. His risk was exactly six minutes. That's what he had to lose, because if he had not received the artificial heart when he did, he would have been dead in six minutes. His benefit so far is 100 days (March 11, when Dr. Peterson was interviewed). So we risked six minutes of Dr. Clark's former life to give him at least 100 more days.

Claudia Berenson, MD, the psychiatrist who has seen Dr. Clark most days since the operation, notes, however, that "In some ways, Dr. Clark was sicker after the operation than before. The seizures and organic brain syndrome he suffered within a week of the heart's implantation put him out of mental commission for almost 10 weeks. He could not think clearly enough to participate in his own recovery. He was confused and disoriented and when his awareness would briefly return, he would often remark, 'My mind is shot. Maybe I would be better off dead.' Sometimes, he would just say, 'Maybe I'd be better off (dead).' Other times, he was more emphatic (about wanting to die). Dr. Clark's mental difficulties did not fully resolve until Feb. 15. I want to emphasize that his brain syndrome was *organic,* relating to his seizures, and was not a reaction to the surgery. Today, he is intact mentally."

Dr. DeVries, the surgeon who performed the implant, plans to send Dr. Clark home soon, but he cautions, "Until we do, our job is not over. The medical team sees no reason to celebrate until we are convinced that Dr. Clark can lead a useful life." Dr. DeVries theorizes that Dr. Clark's seizures, the worst of his many medical complications, "were caused by the sudden perfusion of blood pumped to his head by the artificial heart. Here was a man who had been living with a heart that only pumped about one liter of blood per minute, and, suddenly, the artificial heart was pumping 12. The initial insult from this over-perfusion of blood to the head may have triggered the seizures."

The surgeon describes his patient as a "tough, gutsy, adventurous guy." Dr. Clark has needed all these attributes and more, as he has battled not only the cumulative weakness brought on by his failing heart (to qualify for the implant he had to demonstrate heart failure while at bed rest), but also postoperative complications that have three times sent him back to the OR. His most recent complication, aspiration pneumonia, required him again to be put on the respirator and to resume antibiotics. He remains in fair condition.

The dentist's fight for life is also extraordinary, Dr. DeVries observed, "because the news media are intimately involved with the care of the patient. This is a tremendous demand upon the time of the medical team. A few days ago, I had to explain to Dr. Clark's wife his case of aspiration pneumonia. Then I had to go downstairs and explain the same thing to 385 reporters.

"We don't want to exploit ourselves or turn this whole thing into a circus. We need guidance on how much news the press would like to know, deserves to know, and needs to know. They don't teach these things in medical school. What's right when you're dealing with the press? Do you talk only with the scientific publications? The local papers? Your friends? The people you have come to trust? Everybody? These are important questions because the way the press performs will affect all of us.

"Sometimes, we have been too vague with the press, and they have confused the issue by looking for their own answers. Sometimes, we were too specific and they confused the issue by not understanding our answers. All these things affect people. I read the pathology report on Dr. Clark's heart in *The New York Times* before I read it in his hospital chart. Should we be telling the press Dr. Clark's daily blood chemistry readings? His medical chart? Would they make sense? These are tough questions. We decided early on to keep the press informed, but when I read in the morning paper that he had Cheerios for breakfast, well, that's a bit much."

Dr. Peterson says the press onslaught was assured "when we decided to tell things as they are about Dr. Clark. Before the operation, everyone involved—and that's at least 20-some people—sat down and decided what our media options were. One, we could use the 'Russian astronaut' strategy and do the operation in secret. If the operation failed and the patient died, the report would appear in the back pages of a medical journal. Two, we could lie about it and say the artificial-heart patient was really here for a gallbladder. Or three, we could have open disclosure.

"We chose option 3, of course, and then we had to decide whether to provide minimal information—statements read by a layman—or to tell things as they unfolded, with a physician educating the press and through them the public about heart disease.

"We were mindful of what might happen if we tried to stonewall things. A few years back when (Dr.) Denton Cooley did a famous operation, a reporter jumped out of a hospital laundry hamper and snapped off a few photos before running down the hallway. We can't prevent news leaks. Months ago, Dr. DeVries received a call in the OR from a South American wanting an artificial heart. An hour later in the cafeteria, the man slinging Dr. DeVries' hash asked, 'Well, Doc, are we going to operate on that guy from Bolivia?' We decided to be honest, and I was selected to tell the news. Some people think we have told too much.

"This type of thing is certainly not in my job description, and it's been a terribly interesting challenge. We reported this medical story as it happened. As Dr. Clark was wheeled back to the OR to repair the air leaks in his chest, I went down to the cafeteria to tell the world what was happening. None of us knew how things would turn out. In fact, after Dr. DeVries repaired the air leaks, he turned on the TV to find out 'what I'm supposed to be doing.'

"Most medical articles, you know, are sanitized by delay. The definition of a medical article published in a scientific journal is clear-stepping to a high peak. All the missteps are washed out. Our steps were right there for everybody to see. The medical team decided to hang together and try to educate the press with accurate information, rather than have reporters scurrying after janitors and night watchmen.

"Before the operation, I had everyone on the medical team sign statements that they understood their roles and the roles of everybody else with whom they would be working. That's 20-plus people who had to agree on what they were being expected to do. I have the notes in my file. One nurse, Linda Gianelli, RN, insisted that the nurses be trained to run the heart driver. Somebody said, 'Don't worry, we have technicians for that.' Linda said, 'What if they're in the bathroom when something goes wrong? If we're responsible for the patient, we have to know how to run the heart driver.' Well, she learned, and so did all the other nurses, though it set our timetable back a month. We think our plan worked."

One thing that has worked almost without fail is Dr. Clark's aluminum and plastic heart, the Jarvik-7 that has registered about 14 million beats since being implanted Dec. 2.

"We've learned that the artificial heart works in a human," Dr. Peterson says. "In fact, it works very well, even in the presence of other severe illnesses. And it has worked so far without causing either a clot or an infection, which are two of our biggest fears."

Dr. Berenson says that at first Dr. Clark was disturbed by the "pounding" of his artificial heart. "Until you get used to it," she adds, "it's a little like having a jackhammer inside you. You can put your hand on Dr. Clark's arm or leg and feel the vibration. He used to complain about the 'pounding,' but he eventually got used to it, just like a person with a consistent heart murmur or a person with a heart pacemaker adjusts to the sound. As long as the sound is consistent, it becomes reassuring."

The psychiatrist sticks by her earlier assessment that "we loaded the dice for success when we selected Dr. Clark. He's not only tough, he's highly motivated. During his 2½-minute videotaped interview Dr. Clark clearly was suffering from respiratory distress, as indicated by his pursed-lip breathing. Another reason for his discomfort, though, Dr. Berenson suggests, "is that Dr. Clark very much wants to succeed. He wants to put forth the best possible image, both for himself and the medical center, and he may have been trying a little too hard."

Dr. Peterson believes that the first artificial-heart patient also may be suffering from primary lung disease that predated his heart disease and that, perhaps, may have been caused by his work as a dentist. "Some dentists absorb a lot of metallic residue in their work. It's sort of a metallic aerosol mist. Many dentists who wear glasses will tell you that they often have to stop and wipe this mist off their glasses. Well, Dr. Clark may have suffered a toxic lung infection from years of practicing dentistry. And one of our biggest problems in restoring his health is his lung disease."

Say Dr. DeVries: "Sure, Dr. Clark thought of dying once or twice. But mostly, he's said he's just glad to be alive. Before the operation, he had to be the 'most-studied' patient in the world and he was a 'perfect' patient for this operation, but he was also at death's doorstep. We were afraid he might die before we could get him on the heart-lung machine.

"Since the implant, his recovery has been slowly uphill. His health is so frail that every complication—the nosebleeds, the pneumonia—are a lot more serious than they would be to a healthier patient. But he's going to make it. I've believed that from the start, or I never would have cut."

Caring for Dr. Clark is an ongoing challenge for the three physicians.

Dr. DeVries slept at the hospital until Christmas ("my wife brought the kids to the intensive care unit to see me") and alternated staying overnight there with colleague Lyle Joyce, MD, until February.

"For all of December," he says, "Dr. Clark was my only patient. The surprise in his treatment is that there have been no surprises. That's because we thoroughly anticipated every possible complication before the operation. We had so many dry runs that there have been no surprises. We even had differential diagnoses worked out for the seizures. I talked to a lot of heart transplant centers and about 5% of patients suffer seizures within three to five days of the transplant. But you have to constantly anticipate what can go wrong and be prepared to do something about it."

(The surgeon's colleagues often talk about the "DeVries' luck," how he often happens to walk into the OR exactly when the patient needs him. Dr. DeVries, a former basketball player, knows that it's not luck that the best athletes always seem to be in the right place at the right time. "Bill DeVries," a colleague says, "just happens to make his own luck by always being nearby when a patient needs him.")

Dr. DeVries says that he didn't resume his surgical schedule until January. "I do about five or six a day now. People who are really sick, but people who you're never going to hear about. That's the way it should be. Even Dr. Clark thinks that all this publicity is overblown. What really worries me is that it may frighten away the second artificial-heart patient. The next potential patient may feel that he cannot handle the media barrage.

"We're learning a tremdous amount from Dr. Clark's case. These days, I spend about an hour a day with Barney, about three hours assembling his medical data and figuring out what it means, and about an hour dealing with the press. We're preparing our scientific reports on Dr. Clark's case for presentation this spring.

"Surprisingly, we've learned that Dr. Clark seems to function best when the heart output is at lower levels, six or seven liters per minute, than when we had him up around 10. Mrs. Clark and the nurses were the first to notice that he seemed more alert and lucid at the lower levels. For the past two months, we've fixed his heart rate at 95, which keeps his blood pressure at 105/80. Dr. Clark's vascular resistance seems to adjust to the steady heartbeat to keep a steady blood pressure whether he's exercising or resting. His blood pressure is self-regulated. I think that the earlier higher cardiac outputs may have helped cause the seizures."

Dr. Peterson agrees that blood over-perfusion is "one hypothesis about what may have caused the seizures, but he also had massive metabolic disturbances brought about by toxic antibiotic doses and kidney failure. A tennis player handles 20 liters (of blood per minute), a marathon runner, 30. We're just beginning to sort out the lessons we've learned from the artificial heart. We have x-rays of Dr. Clark's lungs that are a world first. They show his case of pulmonary edema that was cleared up within five minutes, simply by turning his left ventricle up and his right down. Normally, this would require hours of work to clear the fluids."

Dr. Berenson says that counseling her patient in the ICU was "not the optimal medical setting. It's impossible to have any privacy, and much of the time Dr. Clark was on a respirator. Often, I would have to press my finger over his 'trach' (tracheotomy) so that he could talk. It's hard to have a therapeutic dialogue under those conditions. And much of the time, as I said, he was confused and disoriented. There was a period when he didn't know where he was-or why. He recognized me as an ICU regular—most times. The memory loss is what bothered Dr. Clark the most. He not only couldn't remember why he was in the hospital, but he couldn't remember things from immediately before the operation and things going back 10-20-30 years. The memory loss was short-term, intermediate-term, and long-term. I told him 'Don't worry. This will pass. Your confusion will go away. Your memory will come back.'

"The brain syndrome fully cleared up by mid-February. For two weeks—until he came down with the aspiration pneumonia—Dr. Clark just talked and talked to me. Little worries, like will he and his wife be able to operate the heart driver, and big worries, like will he ever feel well enough to get out of the hospital and start really living again. He was amazed by all the medical gadgets in the ICU, and he has a wry sense of humor. He makes a lot of word quips, which shows his mind is sound.

"He remembers his period of delirium, but says it seems 'like it was all part of a dream.' The up-and-down nature of his recovery has been discouraging. But he tells me, 'I'm adapting, I'm adjusting. I want to get out of here.' Now, he's participating in his recovery, and maintaining mental intactness will be the key to his recovery. The brain syndrome is resolved, but kidney failure, liver failure, a high fever could trigger it again. He very much wants to succeed and he takes his public image very seriously. After the pneumonia hit, he told me, 'I feel lousy, but I'm still trying.'"

Says Dr. DeVries: "Dr. Clark really needs to communicate. That's the key to his recovery. He gets bored from time to time just sitting in his room, but yesterday, he was talking to me about golf. He's a six-handicap, and he says he would really love to play golf again. Well, you know, we could fix up a golf cart with the heart driver and take him out on the course. He perked up at that. He could sure beat my golf game. We've got him goal-oriented; this week off the respirator. Next month, out of the hospital."

Was the $250,000 operation (all paid by private donors) worth it?

The Utah team thinks so. Already, the Utah artificial-heart researchers, surgeons, nurses, social workers, hospital administrators, public relations staff, institutional review board, medical consultants, and university administrators are preparing for the possibility of a second operation, should the federal Food and Drug Administration approve.

Concludes Dr. Peterson: "There are two ways to answer that question. As a general matter, we don't know yet, because no patient as yet has had the operation and returned home to lead a useful life. Specifically, we know it's worthwhile because Dr. Clark has said it's worthwhile. Medically, the project is a success. 'Strong heart' is not just a metaphor. Dr. Clark has a strong heart, and it's keeping him alive.

"We've developed a lot of valuable data—how heart drugs and blood pressure perform at given heart rates—but we'll all feel happier when Dr. Clark can go home and enjoy a football game on TV and have dinner with his family. Sure, he's tethered to the machine, but his situation is really not that different from a paraplegic in a wheelchair."

"I hope he's going to make it," Dr. Berenson says. "The ups and downs have been so discouraging to all of us. His health is so frail. But before he was wondering if he might be better off dead. Now, he tells me, 'I want to live.'"

"He's my patient, but he's also become a friend," Dr. DeVries says. "We've seen him through the implant, the air leaks, the seizures, the broken-valve operation, the nosebleed operation, and now, the pneumonia. And still, he's in fair condition. A remarkable man.

"It's not yet time to celebrate. But we're waiting. On Christmas Day, my children and Dr. Joyce's children came to Dr. Clark's room and sang Christmas carols. I could see the joy in his eyes. He was really happy.

"Now, if we can only get him out on the golf course."□

Sadly, Dr. Clark died on March 25, 1983, only three weeks after the U. of Utah medical team discussed their hopes for him. One month later, in the only interview he has given, Dr. Clark's son, a physician, described what the historic surgery meant to him.

THE EYES OF THE WORLD were upon artificial heart pioneer Barney Clark, DDS, 62, but his son, Stephen Kent Clark, MD, 36, could barely stand to see him suffer.

"As his son," Dr. Clark said, "it was not a warm feeling for me to see Dad so uncomfortable and so incapacitated during the last days of his life. I prefer to remember him in the good days, going golfing on a nice summer day or taking a family trip, and not as I saw him in Utah."

During the 112 days he lived with an aluminum-and-plastic heart, the news media made Dr. Barney Clark an international symbol of personal courage and the miracles of medical research. But the medical event that electrified the world was a bittersweet ordeal for his son.

Dr. Clark learned of his father's death from a reporter, just as he had learned of his earlier seizures, nosebleeds, and pneumonia.

"My news from the hospital was always 12 hours old," Dr. Clark said. "Usually, grief and illness is a private matter for the family. But with my father, the family had to share his suffering with the press. People were always asking me, 'Was I all right? Was Dad all right?' It made me feel uneasy, almost embarrassed."

Dr. Clark always told the reporters, "No comment." Only now is he beginning to work his way through the complex feelings he has about the historic surgery. In the only interview he has granted to discuss his father's ordeal, Dr. Clark emphasized, "The whole experience leaves an ambivalent taste in my mouth. I guess I will always be ambivalent.

"There are two very separate aspects to what Dad went through," he said. "On the one hand, let me be very candid. The operation was clearly not worth it for Dad in terms of any useful prolongation of his life, in terms of any added quality of life. On the other, Dad went in with his eyes open. All he expected to do was make a contribution to medical research. He told me that he never really thought the artificial heart would work *for him*. If the entire experience ever made him happy, I imagine it was in the moments right before he would have died had not the Utah team operated. It must have given him peace of mind to know he would be helping others. But the surgery proved to be of no specific benefit to Dad."

Dr. Clark, an otolaryngologist who specializes in head and neck surgery in Seattle, Wash., where he grew up with his father and mother, Una Loy Clark, and a brother and sister, spoke brisky and articulately about his father. Every so often, though, his voice would catch or a sigh would escape. He laughed only when he recalled his father's sense of humor, "which he never lost, right up until the end."

"For me, it is a very personal loss," he said. "I feel a tremendous sense of loneliness, knowing that my father, my friend, my confidant, is not there anymore, that I won't be able to go to his house for dinner anymore. It is a new emotion for me, and I guess it just keeps coming up again and again. We shared so many good things together that I choose to remember him as he lived and not as he died in Utah."

Dr. Clark exempted from his ambivalence the conduct of the Utah medical team and the prospects for the future usefulness of the artificial heart. He gave a "resounding vote of confidence" to both.

"I cannot imagine a medical team," he said, "that could conduct itself in a manner any more upright than did the people who cared for Dad. They were absolutely without blemish, doing everything in a genuinely correct manner. They treated the family with absolute candor, and at no time did I have the feeling that they were trying to keep Dad alive an extra day or two just to set some kind of a record.

"At the very end, I suppose, it might have been possible to have Dad's kidneys dialysized to try to keep him alive. This might have been an option, but it was never recommended. Had it been recommended, I would have been against it. It would have been an absurd situation, with Dad totally dependent for life support not only upon an artificial heart but also artificial lungs, kidneys, and feeding. Kidney dialysis was not a good option and the Utah team never suggested it. They had no interest in prolonging Dad's *death*.

"I think that the artificial heart is a valid concept. I know that some medical people are critical of the artificial heart. A cardiologist here in town wrote an editorial, 'Barney Clark—pioneer to nowhere,' contending that the artificial heart is not clinically useful. I don't resent this viewpoint; I simply do not share it. The Utah team learned a lot from Dad, and I think that in time they will work out the cost and ethical problems. They have to improve the hardware, to make the power unit less cumbersome and more portable. But this is just around the corner, I believe. If the artificial heart is ever to be a good thing, it must be made almost forgettable.

"They learned that the artificial heart works, that the heart itself does not cause pain, that a patient with an artificial heart can sit up and move around, that the patient can do things and begin to try to live a satisfying life."

Was the historic surgery worthwhile?

Dr. Clark carefully considered. "You are asking some very pointed questions. Let me answer from various perspectives.

"The bottom line is that I never advised Dad on the artificial heart. He had his reasons and they were good enough for me. Only Dad can answer the question of worthiness and he's not here. At the time of his March 2 videotaped interview with (the surgeon) Dr. (William) DeVries, Dad said it was worthwhile, and he was the kind of man who always said what he thought. I'm not going to second-guess him now.

"Whether or not something is worthwhile depends upon the final result. Was it worth it in terms of any specific health benefit to Dad? No. Was it worth it in terms of what Dad expected to accomplish, making a contribution to medical research? Yes. Was it worth it in terms of what they learned from the research and in terms of what will benefit others? Maybe. Ask me in 20 years, and we'll all know more.

"I know this. They were very fortunate to have Dad as the first patient. He didn't suddenly become very courageous and gutsy at the time of the operation. He lived his entire life that way. He was the kind of man about whom nothing bad was ever said because there was nothing bad to be said.

"I am 36, and I know that I would never choose to go through what Dad did. But then, if I were to suffer through the states of heart disease, as he did, I might think differently."

Dr. Barney Clark's son thinks his father might be living today with the artificial heart "if his lungs had been good. He had chronic emphysema and that more than anything caused his setbacks. In hindsight, had the Utah team known the extent of the damage to his lungs, he might have been ruled out as a good candidate. But the whole thing developed very suddenly.

"First of all, my Dad's heart disease was a tragic chance occurrence. We think his heart failure was caused by a virus, but that's what scientists say when they really don't know. Dad also had emphysema from his work in dentistry—being exposed during drilling to all the enamel and gases—and from smoking, although he quit completely 10 years before he died. He had primary lung disease independent of the heart disease. At the time, we all thought the lung problems were due to the heart problem.

"A lot of Dad's problems after the artificial heart was implanted were due to his bad lungs—the lung tear and the air leaks that forced him back into surgery; the need to stay on the respirator for long periods of time; and even near the end the aspiration pneumonia from choking on his own vomiting was caused by being on the respirator.

"Also, once Dad realized the extent of his lung problems, he had real doubts about whether or not he and Mom could handle all the medical equipment. He began to doubt whether he would ever be able to leave the hospital simply because of the need to care for his bad lungs in addition to having the artificial heart."

Dr. Clark described his vigil this way:

"As a son, I hoped that Dad would recover and be able to leave the hospital. As a physician, I seriously doubted it.

"I think that the reports in the news media were consistently too optimistic, but I guess that's understandable. Even Mom and the rest of the family were more optimistic than I.

"In my mind, Dad was never the same mentally after he suffered the seizures within a week of the implant. During the times I saw him, there would be short intervals of lucidity and much longer intervals of confusion. He was never quite together, although I think that the physicians had preserved his ability to return to normal mentally. I may not have seen him at his best, but he was never quite himself on the days I saw him.

"A cerebral incident was what Dad feared the most before surgery and what the family feared the most. What bothered Dad the most was the mental confusion he suffered for almost three months after the seizures. Sometimes he couldn't remember things, and other times he would remember things that he had dreamed. There were times when he was hallucinating. He would wake up and he couldn't remember if something had really happened or if he had dreamed it.

"This made it very hard for Mom. She is still trying to work her way through the aftermath. She's a very strong lady, but she'll probably need some counseling before she can come to terms with what happened.

"What made it so hard on her was that Dad was on a roller coaster, with every gain followed by a setback, and much of the time Mom could not talk to him, could not find out how he felt. This was not the way she would have chosen to see him go. Throughout the ordeal, she knew he was suffering, but he was never well enough to really talk to her about it. Worst of all, Mom just felt very helpless to comfort the man she loved.

"Dad was very stoical throughout the entire experience. He was never one to complain. If something bothered him, he would tell you, but he never amplified it.

"Dad was in some pain. There were interminable and unending medical procedures, simply an unbelievable number and all very necessary. He had to be taken back to surgery three times. He was put on and off and on the respirator. He was treated for gout in his right ankle. He needed painful back clapping to clear his lungs. Dad never complained. He never said, 'Stop!'

"Once, the news reports said that Dad had had a 'darned good day.' Well, if you'd been in the room with him as I had, you'd know that 'darned good day' is a very subjective description. Sure, it was good in the sense that he wasn't nauseous or throwing up or having nosebleeds, but he was still confined to bed, unable to do anything. He wasn't up and about, which is what a 'darned good day' would mean to me.

"Occasionally, the news reports said he was practicing his golf putting or walking by himself. Those things never happened. But I think that the news media wanted to believe that he would make it. My mother, brother, and sister tended to be more optimistic than I was.

"The last time I saw Dad was the weekend before he died. I knew he was on an irreversible downhill course, that the painful process was coming to an end. I think that Dad knew, too. Toward the middle and end of his stay, I think that Dad doubted he would ever leave the hospital."

Dr. Clark described the suddenness with which his father was thrust into medical history.

"Dad was always a very proud man, very athletic and very fit. He loved to golf and he was the type of man who would never let himself develop a paunch. Seven years ago, he appeared to be in perfect health. Then his heart disease was diagnosed." The heart failure was chronic— every relapse was followed by a period of apparent stabilization.

"Then, another setback," Dr. Clark said. "He was gradually softened up to the idea of needing something extreme like an artificial heart. When he first began taking steroids for his heart disease, he was bothered that his face became puffy, his tummy became prominent, his legs became very thin. It was hard for him, but he adjusted. He would have been able to handle the psychological trauma of living while tethered to a machine. He had been prepared for it by the stages of his heart failure.

"Understand now, the artificial heart was clearly the least desirable option for Dad. We would have preferred a heart transplant by 1,000%, but a transplant was not an option. Most transplant programs have age protocols, and 50 is the upper limit. Dad was 62. Somewhere, there may be a physician who does heart transplants on a fee-for-service basis for any age group, but we could not find such a physician. The artificial heart was the *only* option, and even it developed accidentally."

Dr. Barney Clark went to the U. of Utah Medical Center in July, 1982, to try an experimental drug. It turned out to be a wasted trip, because he wasn't a candidate for the drug.

"As a sort of consolation, they showed Dad the artificial heart program," Dr. Stephen Clark said. "He saw the animals living with artificial hearts and the research labs and he became interested. He agreed to be evaluated by the university as a possible candidate, but there was no commitment, either from Utah or from Dad. At this time, he could still get around a little, get in the car and go out for dinner. He kept hoping things would not get worse.

"We had Thanksgiving Day dinner with Dad at his house in Seattle. By then, his life was pretty much confined to a six-foot radius. He would have to sit for minutes on the couch just to muster up enough energy to walk to the dinner table. He could barely make it up a flight of stairs to the bedroom.

"We were very worried about the sudden worsening of his condition. The next day, Friday, I called a cardiologist at Utah and said, 'He's really in terrible condition.' The Utah evaluation team decided then that Dad would be the first man to have the artificial heart. They called back Friday night, and said they wanted to charter a plane to bring him down on Saturday. Dad said no. He had some personal affairs to get in order over the weekend. Plus, he decided he was well enough to fly common carrier. On Monday, we took him to a commercial jet and wheeled him onto the plane. He needed oxygen during the flight. In hindsight, Utah had a good idea in wanting to fly him down immediately. Dad arrived in Salt Lake City on a Monday and would have died . . . had they not implanted the artificial heart early Thursday morning.

"The family thought that either Dad would die very quickly or he would make a very quick recovery. It turned out, though, that it was to be a long, agonizing up-and-down ordeal.

"What made it tough for Mom was that one day Dad would look good and the next day he would be back in surgery. She never knew what to think, and Dad was too mentally out of it to talk to her." Social worker Peg Miller became "Mom's advocate," Dr. Clark said. "She spent a lot of time with Mom helping her handle all the pressure and making sure that she was well provided for." The entire Utah team "did everything with class," he added. "the surgeons, Dr. DeVries and Dr. Lyle Joyce, as well as (administrator) Dr. Chase Peterson and (psychiatrist) Dr. Claudia Berenson, did a wonderful job in telling the family what was happening.

"I also want to set the record straight about money," Dr. Clark continued. "A lot of people seem to think that the Clark family was out to make a bundle on my father. The only contract that has materialized so far is a $40,000 foreign-language exclusive with the West German magazine, *Stern*. The family hired an agent for one reason—we knew that if Dad ever got out of the hospital, he might have hospital bills and he certainly would have heavy convalescent bills. Well, the hospital bills were all paid by private donors, and any money paid for rights to Dad's story will be used to, first, help Mom, and, second, fund the artificial heart program. We're not out to make money in Dad's memory."

Dr. Clark paused. He had dwelt too long upon the grim. "Here's how I choose to remember Dad. Seven years ago or so when he shut down his dental practice, there was a big retirement party. The heart disease hadn't hit yet.

"He was in the pink of health and absolutely happy, looking forward to playing golf and running his business. He glowed with health and happiness. That's how I choose to remember him, and I'm sure Mom does, too."

Dr. Clark laughed. "You know, Dad kept his sense of humor right until the end. One day about 5 p.m. the nurse was clapping his back, a procedure he found especially painful. She said, 'Oh, Barney, it's almost 5 o'clock, I'm simply going to have to leave you pretty soon.' Dad said, 'It can't be soon enough for me!' Another time he was told that a cardiac wing in a Seattle hospital had been named in his honor. He told me, 'What an honor, and, just think, I didn't even have to die!' "

The physician warmed to the subject of his father. "Look, here's something real special that I just found out about. They just named a park in Provo (Barney Clark's hometown) in Dad's honor. That's very nice.

"The media interest is starting to drop off sharply now. I imagine they'll let me alone until the second patient gets an artificial heart. They'll want to know what to expect. Well, I'll tell them that if they're interested in making a contribution to medical science and having a slim chance of personal benefit, to go ahead, but to be prepared for some tough moments.

"When Dad left Seattle to fly to Salt Lake City, I knew that I would never see him again back in Seattle, back the way I had known him," he said.

"You know, the entire Utah medical team flew to Seattle for Dad's funeral. Everybody who had cared for him. The family was really touched. Afterwards, we had the Utah team out to Dad's house for a little reception.

"I wanted everybody from Utah to have an idea of what Dad was like before he became a famous patient. Sometimes, you treat a patient as he dies and you never have an idea of how he lived.

"I wanted Dad's doctors to get a little idea of the kind of man he was in happier days. That's how I will always remember him—not as he died but as he lived."□

"Science cannot wait for ethics to catch up."

—Elmer Stackman, speaking as president of the American Assn. for the Advancement of Science in 1950.

MAYBE SO, BUT THE Oct. 26, 1984, transplantation of the walnut-size heart of a 7½-month-old baboon to replace the failing heart of a 15-day-old baby girl who was born three weeks premature and weighed only five pounds has provoked a storm.

As of Oct. 31, the thriving "Baby Fae" was listed as critical but stable, had been taken off all support systems, had become the longest-surviving human recipient of a transplanted animal heart, and was encouraging "guarded optimism" among her physicians at California's Loma Linda U. Medical Center that the controversial xenograft would hold up.

Meanwhile, medical experts in organ transplantation and immunology expressed to *AMN* wide disagreement as to the scientific merits of the bold and highly experimental procedure. Charles McCarthy, MD, director of the National Institutes of Health (NIH) office of protection from research risks, told the press that the NIH would review the transplant, particularly the "question of whether a human heart was available and whether that option was properly considered." He added, "We have no reason to think that anything was wrong, but we will follow up to make sure everything was right."

Xenografts—tissue grafts involving members of different species—have been performed for more than a generation now in the United States, dating back to the 1963 transplants of baboon and chimpanzee kidneys into humans by surgeons Keith Reemtsma, MD, then at Tulane U., New Orleans, and Thomas Starzl, MD, then at the U. of Colorado Medical Center, Denver. In 1964, surgeon James Hardy, MD, of the U. of Mississippi Medical Center transplanted the heart of an ape into a 68-year-old man who died within four hours of the operation.

Baby Fae, however, is the first infant and only the fifth human to receive a transplanted animal heart. She also is one of only two infant heart-transplant patients. The other is London's Hollie Ruffey, who as a 9-day-old baby in 1983 received a human heart transplant and died within three weeks from kidney failure. None of the earlier efforts provoked the excitement that is being stirred by Baby Fae.

Surgeon David B. Hinshaw, MD, speaking for the Loma Linda U. transplant team and for Leonard L. Bailey, MD, the surgeon who performed the historic implant, told *AMN* Oct. 30, "We are exhausted and exhilarated and hoping that the transplant will hold and prove permanent."

Baby Fae is receiving a 40% oxygen mixture nasally and is receiving intravenous doses of steroids and Cyclosporin A, the drug that suppresses the body's immune system, Dr. Hinshaw said. Her heart is being monitored by repeated ultrasound tests. Early on the morning of Oct. 30, Baby Fae surpassed the cross-species heart transplantation survival record of 3½ days set by Benjamin Fortes, 59, who in 1977 received a chimpanzee heart in an operation done by Christiaan N. Barnard, MD, in Capetown, South Africa.

Dr. Hinshaw said the medical team was "delighted that the patient did not have a hyperacute rejection" of the baboon heart and that she had shown no evidence of kidney trouble.

The controversial five-hour transplant began late on the night of Oct. 26 and carried into the next morning. Ironically, during those very hours, the 12,000 surgeons attending the annual clinical congress of the American College of Surgeons were packing their bags and heading for home after a solid week of intensive clinical postgraduate work. There was no mention, however, of xenograft on the formal program. During the first few days after the Baby Fae operation, however, surgeons were being called at ORs across the country to comment on the experiment.

Two of the biggest names in U.S. surgery, Houston's Michael De-Bakey, MD, and artificial-heart pioneer William DeVries, MD, told *AMN* they were fascinated by the transplant.

Dr. DeBakey, reached at New York's Kennedy Airport enroute from Belgium to Houston, said:

"I think that it is very interesting and has considerable significance for the future. Actually, I'm rather optimistic about it. I think that this is a valid concept and presumably, the surgeon (Dr. Bailey) did considerable experimental work. The technical issues have been well-known for some time now.

"The key question, of course, is, how long will the baboon heart last before it is rejected? Because the child's immune system is underdeveloped, there probably will not be a profound rejection, at least not early. They may have several months to seek a human donor heart.

"I think that this is a very significant development, to be able to use an animal heart as a kind of artificial heart for temporary support to keep a patient alive until a human heart can be found. I think the concept of a xenograft as a temporizing procedure is very valid.

"Another advantage of such a temporizing procedure is that the patient will have time to get in better shape for a human organ transplant than is often the case."

Dr. DeVries, who in December, 1982, electrified the world with his pioneering implant of an artificial heart into Barney Clark, DDS, called from his new position in Louisville, Ky., with the Humana hospital, to say:

"I don't know as much about it as I would like, but I think that it is a fascinating thing to do, to use a child because of the underdevelopment of the immune system. It's very interesting and it opens up a lot of questions. I'm going to read more research on it.

"I don't know, however, if this type of transplant will really be able to buy time for an eventual human heart transplant. We'll have to see how long the baby will live and, of course, there are very few size-matched

infant human hearts available. Infants simply do not have the auto accidents and suicides that provide a lot of adult donor hearts.

"We'll all just have to wait and see. As you know, there was only one
artificial-heart operation, and so far there's only been one baboon-heart
transplant from which to learn. I'll be keeping an eye on it."

One of the acknowledged pioneers in organ transplantation is Stanford's Norman Shumway, MD, but he declined to respond to numerous
AMN phone calls. But the transplant immunologist on the Stanford team,
Randall Morris, MD, said, "We knew it was coming. The Loma Linda
people had been up to Stanford and we were aware of their protocols for
human experimentations. . . .

"Some 20 years ago, before anti-rejection drugs and when transplantation surgical procedures were in their infancy, surgeons like Reemtsma
and Starzl were transplanting baboon and chimpanzee kidneys into humans and getting three-to-nine-month survival rates. For that matter,
some 74 years ago, a Dr. Unger did the flip side and transplanted the
kidney of a deceased newborn into a baboon. He also transplanted a
chimpanzee kidney into a young adult, who died two years later. So,
conceptually, the groundwork was laid long ago and the field has been
growing.

"I think that barring complications, Baby Fae has a reasonable
chance of surviving in the short term, maybe at the level of the three to
nine months already reported in the literature for heterografts. The Loma
Linda team acted because of three key assumptions that remain to be
proven:

1. "They assumed that a cross-species transplantation is necessary
because of a shortage of human infant donors. Well, maybe, but I haven't
seen the data.

2. "They assumed that there are no corrective surgical procedures
that might have helped Baby Fae, and some physicians, like Dr. William
Norwood of Children's Hospital in Philadelphia, think that a two-step
surgical procedure might have helped Baby Fae. I don't know."

(Loma Linda medical officials said that Dr. Bailey was not trying to
discredit the Norwood operation but that in Dr. Bailey's hands it was a
very disappointing procedure.)

3. "They assumed that the anti-rejection drugs would not prove toxic
in either the short term or the long term.

"I don't mean to imply that I question these assumptions, but Baby
Fae's chances hinge on whether or not they prove to be true."

Many, however, are pessimisic about Baby Fae's chances.

Sharad Deodhar, MD, a specialist in immunopathology at the
Cleveland (Ohio) Clinic and a member of the AMA advisory panel on

organ transplantation, said, "I think her chances are very poor. The cyclosporine will be helpful, but in cross-species transplantations the rejection impulse is very powerful. I think she will suffer a severe rejection of the baboon heart within 10 to 14 days and probably die."

Transplant surgeon John Najarian, MD, is even more blunt. Dr. Najarian, who is chairman of the Dept. of Surgery at the U. of Minnesota Hospitals and who founded its transplant service in 1967, says flatly, "The operation is doomed to failure.

"I think that this xenograft is premature because I am not aware of any finding in the clinical literature that suggests anything but this prevailing rule—the human body will reject a transplanted animal organ. Baby Fae will reject her baboon heart within the next week or two, and the cyclosporine will not prevent it.

"This is not good clinical experimentation because medical science is not yet at the point where we can cross the xenograft barrier."

Conceding that "we are all strapped for human organs," Dr. Najarian, nevertheless, disagreed with the reasoning of the Loma Linda team that because infant hearts are not readily available for transplantation, the use of an animal heart is justified.

"If we thought xenografts would prove successful, we would use them," he said. "We don't do xenografts because they're not successful."

He also estimated the cost of the Baby Fae experiment. "It's easy to add up the numbers," he said. "You figure $1,000 for the baboon, $5,000 for a five-hour operation, and $2,000 a day for intensive care.

"It's an interesting step, but it is not good clinical experimentation."

Another critic is Paul Terasaki, PhD, director of the Southern California Regional Organ Procurement Agency, who charges that the surgical team did not seek a human heart because they were determined to do the cross-species transplant for which Dr. Bailey had trained for seven years.

Dr. Terasaki's agency provides human organs for transplant teams at Stanford; UCLA; U. of Arizona, Tucson; and the Pacific Medical Center, San Francisco. The agency also works closely with the Loma Linda U. kidney transplant team. The medical centers list their patients with the agency in the hope that a matching donor organ can be located. Loma Linda lists its kidney-transplant patients, but until the Baby Fae operation it never had performed a heart transplant.

The Loma Linda U. Medical Center, which is owned and operated by the Seventh-Day Adventist Church and which counts 85% of its medical staff as church members (though 90% of the patients are not), made its first heart transplant one that was discussed worldwide. Dr. Terasaki argues that if the Loma Linda heart transplant team had signaled its intention to the organ-procurement agency, it would have been notified that the heart of a 2-month-old infant from Salt Lake City was available Oct. 26, the day of the xenograft.

Dr. Terasaki told *AMN,* "We do not harvest many donor hearts, maybe only two or three or four a month, but on Oct. 26 we could have provided the heart from a 2-month-old infant. We didn't know Loma Linda needed a heart because we didn't know they were about to do heart transplants. We work closely with their kidney team, which lists their patients with us, but the heart-transplant team did not list Baby Fae because they were determind to push ahead with an alternate source of organs, the baboons. It came as a complete surprise to us."

Dr. Terasaki emphasized, however, that it was coincidental that the human heart became available the day of the Baby Fae transplant, that this was not a normal occurrence, and that he did not know if the human heart would have been right for Baby Fae. He said he did, however, notify the Loma Linda kidney team of the availability of the infant donor heart, but that apparently the message never was relayed to the heart team.

Responding to this furor was Jack Provonsha, MD, who heads the medical center's bioethics committee. "I think that Dr. Terasaki is being a little unfair," he told the press. "To have a human donor available, you have to know about it and you have to do some tissue testing. I can see they (Dr. Bailey's team) were playing a 'bird in the hand is worth two in the bush,'" he said.

Hospital spokesman Jack Schaeffer said that staff members had been unaware of a human infant donor. Even if they had been, he said, they likely would not have used the human heart because the donor was 2 months old and the heart would be too big for Baby Fae, who was born three weeks premature. Dr. Bailey, who has given only one press conference, responded to the criticism with a printed statement, emphasizing his seven years of research into cross-species transplantation, the scarcity of size-matched human infant donors, and the approval of clinical trials by the hospital's institutional review board. A prior decision had been made to perform the xenograft, and Baby Fae was the strongest of several candidates considered, he said.

Schaeffer told *AMN,* "Dr. Bailey is a shy man and in dealing with the press he has taken Dr. Shumway as his role model. He wants to have only the one press conference." Loma Linda's Dr. Hinshaw was willing to talk about his surgical colleague, however.

"Dr. Bailey is a masterful technician, there is no doubt about that," Dr. Hinshaw said. "He did some of his training at the Hospital for Sick Children in Toronto, and he is one of the leading researchers in the world in the field of neonates. He has done extensive research on the hypoplastic left heart syndrome (this problem, which renders the left ventricle functionless, is what threatened Baby Fae) and, of course, this is a hopeless lesion. But there is more to Dr. Bailey than his technical mastery.

"He is deeply sensitive to the pain and plight of these children. Daily, he sees them cry and die, and he knows that other than the hypoplastic left heart syndrome, they are intact. It is an isolated anomaly. He has a deep emotional commitment to try to help them, and this transplant was preceded by very meticulous and very sophisticated tissue-typing protocols. . . . It is very difficult to obtain a human infant donor in time to complete a transplant. This is Dr. Bailey's attempt to help these dying children."

Dr. Hinshaw added, "We have been a little taken aback by the media attention and by some of the criticism. But many surgeons, including some of the ones you've probably talked to, knew we were apt to do this xenograft. Dr. Bailey has freely discussed his animal trials. (His scientific papers and grant applications were turned down by the medical community—the Baby Fae transplant was funded by private donations, including support from the surgical team.) And many of these surgeons have called to wish us well and tell us 'to hang in there!' "

Many, however, remain skeptical. Houston heart surgeon Denton Cooley, MD, was so besieged by calls that he issued a printed statement.

"I am surprised, even astonished, to learn of the xenograft heart transplant. . . . Because the infant has survived more than 48 hours (with the xenograft), it appears that there is a moderate breakthrough in the rejection process. But serious moral and ethical issues confront the investigators with consequences and repercussions that may offset any rewards and gains. One is skeptical as to the worthiness and practicality of such an effort."

Oscar Salvatierra, MD, president of the American Society of Transplant Surgeons, heads an elite group whose 300 members include most of the leading transplant surgeons in the nation. He said, "I am not aware of any intention by any of our members to do a xenograft transplant."

Xenograft pioneers Drs. Reemtsma and Starzl cheered the operation.

Dr. Reemtsma, now chairman of the Dept. of Surgery at New York's Columbia College of Physicians and Surgeons and director of surgery at Presbyterian Hospital, said:

"I invented this field, and back in 1963, before there were suitable alternatives like dialysis, I transplanted chimpanzee kidneys into humans. In one transplant, the patient lived for nine months and his death was unrelated to the kidneys. I quit doing xenograft transplants many years ago, but I have continued to do lab work.

"I think that the California transplant is an important step in what remains an important field of investigation. The xenograft barrier may not be absolute. This is not a black-and-white area; there are shades of gray. There are wide variations between the compatibilities of some tissue of non-human primates and the tissues of humans. Under certain circumstances, the xenograft barrier may not be as great as in others. That's what the tissue-testing at Loma Linda seems to suggest. I hope so, because if the non-human tissue transplant works, it can be a tremendous help logistically in keeping people alive when donor organs are not available."

Dr. Starzl, now with the U. of Pittsburgh School of Medicine, calls the Baby Fae case "a tempest in a teapot. It's a philosophical problem, not a medical problem. If the protesters are concerned about the use of animals to save human lives, I think that's an unsupportable position. Xenografts are an acceptable medical experiment. Back in 1963, both Dr. Keith Reemtsma and myself were doing heterografts. I was transplanting baboon kidenys to humans; he was transplanting chimpanzee kidneys. As I reported in the literature and in a book, the chimpanzees are actually better—their tissue is less dissimilar to human tissue than the baboons— but, of course, today the chimpanzees are an endangered species.

"Dr. Reemtsma's case in which the patient lived for nine months with the kidney of a chimpanzee is very important. I believe that the patient finally died of pneumoccocal bacterium and that upon autopsy the chimp kidney looked like normal human tissue. The longest one of my patients lasted with a baboon kidney was two months. I also did a chimp-to-human liver transplant, which was reported. By 1970, though, I had started to drift away from xenografts.

"I do not think the Loma Linda surgical team is vulnerable to criticism. It sounds as if they're competent professionals carrying out an acceptable medical experiment upon an otherwise hopeless patient."

AMA policy-makers in organ transplantation and medical ethics stress that the Baby Fae case raises many questions that will have to be answered in the months ahead.

Leo Henikoff, MD, a pediatric cardiologist, is president of Chicago's Rush-Presbyterian Medical Center. He also is a member of the AMA Judicial Council.

"This is not a question of medical ethics," he said. "This is a question of medical practice.

"There are lots of ways to look at this case, and the Judicial Council, obviously, has not discussed it (it meets next in December at the AMA Interim Meeting), but speaking for myself, I think that the use of animal tissue in a human is *not* unethical in any way, shape, or form.

"For 10 years, we have been using pig valves in cardiac surgeries and, obviously, nobody thinks that this is unethical. Now, pig valves are dead tissue; it's like using metal. But if you use animal tissue as a transplant and that tissue survives in a human, that, too, is not unethical. It is not a question of medical ethics. It is a question of what is the best opportunity for the patient to have a viable, surviving heart. Animal tissue is less likely to work than human tissue, but human tissue is not always available.

"It's not an ethical issue, but the Baby Fae case has overtones that are semireligious. Symbolically, many people do not want to see animal tissue in a human. An orthodox Jew, for example, might refuse cardiac pig valves because they come from a pig. But that's a religious reaction, not an ethical reaction. We're seeing a semireligious reaction in this case.

"The Baby Fae case raises many questions. Did the California team have time to find a human infant heart? Does the team have the capability to do cross-species heart transplants with no greater risk than that posed by human transplants? It would have been best if they had had an infant human heart to transplant, but if they did not have time to find one and if the baboon heart were the therapy of last resort, it's hard to criticize them.

"There are many medical questions, too. As a pediatric cardiologist, I know that hypoplastic left ventricle syndrome is a deformation that makes the aorta artery about one-tenth the size of normal. I wonder how the surgeon was able to sew the baboon heart onto that tiny artery. It is this deformation, which is part of the anomaly, that makes the lesion so fatal. I assume that Baby Fae has not yet rejected the animal tissue because newborns' immune system is less well-developed than adults and there is a greater opportunity for the acceptance of foreign tissues.

"If this works in Baby Fae and if infants under one month can get heterografts and have them stick and work, then that's terrific and a real breakthrough. If it only works for two weeks to six months, that's not all bad, either. You're using the baboon heart to buy time to try to cross-match and find a human heart. Right now, all these kids are dying.

"It is very hard to find infant donor hearts. Since you only have about 1 ½ hours from the time an infant dies in, say, Chicago, to the time the deceased's heart must be transplanted in, say, California, it's unlikely we'll ever have a national organ transplantation pool. There'll never be a Chicago-to-California system; it will be limited to local and regional networks.

"But if this baboon heart works in Baby Fae, it will be a positive addition to medical practice."

Ray Gifford, MD, chairman of the AMA Council on Scientific Affairs, said, "It's OK to try an animal heart to save a dying baby. The only thing that bothers me are the published reports that no effort was made first to find a human heart. That bothers me. The AMA does not have a policy on xenograft transplants, but I imagine that we'll soon be developing one."

AMA advisory panel member William E. Braun, MD, is a specialist in transplantation immunology and nephrology at the Cleveland Clinic. He says, "Clearly, there is a lot that went right in this operation. For one thing, we have a living child.

"From what I can tell, the transplant was justified. It was not an impetuous move. It was one for which they had thoroughly prepared. It is true that they would have had a better chance of success had they been able to use a human heart, but they say they could not find one.

"The only ethical issue here is what's best for the infant and if the consent signed on behalf of the infant is truly an informed consent. This is an area where you sometimes need a second opinion, a chance to weigh other options. Once you get in a particular institution, you tend to see only the choices that the institution sees. So the ethical issue here is whether or not Baby Fae might have had a human heart. I don't know.

"But, as I say, they have a living child."

Loma Linda's Dr. Hinshaw has the final word.

"The medical center and the university are solidly behind Dr. Bailey," the surgeon said. "We have learned a lot from this procedure, and we will be sharing our information before we attempt a second heterograft. Baby Fae's parents are bearing up very well, though we're having to work hard to protect their confidentiality. We have never divulged Baby Fae's exact birth date because she was born about 50 miles from here and there are reporters who could track down the parents.

"But our No. 1 hope is that Baby Fae can permanently make it with the baboon heart. Our No. 2 hope is that the baboon heart will last until we can find a human heart.

"We're all holding our breath!"□

When I asked the experts if they thought the Baby Fae transplant was worth it, they answered, "Yes," "No," and "Maybe." A few days later, I flew to the Loma Linda U. Medical Center, San Bernardino, Calif., and talked to the scientists behind the headlines—surgeon Leonard Bailey, MD, and immunologist Sandra Nehlsen-Cannarella. On the day of the interviews, Baby Fae was 10 days old and thriving, and Drs. Bailey and Nehlsen-Cannarella were decidedly optimistic. They explained that the operation was not something they had dreamed up to shock the world, but that it had been preceded by painstaking research and done to help a dying baby.

THE IMMUNOLOGIST WHO OBSERVED the historic surgery recalls that the atmosphere in the OR was "quiet but electric. We had gotten the lab answer we needed to select the right baboon organ donor only that morning at 4 a.m. The baby was dying, and we were racing against time. Everybody's eyes were on the heart monitor."

The surgeon, who took the walnut-sized heart of the "right" baboon, a 7½-month-old female, and implanted it in a 12-day-old, 5-pound baby girl born three weeks premature, recalls:

"There was not one hitch in the operation. It went better than you could have dreamed."

The unique xenograft later would provoke a storm of controversy, but on the morning of Oct. 26, 1984, surgeon Leonard L. Bailey, MD, 41, immunologist Sandra Nehlsen-Cannarella, PhD, 43, and the entire surgical transplant team at California's Loma Linda U. Medical Center were concerned only with helping "Baby Fae," a newborn who by then was on "maximum support" and would have died within hours had the transplant not taken place.

Dr. Nehlsen-Cannarella says: "It was very tense in the OR. Our first goal, as in any heart transplant, was to have Baby Fae's heart start up. Our second was to get her out of the OR without any signs of the new heart being rejected.

"Everybody's eyes were on the heart monitor, and Baby Fae's new heart started to beat almost immediately. As the monitor began to beep and the EKG line began to rise, well, it was quite a sensation and extremely rewarding. There is no applause in the OR, but everybody had their fists clenched and their eyes glued to the monitor. We punched each other on the arm and said, 'It's going . . . it's going.'

"The actual transplant took only about an hour but, of course, Dr. Bailey had to continue to keep working. There was much more to do and I forget many of the details, but we all had an unspoken feeling of unity."

For Drs. Bailey and Nehlsen-Cannarella, the transplant that electrified the world and caused tiny Loma Linda U. to explode on the international medical scene culminated years of each of their dreams.

It was after a serendipity of events that the surgeon from a tiny California town and the immunologist from Montefiore Medical Center in the Bronx, N.Y., found each other only four months before the surgery. Dr. Nehlsen-Cannarella had not heard of Dr. Bailey until spring when she went jogging every morning with another Loma Linda physician while she was in China at a medical seminar.

"I came out to California in June, 1984," Dr. Nehlsen-Cannarella recalls, "as a consultant to Dr. Bailey's team to see if they had covered all their bases, to help determine if a newborn xenograft were feasible. Dr. Bailey and I began to collaboratively work together—rather ferociously, I might add—and I spent almost every waking hour on the project. I came to California believing such a transplant was possible and after a week of reviewing the clinical literature and reviewing Dr. Bailey's experiments with animals, I was *convinced* that it was more than feasible. It could be done."

Dr. Bailey, who preceded his controversial xenograft with seven years of painstaking research on animals, recalls a day back in 1975 "toward the end of my year in training in cardiovascular surgery at the Hospital for Sick Children, Toronto. There were always sick children at this hospital, of course, and it seemed like again and again we would be presented with newborns with hypoplastic left-heart syndrome (the birth defect that would have killed Baby Fae) and it was kind of a routine. The presiding doctor would say, 'Well, it's too bad, but we haven't had too much success treating these babies. I suppose we can try this and that, but . . .' As his voice trailed off, I can recall thinking, in fact, I opened my mouth and said, 'That baby needs a cardiac replacement and we should be looking to solve that problem.'

"Well, I was only 31 at the time and what did I know. This was the kind of naive dream you would expect from a young surgeon piping up to his mentors. I don't think it had much impact upon them, but I know that my thought that day has helped keep me alive over the years. The under-developed left-heart syndrome kills one of every four children who die within one week of birth. I wanted to do something about these cases."

Now, nine years later, he quietly says, "The bottom line, believe it or not, is that this xenograft may work. I have always believed it would work, or I would not have attempted it, so in that respect my attitude has not changed. There was always therapeutic intent. My dilemma has been educating the university and the medical profession. I do not have the time—and there is no need—to educate the world. But I think that Baby Fae is proving that we're in for some interesting revelations.

"I think that we're onto something important!"

Indeed, the two attribute their initial success to sophisticated tissue-typing protocols that enabled them to select the baboon to whose tissues Baby Fae demonstrated the least reactivity—a mixed lymphocyte reactivity culture. "For the first time," Dr. Bailey says, "it appears possible to do a xenograft not by random chance but with science aforethought." Baby Fae's transplant was preceded by six days of meticulously testing her tissue reactivity against that of six baboons and human controls. Implicit in Baby Fae's thriving is the surgeon's and immunologist's belief that for many newborns with hypoplastic left-heart syndrome, a baboon heart not only may be justifiable, it actually may be *preferable* to a human heart.

The man who signed his name to Dr. Bailey's medical degree is David B. Hinshaw, MD, 60, a former dean of the Loma Linda U. Medical School. As the medical center's "old-timer," Dr. Hinshaw says he is proud of and affectionate toward his younger colleague and, as the university representative to the news media, he has supported the controversial surgery solidly. In tempering optimism about the procedure, he told *AMN*, "Well, of course, one has to remember the old adage about surgery: 'Beware of the surgeon with only one case.' The Baby Fae case means a lot, but what does it mean? You can't be sure, not yet."

At Loma Linda, the medical professionals still were taking it a day at a time with Baby Fae. With the infant scheduled to stop intensive care within 12 days postop and then to be converted from intravenous to oral cyclosporine to suppress her underdeveloped immune system, and with the next press conference scheduled to include photos and film footage of a healthy baby, the mood was decidedly upbeat.

On Monday, Nov. 5—day No. 10 with the new heart for a thriving Baby Fae—Drs. Bailey and Nehlsen-Cannarella gave to *AMN* the only interviews they allowed regarding the historic procedure. The surgeon in his scrub suit, taking a hasty breakfast of bagels and cream cheese in the Loma Linda U. Medical Center surgical administrative offices, and, later, the immunologist, breaking away from her test tubes for a taco lunch and interview at the San Bernardino Blood Banking Center, reflect upon their remarkable patient. Officially, they are "guardedly optimistic." Between the lines, however, they indicate astonishment at a historic transplantation that as of the interviews had proceeded without complication.

Here then, for the first time, is the story of the surgeon and immunologist who gambled on the first xenograft ever performed on a newborn.

While Dr. Bailey was taking a holiday with his two sons in San Francisco last month, the young parents of Baby Fae were at their California home agonizing over what to do about their dying newborn. On Oct. 15, her second day of life, Baby Fae had been diagnosed at Loma Linda as having the incurable hypoplastic left-heart syndrome, in which the left ventricle is useless as a pump.

"It's an easy diagnosis to make," he explains, "and she was only hospitalized overnight. Her parents were given a choice—they could let the child die in the hospital or they could take her home to die.

"A pediatric cardiologist made the diagnosis, but, coincidentally, it was raining in San Francisco and I returned home early. The cardiologist was not sure if we were prepared to move yet on our xenografts, but she alerted me that Baby Fae might be a possible candidate.

"Well, again coincidentally, the university's Institutional Review Board had only the week before made the final decision to proceed. We were prepared to move when a desperate situation presented itself. Baby

Fae's parents were notified that one final possibility existed for their child. They were told to think it over and to readmit the child if they were interested.

"Well, I know they went through some difficult moments, but I think that they were awestruck that their child might still have a possibility to live. This has been an awesome emotional experience for all of us, but mostly for Baby Fae's parents," Dr. Bailey relates. "On Oct. 19 at 11:30 p.m., the parents readmitted Baby Fae to the medical center. All we did was put her in a bed. Her parents had not yet agreed to the transplant.

"Apparently, the parents had spent three or four hours in debate at home [before readmitting the baby] and, now, from midnight until well into the next morning, I spent hours talking to them very candidly and very frankly. While Baby Fae was resting in bed, I showed them a film and gave them a slide show, explaining our research and our belief why a baboon heart might work.

"It was 5 a.m. the next morning before they agreed to a workup on Baby Fae, who was desperately ill. It was only then that we began to treat Baby Fae and begin her six-day immunological workup. I called Dr. Nehlsen-Cannarella in New York and she was on the next plane. Dr. Nehlsen-Cannarella and I had agreed that the key to the success of a xenograft would be a full immunological workup—the mixed lymphocyte reactivity culture—which requires six days. Baby Fae was dying, but we were determined that we would not be rushed in obtaining this critical piece of the puzzle, in selecting which baboon should provide the donor heart. By the time we got the answer at 4 a.m. on Oct. 26, Baby Fae's 12th day of life, she was on maximum support and near death. The lab results came just in the nick of time."

Dr. Nehlsen-Cannarella, picks up the narrative. "Our hypothesis," she says, "is that a newborn can, with a combination of its under-developed immune system and the aid of the anti-suppressive drug, cyclosporine, accept the heart of a baboon—if we can find one with tissue of high enough comparability.

"We used human reagents and mixed Baby Fae's lymphocytes into culture with four other broad groups of lymphocytes—her own, her parents and relatives, those of strangers, including myself and several other lab workers, and those of the six baboons we had selected from our outbred colony. We wanted to see how Baby Fae's tissues would react to the other tissues, whether Baby Fae's tissues would 'see' the other tissues as herself or as foreign tissue that must be attacked and, if so, to what degree. We can specifically measure these responses," she explains.

"The control, of course, was Baby Fae reacting against herself and this was negative. She reacted weakly to [the tissues from] her parents and relatives, but very strongly to [those of] myself and the other lab workers. She also reacted strongly and attacked tissues from three of the baboons. But, amazingly, she had weak reactions to three of the baboons, and her reaction against one baboon was very, very weak.

"In fact, her lymphocyte reactivity to this one baboon was very weak, only slightly less so than her reactivity to her own parents. That is the baboon we selected. The comparability of this baboon's tissues to the tissues of Baby Fae was very, very close to the comparability between the tissues of Baby Fae and her parents. Since Baby Fae's tissues had reacted selectively against all the other baboons' tissues, we knew we were not working with an across-the-board antispecies reaction. A weak reaction was what we were looking for and since she had reacted strongly to some of the baboons and to our control group of lab workers, we knew that we were not simply seeing a weak reaction to all the tissues.

"I got the final lab counts at 4 a.m. Oct. 26, and, interestingly," Dr. Nehlsen-Cannarella recalls, "the baboon we selected out as the best donor was the one Dr. Bailey had thought all along would be the best candidate. Baby Fae was dying and I'm sure that if the answer had not come through when it did, Dr. Bailey would have had to do something anyway. We were very fortunate. Hours later, we started the surgery.

"Now, it's true that many humans have a preformed antibody against baboon tissue, but our tests of Baby Fae showed that she did not have this antibody. Had she demonstrated this antibody, the transplant would never have taken place. No transplant team would ever knowingly attempt a xenograft upon a human with a preformed antibody. Our data are very small, but it appears that 30% or less of the human population—perhaps, much less—do not have this preformed antibody against baboons."

"One of every two humans has a preformed antibody against tissue from "another human," Dr. Bailey elaborates, and this helps explain why so many cadaverorgan transplants may not work. There often is not enough time to do a thorough immunological workup. It also helps explain why the xenografts of a generation ago were often not successful. The surgeons were shooting in the dark on the comparability of the tissues."

"We do not use the term 'histocompatibility,'" Dr. Nehlsen-Cannarella adds, "because it is ludicrous to think that baboon tissue and human tissue is 'compatible,' but we found a high enough degree of 'comparability'—a degree higher than found in some of the human tissue—to justify the transplant."

Dr. Bailey continues: "As each day passed, we kept the parents informed of how the different pieces of the puzzle were coming together. We told them that at a certain point, they would have to commit to the transplant. The discussions were very full and very frank. The parents were going through quite a metamorphosis. I explained to them the corrective surgical procedure pioneered by my friend, Dr. William Norwood, at Philadelphia's Children's Hospital. In my hands, the Norwood operation has been disappointing, but I tried to be objective—even supportive—of the procedure. The parents, however, were not interested in palliation, which is all I believe the Norwood operation can offer. Incidentally, I have been in touch with Dr. Norwood and he has no misperceptions about this.

"By Oct. 24, we were ready to pre-treat Fae with cyclosporine, and I would not take this extreme step unless her parents agreed to the transplant," he continues. "That day, they signed our informed consent form, which I believe is a document that reads well and states what it has to state. They signed it once, mulled things over, and, as required by our Institutional Review Board, signed it a second time the next day. It was Thursday, and we began cyclosporine and continued to work Fae up for surgery. By late Thursday night, she was on maximum support and I was having trouble keeping her alive.

"We were sticking to our guns on not rushing the mixed lymphocyte reactivity culture—which was the missing piece in the puzzle—and Friday morning we got our answer. By 5 a.m., we had selected our baboon and Baby Fae was wheeled into the OR.

"Open-heart surgery on an adult is technically not awfully awesome, but for newborns it's a slightly different ball game. Baby Fae had the most severe form of underdeveloped left-heart syndrome, with the aorta arteries very, very tiny, and I had to transplant not only the baboon's heart but its arteries as well. My experience in the lab with newborn goats and juvenile primates proved quite helpful.

"The operation went better than I could have dreamed," Dr. Bailey says, "and I have to thank my colleagues and the institute for that. I lead a luxurious life in the respect that all that is required of me is to think about and treat heart disease among newborns. Three years ago, I dropped the adult side of my practice and, today, my interest, experience, and commitment is to cardiac disease among children. I don't have to worry about the adult with coronary artery disease or the man upstairs with lung cancer. My colleagues do all that."

Ten days after the transplant Dr. Bailey was making plans to keep Baby Fae in her private ICU room, "but to make the intensive care less intensive. We hope to convert her to oral cyclosporine and within a few days all invasive procedures should be halted.

"Baby Fae is a very lusty, vigorous little girl who can scream and squawk with the best of them. She has for days had pulmonary edema and we have had to suck out mucus plugs, but once she starts to cough more her lungs will begin to straighten out and act normal.

"I spent that first night sleeping on a cot right next to her room. But that was only because she is so unique. I still see her several times a day, but every day that she continues to improve the odds become more and more in her favor.

"Yes, I really believe that she will celebrate more than one birthday with her new heart," he predicts. "We're optimistic that within three months, she will be able to go home. Of course, home will be in the immediate proximity. I think it's best to be overcautious for awhile and I will be monitoring her on a weekly basis.

"But for now it's still day to day. Her parents are delighted that something could be done.

"Our worst fear and the worst scenario for Baby Fae was that she would have displayed an uncontrollable rejection of the baboon heart. We had nightmares about that."

Some surgeons had supported the xenograft as a temporizing measure that might "buy time" for a transplant patient until a human organ could be found, but Dr. Bailey is more optimistic about the xenograft.

A question is asked, but the surgeon interrupts. Visibly brightening, he smiles and says, "Let me tell you about the best scenario. In the best scenario, Baby Fae will celebrate her 21st birthday without the need for further surgery. That possibility exists."

In the 10 days since Baby Fae exploded upon the world, the fascination of the news media and public has alternated with the interest, confusion, and criticism of the medical profession. The three members of the Loma Linda team took time to answer some of the questions regarding these reactions.

The potential availability of a human donor heart is "a moot issue" to Dr. Bailey, who says: "The fact is that because of the problematical nature of determining the 'brain death' of newborns (under 30 days of age and, in Dr. Bailey's first protocol, under seven days), the odds of a size-matched infant heart are very, very minuscule. And I have seen too many sick babies who looked very, very awful—but who survived to do quite well—to want to be involved in trying to harvest infant hearts. You can have a flat EEG on a newborn and, yet, the baby will survive. Beyond that, parents do not want to immediately separate from their newborn, even if the CT scan looks bad.

"We were not searching for a human heart. We were out to enter the whole new area of transplanting tissue-matched baboon hearts into new-borns who are supported with anti-suppressive drugs. I suppose that we could have used a human heart that was outsized and that was not tissue-matched, and that would have pacified some people, but it would have been very poor science," he continues. "On the other hand, I suppose my belief that there are no newborn hearts available for transplantation is more opinion than data or science, but it is scientific to acknowledge that the whole area of determining brain death of newborns is very problemat-ical.

"As for this flap with Dr. Terasaki (Paul Terasaki, Ph.D, director of the Southern California Regional Organ Procurement Agency and the man who said an infant heart was potentially available the day of Baby Fae's xenograft), well, Paul simply had the cart before the horse. I believe that Paul's intentions were good, but the human infant heart—became available only *after* we had completed the transplant, not before.

"If Baby Fae were to require another transplant, we would take the best donor organ available, whether human or baboon. That may sound a little harsh around the edges, but that's the way it is. If someone wants to keep grinding the axe about the potential availability for transplantation of newborn human hearts, I suppose that they can, but in my humble opinion the doubtful nature of being able to determine brain death in newborns makes this doubtful. It is a challenge to the organ-procurement agencies," Dr. Bailey asserts.

"Our colony of baboons are among the cleanest, purest strain of donors known to man. They are tested for absence of viruses, parasites, tuberculosis, toxoplasmosis, and given EKGs and lung scans to assure their health. We can tissue-type our baboons for comparativity to a potential human recipient more thoroughly than we can tissue-type most human donors. That's because we have more time. For newborns, the heart of a baboon may well prove to be the organ of choice, even if certain human hearts are available.

"And as for the animal lovers who picket our campus, well, theirs is a sensitivity born of a luxurious society. People in Southern California have it so good that they can afford to worry about this type of issue. I have been in China and third-world countries doing open-heart surgery and these types of issues are not an issue. When it gets down to a human living or dying, there shouldn't be any question. I respect the animal lovers' right to protest, but when they get careless and begin to splash paint upon laboratory doors, I believe their cause becomes a little compromised.

"Some of our critics say that the xenograft barrier is absolute. Well, they ask for my data, where is their data?," he asks. "By late 1983, I was getting such good data on the comparativity of cross-species transplants between goats and sheep that I knew that it was too good not to be partially true. We have extensive data on the underdevelopment of newborns' immune system, and we have relied heavily here on the research of others.

"Our major research contributions were to tissue-type the baboons and select out one to whom the recipient had the least reactivity and to monitor the optimal level of cyclosporine that a newborn can take without crowding her kidney function and other vital organs. I believe that Loma Linda has the original data base in this area. I have found that, with animals, massive doses of cyclosporine can be used without inducing toxicity, except for gastrointestinal problems. Newborns like Baby Fae can tolerate more cyclosporine than adults, and our monitoring of virtually every parameter of Baby Fae that can be monitored indicates no sign of toxicity from the anti-suppressive drugs. In addition to the cyclosporine, which we are keeping at as low a dosage as possible, we have given her two boluses of steroids and will give her a third today.

"I believe that science must develop hand in hand with ethics, and that's because ethics is a human invention. From the start of this formal project 14 months ago, we have clearly insisted upon a therapeutic intent. This is not simply experimentation for experimentation. We believe we are helping the newborn," Dr. Bailey asserts.

"I presented the research case for Baby Fae (titled "Orthotopic cardiac xenografting in the newborn") last June at the meeting of the Western Thoracic Surgical Assn. in Hawaii, and I'm told that it will be published in an issue of the *Journal of Thoracic Surgery*. As time allows, I will be making formal oral presentations to peer groups on the Baby Fae case. As for educating the global population, I do not have the time.

"This is a new frontier, and several of my European colleagues called me to discuss the case before they consented to interviews with the news media. Some of my American colleagues did, but many did not. I wish they had given me this courtesy because it would have made their commentary much more informed.

"You know, back in 1964, in desperation, Jim Hardy transplanted the heart of an ape into a 68-year-old man who died within hours," Dr. Bailey muses. "This is a fascinating story and I've always believed that Dr. Hardy (from the U. of Mississippi Medical Center and a former president of the American College of Surgeons) did exactly the right thing. He had no way of tissue-typing the ape, and he did not have cyclosporine and, yet, he took the gamble to try to save a human life. He's always been my silent champion—oh, he doesn't know me—but he's an idol of mine because he followed through and did what he should have done."

The surgeon adds: "I would say this to the medical profession:

"You can be assured that we did our homework, that we put as much thought and as much science as we could find into this effort, that this is a passionate project intended to help newborns with heart disease, and, most emphatically, that we would not have proceeded had we not believed there was a therapeutic intent and the strong possibility of a therapeutic benefit."

His colleague from across the country, Dr. Nehlsen-Cannarella, adds: "Physicians who are not involved in transplant surgery often do not understand the agony of patients who must wait days, months, and years for the availability of a lifesaving donor organ. And they do not understand the agony of a surgeon like Dr. Bailey, who daily must confront the parents of infants born with heart disease and must tell them there is no hope.

"For the next few months, I will be catching a lot of planes between here and New York. My husband (a photographer) is very supportive and very happy for me. This is the culmination of my dreams that go back to 1964–65 when I began as a nurse at Peter Bent Brigham Hospital in Boston. I was enthralled by the early work in transplant surgery and it led me to a PhD in immunology (from London's National Institute of Medical Research at Mill Hill, under the tutelage of Nobel-prize winning medical scientist Peter B. Medawar, who did his work in tolerance among human transplant recipients).

"It's been a long road, but I believe this: "We may have a new message for those parents. We have found a hope."

Dr. Bailey's mentor, Dr. Hinshaw, concludes this about the controversy over whether Baby Fae's parents truly gave "informed consent":

"Our informed consent procedure for Baby Fae is a specially designed form that is very detailed, that covers all the possible options, and that we feel is adequate and appropriate, solid, and valid. It is university property because, obviously, we cannot have this type of thing dissected in the news media. But many attorneys looked at this form, and we feel very comfortable that Baby Fae's parents knew exactly what they were doing.

"We're hoping that the National Institutes of Health (NIH) will review this case and appraise our consent form for the public. We welcome such a review."

(Charles McCarthy, MD, director of NIH's office of protection from research risks, called *AMN* Nov. 7 to address earlier news reports that the NIH would review the Baby Fae transplant, "particularly the question of whether a human heart was available and whether that option was properly considered." Those reports were in error, Dr. McCarthy told *AMN*, adding, "It is not NIH policy to investigate research work performed without federal funds, unless we receive a formal complaint. We have heard no complaints about the 'Baby Fae' case." He added, however, that because of the heavy publicity, the NIH might investigate if directed to do so by Congress or the NIH's parent body, the Dept. of Health and Human Services. Asked if the NIH would respond to an invitation from Loma Linda to investigate, he responded: "We would have to consider it").

The physician in the news, Dr. Bailey, a Seventh-Day Adventist who did almost all his medical training at the church-supported Loma Linda U. is philosophical. "I am not reluctant," he said, "to see Loma Linda (Spanish for "beautiful hill") thrust into the news. But I can assure my colleagues that there is no attempt here for self-publicity or self-glorifica-tion. As for the merits of our medical center, well, it has an international reputation in perinatology and is the leading pediatric ICU referral center in the state. Stanford was not known for its heart transplant until Dr. (Norman) Shumway began his work. Loma Linda is dedicated to the health professions and we take our motto—'To make man whole'—very seriously.

"We think we're onto something big. It's amazing, but Baby Fae (the name "has significance to her parents," the surgeon says), is doing fine. She may live for quite a while, just the way she is."□

Sadly, the optimism of the Loma Linda team was to prove misplaced; Baby Fae died 10 days after this interview was conducted. One year later, Dr. Bailey told me that a detailed autopsy, published exclusively in *The Journal of the AMA,* disclosed a "complicated, unclear picture." Dr. Bailey attributed the failure to an ABO blood mismatch; Dr. Nehlsen-Cannarella to anti-species antibodies produced by Baby Fae. Several leading transplant surgeons have expressed the opinion that the barrier against cross-species transplants is absolute, but Dr. Bailey counters, "Nothing in medicine is absolute. If medicine teaches us anything, it teaches us that." The surgeon pleaded to his colleagues and the press for patience and emphasized that he will dare to try again.

Laetrile manufacturer Andrew
McNaughton.

Three-year-old Chad Green and family.

Photos (unless otherwise credited) by Dennis L. Breo.

Convicted murderer Jeffrey
MacDonald.

"Death Angel" Jani Adams.

Donald R. Mills, MD, at Dyke Bridge, Chappaquiddick.

"Baby-by-proxy" and her family.

Charles Modica, Chancellor, St. George's University School of Medicine.

Basking student, St. George's University.

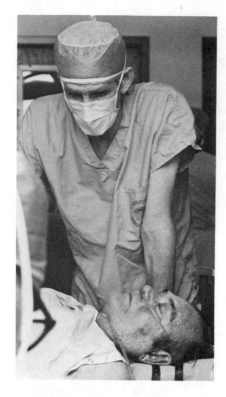

In surgery: Barney C. Clark, artificial heart recipient, and surgeon William C. DeVries.

Barney Clark and physical therapist.

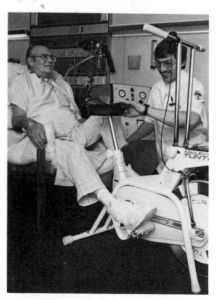

Exercise.

Photos this page by Brad Nelson, U of U Medical Center.

Surgeon William C. DeVries, MD.

Leonard Bailey, MD, Baby Fae's pioneering surgeon.

Immunologist Sandra Nehlsen-Cannarella, PhD: "There is no applause in the OR, but. . . . We punched each other on the arm and said, 'It's going. . . .'"

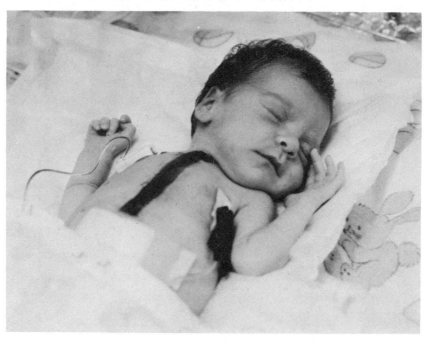

Baby Fae recuperates in the pediatric ICU.   Photo: Loma Linda U.

3. Personal Quests

DOCTORS ARE a remarkable lot.

Glamorous to the outside world, theirs is a world marked by the grim realities of dying, death—and, often, the inability to do anything about it. Most work hard and think hard—products of an educational system that puts them through an extended "boot camp" and that puts a premium on self-reliance.

Doctors, in fact, may very well be the real cowboys, the last of our rugged individualists. They are trained to think for themselves and to act according to their consciences.

Small wonder, then, that so many end up doing unusual things:

Richard Raskind, one of the world's best eye surgeons, became Renee Richards, the world's most controversial transsexual tennis player. Story Musgrave, a physician with five advanced degrees, opted for a career flying in space. Roman Vishniac used a hidden camera and risked his life to record the memories of a "vanished world," that of World War II's Eastern European Jews. John Rock set out to find a way around infertility and ended up changing the world by discovering a way to prevent pregnancy, "The Pill." George Sheehan grew bored reading electrocardiagrams and launched a revolution—running. Walker Percy forsook medicine to diagnose society by writing novels.

Mort Copenhaver built—by hand—a castle atop a mountain; Chris Chandler climbed the world's highest mountain, Mount Everest; Alex Comfort achieved fame with "the Joy of Sex," but remained at heart a gerontologist, seeking improved ways to care for the elderly; and Jim Sammons turned the AMA from a paper tiger into the world's most powerful medical organization.

Their stories, and others, follow. They are stories about courage—and about dreams.

Papa's Son

Gregory Hemingway

I had been attending an AMA seminar on medical negotiations in San Francisco, a rather boring affair, when the idea hit me to try to arrange an interview with Dr. Gregory Hemingway, the youngest son of novelist Ernest Hemingway, and, at this point in time, a rural physician in tiny Fort Benton, Mont. Dr. Hemingway had just written his account of "Father knows best," called *Papa: A Personal Memoir*.

He was not too excited about the idea, pleading a busy medical practice, but he agreed that if I cared enough to come out to see him, he would somehow find time to see me.

That evening I flew into Great Falls, Mont., rented a car, and made the short drive to Fort Benton, arriving around 8 p.m. My hotel was the once-proud Grand Union, built in 1865 and named in commemoration of the end of the civil war. It was right down the block from a Tastee-Freeze, where the kids were gathered, and across the street from a saloon, where the adults were gathered. Dr. Hemingway's medical clinic was located between the saloon and the Tastee-Freeze.

Fearlessly, I strode into the cowboy bar, sporting my San Francisco outfit: sunglasses, seafoam green silk suit, striped shirt, paisley tie, tangerine suede shoes (this, after all, was the 1970s). A long line of cowboys, in plaid shirts, jeans, and boots (with spurs), all drinking Pabst Blue Ribbon in cans, looked me up and down. The bartender, a roly-poly woman approximately five-by-five, rolled over in my direction:

"Podner, you're not from these parts?"

"No," I conceded, "I'm with the American Medical Association in Chicago and I'm here to see Dr. Hemingway." I resisted my impulse to order my usual kir on the rocks and asked for, what else, a can of PBR. I figured that dropping the Hemingway name was enough to justify my presence in the bar.

She brought the beer, adding, "Well, when you find the SOB, tell him to stay out of here. He's caused his last ruckus in my bar."

I finished my beer quickly and adjourned for the night. Dr. Hemingway, it seemed, had a bit of his father's brawling nature.

I would have to spend the entire next day walking the three streets of Fort Benton and the nearby banks of the Missouri River, while Dr. Hemingway held office hours. He did not want a visitor from the AMA to watch him practice medicine. By 4 p.m. or so, though, he became a gracious host, explaining for me his move from Manhattan to Montana and the nature of rural medicine. He, in fact, discussed everything with great ease, except the reason that had brought me—his relationship with the greatest writer of the 20th Century, his father, Papa Hemingway.

Gregory Hemingway was still having trouble coming to terms with this special relationship. I had meant to push for drinks that evening (though at a different bar!), perhaps, even dinner. But Gregory Hemingway declined; he was in no mood to prolong his painful memories.

"I never got over a sense of responsibility for my father's death, and the recollection of it sometimes made me act in strange ways."

—Gregory Hemingway, MD, in *Papa, A Personal Memoir*

EYES CLOSED, HANDS shadowing his face, Gregory Hemingway, MD, sat in a park in Fort Benton, Mont., in September 1976, and tried to bring it all back.

The days with his father in Key West, Bimini, Sun Valley, and Havana, the experiences he so movingly evokes in his recent book. Ernest Hemingway, the Nobel Prize-winning author who influenced a generation, still casts a spell over his youngest son.

"For a child who often considered himself neglected," Dr. Hemingway said, "I've had all the attention I'll ever need while traveling the country promoting this book. God, I'm getting so tired of it.

"It was easiest on the radio talk shows, when I could close my eyes and concentrate. Almost every interviewer said, "Well, that was a good one.'

"But television was something else. I was overwhelmed by the process: all those cameras, all those technicians, and the smooth moderators. And on prime time, you only get a few minutes, and I'd be cut off in the middle of an answer.

"You know, I recently saw a dermatologist on a TV talk show discussing the effects of sunlight on the skin. He was so smooth. How nice it would be if I could have discussed something I know like medicine.

"But a father-son relationship, that's something else.

"I wrote the book to show my father's human and loving side. He wasn't always an SOB, and I hope readers enjoy him as much in his youth as I did."

"The Carlos Baker biography of my father was so detailed, piling incident upon incident, that it makes his life seem almost dull. It doesn't really capture the spirit of the man. And the A. E. Hotchner biography covered only his later years when he was starting to decline.

"Baker never knew my father; Hotchner knew him at the wrong time. I knew him and loved him."

Intense, restless, Dr. Hemingway signals it is time to move on. A few quick strides and he has traversed the tiny park that marks the site of the old fort on the Missouri River. Dr. Hemingway's office, the Fort Benton Health Clinic, is in the middle of the old Main Street facing the river. Signs flanking his office door promote a tractor pull at the upcoming Chouteau County Fair and classes in transcendental meditation.

He came to Fort Benton, population 2,000, last summer, and as one of only two physicians, carries on a busy general practice. Royalties from the book helped finance his move from New York City.

"I was doing industrial medicine," he said, "for big companies like General Motors and Exxon. It's not very demanding work. Annual physicals and the like. Anything difficult at all is referred.

"I came here to get out of the city, get out of a rut, and take on a more demanding assignment."

His move to Montana was influenced, Dr. Hemingway said, by having his two brothers nearby. His older brother, Patrick, a former African big-game hunter with a Harvard degree in classics, lives in Bozeman, Mont. His older half-brother, Jack, is the fish-and-game commissioner in Ketchum, Idaho, where Ernest Hemingway died.

There is irony in the fact that all three Hemingway sons are now back in the West, in the Hemingway country of big sky, big game, big fish, all the things Papa loved and wrote about.

But there is also loneliness.

Dr. Hemingway's wife and their three children have just left Fort Benton after a short visit. (He has four other children by his first wife.)

"When my wife was here, however briefly," he said, "things all made sense." Providing medical care for children, studying to deliver children into the world, being with my family, enjoying the land. When you get right down to it, that's all any of us really have.

"I think with a good stereo, some books, and my family, I could be very content here. It would make up for the lack of cultural activities, educational opportunities, intellectual stimulation. I'm sure I can make three or four really good friends here and that's all you're usually going to have anywhere.

"But without my family, I'm going up the wall."

Dr. Hemingway's wife, Valerie, and the children have returned to New York. "I hope they can return for the Christmas holidays," he says. "I hope."

The practice is going nicely.

"People here are healthy," he says. "I've yet to prescribe a tranquilizer. That was half my business in New York. You see very few heart problems. The National Health Service Corps physician I replaced saw only one tumor in two years. Might have been worth an epidemiological study. The other physician in town hasn't had one malpractice suit in 15 years.

"Mostly it's trauma you see. People kicked by horses. Auto accidents. Although the roads are excellent, the landscape can be so flat, it has a hypnotic effect."

He moves to the banks of the Missouri, where river boats unloaded during the town's heyday in the late 19th Century. Dr. Hemingway's thoughts ramble.

"Don't be too hard on industrial medicine," he says. "I may be back in New York doing it before long. Then again, I may specialize in emergency medicine back in the city."

For the moment, however, he is reading late at night about obstetrics-gynecology, and plans to take some refresher training at the hospital in nearby Great Falls. "It should come back quickly," he says.

Dr. Hemingway started medical school late, enrolling at 29. He was graduated in 1964 from the U. of Miami.

His studies were delayed, as he describes in his book, by some ugly memories.

His father blamed him for the death of his mother, Ernest Hemingway's second wife, Pauline, after a family quarrel over a mind-stimulating drug that Gregory had taken. The discussion took place at Hemingway's farm in Cuba. Gregory was never to see his father again.

Gregory stumbled through the next seven years with a "blurred focus," he recalls, spending much of the time killing elephants in Africa.

When he returned to resume his presumed studies, he obtained his mother's autopsy report. It convinced him that it was his father's brutal telephone conversation with his mother eight hours before her death—and not the drug incident—that triggered the fatal secretions of her adrenal gland tumor and led to pheochromocytoma.

Gregory so wrote his father and, as the book notes, "According to a person who was with him in Havana when he received my letter, he raged at first and then walked around the house in silence for the rest of the day.

"About three months later, his first noticeable symptoms of paranoia began, with the worries about the FBI chasing him for income tax evasion. Or was it the great FIB, finally coming home to roost?"

Gregory remarks in the book, "I hope that this whole seemingly fatal time sequence was coincidental . . . God knows I would never have written my father if I had thought it would upset him as much as it did. There's a tremendous difference between wanting to kill someone in your unconscious and actually committing the deed. It is a difference that makes us human."

By the time of his father's funeral, Gregory was starting to pull himself together. "I had the damndest feeling that now I would really become a doctor," he wrote.

This day, Dr. Hemingway, 45, turns his thoughts to writing and to some of his father's Paris contemporaries, described in Hemingway's *Moveable Feast*.

"Scott Fitzgerald, God how the man could write," he says. "What a terrible life he led, but I consider *The Great Gatsby,* perhaps, the greatest book by an American in this century."

Dr. Hemingway gives high marks to *Moveable Feast,* except for "father's turning on Gertrude Stein." Ernest Hemingway's professed incredulity and shock at overhearing a conversation revealing Ms. Stein's lesbianism is unlikely, his son says.

"He was pretty shock-proof in those days."

Perhaps he will write another book, Dr. Hemingway says, "a non-fiction book about medical school. There hasn't been a real good book about this since Sinclair Lewis' *Arrowsmith.* Bill Nolen's book, *Making of a Surgeon,* was good, but only covered residency training."

Good writing is difficult, Dr. Hemingway adds. "In the end, I think that was what got my father. He was such a perfectionist. And to write four to five hours daily, and know it's no good. And once it was so easy."

Dr. Hemingway's prescence has not caused a great stir in Fort Benton.

"This is not a celebrity-conscious town," he says. "I'd say about four-fifths of the people here don't know I've written a book. A policeman came up to me at the hospital emergency room recently and said, 'Hemingway, oh yeah, you're the one whose relative was that newspaper reporter.' "

It's time for Dr. Hemingway to visit a patient at the hospital. It is not to be very pretty.

The patient's visitor is reading Jack London.

"Isn't his writing marvelous?" Dr. Hemingway asks. "You can almost feel the cold." The lady replies, "Being from Montana, I can really feel it."

The patient is dying.

"I want to die," he says. "There's no sense in hanging on like this. I seem to have just enough strength to keep from dying. When you get to the end, it's hard to want to keep going."

Dr. Hemingway can only ask if the pain killers are working. The patient says they are.

It is late. There are charts to be dictated, reading to be done. Is there time for dinner, a drink, perhaps?

Dr. Hemingway, distracted, considers. Then, "No, no, I'm really not good company with my mind on my wife and family. I'd better leave you now."

A listener wishes him well.

"Yes, yes," Dr. Hemingway says, "sometimes I think it will all work out. But the ability to carve out one's own destiny—I find myself believing it less and less."

A flashing smile, a quick handshake, and Gregory Hemingway is off. To make it through another night.□

Crusaders

Renee Richards

"Transsexualism" was hardly a household word until Dr. Richard Raskind decided to change his name (and sex) to that of Dr. Renee Richards, who in 1976 was petitioning to play tennis in the prestigious U.S. Open, woman's division. The prospect of a match between Dr. Richards and a prominent woman pro, perhaps Chrissie Evert, had provoked enormous controversy, and I had chased Dr. Richards across the country, from Manhattan to Newport Beach, Calif., where on this day, she was taking tennis lessons. She had agreed to an interview "to clarify what a transsexual is and is not."

For five hours or so, I taped an interview in which I attempted to understand both the physical and psychological dimensions of changing one's sex. It was a laborious interview and we both wore frowns on our faces. Toward the end, however, I reached for my Nikon and began to photograph the world's most famous transsexual. Suddenly, Dr. Richards, who had very matter-of-factly been describing the intricate details of her odyssey from man to woman, became very flustered.

"Oh, dear," she exclaimed. "We've been talking so seriously that I'm not going to look very feminine. It's hard to smile about some of this." Looking through my viewfinder at her strong sinewy arms, the rope-cord arms of a male athlete, I could appreciate her predicament. I stopped shooting, so that she could compose herself and apply makeup.

Since I play tennis myself (poorly), I had hoped to get a lesson or two, but I had to return to my hotel to write a story that would be sent by plane (with the film—which was never used) back to our Chicago offices that very night. Next time, I promised myself.

Next time would be six years later, after Dr. Richards had resigned as coach to the phenomenally successful Martina Navratilova to resume her medical career as an eye surgeon. I was her guest at the U.S. Open in Forest Hills, N.Y., and, this time, the interview was considerably more relaxed, concentrating on her medical career. She referred to the autobiography she was writing and confided that it would have one of publishing's greatest titles, "Second Serve." She still was not sure whether or not she was winning the game, but she liked the way she was playing.

I never did get my tennis lesson.

THE JOHN WAYNE TENNIS CLUB in Newport Beach, Calif., is a tasteful blend of tradition and today: whites only and art prints of the game's past, television consoles monitoring the court action, and the latest in instructional equipment.

And the club's best player, perhaps, is Renee Richards, MD, formerly Richard Raskind, MD, who provoked an uproar this summer when she unsuccessfully tried to enter the women's division of the U.S. Open tennis championships.

Next year, Dr. Richards says, "I'm sure I'll be invited to play the U.S. Open, but I'm going to turn my nose up at the tournament. I was very disappointed that I wasn't allowed to play this year."

Interviewed by *American Medical News*, Dr. Richards said she is taking a one-year leave of absence from her ophthalmology practice to hit the tennis tournament trail "and keep transsexualism in the news. I want people to know we're people, that we have feelings, that we have rights— like playing in tennis tournaments—and that we're not two-headed or psychotic or freaky."

"I've found the hard way," Dr. Richards said, "that people in sports or entertainment can have a public impact far greater than the normal person. I am a talented tennis player, and I tend to take advantage of this to enlighten people about transsexualism. I expect to be very visible during the next year."

Dr. Richards, 42, was leaving for La Costa, Calif., for two weeks of tennis training under Pancho Segura, who trained men's champion Jimmy Connors, among others.

Next year, she expects to win or place high in several of the major woman's championships, including the Australian, French, and Italian opens, and Wimbledon. Such a record, she believes, will bring her an invitation to the U.S. Open, which, ironically, is held at Forest Hills, N.Y., where the former Dick Raskind grew up into the epitome of male success.

"In the abstract," Dr. Richards told *AMN,* it might well have appeared that I had it all as Dick Raskind: big career, big income, big professional reputation, beautiful wife and son, considerable success as a tennis player. But I was miserable, I wanted to be a woman, had always wanted to be a woman."

By next spring, Dr. Richards plans to have published two books, one on strabismus, a field in which she has particular expertise, and the other describing her odyssey from man to woman. Both will be written, the autobiography with the aid of a professional writer, as she travels the world playing tournament tennis. And she will be giving interviews and making the talk shows to promote her views.

"I expect to win at tennis next year," Dr. Richards said, "because I'm in much better physical shape now than I was last month when I lost to another woman in the Tennis Week Open preceding Forest Hills, and, most importantly, because all the publicity pressure is starting to fade now. I'll never again have to go through what I did this summer."

Dr. Richards was always a star athlete as Dick Raskind.

"In high school," she recalls, "I was a star pitcher on the baseball team, good enough to attract attention from major league scouts. And I was a good end on the football team. I had great anticipation, hands like glue, and good eye-and-hand coordination. But I couldn't stand the physical contact, which is why I gave up wrestling, at which I also excelled."

Tennis was her real game, though, and as Dr. Richards remembers, "I was always captain of the tennis team: at Yale, in the Navy, during the Maccabiah Games (the Jewish olympics)."

"I was a very good tennis player as a man," Dr. Richards said, "but I certainly did not become a woman so that I could become the best woman player."

In 1973, Dr. Raskind was a finalist in the U.S. national finals for those 35-and-older. "I was the only one of the top 10 seeds who did not make his living from tennis," Dr. Richards recalls.

At that time too, she recalls, "I had been on female hormones for about eight years and looked pretty strange. Many people thought I had cancer or something and had to take the hormones as therapy."

Dr. Richards traces her quest for fulfillment as a woman.

"My mother was a Freudian psychiatrist," she said, "and when I was 16, my freshman year at Yale, I told her about my psychosexual difficulties.

"Well, Freudian interpretations were the vogue then, and she suggested analysis, which I started my senior year at Yale.

"When I entered medical school at Rochester, N.Y., I went into full-scale analysis. I was very innocent, very naive about transsexualism, but I learned that psychiatry had little to offer me and that this particular therapist had scarcely a clue as to what my problem was.

During my internship, I declared a moratorium on therapy, because of the rigors of the internship year. After completing it, however, I took 4½ years of therapy with a prominent New York psychiatrist, Robert Bak, MD. He thought I was a normal young man except for the compartmentalized, isolated crazy wish to be a woman.

"By this time, I was becoming increasingly anxious and dissatisfied with psychotherapy. I talked to Wardell Pomeroy, MD, a co-author of the

Kinsey Report, and he was disturbed by my lack of homosexual relationships. On a scale of zero to ten—homosexual to heterosexual—I was a
10 heterosexual.

"It was then that I started my odyssey toward becoming a woman by
seeking out Harry Benjamin, MD, the man who coined the term 'transsexual.'

"I later talked with Robert Laidlaw, MD, a psychiatrist at New York's
Roosevelt Hospital who, along with Dr. Benjamin, was the first to really
understand my predicament.

"And there were other therapeutic forays. I went to Europe and
sought out Paris showgirls who were transsexuals. I lived abroad as a
woman. I dated men. I talked to Christian Hamburg, MD, the physician
who looked after Christine Jorgensen. And, finally, I ended up at the
Casablanca clinic of Georges Borou in 1968, intending to have male-to-
female surgery. But as a medical doctor, the lack of standards there turned
me off. I pulled back and returned to the states.

"I tried Johns Hopkins in 1969 and was very frustrated. Johns
Hopkins had called a moratorium on transsexual operations at that time
and they held my case in abeyance."

"I don't mind saying that I think their attitude at that time stinks. I
was ready for surgery then and I think it's just as bad for Hopkins to hold
off on surgery that is indicated as it is to operate when it's not indicated.

"Because of all these disappointments—nine years of futile psychotherapy, the pullback at Casablanca, the reluctance of Johns Hopkins to
act on my case—I was very distraught. In the backlash, I married.

"I can recall going to Chicago once in 1969 on a cold, cold day to
visit a private hospital and having to be furtive, dressing one way on the
flight, another for the hospital interview, trying to sell them on my need,
seeing that they knew little about the problem; the hiding, the furtiveness
is painful.

"I gave up and got married in 1970 and fathered a son. Since the age
of 18, I had always been living with one girlfriend or another. They were
all aware of my dilemma, but thought they could take me out of it.

"However, since 1965 I had been on female hormones and looked a
little strange in men's clothing. In many ways, I looked then just as I do
now, except that I dressed as a man. Once, in 1969, I was visiting a state
park with a girlfriend and when I came out of the men's room, a state
trooper wanted to know, 'what the devil did I think I was doing.'

"I was married for four years, but by 1974 I knew I couldn't continue
as a man. I went back to Dr. Laidlaw and Dr. Benjamin, who was in his
80s by now. They decided, 'You know, Richards, the last thing you need

now is the screening program offered by a university gender identity clinic. You've had that ad nauseam. You need three things: skilled surgery, minimum red tape, and anonymity.'

"I was thinking of going to Stanford, but I found all three requirements right at home in New York. Three days later, my surgical reassignment was performed by Roberto Granato, MD, at a private hospital in Queens.

"God, the post-operative recovery was painful, unbelievably so. But I was happy, wonderfully happy that it was done. I'm not foolish to think I'm a total woman, like one with a uterus and ovaries, but I'm happy being 80% a woman, or 75%, or 25%. It's better than zero, and I'm as much of a woman as one who has had a hysterectomy.

"You know, some psychiatrists think that transsexualism is caused by a castration complex, that the cross-dressing is symbolically, ceremoniously acting out the fear so as to be relieved to find later that the male genitals are intact. Well, after I had my surgery (Aug. 4, 1975), I thought, God forbid, that that will be the case with me. That I'll miss my male genitals, break down, become psychotic.

"That certainly hasn't been the case. I don't regret for one moment becoming a woman. Except when I reach back for that extra power on a first serve and wish I still had Dick's strength.

"I've been very fortunate in terms of receiving support, my father's been super. My son adores me and I adore him. My ex-wife has been very understanding, as have my uncles and aunts.

"And I've received great support from the tennis friends I've made since relocating to Southern California this summer. I had made a lot of male friends, and it was great to be fussed over as a woman. When my story broke, I thought they might be humiliated or embarrassed, might turn against me.

"One friend in particular called my office right after the wire services reported I had won a woman's tennis tournament in La Jolla, Calif., although I had formerly been a man. I thought, "Well, here goes, I have to face the music.' But all he said was, 'Richards, can you play tennis at noon?' I said, 'Sure,' and that was that. The matter was never brought up.

"Other transsexuals aren't as fortunate; the loneliness, the social ostracism is terrible. I have a chance to improve their plight by enlightening the public—and the medical profession."

Dr. Richards says that she knows as much about transsexualism as anybody in the world.

"I am a physician," she says, "a transsexual. I researched everything about the condition to the nth degree. I began studying it 20 years ago when the phenomenon was barely understood, and I've met hundreds of transsexuals. Whenever a transsexual was passing through New York, Dr. Benjamin would suggest that I talk with him or her."

At the same time, she cautions that, "I'm a transsexual patient first and only a physician by happenstance. Whenever a patient tries to be his own physician, there's the risk both the patient and physician can be a fool.

"In 10 years of hormone therapy, I never once prescribed for myself. I just don't think that's intelligent."

With that caveat, she describes what a transsexual is—and is not—and what she thinks can cause a person to want to surgically change his or her sex.

Dr. Richards thinks a combination of prenatal disposition or vulnerability and a strong identification with her mother caused her transsexualism.

"If you expose a person to a potent dose of pneumococcus, he's going to contract pneumonia," she said. "But if you expose an entire community to the tuberculin bacillus, some will contract tuberculosis and some won't, depending on a number of circumstances. I think transsexualism is of multiple etiology.

"All children start out identifying with their mother, and most normal boys later re-identify with their fathers. In my case, I had a strong, domineering, loving, all-powerful mother.

"I was given a potent dose of exposure to this all-powerful figure and, many years later, here I am reborn in 1976 in my mother's image as a powerful, successful woman physician."

(Dr. Richards' mother, now dead, was a psychiatrist; her father is an orthopedic surgeon.)

Dr. Richards continues: "My case was compounded by having an older sister whose purposes were served by having me be viewed as a young girl. But the overwhelming influence was that of my mother, who dominated my early impressions. My sister merely aided and abetted the identification."

Noting that she thinks her mother, were she alive today, would agree "100%" with this interpretation of what caused Dr. Richards' transsexualism, Dr. Richards says, "This area of possible causation is largely untouched by current psychotherapy."

Dr. Richards also says that, "With apologies to my good friend Dr. Benjamin, who coined the term, 'transsexualism' is not a very good description of the condition, but, unfortunately, we don't have anything better."

Dr. Richards thinks of transsexualism as a spectrum ranging from "the pure transsexual at zero" to "the pure transvestite at 10." The pure transsexual, she said, wants his physique and psyche to harmonize; the true transvestite uses cross-dressing as an erotic turn-on and is almost always heterosexual or bi-sexual.

On such a scale, she rates herself as a three.

"I had always dressed as a woman from time to time," she said, "but it was seldom for erotic gratificiation. It was make-believe. I wanted to be a woman, and this was the only way I could pretend.".

Most male-to-female transsexuals, she said, follow one of two routes: "Either they are very effeminate boys who can't make it as males or they practice episodic transvestism." Dr. Richards, of course, was the latter.

Dr. Richards stresses that, "your garden-variety transvestite, however, is overwhelmingly heterosexual or bisexual and dressing as a woman is nothing but a turn-on. For the true transsexual, cross-dressing has little erotic gratification."

Dr. Richards believes transsexualism is an illness.

"Today, I feel so healthy physically, emotionally, psychologically," she says, "that to think I have a major illness is a bit mind-boggling, but in all honesty I have to admit that's a fair statement."

She continues, "anytime you have to undergo the extensive drug therapy I had and go through major surgery, you have to consider that an illness. Homosexuality was once considered an illness and, yet, homosexuals don't require drugs or surgery or even, necessarily, counseling.

Turning to predictions by some physicians that transsexuals will, after an initial period of elation, become depressed "by realizing they are not really women," Dr. Richards said, "this does not have to be so for two reasons.

"First, if an individual is successful as a man, as I was, then he has more to work with in being successful as a woman. Second, if one is fairly sophisticated you realize that you don't have to be totally a woman, or totally anything to be happy. Being 80% a woman is good enough for me. Wouldn't it be a dreary world if anyone were totally a man or totally a woman or totally anything."

For her part, Dr. Richards said she intends to be open about her past as a man.

"Frankly," she said, "I would be contemptuous of a man whom I had fooled about my past. I don't want to live as an ex-convict with my past walled off from me, having to bite my tongue every time I remember something about life as Richard Raskind. Why try to fool a man? I want a relationship with a man who understands everything about me, as I want to understand everything about him."

A successful transsexual, she said, must achieve "somatic compliance. In other words, a man who is six-feet-six, with an extremely hairy body, will, as you can imagine, make quite a man. Maybe a truck driver or a basketball player. But he can never be a successful transsexual. For him, the surgical reassignment alternative is out. Only drugs or psychotherapy can be used. Such people are tragic. God has played a dirty trick on them.

"I was lucky. I can pass as a woman, barely. I'm six-foot even and very broad-shouldered, but I'm relatively hairless, have a good complexion, an appealing face, and have always had soft manners."

Dr. Richards says she has a boyfriend, but "I'm not getting married tomorrow."

She has mixed feelings about the duration of her quest for womanhood. There are pluses and minuses, she said.

"I have many happy memories of my life as a man and I fathered a son whom I adore and who adores me. And the surgery is much better now. On the other hand, I endured 12 years of hormone treatments, 20 years or more of anguish over wanting to become a woman, and spent years as a pretty weird-looking man."

She is disappointed by the lack of progress medicine has made in treating transsexuals. Johns Hopkins, in particular, which Dr. Richards views as one of the world's leading institutions "has been mired in a morass of uncertainty, wasting what could be valuable therapeutic efforts in minutiae and moratoria."

However, she adds, "I except Dr. John Money from this judgment, as I think he has tried to be very progressive in understanding the condition."

She urges family physicians to learn the terminology, the subleties of the transsexual condition. The scope is small, she says—perhaps 10,000 American transsexuals in a population exceeding 200 million.

"The family physician will never miss the true transsexual," she said, "but he should be acquainted with the many medical conditions that can mimic or co-exist with transsexualism so as to refer patients for proper care."

"By the year 2000," she concludes, "we may have better treatment for the transsexual than surgery. But for now, it's the best we have.

"I am an expert in operating on the eye muscles to cure strabismus, but the real problem is in the head where the muscles of convergence are controlled. Someday, we may be able to cure cross-eyes without surgery, and similarly, someday we may be able to treat transsexuals without operating on the end point.

"But transsexualism must be caught early because once it progresses beyond a certain point, the game is over. We need more medical research, starting with the basics. You can't duplicate the workings of the human

mind in studies on animals, but you can use animals to study sex behavior, and we need to do more of this."

But Dr. Richards adds, "I've had my fill of transsexualism as a disease
entity. God knows my psyche has probably been probed more than any
other transsexual. I've done my thing now and I'm happy. The rest is for
someone whose thing is studying transsexualism as a disease entity. I've
paid my dues."

Dr. Richards will close her practice for a year. "Acceptance to a male
MD comes almost automatically," she noted. "As Renee, I had to prove
myself as a surgeon for the first few times, but then I was accepted as well
as Dick Raskind had been."

Dr. Richards is uncertain about how she will return to medicine.
Today, she is off to practice her tennis serve.□

HER MOTHER ALWAYS SAID that he was "born under a star," but for Renee
Richards, MD, the world's most celebrated transsexual, the luck always
has been good and bad.

This month, September, 1982, Dr. Richards returned for good to the
place where it all started, Forest Hills, N.Y., and swore off big-time
competitive tennis for a return to the other great passion of her life—
medicine. She says, "In the future, medicine will be my profession and
tennis my sport. I could have turned my sport into my profession, but I
guess I must believe in unconscious determinants—my mother was a
physician, my father is a physician, my sister is a physician, and I will be a
physician."

As a man, the former Dick Raskind grew up in Forest Hills, site of the
U.S. Tennis Open, into the epitome of male success: big career, big
income, big professional reputation as an eye surgeon specializing in
strabismus, beautiful wife and son, and considerable success as a tennis
player.

And as his mother, a psychiatrist, pointed out, whenever disaster
threatened—as it did in a head-on auto collision that broke Dick's jaw or
in an emergency landing when the plane he was piloting ran out of gas—
providence was there to watch over him.

The luck ran out, however, when Dick Raskind finally came to terms
with his transsexualism.

In 1976, Dr. Richards was denied permission to enter the U.S. Open
as a woman, and the controversy that has followed her ever since began.

Six years later, all that is behind her. This day in the players' lounge of
the 1982 U.S. Open at Flushing Meadow, a deep lob from the Forest Hills

home where Dr. Richards grew up ("I used to walk my dog right about where the main tennis stadium now stands"), Dr. Richards says:

"I've made my statement about transsexualism. I've paid my dues. Those who were listening heard what I had to say; those who weren't listening never will."

She is again embroiled in controversy. During the past year, the 48-year-old physician coached 26-year-old Martina Navratilova to one of the greatest years enjoyed by any athlete—a 76–1 singles record, including championships in the Australian, French, and U.S. Indoor Opens and the coveted Wimbledon (All-England) Championship. The game plan was for the physician-coach to stay with tennis' newest prodigy until she had won the 1982 U.S. Open and the 1982 Australian Open, completing tennis' fabled Grand Slam.

The game plan went out the window at Wimbledon when Dr. Richards, anxious to resume her medical practice, was snubbed and not invited to Navratilova's birthday party.

"That moved up my timetable," the physician recalls. "I quit. People think that I was ousted by Martina and her entourage (notably Navratilova's good friend, basketball star Nancy Lieberman), but that isn't the case. I had intended to resume my ophthalmology practice anyway, and the Wimbledon incident simply made me act sooner. I quit as Martina's coach. I was no longer in charge, so I had to quit."

On Sept. 8, Dr. Richards regretted her decision. That was the day Navratilova was upset by her doubles partner, Pam Shriver, and lost her chance at the Grand Slam. The next day, Dr. Richards told *AMN*, "I was in the stadium and saw Martina lose, and I felt very badly. I had a job to do and I let her down. All right, so she didn't invite me to her birthday party, so what? I was her coach and I should have stayed with her.

"She never should have lost. She was ahead 6–1, 5–4, and serving for the match. She never should have lost her serve. Yes, if I had been with her, I think she would have won."

A few minutes later, Gary Wadler, MD, the U.S. Open's internal medicine consultant (Dr. Richards is the ophthalmology consultant; both work under head physician Irving Glick, MD), stops by to confirm to Dr. Richards a rumor that has been sweeping Flushing Meadows—Navratilova was weakened during her matches by a toxoplasmosis infection picked up from a friend's cat.

Dr. Richards, the coach, tracks down her former student in the ladies' locker room: "All right, Martina, let me feel those swollen nodes. Why didn't you tell me?"

Navratilova: "I guess I just never thought of it. What are you doing here? Are you playing in the over-35s?"

Dr. Richards: "No, I'm through with playing competitive tennis."

Navratilova: "You know, Renee, I warmed up 50 minutes for Pam (Shriver). Maybe, I warmed up too much. I knew that if the match went three sets I was in trouble."

Dr. Richards: "Oh, Martina. You should have warmed up 15 minutes. And you should have taken her out 6–1, 6–4. But now, forget about it. If your goal is to be considered one of the all-time greats, forget about the U.S. Open and concentrate on winning the Australian. You only need five more major championships to be considered among the all-time greats, and that's only one a year for the next five years. You will do it. Without me."

Dr. Richards is philosophical about her famous former player. "When Martina came to me for coaching, she was already one of the world's best, but she had several weaknesses. Her backhand was strictly a defensive slice; I taught her how to hit passing backhands. She couldn't hit an offensive lob; I taught her to use topspin. She rocked backward too much on her serve; I taught her to move forward more. Her volley was like a lottery ticket—nobody knew where it would fly; I taught her to hit compact winning volleys. Before, she never had a strategy for different matches. I taught her to use her head, as well as her natural ability.

"Working with me, she had the greatest year any athlete has ever had. But it's all over now. Martina has a brilliant mind, but, like many brilliant people, she doesn't always think as consistently as she should. But she will remain one of the game's greats. With me, she would have beaten Shriver, but she may not have had the stamina to win the Open."

Dr. Richards, who ruthlessly can dissect the games of some of tennis' biggest stars, is equally candid about her own game.

"My shoulder seems dead and I can't get around on the serve the way I should. My eyes can't pick up the ball as fast as I should, and my legs can't get me to the ball as fast as I should. I won my first tennis tournament in 1947 (at age 13), and my best games are behind me.

"If I had stayed a man, I could have made a living from tennis. I don't think I was ever quite fast of foot enough to have been No. 1, but I would have been up there among the best.

"As a woman, I had my moments. In 1977, Betty Stuart and I made it to the finals of the U.S. Open (losing to Navratilova and Betty Stove). In 1979, I defeated Nancy Richey to win the woman's over-35 championship at the U.S. Open. The backlash was so great that I vowed never to play in the over-35s again. They said I was too big and strong for the other women.

"In 1979, I also made it to the semi-finals of the U.S. Clay Court Championships (losing to Chris Evert-Lloyd) and to the finals of the Avon

Open in Seattle (again losing to Evert-Lloyd). I won a few tournaments in South America, including one from (Wimbledon champion) Evonne Goolagong. I played team tennis with the New Orleans Nets. I'm proud of what I did with my tennis game. And it will always be part of my life. You know, my father (an orthopedic surgeon) is playing today in a tournament for those 80 and over!

"I could easily stay in tennis. As a coach, I can hand-pick the best young players. They all want me to train them, including a few men. I had offers to open a tennis ranch. I could go back as Martina's coach, but I decided I had to leave when I was no longer in charge, when she wouldn't listen to me. I was tempted to stay in tennis, but I remember what Pancho Segura (a tennis teaching great) told me when I visited his home in Palm Springs, Calif. 'Richards,' he said, 'how do you like my beautiful home? I had to hit 20 million tennis balls to pay for it.' No thanks. That's not for me."

Dr. Richards breaks off the interview to give a teaching lesson to Barbara Potter, the 10th-ranked woman's player who, this night, has a doubles match. The next morning, however, the tennis teacher is dressed in a white doctor's coat and resumes her reminiscences in her Manhattan office on Park Avenue, which she recently purchased from another physician. Curing cross-eyes among children is her game today.

"I had considered being a country doctor out on Oyster Bay in Long Island, but when this opportunity came up, I knew it was for me. This is where I belong. Tennis will always be part of my life, but from now on I will be making my mark in medicine. I have some ideas to improve the diagnosis and surgical correction of strabismus.

"I'll be going out to the annual meeting of the American Academy of Ophthalmology next month in San Francisco. Maybe they'll have a physicians' tennis tournament there. The last time I played tennis with doctors was when I took my New York licensing exam. Another candidate who was a good player and I played doubles with the two senior examiners. We made sure the two sets were split.

"I've been taking refresher courses and I will soon apply for clinical privileges at the Manhattan Eye and Ear Hospital, where I did my residency. I also have surgical privileges at the New York Eye and Ear Hospital (Dr. Richards received her medical degree from the U. of Rochester, N.Y.). Minor surgery I do in the office.

"A few days ago, I cured a small boy of cross-eyes. To me, that's like winning the Open. Better, because it's a shared, not solitary triumph."

She has to break off the interview again to pick up her 10-year-old son. "I'm very protective of his privacy, but I'm proud to say that we have an excellent relationship. But it's only recently that he's let me teach him tennis. I think he may be a little too big and muscular for tennis, though. Football may be his game."

The final question: Is she happy?

"I'm not there, yet. I'm pretty comfortable with who I am, but I'm still growing. Medicine and tennis can be glamorous, but I've been pretty miserable in these glamorous worlds.

"But I've made my statement. It may seem that by coming home I've completed a big circle, but I feel that I'm only halfway there. I've got a long way to go to do what I want to do. I'm not married. I haven't had a stable home life for years. I haven't made a lot of money in tennis.

"At least all those years in limbo are behind me now. I can get on with my life. I no longer think of myself as a transsexual. I think of myself as a woman physician, and that is a role with which I am very comfortable. It's been a very unusual life.

"But happy? Well, I'm only halfway home."□

Story Musgrave

In spring, 1983, Dr. Story Musgrave, NASA's senior physician-astronaut, rode on the maiden flight of the space shuttle, Challenger, and became the first American in nine years to walk in space. He told me that the experience of flying high above such Earth-bound concerns as politics, pollution, and wars is "incredibly positive."

Three years later, of course, Challenger tragically exploded into a fireball that was fatal to its seven passengers, including teacher Christa McAuliffe. I returned to the Johnson Space Center in Texas to again talk to Dr. Musgrave. At the time, I was one of 100 national finalists in NASA's competition to select a "journalist-in-space," so I listened with special interest.

Dr. Musgrave, I found, is still a believer.

HIS FIRST WEEK BACK on Earth "was a bummer," but Story Musgrave, MD, has regained the exuberance that marked his five days last month aboard the space shuttle Challenger.

"For 16 years, I've waited for this experience," Dr. Musgrave said. "This is why I got into this business—to be on the intellectual and physical frontier. This is why I took the job, what I'm supposed to be.

"I can't say that I expected it, but I wanted a transcendental experience, an existential reaction to the environment. I'm not talking about an illusion, of seeing something that wasn't there. I'm talking about a magical emotional reaction to the environment, to what's there. This is what I've been after all my life, to experience and feel new sensations. You know, I did my first airplane solo about 30 years ago, so I've been in the business of challenging physical frontiers for a long time, whether it's scuba diving or parachuting or skateboarding or walking in space. I wanted something to remind me that I was no longer practicing in the water tank."

At precisely 4:15 p.m. (Eastern time) on April 7, 1983, Dr. Musgrave, 48, cracked the hatch leading to Challenger's cargo bay and, with fellow astronaut Donald Peterson, became the first Americans to walk in space in nine years. Bundled in thick white $2.5-million space suits, the two astronauts stepped out of Challenger's cabin like two children going for a romp in the snow. For 3½ hours, the two floated, somersaulted, and tumbled through the vacuum of space—restrained by tethers—while successfully testing their abilities to serve as space repairmen.

Dr. Musgrave, the first one out, all but swung himself over the side of the spaceship, doing a handstand on the rail, restrained only by his tether. The Earth, 176 miles below him, was spinning brightly. His space suit and backpack, formally known as the extravehicular mobility unit, is a personal creation, largely designed by the physician-astronaut during his days on the ground. At the time, Dr. Musgrave told mission control in Houston, "It's so bright out here. It's a little deeper pool than I'm used to working in" (astronauts practice for space walks by swimming underwater).

Today, he recalled, "I guess I was hoping for a kind of religious experience out there. I didn't expect anything particular, I was just openminded about it. Now, this is a funny thing to say, but things went so smoothly that in a sense I was disappointed by what I felt. I never got that transcendental jolt.

"I never experienced a separation phenomenon, either from the spaceship or the Earth. I had no sense of the Earth being down. In fact, I had no down reference at all. My frame of reference was the cargo bay of the orbiter. There I was, 170 miles above Earth floating on a thin tether and I felt perfectly at home. I had no feeling of falling.

"Now, don't get me wrong, I was terribly excited. I found the zero gravity very appealing, being able to glide to wherever I wanted to go with no feeling of up or down. For those 3½ hours, I did the work I had to do and I grabbed for all the sensory inputs I could grab."

With fellow astronauts Peterson, Paul J. Weitz, the crew commander, and co-pilot Karol J. Bobko, Dr. Musgrave had just met the press for a formal report on the mission. Now, in his first one-on-one interview, he discussed the personal experience. The Challenger crew members still are committed formally to debriefings, and their general media tour is months away, but Dr. Musgrave said simply, "Let's talk.

"You ask me what will I have to say to doctors about this mission. Well, when I meet with medical groups, I'll talk about everything *except* medicine. Doctors go to conventions and hear about medicine all day long. When they talk to an astronaut, they want to know what did I feel, see, think. What was it like? They want to know what it would be like if they were to walk in space. Well, here's how it felt to me.

"I had absolutely no butterflies about this mission. I had total confidence in myself and the mission. I knew what was going to happen, and it happened. I knew every valve, every switch, and every number on this flight. It was sheer play for me to be able to so completely interact with my environment.

"The entire experience tremendously turned me on. I was on a five-day high. I had to be commanded to go to bed. I was so hyper and there was so much to do and see that I seldom got to bed before 5 a.m. Houston time.

"Technically, the mission was extraordinarily exciting, because we accomplished everything we set out to do—launching the TDRS (tracking and data relay satellite—the communications station), performing the EVA (extravehicular activity—the space walk), conducting the medical experiments (electrophoresis to use electrical charges to separate blood components to a purity 400 times greater than can be achieved in the presence of gravity), and bringing the shuttle home in great shape (this was Challenger's maiden flight and it joins Columbia to create a two-shuttle fleet to carry out NASA's Space Transportation System (STS) goals, which include 15 shuttle flights in the next few years). It was also personally fulfilling, because I've been waiting for this for a long time. I've been working on the design of the space suit I wore since 1972, so I guess it's only poetic justice that I should break it in.

"The entire five days were exciting, but the space walk was the highlight. It sure was a spectacular sight. I was taking in the sunrises and the sunsets—you can't tell them apart from up there. Even such a simple thing as our flash evaporator was making things of beauty. It would throw out little icicles of water, and you would see a tremendous blizzard of sparklets of light of all sizes, shapes, and velocities come tumbling at you.

"Every hour and a half, we made a complete orbit of the Earth, and it was just like getting a crash course in world geography. Seeing entire continents with the naked eye is something special. We saw oil slicks off

India, oil tankers in the Persian Gulf, the swirls in the Earth's crust where Iran, Pakistan, and India collided years ago and the mountains were thrust upward by the force. We saw the White Nile and the Blue Nile converge in the Sudan, the dust storms in Mexico, the thunderstorms over Africa, the tranquil beauty of the Bahamian Islands. These are all 'gee whiz' things."

When Dr. Musgrave's "airlock egress" or space walk commenced, Weitz described it: "Story seemed like a butterfly coming out of a chrysalis, only he's not as pretty."

Dr. Musgrave said, "I couldn't wait to get out. Space is a career to me, and this was to be only three hours of experience on top of 48 years, but it's like a surgeon who's been training 16 years to operate. Sooner or later, a surgeon has to operate. Sooner or later, I knew I was meant to walk in space."

In describing his extraterrestial experience, Dr. Musgrave excitedly shifted into the conversational rhythms of his native Kentucky. He holds five college degrees (bachelor's degrees in math and chemistry, master's degrees in biophysics and computers, plus the MD), but now he excitedly was dropping his "gs."

"I was lookin' at the sunrises and lookin' at the sunsets—they never got tiresome—lookin' at the Earth spinning, and realizin' how fast we were really goin'. Even at our high altitude, we were goin' very fast. We were really haulin'."

A common medical problem encountered by astronauts is motion sickness, or space adaptation syndrome (SAS). Remarkably, Dr. Musgrave never experienced a moment's discomfort.

"I've done a lot of research into SAS," Dr. Musgrave said, "and I favor the theory that it's due to sensory conflict at the level of cerebral integration. The brain cannot understand the signals it's being sent in a zero-gravity vacuum, and it responds by commanding nausea and vomiting. It's a lot like seasickness.

"For some reason, I immediately oriented to weightlessness. I was totally at home in zero gravity and felt extraordinarily comfortable in a no-down environment. I trained myself not to expect to see a 'down.' I was prepared to tell myself that the floor of the spaceship was down and to keep myself oriented that way, but I found that I didn't need a down. To me, the Earth was neither down nor up. It was just there.

"Some people are different and get confused by all the sensory inputs telling them that down should be here, but, wait a minute, it should also be there, and the two don't match. I had done a lot of work on integrating the vertical and horizontal parts of the spaceship, and I had no need to see or feel an up or a down. Since I had no fixed notion of down, it never bothered me to see things up that should have been down. The usual treatment for SAS is drugs, but based on a subjective data point of one—me—we may be able to handle it by never having a notion of down.

"The only time I missed gravity was when I got into my sleeping bag. I tied it horizontally to a structure inside the spaceship and I slept horizontally across the shuttle. I slept up front near the commander just to keep him company, since Bo (Bobko) and Don (Peterson) were sleeping at mid-deck. Now, I'm a 'side sleeper,' and I like to change to different positions throughout the night. But since there's no up or down in space, I really couldn't sleep on my side. No matter what position I tried to take, the zero gravity would keep me locked in a neutral position—neither up, down, or sideways. I couldn't twist and turn and hold a new position. I was tempted to take a strap and lock my knees in a crouched position, just to get some variety, but I never did. You know, the space program inspired all the medical research on sleeping, on what happens to you when you go to bed.

"It's absolutely amazing that man, a creature genetically coded to live in gravity, can survive in zero gravity. When the space program started 25 years ago, there were people who said that man wouldn't be able to breathe or swallow in zero gravity. There were a lot of straw men in those days who said that manned space travel would be a disaster, that it was not survivable.

"As you can tell, I'm an optimist, not a pessimist. I had absolute confidence that this mission would go as smoothly as it did. This is my career, and though I'm not scheduled for another flight as yet, I hope I don't have to wait another 16 years. I want to go up again.

"What did it mean to me? Well, you're talking about five days' experience on top of 48 years. I've kept myself pretty busy and pretty excited all my life, but there's definitely a 'delta' value to those five days in space. It means something to me. I'd talked to all the other astronauts who'd been up and I'd read all the mission reports, but being there is something else. It's the intensity of the experience. It's like being told how to fly an airplane and what it's like and then really doing it. You have to do it to feel it.

"You remember the little things, too. Like sound. Even though there's a vacuum in space, if you tap your fingers together, you can hear that sound because you've set up a harmonic within the space suit and the sound reverberates within the suit. I can still hear that sound today.

"But the main impression is visual. It's like seeing the totality of humanity within a single orbit. It's a history lesson, a geography lesson—

a blue ocean here, a brown continent there, clouds and mountains and ships and seas and trees. It's a sight like you've never seen. I hated to come down."

During re-entry into the Earth's atmosphere, Dr. Musgrave stood up in Challenger's cabin, an action usually prohibited by standard operating procedure. The question came up at the press conference, and Weitz said, "Sure, Story did it on the spur of the moment, but we all knew what he was doing and nobody's quarreled with him—at least until now."

Dr. Musgrave didn't comment at the press conference, but now he explained, "I was conducting my own experiment. The whole flight had been so totally exhilarating and I was on such a high that I decided to stand throughout re-entry. It's my nature to press and push, to go beyond what's expected. I had my Hasselblad camera and I was taking some photos. Also, I wanted to prove that you can stand while going from zero gravity back into gravity. That's important if an astronaut ever has to leave the top deck and go below to throw a switch or circuit breaker. I wanted to show that the cardiovascular system doesn't have any problem going back into gravity and that you don't have to be strapped down.

"My standing was smooth and steady, and it shows how the STS system is maturing. We all had total confidence. Standing up throughout re-entry, instead of being strapped down, was the perfect end to a perfect trip. I was having fun. As always.

"When I came off the shuttle, I was a little wobbly. I had sea legs. But nothing serious. Within 24 hours, I was running. I played racquetball 24 hours before I left Earth and played 24 hours after returning. I played equally well both times.

"The most surprising thing about this whole mission was the lack of surprises. There's an inverse relationship between productivity and surprises, and we had very few surprises."

Dr. Musgrave has to get back to the debriefings. Dressed in a turtleneck sweater and sport coat and carrying an umbrella as if it were a walking stick, he looks more like a suburbanite who has come in out of the rain than an astronaut who has come in from outer space. In photographs, his clean-shaven head often gives the appearance of fierceness, sort of a Kojak of space. In person, though, he appears much gentler, soft-spoken, and a bit of a dreamer. Like all the astronauts, he is the "right stuff," a believer.

"The next thing that will rival our landing on the moon in terms of public impact," he said, "is when people take space to their hearts, when they realize it's the way of the future."

There is time for a final question. How does he view the use of space-age technology for war?

"I'm an optimist," he began. "I like to think positive. But man is simply not a social animal. One of my biggest disappointments is the absolute failure of the human being as a social animal. You get back here to Earth and open the newspapers, and every week there's 10 or 12 new wars breaking out around the world.

"When I was in space, I never thought about war. I never had one negative thought. It was an incredibly positive experience, my five days in space. I don't think that one negative thought ever intruded upon the wonder of what I was doing. There was no time or inclination to think of war or problems, disease or death.

"Say, you know, maybe it did happen to me. Maybe I had it. It just took time to bring it home to me. I did have my transcendental experience, after all."□

HE ALWAYS KNEW that it *would* happen sometime, but for astronaut Story Musgrave, MD, the Jan. 28, 1986, explosion of the space shuttle Challenger provoked initial disbelief.

"I was sitting in the astronauts' room [at the Johnson Space Center, Clear Lake City, Texas] watching the lift-off on NASA-Select, our special TV station," Dr. Musgrave told *AMN*. "My view was from the back of the shuttle, not the side view that was replayed again and again after the explosion. I watched Challenger's contrails widen into a mushroom, and my mind reacted with disbelief, blocking out the fact that there was supposed to be a nice straight trail of smoke. But when I saw the two little horns coming out of the mushroom, and the two solids [booster rockets] still firing and shooting off in different directions, I instantaneously knew that something was wrong. My words were, 'That is bad. That is very, very bad.'

"I was in a room with other astronauts and wives and secretaries, and I was the first one in the room to say the words. I knew that Challenger was lost, and I knew that we'd lost seven very good people, some of whom I was very close to.

"I knew what had happened, but there was still the matter of accepting what had happened. You've seen it, but you've still got to soak it all up.

"On the TV, the debris was still streaming down from the sky. Everything was evaporating. My mind started to numbly walk through some programmatic things, but, suddenly, the loss became overwhelming.

"We'd lost the crew and that is the main thing. But for me, even though it's an inanimate object, the loss of Challenger itself was a personal loss. I'd flown on Challenger twice [a walk in space in April, 1983, and a second flight last August], and she'd taken spectacularly good care of me. I'm the kind of person who hugs and kisses airplanes. They're part of me and they're what has enabled me to be me. I've flown 15,000 hours as a test pilot and done 500 parachute jumps and, believe me, you become close to your vehicle.

I went back to my office, stared out the window, and cried like a baby.

"But, no, it was not totally unexpected. I've been in this business too long not to know that the shuttle system is terribly vulnerable and terribly unforgiving of any mistake. And you can't test many of the critical systems. You can only model them.

"I didn't think that something like this *could* happen. I knew that it *would* happen. Of course it would."

Dr. Musgrave, the senior physician-astronaut, has been with NASA for 20 years and in the test-flight business "all my life." In 1983, he became the first American in nine years to walk in space—and the first physician to fly on the shuttle—when he accompanied Challenger on its maiden voyage. In this February, 1986 interview with AMN, Dr. Musgrave says that despite the risks, he intends to fly in space again. At the age of 50½, he said, "I'm absolutely at my peak right now. In this business, experience counts. This is not a business about reflexes. It's a business about computers and electronics and design and guidance systems and navigation and flight control. It's not like running a little dragster. You need experience, and I'm going to get into space again, even if it takes me another five years. Space travel is a wonderful privilege, and I'm roaring to fly again—once NASA completes its reassessment of the shuttle's safety."

Like his colleagues, Dr. Musgrave has the "right stuff." He shrugged off vulnerability by saying, "This is my business. I'm paid to fly.

"Dying—I think about it all the time. That's why I don't have a scratch on my body. I take very good care of myself. I eat right, I exercise. I have the right attitude. My pulse rate is in the 40s, sometimes the 30s, and when I walked in space, my heart beat stayed at 45 to 60 beats per minute. I do everything I can to put the odds in my favor."

But the astronaut is vividly aware of the risks he faces in his chosen profession. "Space travel will always be risky," he said. "It will *never* be routine. We will never eliminate the risk, and what happened last January may happen again. There will always be an element of vulnerability.

"Space flight is a scary thing. Oh, I don't lose any sleep over it. The nights before I was scheduled to fly I fell asleep within 10 minutes. Space is pulling me on, and I'm roaring to get out on that pad. That's why I'm here in life. But when I get in that cabin aboard the space shuttle I'm scared— just plain scared. It's not butterflies, but it's fear. I cope with it by concentrating on my checklist—the things I have to do. You have to carry on, and I try to remember where all the steps are leading. They're leading me to space. I can't wait to start trekking around the world at 200 miles a minute.

He added, "I've always been terribly aware of the vulnerability of the shuttle concept, and I've not liked it. The shuttle design evolved as a compromise. The vehicle had to be able to land on land, and that is a very heavy requirement because it means having an airplane. The old vehicles were nice rockets that were shaped like rockets, or arrows, and flew like arrows right through the atmosphere with a nice uniform stack. Not so the space shuttle, which is an airplane sitting on struts and strapped to a large tank of 500,000 gallons of fuel and to the two solid-fuel rocket boosters. Every component has to work perfectly. The concept behind Challenger is terribly unforgiving of any mistake. If one thing malfunctions, you've lost the mission.

"The shuttle is also a transportation system and a space lab. And it had to be built with the dollars available, and it has had to maintain a very demanding schedule. So it has evolved into a very vulnerable system.

"Intuitively, you know the shuttle is vulnerable. It looks vulnerable, like a butterfly impaled on a stake.

"I don't know the cause of this accident, but in general, I have always been fearful of four things that have to work perfectly, or you've lost everything:

"First are the solids. I mean they're right there, so big and visible that they demand your attention. At lift-off, the noise and vibrations and violence of the solids are so significant that you know everything has to work perfectly with them, or you're in trouble.

"Second is the shuttle's main engine. I know how hard that engine's been pressed to do the work required to meet the demands and pressures put on it to meet the shuttle's schedule. I know about all these things and I know that, if the engine fails, you've lost it.

"Third is maintaining the structural integrity of the spacecraft at maximum dynamic pressure shortly after lift-off.

"Fourth is maintaining the integrity of the cabin pressure at lift-off."

"All four of these concerns center on the ascent. The first eight minutes and 34 seconds are critical and the first two minutes and 10 seconds are very critical. This is the time when you have to withstand maximum dynamic pressure. The loads are awesome, and everything has to work perfectly.

"All these things are on the edge of my mind when I'm ready to lift off. Space travel is like an obstacle course, and I look at those first 8½ minutes as a series of hurdles to clear to get to where I'm going. Space is my haven, and I sweat getting there. I don't sigh, but, emotionally, I do have a sense of relief when the shuttle breaks through the atmosphere and gets into Zero-G.

"During the first 8½ minutes of ascent, safety is out of the hands of the astronaut. You must have faith in the team that's put everything together. On Jan. 28, Challenger never made it. The accident happened right after she would have reached maximum dynamic pressure."

Does NASA deserve the faith its astronauts have placed in it?

Dr. Musgrave mused. "You have to have faith, or you cannot fly. Whether the faith was breached in this one case, I do not know. The media have done a heckuva job of reporting all the data, and, definitely, there's a trail of evidence there. But I will have to wait for the written conclusions of the investigating committee. If there has been negligence or shortcuts, wait until I have the committee's paper in my hands and then come down and talk to me. I'll tell you what I think right from the heart. But it is inappropriate for me to second-guess the commission's findings.

"NASA's image is tarnished. Sure, it is. When you have a national magazine headline, 'Clearly Flawed,' as *Time* did [based on the investigating commission's testimony] about the decision to launch Challenger, you've got a tarnished image. But what is NASA? Many thousands of people make up NASA. I, too, am NASA.

"NASA has one of the greatest engineering teams on Earth, an incredibly good team. I've put my life in their hands many, many times. As I said, I've flown 15,000 hours, parachuted 500 times, and spent countless hours in vacuum chambers, pressure chambers, and pressurized suits. You don't do all that unless you're a believer.

"But they're not perfect. Maybe, in this instance, everything was not handled as explicitly as it might have been. But before I say so I've got to get that final report. And if I find that there's been negligence, that this accident was preventable, sure, I'll be angry and disappointed and let down."

Dr. Musgrave discussed one reported possible cause of the disaster—the decision to launch in cold weather despite engineers' warnings that the O rings on the booster rockets' safety seals might not seat.

"The weather factor should have been known," he said. "The principle has been known for as long as we've understood hydraulics. In cold weather, you look for leaks—and you do find leaks. When we test planes up in the North Country, after I crank up the engines in the cold, I have the mechanics go all around the plane looking for leaks. And they find them.

"The link between cold and O rings has always been known. The function of an O ring is compliance, to have the ability to mold itself to fill the crack between two hard objects, like the steel ends of a rocket. The soft material must mold itself to slip down between cracks and to seal off joints. By definition, that compliance is a function of temperature. It's always been known."

But, surely then, there must have been weather protocols? This seems like a pretty straightforward requirement, doesn't it?

Dr. Musgrave smiled. "It does," he allowed. "But there were no launch-commit criteria based upon the temperature and the ability of the O rings to seal the solids. Maybe there should have been, though, and the panel will get to that. I'm not sure that the engineering tests on the O rings were acknowledged before launch. The fact that prior launches worked at certain temperatures should not establish a launch-commit criteria. That only means that you got away with it then. Criteria should be established by engineering and lab data and ground tests."

But, surely, this data was known?

"I'm not so sure they were aware of it," the astronaut replied. "But I've got to have the board tell me that. I cannot yet address the cause of the accident."

Dr. Musgrave reflected on the tragedy. "Surely, having all those millions of kids watch the lift-off to see a teacher go into space was very unfortunate. And all this at a time when the media had *quit* covering the launches because they seemed so routine.

"But they can never be routine. If you drive an auto long enough or fly enough on commercial planes or parachute out of airplanes long enough, you're going to have an accident—and these are terribly simple systems. The shuttle system is terribly complicated, much more complicated than Apollo, and Apollo was extraordinarily complicated.

"I have to think that [schoolteacher] Christa McAuliffe did not understand the risks. Challenger had gone up and down 24 times, without a major incident. Me, I understand the risks. I've thought about them every day."

He added, "The attitude here at NASA is, 'We're going to find the cause, we're going to reassess all safety risks, and we're going to fly again.' It's a can-do attitude. 'When the going gets tough, the tough get going' type of thing.

"We're going to get a real good reassessment of the entire shuttle system, and if it means going back to redesign and the drawing board and manufacture and testing, we're looking at a delay of at least one year, probably more.

"In the normal schedule, I probably would have flown again in January 1987, but now I'm looking at 1988, maybe 1989. Selfishly, I'd like to fly again soon, but I have the patience to let them do a very thorough safety job.

"I'm going to be here at least another five years, maybe 10. If I ever leave, it will not be because I don't still love the work, but because other things are pulling me away. For me, NASA has been both a mental and a physical frontier. In this job, I've been able to use everything I've ever learned—the flying and the parachuting and the math and the computers and the physiology. I didn't plan my education that way, but NASA has enabled me to be me.

"I may leave someday to fill a few vacuums in Story Musgrave's life. There are a few gaping holes. I've done the doing, but I'd like to spend more time on the being—studying art and music and literature. More time for relationships and travel. My five children are going to college now and they're scattered all over the country. I'd like to spend more time with them.

"Next month, I'm marrying again. [He's divorced.] Oh, she works for NASA and she understands the risks. Just like me, she'll be sweating out those first 8½ minutes. But I've never had any pressure at all from the family about my business. They all figure I'll come out OK. They don't worry about me.

"And I love space. It's an incredibly positive experience. For me, it's a haven. It'll take awhile longer now, but I'm going to get back up there.□

Roman Vishniac

I have really been nervous about my photography only two times. The first was when I attempted to take a picture of the world-famous portrait photographer, Yousuf Karsh. The second when I took out my camera to photograph Dr. Roman Vishniac, whose magnificent book of photos, *Vanished World*, is a tribute to the Eastern European Jews who were systematically killed during World War II. Dr. Vishniac had over decades risked his life to record with a hidden camera a lifestyle that otherwise would have been forgotten.

Fortunately, their wives saved the day. Estrellita Karsh told her husband to be patient with the novice, and Edith Vishniac told her husband to stand still. Only moments before, Dr. Vishniac had been deploring "this journalistic nonsense of posing people for pictures." He explained, "If a photograph is to endure as art, it must capture people as they live." I stammered, "Well, I just need a shot of you standing over there by the bookshelf. . . ."

We compromised. Dr. Vishniac retrieved from the studio his 1942 photo of Albert Einstein, which he had printed only that morning, and agreed to pose with the photo. At least that way, my picture would show how a candid photo should look.

I also had to enlist the wives' help for my other request—that I be allowed to carry back with me to Chicago for reproduction in our newspaper custom prints of some of the priceless photos taken by Karsh and Vishniac, two of the giants of photography.

Overruling her husband, Edith Vishniac allowed: "Of course, you can borrow some of his photos. That's why he took them. So people can see."

"I was unable to save my people, only their memory."
—Roman Vishniac, MD, in the preface to his book of photographs, *A Vanished World*.

TODAY, DR. VISHNIAC, 86, says softly, "I wanted to save their faces, not their ashes."

And in *A Vanished World,* a luxurious book of 180 bleak black-and-white photographs, published in October, 1983, by Farrar, Straus and Giroux, he has done what he set out 60 years ago to do.

"I was living in Germany in the '30s, and I knew that Hitler had made it his mission to exterminate all Jews, especially the children and the women who could bear children in the future. . . . The memory of those swept away must serve to protect future generations from genocide. It is a vanished but not vanquished world."

Dr. Vishniac's book, a publishing success in 1983, actually had its beginning in 1923 when Adolf Hitler published *Mein Kampf.* Most people ignored it; Dr. Vishniac, a Russian Jew who had escaped the brutalities of the Czars, took it to heart.

For eight years, from 1932 to 1940, he traveled 5,000 miles through Czechoslovakia, Hungary, Latvia, Lithuania, Poland, and Rumania to record with hidden cameras a Jewish civilization that he knew soon would be annihilated. He could not get back behind the Iron Curtain.

"Why did I do it?" he asks in the book. "A hidden camera to record the way of life of a people who had no desire to be captured on film may seem strange to you. Was it insane to cross into and out of countries where my life was in danger every day? Whatever the question, my answer is the same: It had to be done.

"The pictures depict people and places that no longer exist, yet in my memory they do exist. I hope that you will look at each picture with its story, and perhaps you, too, will see the world that I saw."

It is a crisp fall day in Manhattan, and the sunlight streams through a small window, dancing about Dr. Vishniac's study and lighting up the memories of a lifetime spent in the pursuit of knowledge—books, photographs, and Oriental art.

He speaks very softly and with the heavy accents of his native Russian, Yiddish, and German. His travels also made him fluent in French, Italian, and Rumanian, and occasionally he will get lost in thought as he gropes for the best English expression.

Tonight, he is to be made an honorary citizen of New York City. The ceremony will take place at the International Center for Photography, where his photographs of the East European Jews are the subject of a major exhibition. He holds doctorates in zoology and Oriental art and he teaches humanities at Brooklyn's Pratt Institute. But his thoughts are with other times, other places.

The medical degree is from Moscow U. and Dr. Vishniac, an endocrinologist, has made substantial contributions to medicine with his pioneering photographs of microscopic life. He no longer has the medical diploma.

"It was lost in Berlin," says Edith, his wife of 52 years and the woman he describes as "my reason for being." "I went out for a walk one day and when I returned everything was gone. Everything."

Dr. Vishniac adds: "I would not have kept it anyway. It had a photograph of Lenin."

A supreme realist, Dr. Vishniac joined the army of the Czar before escaping from Russia to Germany by way of Latvia. "I had to join the Red Army," he says. "It was the only way for a Jew to survive in Russia." Later, he would bribe German officials to obtain his cameras and film and to escape jailing for his photographic safaris.

"Danger was my business," Dr. Vishniac says. "I don't know this feeling of danger.

"None of my colleagues was ready to join me. Rather, they warned me of the danger and called my project impossible. A man with a camera was always suspected of being a spy. Moreover, the Jews did not want to be photographed, due to a misunderstanding of the prohibition against making graven images (photography had not been invented when the Torah was written). I was forced to use a hidden camera, and there were other problems as well. . . .

"My means were meager, but my will was unbreakable."

He leans across the table and speaks these ironic words:

"My friends told me to adapt, adjust, accept. The tragedy is that despite all the danger I pursued, it is I who am alive today and my advisers, my friends, who were all very careful, are now all dead.

"Yes, I am a fatalist. It is impossible to predict what life has in store. I would never have thought that Wolf, my only son (from a first marriage), would have gone before me, but so he did (falling to his death from a glacier in Antarctica while leading a scientific expedition). I wanted to leave everything to him, but, no, it was to go the other way.

No, this sense of danger never held any fear for me."

He used a primitive Rolleiflex for outdoor shots, a primitive Leica for indoors. He traveled with a Latvian passport—"no religion was noted." Now, he explains his technique.

"Once I decided to limit myself to taking pictures, not saving my people, I decided that I would take pictures not with all this journalistic nonsense, people holding hands and posing, but as historian. I wanted the people to have the proper expression at the proper moment. All my photos are unposed. I photographed things as they are and I tried to make it art, so that this photographic record could survive the centuries.

"It was very difficult. I would have only seconds to compose the photograph. The Rolleiflex I kept under my coat against my breast, with the lens opening through a large buttonhole. I would focus with my left hand, always looking straight ahead. I became expert in judging distances, whether the subject was three feet or five feet or 15 feet or to infinity, which made focusing not so critical.

"Even today, I can look at your eyes and tell that you are four feet away, almost to the inch. I had a cable release in my right pocket and I would use this to take the picture.

"Sometimes I would use a suitcase that weighed 115 pounds to carry my camera beneath some second-hand clothing that I pretended to sell. There was an opening on one side of the suitcase.

"Indoors, I would hide my smaller Leica behind a handkerchief. It was a very large handkerchief, almost a scarf, and this worked well if things were either very hot or very cold. I would wrap my camera in the scarf and raise it to my eyes to photograph. Occasionally, I would be caught, and arrested as a Jewish spy."

Only 2,000 of his 16,000 photographs survived. "I sewed some of the negatives into my clothing when I came to the U.S. in 1941," he says. Most he left with his father in central France who survived the war by hiding, and who hid negatives under floorboards and behind picture frames.

"After the war, I was able to recover them," Dr. Vishniac says, "My father came to the United States and died here in 1957. He was very proud that he had saved this record of the Jewish people."

For his book, Dr. Vishniac chose 180 photographs, each a haunting image of a doomed way of life. This testament to a lost people haunts him even today. As he turns the pages of his books, his life's work, he caresses each page.

Shoes are a grim motif.

"In Poland," he explains, "the authorities began an economic boycott against the nation's three million Jews. The only jobs permitted the Jews of Warsaw were as peddlers or porters. The porters, who were permitted to carry freight by handcar or on their backs, banded into cartels.

"In the past, carts were pulled by horses. But in prewar Poland, humans had to take over the job. They were more economical and more dependable. Horses had to be fed before they would work; humans had to agree to carry the goods first and eat later.

"The porters had to use all their strength. Their carts lacked tires, their shoes lacked soles. And only the wage earners had shoes. Leather soles lasted only six weeks on the cobblestones of Warsaw. How important was the shoemaker? One shoemaker I photographed told me:

"Without soles, nobody can exist, neither porters nor peddlers. Even to go to synagogue, you need soles on your shoes. And to feed you family, you must walk on the cobblestones—everybody needs soles. To buy leather, I need mezumen (cash). But all my customers are Jews; no one has money. To pay me, they must earn, and that means they need shoes. Leather soles last six weeks on stones. I work day and night; all my customers work hard. It's hard to be a Jew."

Some Jews without shoes spent entire winters indoors, often with as many as 26 families living in a basement partitioned into tiny cubicles with wooden boards. One of Dr. Vishniac's most compelling images is a photo of Sara, age 10. The photographer explains:

"She had no shoes and she could not go outside. She longed to see the flowers, so her father painted the flowers you see above her bed."

Another photo, of Jewish girls arranging their shoes in a circle, brings tears to the old man's eyes. "The Jewish Health Society helped handicapped and retarded children. They brought a ray of hope to the children of poverty. In this photo, the children are placing their shoes in a circle—as they have been taught—before taking their afternoon nap. After the war, I saw huge heaps of such shoes, taken from the child martyrs of the Holocaust and intended for the use of Aryan children."

"It was a madness, a successful madness," he adds. "The Nazis killed six million Jews, including 1½ million children. It is the children I love the most. The children did not understand about the ban against work. They simply asked for food."

Dr. Vishniac turns to a photograph of a young Jewish woman talking with her grandfather. "At home, her parents are in poor spirits. Her father has a severe hernia from carrying heavy loads, and her mother has a weak heart. The grandfather listens, always silent—what can he say? After the war, I heard about this family from a survivor. They all died after being seized by the Nazis. The daughter was shipped to a camp where she was raped and later gassed.

"It was an ordinary story," he adds, "but this picture and its story will remain when I am gone."

He turns to a photo of a tax collector paying a call on a Jewish peddler. "She had nothing to bring to her stand in the open-air market. But she had come for countless Thursdays, so out of habit she was there, she just couldn't stay home. She sat in the snow, without a single customer. I was there when the tax collector appeared and demanded three zlotys, or else he could confiscate her merchandise.

" 'I don't have anything,' 'Then I'll take your food.' 'I don't have bread and the sugar tin is empty. Only salt is left; to eat it alone is too bitter.' I heard her story and took the picture."

Suddenly, the old man shoots out his right arm and exclaims to the cluttered room:

"Heil Hitler!"

He explains: "Oh, yes, I was able to join the Nazis and become one of them. It was easier to buy a brown shirt in Berlin than a Jewish caftan. I drank beer with them and declared my hatred of the Jews. It was the only way I could photograph the Nazi demonstrations and storm troopers."

One of his photographs shows a young girl standing before a Berlin store window that displays Nazi posters. He points out a strange device in the store window. "It was something called a plastometer that was part of the Aryan mythology. An instrument to measure skulls to prove that you were not a Jew but a good Aryan. I had to pose my daughter, Mara, then 6, in front of the window to take the photo. Aryans were supposed to have long, thin skulls. What lunacy!"

Dr. Vishniac used the customs of his time. "I came to learn," he says, "that bribery can be important in human life and that it can be used for good purposes. My father used to pay 25 rubles to the Czar to escape persecution, and in Berlin I paid 200 marks every month to the secret police. It was the only way I could obtain cameras and film and escape being jailed.

"Once, a policeman warned me that I was about to be seized as as Jewish spy. He suggested that I might try to 'persuade' the secret police captain against the arrest.

"Well, I spent a sleepless night, and the next morning I went to the secret police headquarters, which was located in the former Museum of

Far Eastern Art, where I had previously worked. An ironic touch. I met
this brutal-looking man, and told him that I was interested in making a
donation to the party.

" 'How much?'

" '5,000 marks.'

" 'Where is it?'

" 'Right here.'

"I placed it on the table, and he took it without saying a word. Then,
he leafed through a list until he came to my name. He drew a line through
the name. I was safe.

"Now, I doubt if the money ever got to the party, but that was the way
things had to be done. Bribery was a way of life, later to be followed by
killing."

Even when he reached the United States, Dr. Vishniac had to fight to
get his book published.

"After the war, there was no interest," he said. "People said that the
Jews must forget the past, that in America they must assimilate. I was
offered money to destroy my negatives. They said that such a book would
be bad, that I was *too* Jewish.

"But I had been jailed 11 times and I had been in prison. I had seen
the Germans hand out 'concentration camp money' to the Jews. It was
German sadism. What can you do with it? You can cry.

"I lost 101 relatives during the war. The Russians killed half, the
Nazis the other half. I would not stop.

"One publisher wanted to run only the text, not the photographs.
Finally, I found a good publisher and good editor. This interest in the old
Jewish way of life is a recent thing.

"What were the Nazis all about? It was the movement of the majority
against the minority, against a minority that resisted assimilation, that
insisted on its special culture, dress, and religion.

"Now I have been invited by the president of West Germany to come
and lecture on the Holocaust. I will go because I think that Germany must
teach the true story of the Holocaust. The Nazis also murdered 60,000
non-Jews. The German people, too, suffered."

Dr. Vishniac's wife, Edith, brings the old man a lozenge for his throat.
He has been talking for a long time now, and it is Edith who is his
protector. During his lectures, she will put the microphone around his
neck, run the tape recorder, show the slides—and slow him down when he
moves or talks too fast.

"My wife is my life," he says. "We have been together 52 years, and
that is a considerable time. I met her in 1932 in Berlin, when not only

Hitler, but Paul von Hindenburg was alive as well. Her father was German, though he was never there, and her mother, a Czechoslovakian, was a saint. My wife is a saint. I often think of divorce, but only of divorce from myself. I often get upset with myself, but my wife and I have not had a disagreement in 52 years.

"Because I was Jewish and she was not, we could not get officially married until after the war in 1946. I went to Reno, Nev., where I waited six weeks to officially divorce my first wife. I think I was the only person there who did not play. I do not drink, I do not smoke, I love only my wife, to whom I have been faithful ever since meeting her in 1932. When I sign my books, 'Roman E. Vishniac,' that 'E' is for Edith. We are one."

The Vishniacs have a happy life together. They are both naturalized American citizens, and she long ago converted to Judaism. Recently, they traveled to Japan, where Dr. Vishniac studied art. They spend the summers in Switzerland, where Dr. Vishniac still climbs mountains. "Oh, not the highest mountains, and not to the top, but I climb up two or three thousand feet, and I regain all the red blood cells that I lose in New York." Dr. Vishniac's lectures on "creativity" and the "philosophy of the open-mind" are the best attended of all the Pratt Institute courses, but his special student is always Edith.

He concludes: "I feel good, yes. My book is being celebrated as a work of art. I am receiving letters from people saying, 'I discovered that I am a Jew because of your book,' or 'I am returning to Judaism because of your book.' And we are so happy to be in America. I do not agree with everything that this country does, but mankind has found nothing better than America. I hope that everybody realizes how lucky we are to be in America!

"The people I photographed were saints—I only wish they could be here."

The old man stands.

"Now, if you will say, 'Oh, boy, Oh, boy,' I will show you a surprise." Moments later, he emerges with a photo of the young Albert Einstein, taken in 1942. "You are seeing it first," he says, "because I printed it only this morning. It was 1942 and Einstein was happy to be in America and so was I."

The reporter wants a photograph of Dr. Vishniac holding the blowup of his cover photograph, a dramatic image of a Jewish village elder.

"Yes," Edith says. "This is a special photograph. It was always special to you, but now because of the book this photograph is being accepted and understood by others. Before, it was not known. Now it is."

Dr. Vishniac calls for his wife to join him in the photograph.

"Oh, no," she says. "It is your book."

"We are one. I love you."

Coming to his side, she whispers: "And I love you."□

John Rock

I must have gotten lost and stopped for new directions at least six or
seven times, as I tried on a snowy fall afternoon in 1980 to drive up
Green Mountain to the remote New Hampshire home of Dr. John Rock.
He had given me directions, of course, but the retired physician was 91
at this time and he figured, "any fool can follow the mountain trails." I,
on the other hand, knew from experience that if someone said, "You
can't miss it," that I would miss it.

Finally, an hour or so late, I arrived at the door of the man whose
discovery changed the world. I began, "I must have gotten lost seven
times. You cannot believe the twists and turns I took." He replied,
"Hey, that's my story. Let me tell you about how we found oral
contraceptives. . . ."

IT WAS A GENERATION AGO that John Rock, MD, took a wild Mexican
yam, turned it into a miracle contraceptive, and changed the world. His
identity was forever set, "The Father of The Pill."

He will be 91 in a few months and he says he is glad "to lose hold, to
let the world pass me by. I've earned a rest."

Those who are interested, however, can find him among the pine and
maple trees of Temple, N.H., living in an 18th Century clapboard house.

In coat and tie, he formally receives visitors in a book-lined living
room graced by a roaring fire. There will be a pitcher of martinis, though
he ruefully adds, "Mine are mostly vermouth and water these days."

Then, with every strand of silver hair in place and the smoke from his
pipe encircling his head, he settles back in his rocking chair and begins to
recount his 50-plus years in medicine.

"You're getting to me a little late," he says. "I don't cerebrate as well
as I used to. And excuse me for just a minute, you are mumbling your
words and I have to put on my hearing aid." Then, with a grin, "I was
tempted to take some Ritalin before you came so I would appear alert."

John Rock's mind and memories may wander from time to time, but
they focus with exquisite clarity on the towering achievement and terrible
controversy of his otherwise quiet, orderly life.

The Pill.

"I am not the father of oral contraceptives," he says. "If anything, I
am the stepfather. But, as my good friend and colleague Dr. Celso Ramon

Garcia has said, I am the man who put it across, who popularized it to a skeptical world."

He is a Catholic who loves his church and John Rock, MD, went through agony in standing up for the right of women to decide whether and when to have children. Caught in the conflict between science and ethics, religion and research, Dr. Rock had no doubts about his mission.

"When I was 14," he said, "and wearing my first pair of long pants to a 9 a.m. mass, I was called aside after the service by my parish priest, Father Finnick, who asked if I would like to drive with him on his regular visit to the Poor Farm outside Marlborough, Mass., where a few very elderly men and women lived. It was there that he told me, 'John, always stick to your conscience. Never let anyone else keep it for you. And I mean anyone else.' "

John Rock was to keep his own conscience during those controversial early years of the Pill in the 1960s. No one, including Pope Paul VI, was to keep it for him. Today, the Pill is a fact of life. There are 10 million women in this country alone who for 20 days or so a month will take an oral contraceptive and get on with their lives. One once told John Rock, "You have changed my life. You have ended the fear and uncertainty."

However, when the Food and Drug Administration approved the first oral contraceptive in 1960, it unleashed a storm of medical and moral controversy.

Sitting in front of his New Hampshire fireplace, John Rock remembers those days. "No, I was never afraid of the criticism. I was straight with my conscience and I was sure of my motives. The rising birthrate was about to ruin humanity.

"I remember it like it happened yesterday. I was in Washington to see the FDA and an official said, 'Well, we'll get back to you.' And I stood there and shook my fist in his face and said, 'You will not get back to me. You will license this drug and you will license it now. We have waited long enough. It is time to act.' "

And so they did. The Pill coincided with a watershed period in American history—the 1960s when social and sexual revolution shook the nation to its foundation. Feminism eagerly embraced Dr. Rock's discovery and, today, the U.S. birth rate is at an all-time low, divorces are at an all-time high, and more than half of all women are in the workforce.

Dr. Rock isn't happy about all of this. "Sometimes," he says, "I wonder whether or not all this liberation is not making women lose some of their valuable femininity." But, with a shrug, he adds, "What will be will be."

They say John Rock was a wonderful doctor. One woman said, "He always had time for his patients and the women knew it."

His early work was in infertility. The Rock Endocrine and Fertility

Clinic established in 1924 at the Free Hospital for Women in Brookline, Mass., was a first for the nation.

But, Dr. Rock reminds, "The drama of human fertility is not a one-dimensional view. Any investigation is research into the whole process of conception."

It is ironic that Dr. Rock's early work in infertility laid the foundation for the Pill. He holds up a sheaf of yellowed pages that list his scientific articles, over a 40-year period dating back to 1925. "It is a continuum," he says, "this research into human reproduction. It is always inclusive.

"When reproduction fails, we try to discover where there is a break in the chain of events associated with its normal functioning. When this is found, we try to repair it, to weld the chain together for women who want to conceive.

"The facilitation of contraception poses just the reverse problem: To find harmless ways of creating such a break. . . . In the development of the oral pill, those of us who were working on welding the chain together joined with investigators seeking a way to sever it to bring forth a medication of great value for both objectives."

The medication was known to the FDA as SC 4642, to chemists as norethynodrel, the most effective of the nineteen-nor-steroid group, and to the public as Enovid, marketed first by G. D. Searle Co.

For Dr. Rock, it was the culmination of almost 30 years of research. Today, however, he wants to stress two things about this remarkable medication.

"First, we must remember that oral contraceptives not only can prevent births, but they also can treat various menstrual disorders and prevent miscarriage. By preventing repetitive miscarriage, the so-called 'habitual abortion' that plagued many childless couples, the pill has also helped give life.

"Second, the discovery of the oral contraceptive was truly a team effort. Gregory Pincus, ScD, and Min Chueh-Chang, PhD, performed all the complex chemical testing to determine the best synthetic pro-gesterone-like steroid. And Celso Ramon Garcia, MD, and Edris Rice-Wray, MD, helped me with the necessary clinical testing of women. Together, our clinical work produced a medication that researchers would agree documented a record of effectiveness and safety that no other contraceptive has matched.

"One reason I have always been so sensitive to the problems of women," he says, "is that for the first five or six years my best pal was my twin sister. I didn't play ball or anything. I played with her. Played dolls. I even went to sewing class."

His first experience with international overpopulation—and poverty—came after his graduation from high school, when he took a job in Guatemala with the United Fruit Co. He was first promoted and then sacked from this position, a pattern he was later to repeat with a Rhode Island engineering firm. "I began to realize," he says with a twinkle, "that commerce was not my field."

He received his medical degree from Harvard. "It was perfectly simple to get into then. I just went over there. I think there was one personal interview. And you just signed the book and were in."

The doctor-to-be had already determined that only two areas of medicine were worth devoting a lifetime—psychiatry and human reproduction. He took a residency in obstetrics at Boston's Lying-In Hospital in 1919.

In 1921, he began the private practice of obstetrics and gynecology in Boston. He was 31 and decided it was time to support himself, get married, and raise a family. He met his wife of 36 years, Anna Thorndyke, upon her return from France, where she had been an ambulance driver for the Red Cross during World War I.

The old man's mind is distracted by this reference. He walks into his office-study, where he points to faded black-and-white photos of his wife and four daughters. "That's quite an array of pulchritude, isn't it?" he remarks. "I'm sure my daughters used the pill," he adds, "but not to extinction. I have 19 grandchildren. The irony is not lost on me that the man who helped make widespread contraception possible also is the grandsire of this vast tribe."

There is another photo. His son, John, who in the late 1940s on a rainy evening was on an errand for his father when the car spun out of control and hit a tree. He was killed. "If I concentrate on it," he says, "I don't break down anymore when I look at his picture. Finally."

He returns to the safety of the fireplace and the pipe and resumes his reminiscences. "At the family dinner table, we used to have some pretty frank discussions about sex and reproduction. I always shared my work with the family."

That work was putting Dr. Rock into prominence—and controversy.

In 1931, he was the first Catholic among 15 Massachusetts medical men who signed a petition endorsing birth control. He was attending mass every morning and a crucifix hung over his desk, but Dr. Rock "was flying right in the face of my beloved Church. For it had become apparent to me that contraception is a necessary instrument for family welfare, essential to health, and, when otherwise justifiable, does not contravene Catholicism."

During the 1930s, he and his Harvard colleague, Miriam F. Menkin, recovered and preserved a series of 30 human embryos from 2 to 17 days after fertilization—a classic grouping whose pictures were studied throughout the world. The physician asked his patients scheduled for hysterectomies to discontinue contraception—usually the Church-approved "rhythm method"—for a month prior to their operation. That made it possible to photograph embryos as early as the two-cell stage, a remarkable achievement for the time.

The Church was in an uproar and Dr. Rock was "disturbed by the realization that the voice of my conscience was not always telling me what the priests of my Church were saying. . . ."

Meanwhile, his work with infertile couples was making startling progress. He made known today's commonly accepted fact that many supposedly infertile women are really married to infertile men. He emphasized the "bipartisanship involved in conception."

Noting that many infertile women suffered from hypoplasia, he theorized that the underdeveloped uterus and fallopian tubes might be preventing pregnancy. He knew that in a normal pregnancy the rise in the body's output of estrogen and progesterone expanded the uterus and the tubes. Perhaps "a false pregnancy" stimulated by doses of the two hormones would correct the problem.

Eighty childless women agreed to try treatment. Daily, for three months, they took massive hormone doses. After treatment was discontinued, there were within four months 13 pregnancies. There were also 13 joyful women. The phenomenon became known as the "Rock rebound."

Dr. Rock knew he had demonstrated that the use of the female hormones could suppress ovulation. None of the 80 women had menstruated during the months of treatment; they had some of the signs and symptoms of a genuine pregnancy.

It was at this point that he and Dr. Gregory Pincus, the renowned scientist and an old friend, met at a scientific conference. Dr. Pincus and his assistant, Dr. Chang, working at the prodding of Planned Parenthood leader, Abraham Stone, MD, in a search for "the ideal contraceptive," had duplicated earlier work confirming that ovulation in rabbits and rats was halted when they were given large enough doses of progesterone.

Drs. Pincus and Rock exchanged ideas. Dr. Rock returned to Boston for another try at stimulating the rebound reaction in his infertile patients, this time using progesterone alone. To avoid the trauma of missed menstrual periods he instructed his patients to began taking the pills the fifth day after the start of their menstrual periods, take them for 20 consecutive days, and resume again the fifth day after the next period.

He chose 27 chronically infertile patients, explained the experimental nature of the treatment, began the 20-day course of oral progesterone, kept each woman under close watch, and at the end of three months had his answers.

The medication appeared safe, the fertility rebound was confirmed—4 of the 27 women were pregnant within four months of first taking the pill—and progesterone definitely could temporarily inhibit ovulation.

All that remained was finding the best and most inexpensive form of a synthetic version of progesterone and conducting large-scale human trials.

Dr. Pincus and his lab assistants solved the first problem. A batch of SC-4642, norethynodrel synthesized from a wild Mexican yam, was found to be 10 times more active than natural progesterone and much cheaper. Thus, it could be effective in tiny—and inexpensive—doses. A batch of the synthetic progestin was sent to Dr. Rock and Dr. Garcia.

In 1956, with the help of Dr. Edris Rice-Wray, medical director of Puerto Rico's family planning association, Drs. Garcia and Rock found 265 women in Puerto Rico who volunteered to take a pill a day for 20 days for six months.

The six-month trial included 1,700 mentrual cycles for thse women to whom pregnancy had been an annual event. The results were astonishing.

Not one who had taken the pill became pregnant. Dr. Rock would write, "The drug has given 100% protection against pregnancy in 10-milligram doses taken for 20 days each month."

The Pill was about to burst on the world and the physician turned his mind to the hardest task—convincing the world and the Church that it was acceptable.

Today, he lowers his strong-boned Irish face over a dusty copy of his 1963 book, *The Time Has Come*, which presents his case for the pill, and reads:

"It is the voice, as I hear it, of the conscience that has thus been formed within me that I am impelled to follow. I fervently pray that in doing so, I injure nobody; I give no scandal; and that, if, inadvertently, I do either, I shall be forgiven."

He crisscrossed the country with the message. The Church wouldn't listen, but the women did. Dr. Pincus called his efforts "fearless." In 1968, Pope Paul VI attacked both birth control and the pill.

Today, he is not bitter. "My church teaches charity," he says. "Besides, as you can tell, I am completely out of it now. Both medicine and the Church have passed me by."

A young college student who is a friend of the family lives with the physician and helps see to his needs. Firewood is stacked against the house, trails and bridges are built so he can walk the grounds. In the summer months, the physician is still known to go skinnydipping in a nearby mountain brook, slowly sipping a beer later and dozing off in the afternoon sunshine. He has his birds to feed and his garden to fuss with. And his memories.

"Had my name been Elgin R. McGillicuddy," he muses, "none of this notoriety would have happened. But it was an easy name for the press—John Rock. And, of course, I am Catholic.

"The Pill is perfectly safe and it is one of the most important achievements of gynecological medicine."

He stands and looks out the window toward the beloved mountains that drew him here years ago upon the death of his wife ("In 36 years, we were seldom apart more than 20 minutes") and concludes:

"I still go to mass now and then. I keep the crucifix above my desk. The Church always comes around to the truth. But it can take so long. Galileo learned that. I shall be vindicated by the Church.

"You know, the doctors always supported my work. Always. But there was this Catholic physician in Boston."

His blue eyes twinkle as he recalls:

"Seems to me he was a fellow by the name of Good. Another irony. But he didn't think I should be allowed to take communion every morning.

"I did, of course. I went to communion every morning. I never paid him no mind. No mind at all."□

George Sheehan

Naturally, Dr. George Sheehan, the Pied Piper of Running, whose best-selling books have helped motivate millions of Americans to take up the sport, wanted to do this interview on the run.

Not a chance, I responded. The importance of the message demanded a sit-down session.

We compromised—and did it on the walk. For two days, I chased him around Chicago, as he gave a running clinic, answered runners' questions, and gave the keynote speech at a runners' banquet. Then, I stood in the rain on Lake Shore Drive and waited for the 59-year-old physician to finish running the 12.4-mile Chicago Distance Classic in an average time of six-minutes, 37-seconds per mile—just as he had predicted.

Finally, over a post-race beer, he agreed to stand still for awhile to talk to me. His message, however, had already been made loud and clear:

You should really begin a running program, he advised.

DIXIELAND BLARES and booze flows as Chicago's captains of industry and politics convene to enlist the nations' newest craze—running—on behalf of the oldest of causes—the fund-raiser.

The event is the 12.4-mile 1978 Chicago Distance Classic and the beneficiary is the Chicago Lung Assn. ("We care about your breathing.") Tonight, no one dances and few drink. Tomorrow's run is the thing.

This year's run includes the first National Corporate Long Distance Running Championships, and tonight's dinner honors the 50 corporate teams who have contributed $250 each to the lung association. Running is in, and the Beautiful People are out in force to mingle with the likes of Chicago's No. 1 runner, Mayor Michael Bilandic, and that perennial athlete, Sen. Charles Percy (D, Ill.), plus the chief executives of the seven corporations co-sponsoring the classic.

Wandering unnoticed amid this assemblage of power and pomp is the evening's featured speaker. He describes himself as "middle-aged enough to have a body that allows me to do what I want and a face that lets me get away with it."

"You know that look. The hair is short and graying, the face just skin and bones, the general impression that of an ascetic who began the fight with the Devil in the Garden, decided it wasn't worth it and walked away."

He is dressed in faded corduroy jeans, a buttondown shirt from the 1950s, and a threadbare seersucker sport coat. His club tie is firmly held in place with a jumbo paper clip ("I tell people it's made of platinum," he says). On his feet are tennis anklets and his beloved Tiger running shoes.

He notices that one young man has come without a tie. "If I had thought I could get away with it," says George Sheehan, MD, 59, "I would have dressed informally."

A cardiologist from Red Bank, N.J., Dr. Sheehan resumed his running career 14 years ago, ever since he discovered his heart was in more than just practicing medicine "and getting bombed weekends watching TV." He had been a varsity miler during his undergraduate days, but since medical school had given up the sport. Then came his renaissance.

With the publication this year of his second book on running, *Running and Being,* and its condensation in *Sports Illustrated,* Dr. Sheehan has emerged as the Pied Piper of running, itself the nation's newest leisure time industry.

Dr. Sheehan himself "will make a lot more money than I need from the book." "It's already No. 5 on the *New York Times'* best-seller list. It'll go a million copies, counting paperback sales. My first book has now sold 100,000.

"I don't know what to do with the extra money. I really don't need it.

The money from the book adds up to a real good year for an internist and a pretty fair year for a surgeon."

He is an unlikely guru, more iconoclast than evangelist. But running to Dr. Sheehan is a "wordless religion" and he observes, "Wake me up at 3 a.m. and hand me a mike and I'll talk for you."

Dr. Sheehan feels strongly about the positive value of running and athletics. "Sometimes I get choked up and cry," he says, "especially when I'm talking about something like my daughter Sarah, who just completed the Boston Marathon, or a great competitor, like the Boston Celtics' John Havlicek. Running strips down your personality, lets you know who you are. It has brought out the feminine side of me, and I'm not ashamed to let people see it."

Will he become emotional tonight? "I never plan on it. But sometimes it just happens."

For two post-dinner hours he sits through the interminable back-slapping that must precede the running of the Chicago Distance Classic. He winces only slightly when Sen. Percy tells the crowd he tried unsuccessfully to convince his wife to take up running by buying her a running book written by James Fixx (Dr. Sheehan's chief competitor as a runner-author. Fixx only tells you how to run," Dr. Sheehan says. "I tell you why.") The wince is more noticeable, however, when former Olympic runner Rick Wohlhuter finally tells the crowd, "We want to introduce our featured speaker now so everyone can get to bed. . . ."

Dr. Sheehan is on his feet. "Sen. Percy has told you," he says, "that today he has swum, walked a few holes at the Western Open (golf tourney), and played in a tennis tournament, not to mention running in the morning. Well, most of us can only run. In my family, those who can, play basketball; those who can't, run."

He continues, "We've heard a lot about how this event is being mass produced, but it remains for each of us a very personal thing."

In the next five minutes, the New Jersey cardiologist has invoked the words of no fewer than 10 authorities to buttress his belief that only through athletics—and running—can man (woman runners are still scarce in competitive meets) regain the state of grace his Creator intended.

We are told of Emerson ("Become first a good animal"), Nietzsche ("Never trust a thought you come upon sitting down"), Thoreau (Why lead "lives of quiet desperation" when running offers salvation?), plus Kierkegaard, Santayana, Gandhi, Ortega, Tielhard de Chardin, St. Thomas Aquinas, Ecclesiastes.

Sometimes, the reference is closer to home. The message, Dr. Sheehan notes, is "what Fordham (College basketball) forward Charlie

Yelverton once said was the principle of being an athlete—'the principle that makes you dig your guts out no matter what kind of game you're in.' "

The running game is what Dr. Sheehan is into. Ten miles a day every Tuesday and Thursday on a course outside Red Bank's 600-bed Riverview hospital, where he now works only 40 hours a week reading x-rays and giving stress tests.

Weekends are for competition, like this event in Chicago. Dr. Sheehan usually combines the run with an instructional clinic.

In Chicago, he shared the podium with world-class runners, but it was the physician whom runners sought out afterwards with their questions about training, equipment, and injuries.

Pain is part of the game. "You know," he says, "a reader of my column (in the Red Bank, N.J., *Register,* the best of which are reprinted in *Runner's World.* His books are collections of his columns, which are "written on the run") complained that this 'claptrap about pain by Dr. Sheehan is simply irrational.' Well, to him it is irrational. He has no reason for pain. But to me it's supra-rational. Reaching the edge of what I can do, and then pushing on for more."

There is also play. "Adults," Dr. Sheehan says, "have forgotten how to play. Life is, after all, a game, and running is play. The essence of the running game for me is the feeling I get when running alone occupies me.

"I am comfortable, calm, relaxed, full of running. I feel like I could go on like this forever. I am suspended, content with the nothing. And the peace that comes with it.

"That is the essence of the running experience for me. The lack of anxiety, the complete acceptance, the letting go and the faith that all will be well. In running, I feel free. I have no other goal, no other reward. The running is its own reason for being.

"Only the child still lives in a world where such days are possible."

Dr. Sheehan is now turning to his favorite philosopher, William James. At a nearby table, his wife, Mary Jane Fleming Sheehan, who has presided over the raising of their 12 children, observes: "He quotes so many philosophers because people said things better in those days. We've lost our philosophers." Mrs. Sheehan does not run, "except up and down stairs," but eight of their children do.

"However I phrase it," Dr. Sheehan says, "it comes down to one of the Jamesian expressions: 'The nobler thing tastes better. The strenuous life is the one we seek.' "

And there is vanity. "Everything we do," Dr. Sheehan says, "is vanity. Whether we be U.S. senators or mayors of big cities or presidents of corporations, we are all just chasing the wind. But we must do it with all our might, with every fiber we have. Only then do we know what we are." He concludes (without tears):

"Only one man can win this race, but each of us who tries is a winner. Man was born to be a success, but the only time he believes this is as an athlete."

Off-stage, Dr. Sheehan is disarming but firm. "I quote from so many sources," he says, "that when I come up with a good original line my son says, 'Who did you steal that from? Running is here to stay. It's not just a fad. I just hope it doesn't become a cult thing."

He is direct about his ability. "I can give most people a five-minute start and run them down in 20 minutes. Tomorrow, I'll do the 12 miles in an hour, 22 minutes, and probably finish second in my age group.

"This race has an unusual out-and-back feature, so that you can see the leaders running back at you. The thing I remember about this race last year is (Olympic champion) Frank Shorter running back toward us. I was trying as hard as Frank, but I had to marvel at his speed. I can still see him: his crazy tangerine costume, El Greco face, and angelic lope."

His competitiveness returning, he adds, "Of course, not only can you see the leaders coming back at you, but when you make your turn, you can see how many people you're running ahead of."

The idea, Dr. Sheehan said, is the "athlete-saint. By that I mean being fit and having a sense of humor. The athlete has the balance, the perspective to tell the Mickey Mouse from the meaningful."

In medicine, Dr. Sheehan observes, the "Mickey Mouse includes the paperwork, the bureaucracy, the chart committees, the accreditation busywork, the continuing medical education fraud."

"I just can't stand it. Here I am, traveling the nation to educate people about taking care of their health, moving past health to fitness, and the medical administrators are about to chastise me because my CME hours are not up-to-date. Now mind you, I've acquired the classwork hours; I just haven't reported them. Then, there's the commercial ripoff. you've got schools using CME to defray tuition. CME, after all, is deductible. Then, too, I'm a gadfly to some doctors. I tell runners that a podiatrist can do more for them than an orthopedic surgeon, that hypertension is better treated with diet and exercise than medication."

He would never give up medicine, though. "Those 40 hours a week in the hospital are important to me. But we need to reach people with the fitness message. If you keep at running long enough, you're going to become the person you're supposed to be. Everybody's searching for something. With running, you no longer need TM and EST, Outward Bound and Librium."

The night before the race, he is pretty loose about the whole thing. "I'll probably have a beer or two," Dr. Sheehan says. I tell my clinics that beer is good for liquid near the end of a race.

"I've run in 50 marathons (26 miles) now. Fifteen years ago when I ran in my first Boston Marathon, there were only 225 of us, many of whom had come on a dare or as a joke. I finished 96th in three hours and ten minutes, and because of this considered myself one of the top 100 marathoners in the country. Now, with nearly the same time, I am not even in the top 5,000.

"Back then, there were about seven marathons a year; now there are more than 200. Last year, there were 25,000 people who ran a marathon. Boston had 4,000 entries, and that's only the tip of the iceberg. For every marathoner, there has to be at least 100 serious runners. Some people estimate that as many as 20 million Americans are running. I'd say more like five or six million. When *Runner's World* first came out a few years ago, it had 250 subscribers; now, there are a quarter-million.

"I have a friend who calls and tells me, 'I know of a great race next week up in Bayonne (N.J.). Nobody's coming!"

The next morning in Chicago, there are 8,000 runners who ignore a driving rain to line up in the city's Loop for a prompt 8 a.m. start. Kibitzing before the race, Dr. Sheehan says, "This may ruin my cookout with friends later in the day, but I've never seen a race cancelled." As he talks, the starter's gun fires and a surge of humanity roars toward Lake Michigan.

An hour later, Olympian Garry Bjorklund leads the pack to the finish line. Mounted policemen hold back the cheering crowd lining the finishing lanes on Lake Shore Drive. A school band is alternating the theme song from "Rocky" and "My Country Tis of Thee." Mayor Bilandic, who fired the gun to start the race, is at the finish line with Sen. Percy. TV cameras and news photographers move in.

At exactly one hour, 22 minutes (6 minutes, 37 seconds per mile), as predicted, Dr. Sheehan sprints to the finish line, just behind a muscular lad tearing along in a wheelchair. As predicted, Dr. Sheehan is second for his age group. While junior executives rush for yogurt, Dr. Sheehan has a beer. "In three months," he says, "I'm eligible for the 60–70 age group. Watch me then!"

Glory is not what drives him, however. Standing apart from the thousands of runners who have finished their races and are now milling about Buckingham Fountain, where the awards will be presented, he reflects on running—and runners. The words are from his book, but he rewrites them every time he runs.

He runs for his soul. "It seems like such a simple thing, running does," Dr. Sheehan says. "Really only a bit above breathing. And such a lonely calling.

"But the real loneliness that pursues me this day and every day begins long before I put on my running shoes. It begins with my failures as son, husband, father, physician, lover, friend. It begins when those other gods have failed, the loved ones, the career, the triumphs, the victories, the good life. The heartbreaking loneliness begins when I realize that no one can think for me; no one can live for me; no one can die for me. I can count on no one for help. The true loneliness, then, is me seeing that nothing I do is true."

At these times, Dr. Sheehan says, "I run so that I am caught up in the life of the universe. Then, finally, loneliness is dispelled. I know I am holy, made for the greater glory of my Creator, born to do His work.

"Which for this day and this hour is running, a lonely figure on a lonely road."

On this rainy morning in Chicago, George Sheehan, MD, slips back into the crowd.□

Walker Percy

New Orleans' seamy French Quarter is an unlikely place to shop around for a book on high philosophical ideas, but that's what I had in mind. In town in 1977 for a medical convention, I had grown restless and decided to take a shot at trying to interview the reclusive Walker Percy, a (non-practicing) physician who is one of America's finest writers of serious fiction.

The good news was that Dr. Percy lived right across the Lake Pontchartrain causeway in Covington, La. The bad news was that he had sworn off all interviews. With the exception of the legendary J. D. Salinger, Dr. Percy had become America's least-accessible author.

I made the phone call and was told, no, he was not interested in discussing his writing. Well, then, I countered, would he discuss the medical career he had abandoned to pursue his muse. There was a long pause. "I'm going to play golf tomorrow," the writer said, "but if you can get here early in the morning, we can talk before I leave to tee off."

Moments later, I was out in the quarter tracking down a copy of Dr. Percy's then-current book, "Lancelot," a diagnosis of the spiritual ills confronting America. It is Dr. Percy's contention that philosophical ideas are best expressed in fiction, not in philosophy quarterlies, and "Lancelot" is powerful proof. I found the book in a store sandwiched between, what else, a strip joint and a jazz joint, and I stayed up most of the night reading it.

The next morning, Dr. Percy, as agreed, discussed why he had turned his back on medicine. He also, as hoped, discussed why he writes.

"Tell me the truth now. Is everyone cold or is it only I?"

—*Lancelot,* by Walker Percy

THE SPEAKER IS Lancelot Andrewes Lamar, scion of Louisiana's Belle Isle. He speaks from a prison cell, his home since discovering his wife's infidelity and killing her and her lovers by burning down Belle Isle.

The question, however, belongs to author Walker Percy, MD. He says he would have been miserable as a physician, but has taken a "diagnostic stance" toward American society, a society he believes is terminally sick.

Walker Percy started writing some 36 years ago, shortly after he received his medical degree. This year's critically acclaimed *Lancelot* added to his reputation as one of America's most important writers.

He has quit giving interviews ("I've developed amnesia about *Lancelot;* it's time to move on to something else"), has, in fact, recently "interviewed" himself for a satirical article to be published in the December *Esquire.* But he has relented for this one last interview by a publication about medicine, the profession he left behind.

It is a bright sunny day in Covington, La., the small community across Lake Pontchartrain from New Orleans where Percy came to write in the early 1950s. He rocks gently back and forth in a swing outside the Kumquat, his daughter's book-and-antique store.

"I'm afraid my entry into medicine will not prove very inspiring to your readers," Dr. Percy says. "I grew up in a family of lawyers and there were only two professions considered respectable—law and medicine. I couldn't stand law, so I went into medicine (graduating in 1941 from New York's Columbia College of Physicians and Surgeons).

"During my internship (at Bellevue Hospital in New York City), I picked up tuberculosis while working on the TB ward. I was sent to the Adirondacks to recuperate.

"Well, there wasn't much to do, so I spent a lot of time reading: Kafka, Dante, Sartre, Dostoevski. You know, during your medical education there isn't much time for outside reading, although I guess now there's more of an effort to broaden the curriculum, include some humanities.

"I found that I enjoyed reading and for two years I read everything I should have before. I began to write for the psychiatric and philosophical journals."

Dr. Percy said that his late uncle, William Allen Percy, who wrote a

classic book about the South, *Lanterns on the Levee,* had turned him
toward music, literature, art. Percy and his brother had gone to Greenville,
Miss., after the death of their father to live with their uncle.

Percy went on to do his undergraduate work at the U. of North
Carolina. An avid athlete, he recalls that he grew up in Birmingham, Ala.,
in a home "right next to the sixth hole of the Birmingham Country Club."
(Though he savagely put down the game in *Lancelot*—"But golf is a bore.
I quit"—Dr. Percy will be off for a round later this afternoon. "When I
wrote that sentence," he recalled, "I had just had a bad day on the
course.")

After his convalescence, Dr. Percy decided "that I would rather write
than practice medicine. I really didn't have a gift for medicine, though I
believe that if I had stayed I might have enjoyed pathology or psychiatry.
But I believe you have to do the things that make you happy. And I wanted
to write."

Support from his father's estate and his uncle "gave me the time to
find my way," Percy said. "By the time I came to Covington in the early
1950s, I had written two unpublished novels.

"They were both pretty bad and, fortunately, no one would publish
them. I call them my apprentice novels. They were kind of the young-man-
grows-up-in-the-south, goes-to-New-York type of thing. I copied a little
bit from the writers I liked, a little Thomas Wolfe, a little William
Faulkner.

"My real aim was to write like the French Existentialists, Sartre,
Camus, Marcel. I had decided that rather than write for the philosphical
quarterlies, I would try to write novels expressing philosphical ideas."

In 1961, Dr. Percy's first published novel, *The Moviegoer,* won the
prestigious National Book Award.

"I was astonished," he recalls. "I had decided to write a book about a
man who is fairly typical in the South and elsewhere. A book about a man
from an upper-class family in New Orleans' Garden District, a man with a
good family and education but who is generally disenchanted with life.
After college, he moves to a middle-class neighborhood in New Orleans
and takes a nominal job as manager of the branch office of a brokerage
firm. He lives alone and is secretive. To get through life, he goes to the
movies."

Dr. Percy tells an unusual story about how *The Moviegoer* may have
won its laurels. "I sent the book to Alfred Knopf, Inc., which had published my uncle's writings," he recalls. "I'm told that when the manuscript
was mentioned to Mr. Knopf, he said, 'what's this fellow's name, Percy,
must be related to old Will Percy. I'm sure he must be a fine boy.' " Knopf
decided to publish the book without reading it, Dr. Percy said. Later,

however, the publisher read it and was not impressed. He did nothing to promote the book.

Luck was on Dr. Percy's side, however. "I'm told," he recalls, "that A. J. Liebling (the caustic critic and journalist) was in New Orleans researching a book on Huey Long and he just happened to walk into a bookstore on Basin Street and buy *The Moviegoer*.

"Liebling really liked the book. Now, it just so happened that his wife, Jean Stafford, was one of three judges for the National Book Award that year. Liebling gave her the book and told her to consider it."

The hardcover version of *The Moviegoer*, Dr. Percy said, "was a moderate financial success. The paperback did quite well." A movie option was recently obtained by actress Karen Black ("Five Easy Pieces") with filming to start this January in New Orleans.

Completing a book about every four years, he followed *The Moviegoer* with three novels, *The Last Gentleman, Love in the Ruins,* and *Lancelot,* and a collection of essays, *Messages in the Bottle*. He is at work on another novel.

"The Moviegoer," Dr. Percy said, "was about an intelligent but ineffectual man searching for meaning in his life in the South. *The Last Gentleman* is sort of like *Roots*. It's about a young Southerner returning home to rediscover his roots and finding that everything has been changed. *Love in the Ruins* is a satirical look at life in the Sixties."

Dr. Percy is a great believer in turning philosophical questions upside down. The moviegoer finds life by studying art; his new book will have a schizophrenic girl discovering that she is sane and the world is crazy.

In *Lancelot,* Dr. Percy has created a hero who, despairing of finding the holy grail of God, searches for the unholy grail of sin.

"One conclusion I have reached here after a year in my cell," says Lancelot-Percy, "is that the only emotion people feel nowadays is interest or the lack of it. . . . Even the horrors of the age translate into interest. Did you ever watch anybody pick up a newspaper and read the headline, "Plane crash kills 300.' "How horrible, says the reader. But look at him when he hands you the paper. Is he horrified? No, he is interested. When was the last time you saw anybody horrified?"

It is Dr. Percy's belief that society has become so sick that no longer can we be shocked. Moral atrocities are met with numb acceptance.

Lancelot has discovered by chance that the blood type of his daughter means he cannot possibly have fathered her. "I can only compare it (the discovery) to the time I discovered my father was a crook," Lancelot says. "I discovered my wife's infidelity and five hours later I discovered my own life. . . . Can good come from evil?"

Lancelot—and Dr. Percy—come to their point: "It is the banality of the past which puts me off. . . . It is because the past, any past, is intolerable, not because it is violent or terrible or doomstruck or any such thing, but because it is so goddamn banal and feckless and useless. And violence is the most banal and boring of all. It is horrible not because it is bloody but because it is meaningless. It does not signify.

"The mystery is: what is one to do with oneself?"

For Lancelot and, Dr. Percy fears, for far too many Americans, the thing to do has become mindless violence, an impotent yielding to self-destruction rather than searching for new alternatives. The discovery of evil is a call to arms for Lancelot.

Lancelot starts his quest for evil: "The mark of this age is that terrible things happen but there is no 'evil' involved. People are either crazy, miserable, or wonderful, so where does 'evil' come in? Is evil to be sought in violence or in sexual behavior?"

Lancelot concludes that The Great Secret of Life is "that man's happiness lies for men in practicing violence upon women and that woman's happiness lies in submitting to it. The secret of life is violence and rape, and its gospel is pornography. The question is, can we bear to discover the secret?"

Lancelot decides—and this is the most-quoted sentence attributed to Dr. Percy in all the reviews of his writing—that:

"I will not tolerate this age."

Lancelot's search for salvation through the study of evil fails. He asks his friend, the priest-physician, "Why did I discover nothing at the heart of evil? There was no 'secret', after all, no discovery, no flickering of interest, nothing at all, not even any evil . . . so I have nothing to ask you after all because there is no answer. There is no question. There is no unholy grail just as there was no Holy Grail."

However, Dr. Percy says, the priest has been "rehabilitated by the horror of what Lancelot has done. He is horrified at the logical basis to Lancelot's action, if we accept the fact that if there is no God, then anything goes."

Religion, Percy says, "no longer works. The words have become worn out, meaningless. That is why for 257 pages, the priest does not offer one word of rebuttal to Lancelot."

Dr. Percy, however, gives the last word of the book to the priest. Lancelot asks, "Very well. I've finished. Is there anything you wish to tell me before I leave?"

The priest replies, "Yes."

Jogging his memory about the book he has attempted to forget, Dr. Percy explains, "The priest's reply is about alternatives. That one doesn't have to submit to the horrors of the age." He adds, "A friend recently sent me a review of *Lancelot* in the *London Times* and the reviewer caught this message. That there are alternatives. That priests and men must try to recreate."

Dr. Percy believes "that the whole world really blew up about World War I and we still don't know why. Before then, men thought that utopia was in sight. There was peace and prosperity. Then everything blew up. We've been in a state of suspended animation ever since, a kind of purge before the next big revolution in American life.

"No, I don't know what the next revolution will bring. I'm not a prophet. But we need to recreate belief in human possibilities, to find an alternative to boredom other than violence. You know, people are always deploring violence, but the happiest I have ever seen the people of my generation was during World War II. More people have been killed in this century than in all of history. It has to get better."

Dr. Percy is working about three hours every morning writing in longhand (he types it in the afternoon) the beginning of his new novel. "It will be about a young, schizophrenic girl," he says, "a sane person in a crazy world.

"I'm still working on the first chapter, which I've rewritten about five times now. It's tough to get the first chapter right, in fact to get the first paragraph right. It will take another three years to complete the book."

Dr. Percy says he is one of maybe "a hundred serious writers in America today, people who make a living strictly by writing literature." He is near the pinnacle of his art and yet his earnings "are maybe half what the physicians earn in this town." Percy has no regrets.

At a recent autographing party, he recalls, his neighbors bought 300 copies of *Lancelot*. "How many will read it, I'm not sure," he says. "The people here still call me Doc and although they know I'm a writer they still ask, 'Come on now, Doc, what do you really do?' "

Percy intends to continue to diagnose society. As Lancelot says from his prison cell, "You like my little view. Have you noticed that the narrower the view, the more you can see?"□

Jim Owens

I started out thinking that I would travel to Ethiopia to join Jim Owens, MD, a missionary physician, and spend a few days with him in the primitive tent cities high in the hills of the ancient land that had been stricken with a killer famine. I knew that World Vision, the international agency that had arranged for Dr. Owens' trip, would facilitate my travel, and, since politicians and rock stars were flying into Addis Ababa on a daily basis, I foresaw no problem.

I had overlooked a medical technicality, however. In order to live in the tent cities, where the life-saving feedings and medical care were being provided, I would first have to submit to inoculations against nine major diseases (the politicians and rock stars were staying at the Addis Ababa Hilton and going nowhere near the countryside). Ideally, the inoculations were to be spread out over months. However, Dr. Owens' tour of duty was to end in three weeks, so that if I wanted to join him I would have to take all the shots within two or three days. A nurse at the Northwestern U. Medical Center Dept. of International Travel told me that, "In good conscience, I cannot inject so many live diseases into the body of one person at one time."

I saw her point. I settled for catching up with Dr. Owens upon his return in February, 1985, to his hometown of Seattle. Instead of a tent, I stayed in the opulent comfort of the Sorrento Hotel, one of my favorites.

I missed out on the eyewitness reportage, but Dr. Owens' memories of the suffering—and salvation—he witnessed are powerful enough.

"To serve in Ethiopia today, you have to be able to see the trees for the forest."

—Missionary physician Jim Owens

HE WENT TO SLEEP every night to the sweet sounds of religious hymns sung by the Ethiopian Christians with whom he worked at the refugee camp. But 50-year-old Seattle pediatrician Jim Owens, MD, was awakened every morning by a different sound—the mournful wails of mothers who had lost their children during the night. The high-pitched wails would begin at the first crack of light—about 5 a.m.—and Dr. Owens would climb out of his cot in a makeshift plaster hut to begin another long day in the World Vision feeding center at the refugee camp at Alamata.

The day's work actually would have begun the night before when Dr. Owens cut into little squares some 100 pieces of paper. In Ethiopia today, these little tickets are more valuable than gold—they are used to admit children to either the feeding center or medical clinic, and they often are the difference between life and death.

Alamata, which sits on a 5,000-foot high plateau 80 miles north of Addis Ababa, the capital of this ancient African land, is a village of 12,000, but refugees fleeing the famine have swollen its numbers to 60,000. The Alamata center has been set up to try to save the children, and most have walked for several days, carrying only the rags on their backs, to reach it. Most have come with their mothers and fathers, but many are orphans and have come alone or with only their brothers and sisters.

Now, in the early-morning hours, Dr. Owens walks outside the barbed-wire gate enclosing the feeding center and begins to walk among the thousands who huddle on the ground outside the gate, hoping for a ticket to get inside. The medical triage is crude—and often cruel.

"They're all in terrible shape," Dr. Owens recalls, "and out of the thousands who wait, I could choose only 50 each morning. For some, I would write out a ticket for feeding; for others, a ticket for the medical clinic. The selection process would take about an hour, and it was agonizing. For every child chosen, many more had to be ignored.

"I did not have to do any sophisticated testing to determine the state of malnourishment. Mostly, I would just put my fingers around their upper arms. The ones who had only skin and bones, instead of fat and muscle, were admitted. When I ran out of tickets, the mothers and children who had not been selected would start to scream and wail and clutch at me with their hands, imploring me to save their lives. It was frightening—not that I felt any personal danger, but that the need was so overwhelming, and often, so beyond me."

The medical terms are "stunting" and "wasting." According to the World Health Organization, any child whose height is less than 90% of average for his age is stunted; any weight less than 85% of average for the height is malnourished, or wasted. In Ethiopia, the children typically are stunted as an adaptation measure to their bleak lives. After the famine of the last year, they also are wasted. Dr. Owens will admit to Alamata only the sickest and the starving:

Those children whose weight is less than 60% of what is normal for their height will be assigned super-intensive feedings five times a day; those weighing 60% to 70% of normal will be assigned intensive feedings four times a day; and those weighing 70% to 85% of normal will be assigned supplemental feedings three times a day. The goal is to admit every child whose weight is 85% or less of normal, but the feeding center can hold only 10,000 and the children already are crowded side by side.

Dr. Owens will assign those children who are both starving and very sick to the medical clinic run by the Sisters of Charity on the other side of the compound. The Sisters of Charity also are caring for 10,000 refugees a day, and they have one supplemental feeding that lasts all day. They also have wards so that the sickest children can stay overnight.

The rest will have to leave at 5 p.m., banished from the feeding center to have to sleep overnight on the unprotected hillsides. They will, however, have hanging around their necks the yellow cards that will entitle them to return the next morning—and the mornings after that—for the precious feedings.

Dr. Owens will leave the feeding center at 5 p.m., too, to return to his makeshift living quarters down the road. The children will chase after him, clinging to his hands and imploring, "Father, feed me, " or "Father, fix my foot." Dr. Owens will think, "I only wish I could," before the guards will force the children away.

For two months last December and January, Dr. Owens was one of five medical missionaries who worked in the feeding center at Alamata. Amid a sea of sickness, he survived outbreaks of meningitis, measles, and pneumonia, a shortage of water for all but cooking for six weeks, and the profound sadness brought on by seeing a proud, dignified people reduced to unspeakable suffering.

"In Ethiopia," he says, "I had to be able to see the trees for the forest. Every day, 15 children would die inside our gates, and many more on the outside, so you had to be able to draw satisfaction from the children you could help, the ones you would see pull through."

It is a Sunday night in Seattle, and Dr. Owens has been back from Alamata for about a week. He has bronchitis from inhaling the contaminated air around the refugee camp, and he has amebiasis from drinking polluted water, but both are responding to medications. That morning, he had heard that one of the World Vision volunteers had contracted meningitis. Dr. Owens' service at the World Vision camp was co-sponsored by Seattle's University Presbyterian Church, of which he is a member, and this night he is on hand for an Ethiopian Benefit Concert.

The program opens with some powerful selections from Handel's "Messiah" and concludes with the Ethiopian Fellowship Choir performing some haunting songs from their homeland. Dr. Owens is scheduled to give a special report on his mission.

"The music moves me," Dr. Owens begins. "First, the passion and suffering of the 'Messiah,' and then the music of Ethiopia. I cannot tell you how good it feels to hear Ethiopian music that is joyous. The joyous sounds we have heard tonight are very different from the lamentations we heard every morning outside the refugee camp.

"Someone asked me, 'If God is just, then why does He let the Ethiopians suffer?' I told him, 'The God I know weeps over what is happening in Ethiopia.' I want to share with you my joys and sorrows, and, yes, hopes over what I have seen in Ethiopia. There is great suffering, but there is also great kindness, and most of the aid from the West is getting through to help the people it needs to help.

"The slides I am going to show are not meant to horrify you with how bad off some of these children are. I assure you that I met hundreds of children like these every day, and many of them are going to make it, thanks to the help people like you are making possible."

Dr. Owens is the medical director at the Echo Glen Children's Center in Snoqualmie, Wash., where he cares for teenage juvenile delinquents. He also coordinates the care of other juvenile treatment centers in the state. He is a former chairman of the AMA task force that developed guidelines for medical care in correctional institutions.

He has been a missionary physician in Cambodia, Thailand, Lebanon, and Somalia—none of which prepared him for the suffering of Ethiopia. "It is 10 times worse than anything I have ever seen before," he says.

With an average per-capita income of only $140, Ethiopia is one of the five poorest nations in the world. Average life expectancy is 40 years. Fewer than one of three Ethiopians can read or write. Only one of nine Ethiopians has access to clean water. Only one of eight children attends school. Most Ethiopian girls are engaged at age 8, married at 10, and mothers at 12. Three of every four Ethiopians live in villages too remote to be reached by ground transportation.

During the past year, the crop failures of the nation's Marxist government have averaged 80% to 100%. It is estimated that 10 million Ethiopians are being victimized by the famine, and that 2.2 million have left their rural homes in search of food and water. At least 2,000 are dying every day, and some estimates run as high as 7,000. One of every two deaths is a child. During 1985, it is estimated that as many as one million Ethiopians may die from a malnourishment—and its cousin, sickness.

"We lost about 15 every day," Dr. Owens recalls. "It's hard for an American to imagine how these people are forced to try to survive. Their entire lives are being spent waiting in line.

"They walk for days or weeks just to get to the camps. Then they wait in lines to try to be admitted to the feeding center or clinic. Then they wait in line to be fed. Many die while they wait.

"Some people say the Ethiopians do not care for their children. Nothing could be further from the truth. The Ethiopians are a very magical, loving people, with beautiful smiles. They have a deep and abiding love for their children, and they have a deep and abiding faith in their Christianity. In Addis Ababa, you see every few feet a garish poster to Marxist revolution, but the people are Christian. They trace their Christianity back to the first century A.D., and they take it seriously. I have never seen a more radiant faith than among the Ethiopians with whom I worked. After doing back-breaking work all day, they spent an hour and a half every night giving devotions and singing hymns.

"Our biggest problem in the camp was overcrowding and a shortage of water. We got our vaccines just in time to head off an outbreak of meningitis. The camp was swept with outbreaks of measles and pneumonia. Many of the children were suffering from diarrhea and were dehydrated. Our water was brought by truck and by women who hauled enormous cans on their backs. But that was enough water only for the cooking. The children were infested with lice and scabies, their eyes encrusted with infection, and there was no water to help them.

"Our water engineer was a wonderful Australian Christian named Rod. He needed one last part for a pipe-fitter to bring water from the village reservoir out to the camp. But in Ethiopia, everything takes time, and the Marxist government sees to it that there are bureaucratic delays. What might have taken hours in Australia was taking weeks in Ethiopia. We would pay double for a "lightning" telephone call, then wait an hour or more for a connection that was so bad you couldn't hear.

"The Ethiopian Christmas is celebrated on Jan. 7, and the two weeks right after that were the worst we experienced. We came within a day or two of having to close the camp. There are three wars going on in Ethiopia: The government is fighting the neighboring country of Somalia, and the provinces of Tigre and Eritrea are fighting the Marxist government. Alamata is located near Tigre, and the Tigrevian rebels were stopping our truck shipments of food, water, and medicines. Our relief planes were being turned back for 'security reasons.'

"Our water supply was running very low, and we were almost out of everything. We had to limit the number of children we could admit for feeding. Finally, at the 11th hour, our supplies arrived.

"The next morning, something even better happened. Every morning, we had been going down to the camp reservoir and looking for water. Nothing. This morning, we went down and our prayers were answered. There was water, fresh clean water to wash our children and help fight off infection. It happened on Jan. 19, which, coincidentally, is the Ethiopian holiday to celebrate baptism. One of the Ethiopian priests came down to bless our water supply.

"The professional staff had been limited to three 'splash baths' a week, and I was in such terrible condition that even the ever-present flies were avoiding me. Rod was the man of the hour."

Rod is only one of the characters Dr. Owens fondly recalls from his Ethiopian mission.

There also was Mother Theresa, who heads the Sisters of Charity mission of Alamata. She stopped by to bless Dr. Owens and tell him how to reach her order in New York and obtain some soy flour. It is soy flour that is the lifeblood of the feeding effort. Soy flour is combined with dry skim milk, oil, sugar, and salt to make the high-calorie brown porridge called "fafa" that is the staple of the feeding program. Every day, scores of shifts of children stand in line to be given the life-saving fafa, though some are so sick that it must be administered by nasogastric drip.

Dr. Owens remembers one starving child who was given a high-energy Australian biscuit, but who was so dehydrated that he almost choked on it. "We had to give him oral hydration salts before we could feed him," Dr. Ownes recalls. "This is only example of how a minor U.S. medicine like oral hydration salts can make a life-saving difference. Many of these children are severely dehydrated from diarrhea."

There was Abade, a young boy who, while standing in line waiting to be fed, was hit in the elbow by a rock thrown by another boy. The elbow became severely infected, and Dr. Owens thought his arm would have to be amputated. The physician prevailed upon Mother Theresa's order to put the boy on a Sisters of Charity plane and fly him back to Addis Ababa for hospitalization.

On Christmas Day, while taking a rest break in the capital city, Dr. Owens tracked down a healthy, smiling, two-armed Abade. The arm had been saved. "He jumped at me with a joyous yell," Dr. Owens says, "and he threw his arm and cast around me and hugged me again and again. It was quite a Christmas present."

There was the old man who sat outside the feeding center, ignoring the dust and the flies and solemnly reading his Bible. He would die soon.

There were the two orphan children, a 12-year-old girl carrying on her back her tiny brother who was so shrunken that he looked like a rag doll. The girl had walked for days—carrying her brother on her back—to reach the camp.

There was Esther, the Ethiopian nurse who would lead the children in humorous singing of the "Diarrhea Song," a musical tool used to teach the children about their diarrhea.

And there was the mother whom Dr. Owens encountered one night outside the camp gate. "Big, huge tears were coming down her cheeks, and her body was wracked with wrenching screams. She had walked for days to bring her child to the camp. She had not been admitted and when she appealed to the guard, he turned on her and whipped her across the face with a stick. She had angry red welts on her face, and the whipping was simply the last indignity. To be whipped for trying to save your child was simply too much. By the next morning, she was gone."

Dr. Owens knows that his experiences and his report are but a snapshot of the panorama of suffering going on in this ancient African land. On the day he left, the camp was preparing to try to ward off an outbreak of cholera. Because the dreaded disease is taboo in Ethiopia, the Soviet-influenced government will not officially admit that it exists. But it, too, is there, waiting to prey on the weakened children.

Ironies abound. The nation is suffering from a terrible drought, but three times during Dr. Owens' stay, monsoon rains washed down upon

Alamata—too late to help the crops, but in time to bring pestilence upon
the thousands of refugees huddled against the hillsides. The Alamata
camp feeds 20,000 a day and for 37 cents an Ethiopian child can be fed
one day, and yet every day thousands are dying for lack of food. During his
rest and recreation breaks in Addis Ababa, Dr. Owens could live in a
world where the suffering and starvation of the countryside are neither
recognized nor regretted.

It is the children that drew the pediatrician to Ethiopia. "When I
showed slides of the Ethiopian children to my patients at the juvenile-
treatment center," Dr. Owens recalls, "they were dumfounded. Many of
the teen-agers at Echo Glen are street kids and have been in trouble with
the law. They looked at these sad faces staring from behind barbed wire
and they asked me, 'What did they do to deserve this?' I had no answer.

"Being in Ethiopia often made me feel as if I were in the middle of
Dante's *Inferno*. But I was able to help make a difference for at least some
of these people. We were able to get tents to shelter some of the sickest
children, instead of having to turn them out to the hillsides. We were able
to build additional feeding wards, so that we could space out some of the
children and not have the terrible overcrowding that can cause epidemics.

"And we finally got our water. Mother Theresa and the Sisters of
Charity do not allow photos to be taken of their compound, and we
always respected their wishes. But the day our water came, Rod and I took
a bucket over to the sisters' mission. The sister looked at me and said, 'Go
ahead, take a picture, take a picture!'

"Why did I go? I guess it is something I felt I had to do. I've seen the
pictures and read the stories that everyone else has seen and read, and for
me it was the faces of the children that stood out. It was easier for me to be
a part of it, to try in a small way to help, than to have to watch it."

Dr. Owens is a deeply religious man, and he thinks that there is hope
as well as suffering coming out of Ethiopia. "Already," he says, "some of
the workers in Ethiopia are talking about trying to turn a disaster into a
development. There is talk of irrigation, of restoring the fertility of the
valley. We know that many of the 10,000 kids we are feeding at Alamata
are going to make it, perhaps as many as 80% to 90%. That's how many
are on supplementary feeding and not intensive. They're going to make it,
that is, unless there's a war-caused shutdown of supplies."

He praises the relief effort being made by the West. "When I arrived
at Alamata, the construction supplies for the feeding center had not yet
been shipped. So, the sides of the shelter were made out of wheat bags
shipped from Canada, and the floor matting was made out of wheat bags
shipped from Australia. When the Canadian news reporters arrived, they
were gratified to see all those maple leaves on the sides of the shelter.

"I guess I do it because I believe I can help make a difference. A few years ago, I volunteered for work at a hospital in Kampuchea (formerly Cambodia). They chose me because I can speak French. Well, the Kampucheans are given two hours of 'political education' a day teaching them to hate Americans and the West.

"Months later, I received a letter from a Kampuchean intern at the hospital. She wanted to thank me for what I had done to help the children. She said, 'We are taught to hate you, but we not only were able to listen to what you had to say, we were also able to see what you did. That made the difference. We could see that you cared about our children.' I still have that letter.

Dr. Owens lost 30 pounds in Ethiopia from his daily diet of ingerra (spongy bread) and wat (stew). He is still recovering from bronchitis and amebiasis. As he talks to a youth group at his church and as he talks to his patients—he thinks of them as his friends—at the juvenile-treatment center, it is plain to see that they are frankly amazed at what he has done.

But it is all part of his life. For years, Dr. Owens' home has been open to homeless children. His wife, Ann, was once a Peace Corps volunteer in Ethiopia. Dr. Owens' only regret is that his time in Ethiopia took him away from the youngsters he is trying to help at Echo Glen.

"I believe that you should use your skills to help others," he says. "Whatever I may have done to help children is nothing compared to what they have meant to me."□

Characters

Alex Comfort

Somewhere on my bookshelf is an autographed copy of the *Joy of Sex,* the sensationally successful how-to manual written by Dr. Alex Comfort (to be honest, I know exactly where it is). The various "Joy" books, as Dr. Comfort calls them, continue to sell well today, 14 years after their initial publication, and remain a publishing phenomenon.

However, in 1979, when I paid a call on Dr. Comfort at his lovely home in Santa Barbara, Calif., sex was the last thing he wanted to talk about.

Dr. Comfort, a very proper British physician, had during World War II been a writing prodigy, whose works of fiction were held in higher esteem than those of his contemporary, George Orwell, who would later write *1984.* Dr. Comfort was also one of the first, along with Sir Bertrand Russell, to warn of the potential threat of nuclear war (getting thrown into jail for the effort). The sex books, he explained, were written almost by accident during a three-week period in the late 1960s. What took time, however, was finding the right artist to graphically illustrate what would become a sexual manifesto.

So, on this day, Dr. Comfort was willing to describe how he put together the *Joy* books, but his heart was in a different crusade— providing better medical care for the nation's rapidly growing elderly population.

In hindsight, Dr. Comfort is once again proven a prophet of honor. In 1986, as our "baby boomers" turn 40 and begin to look forward toward "golden pond" and retirement, America is being confronted for the first time with a new crisis—how to care for the one in five people who will by the year 2020 be 65 or older. A longevity revolution is following the sexual revolution.

Dr. Comfort knew all the time that there's much more to life than sex.

HE WAS THE LEADING literary figure of the "New Romanticism" school that flowered in Britain during World War II. A contemporary of George Orwell, Aldous Huxley, and Franz Kafka, he wrote six novels, seven

306

volumes of poetry, two plays, a short-story collection and—at age 18—an autobiographical travelogue. All his writings were against war, death, and power, and for peace and anarchy.

He was trained as a pediatrician, but his medical and scientific interests soon shifted to gerontology, a field in which he was to become a leading figure. He has written 19 non-literary books, including the benchmark text on aging, *The Biology of Senescence* (twice totally rewritten), and *A Good Age*, described as a self-defense manual for the elderly. A rundown of his scientific papers requires 11 single-spaced pages.

As a young literary man, he was called "the Voltaire of neo-Romanticism." As a mature medical scientist, "the foremost gerontologist of the 20th Century." He was a conscientious objector during World War II while pursuing his medical studies at Cambridge. Because he headed the agitation against indiscriminate Allied bombing, he was blacklisted by the British Broadcasting Corp. His first novel, *No Such Liberty*, examined the neglected and unpopular subject of Allied mistreatment of aliens, and prompted George Orwell to write a critical review that concluded, "There is no such thing as neutrality in this war . . . Objectively, the pacifist is pro-Nazi." In later years, he would be jailed along with fellow libertarian and friend Bertrand Russell for organizing an anti-nuclear sitdown in Trafalgar Square.

Strange, then, that Alex Comfort, MD, PhD, ScD, should now be living in Southern California and best known—in fact, known at all—only for two books about sex.

His sprawling home is nestled beneath the mountains in a fashionable, wooded area of Santa Barbara. Roses bloom in the backyard garden and gracefully spreading trees canopy the driveway. It is here that the old war protester and sexual libertarian now practices his personal revolution.

Dr. Comfort's *Joy of Sex* and its companion, *More Joy of Sex*, have sold in hardback and softcover versions some five million copies, and are the titles that have been on the best-seller lists longer than any other in American publishing history. The sales dwarf those for all his other books combined.

This day, he is like a caged tiger.

"I do not enjoy living only off royalties," says Dr. Comfort. "I have always had a 9–5 medical job, in addition to writing."

Adds his wife, Jane: "Frankly, I have been exploiting him as a domestic help the past few months."

They are a very British couple. Dr. Comfort is dressed in grey slacks, navy blazer, club tie, and ever-present pipe; Mrs. Comfort serves tea and cucumber sandwiches.

His library/writing room long ago overflowed and now spills into another room that is reached by passing through the garage. This room is stacked high with back issues of *Lancet* and the complete file of the *Journal of Gerontology*. On one wall is a huge chart tracing the Comfort family genealogy. Any famous members? "Not really," he says. "But we take great pride in the family motto: 'Take Comfort or take heed!' "

Meticulous research was one key to the success of the "Joy" books, as Dr. Comfort calls them. Thumbing through a voluminous drawer of file cards, he notes: "It's all in here, the documentation for everything written in 'Joy.' "

His wife adds, "The idea for the book began when Alex and I started making notes on our erotic relationship. His original idea was to write a long, scholarly tome, but the publisher talked him out of it."

Dr. Comfort says, "My original draft included both books—the first is a 'how' book and I thought a 'why' book was needed, too—plus the biography. An old publishing friend, James Mitchell of London, and his company, Mitchell Beazley, talked me into splitting the books up and forgetting about the bibliography. It's still here, if anybody's interested. I doubt it.

"Writing is easy; it's the research that's hard. I wrote both 'Joy' books in three weeks. But they were based on my 30 years as a doctor discussing sex with patients, family, and friends."

Mrs. Comfort says, "He's amazing. It's all in his head and he just sits down and writes until he's completed a book. He does his fiction in nothing flat."

Dr. Comfort is a five-fingered typist, the result of a boyhood gunpowder accident that blew off most of his left hand. In 1978, he rattled off four books (*I and That*, which he calls a study of the biology of religion, and a three-book, science-fiction saga "based loosely on the writings of William Blake," the late British mystic poet), edited a book on the sexual consequences of disability, and developed a textbook on geriatric psychiatry. His wife, a psychiatric social worker, edited a book on adolescent sexuality ("I had to take great pains to get the American slang down right," she says. "Americans may speak English, but we'll have to rewrite the book for the British readership.").

Despite the prolific output, Dr. Comfort is disappointed that he did not have time to get around to the project that really interested him: "Doing a historical novel about the physician to Nero, Rome's clown prince emperor. Do you know that Nero was trained as a pop singer? Actually, they just mimed the words in those days. But he always fancied himself a singer, sort of a classical version of Elvis Presley. That's why he was fiddling while Rome burned. That's what he did best. I think a story about Nero's physician would be fascinating."

Dr. Comfort sounded an early call for what came to be known during the 1960s as the 'new morality' or the 'permissive society' when in 1950 he wrote *Sexual Behavior in Society*. His theory—then and now—is that human sexuality should always be a liberating counterpoint to what he perceives as man's unrelenting struggle against an always-hostile environment.

In the late 1960s, he began to think that the time had come for an open book about sex. "I was traveling regularly back and forth to the States," he said, "and I noticed how open people were becoming, particularly in California."

Dr. Comfort wrote the text for what he called a "cordon bleu guide to lovemaking." Distinguishing the book were explicit illustrations done with air-brushed exquisiteness by a pair of artists finally selected after 31 go-rounds.

Dr. Comfort's advice basically boils down to: "Whatever you're doing, chances are a lot of other people are, too, and it's all right." The style is upbeat and non-judgmental (oral sex is referred to as "mouth music" in one place and "gamahuche" in another).

"There's nothing new in the book," Dr. Comfort says. "It's just reassurance, telling people it's OK. The book succeeded because it became the first coffee-table book about sex. People could put it on their coffee tables right next to 'Great Art of the Western World.' "

Publishers were initially skeptical, and Crown, the house that took U.S. hardback rights, made Dr. Comfort "tone things down a bit" before agreeing to put it out at Christmas, 1972. First printing was only 15,000 copies, and the elated people at Crown had to airlift from the printer in Holland tens of thousands of copies to satisfy the Christmas trade. It has been a best-seller ever since—1.25 million in hardback, 3.75 million in softcover (published by Simon & Schuster).

Jane Comfort says, "When 'Joy' first came out, everybody was embarrassed at even considering some of the techniques. Now they're embarrassed if they haven't tried most of them.

"The book, after all, is based on much more than just our experiences. We don't swing from the chandelier, you know!"

Dr. Comfort says, "When 'Joy' came out, we thought of it as a counseling guide, but we did not identify ourselves as the medical couple upon whom the book is based. We avoided identifying ourselves, not because of the subject but because any form of self-advertising by medical professionals is absolutely forbidden. We didn't want the publicity anyway because we never had any intention to run a sexual counseling service."

Dr. Comfort turned 59 in January, and he is anxious to get on with new things.

The 'Joy' books are behind him now, Dr. Comfort stresses. His immediate interests are finding a full-time faculty position in the United

States and teaching geriatric medicine. He is an affiliate professor at several universities, but notes, "They're happy to use your name and let you lecture, but they don't want to pay you any money. Many of these faculties are closed shops."

He is licensed to practice medicine in England and Canada, but not in the U.S., and he is not eager "to repeat my medical training. Some of these requirements are unrealistic. Take continuing medical education. The way it stands now I can get more credit for sitting through one of my lectures than for actually delivering it.

"What I'd like to get is a university medical school position where I could work in the hospital without a license to practice. I don't want to practice private medicine; I just want to be able to teach and practice geriatric medicine under the aegis of a medical center. I'm negotiating with one right now, but you really have to prod them. We love Santa Barbara—who wouldn't—but if I can't do the kind of work I want to do, we'll just have to go elsewhere."

Unlike his earlier literary works that were characterized by the inescapability of death, or the triumph of death and physical decline, Dr. Comfort now believes there is both growing interest and growing hope in combating death and the aging process through scientific research. "Prolonging vigor" is what it's all about, he says, "and we have every reason to believe that the span of active life can be increased."

Dr. Comfort's art is an art of protest. He protested war, and his writings received an unusual amount of hostility, though Vietnam would later vindicate much of what he was saying. He protested sexual repression, and his writings reaped enormous rewards.

He emigrated to Santa Barbara with the profits from 'Joy' in 1974, investing in a think tank called the Center for Democratic Studies. The think tank collapsed, though Dr. Comfort and two others hang on in what is now called the Institute of Higher Studies. In the meantime, he has become one of those exiled expatriates who were the heroes of his early novels.

He is now protesting social bias against the aging. And looking for a forum to wage the fight. "Let's face it," says Alex Comfort, "my work is my life."

In the meantime, there's always that book to be written about Nero.□

Mort Copenhaver

I've only spent one night in a real castle, and, frankly, one night was enough.

Dr. Mort Copenhaver, an orthodontist who calls himself a recluse, agreed in 1978 to show me the castle he built by hand atop Phoenix' Camelback Mountain on one condition—that the story publicize his foundation to fund orthodontia for needy youngsters.

I quickly accepted, and days later we were wending our way up boulder-strewn roads to reach the drawbridge (though, perforce, there was no moat). The next morning, beneath a ferociously hot Arizona sun, his good friend, Bev, drove me hither and yon in a silver Mercedes, while I photographed the castle from various angles.

Believe me, it's quite a place. If you're ever in Phoenix, look for Dr. Copenhaver's castle. It will be the highest structure on Camelback Mountain, as high up as one can see. That was the vision that sustained him over 12 long years.

"It is a bit different," says Mort Copenhaver, DDS.

It started as a magnificent obsession and now sits high atop Phoenix' landmark Camelback Mountain. It is Dr. Copenhaver's home and it literally is a castle.

Working in fits and starts over the last 12 years, Dr. Copenhaver (and anyone he could talk into temporarily sharing his dream) built his castle rock by 100-pound rock.

Armed only with a jackhammer, he started his assault on the huge rounded boulders atop Camelback. The site he had purchased was far above the other homes and, to all but the eye of a dreamer, totally uninhabitable. It took him three years just to carve out an access road up the steep grade to the building site. Then he had to rebuild it because an irate neighbor refused to allow a zoning variance permitting the road.

"Things like that don't stop me," Dr. Copenhaver says. "In a way I was glad. It gave me a chance to go back and build the road right.

"What really bothered me was that I might not be able to finish things. About the time I was getting started, Lady Bird Johnson and some others came down here and declared Camelback a landmark. The save-the-mountain people were up in arms. I had gotten my building permit just in the nick of time.

"It took me eight years just to get one zoning variance permit. Every time I'd go in for a hearing, one of my neighbors would be there to oppose it. He had it written right in my permit-to-build that he would be notified every time I sought another variance. But now my neighbors all say how much they admire the way the castle blends right into the mountain landscape. At night, you can hardly see it. At this last hearing when my permit was granted, all my neighbors showed up and talked in my favor (the holdout recently died)."

Fearing to rattle his neighbors and the zoning people, Dr. Copenhaver has held off on publicity about his unusual home. This month, however, he is opening his home to the press on behalf of another dream—providing orthodontal care to needy children.

As a man who has practiced general dentistry in Phoenix for 18 years, Dr. Copenhaver estimates that "about half my time is spent in orthodontia. It's amazing how many people, especially children, need orthodontia. But many can't afford it. What this country needs is preventive orthodontia at reasonable cost. Too many people cannot afford the prices being charged by orthodontists."

Dr. Copenhaver has set up a nonprofit foundation, the Castle Foundation, to raise money for "orthodontics for the underprivileged." On Friday, Oct. 27, he will host a $100-a-plate cocktail buffet at his castle to raise funds. That weekend, he will open the castle to public tours at $10 daytime, $15 twilight. If successful, the format will be repeated later. He has also enlisted the Phoenix Ski Club and Optimist Club to aid the foundation.

Here's what visitors to Dr. Copenhaver's castle will see:

A narrow, winding road up a 25-degree grade to a remote-controlled gate. Beyond the gate, two German Shepherds patrol the road, which leads to the fortress-like castle, complete with battlements and walls six feet thick.

"I've always associated steep grades with castles," says Dr. Copenhaver. "You look at all those Scottish castles, and they're always on top of a hill, in position to be defended. It was the slope of the mountain that made me decide to build a castle."

The view is breathtaking—a sweeping look at metropolitan Phoenix.

"As a boy growing up on a Colorado ranch," says Dr. Copenhaver, "I promised myself that someday I would own a big house on a big cliff overlooking a big lake. I don't have the lake, but this will do."

Everything is king-size. Rooms have 15-foot ceilings. There are five bedrooms, 7½ bathrooms, living quarters on eight different levels, including luxurious servants' quarters underneath the castle.

Colored lights play on a 20-foot recirculating waterfall that cascades in front of a huge fireplace in the living room. The living room also boasts a dining table that would do a feudal baron proud and two gilded throne chairs that would do his lord proud. There's a similar waterfall-over-fireplace unit in the bi-level master bedroom, which opens onto a terrace.

"Actually when I started to build this," says the thrice-divorced Dr. Copenhaver, "I was thinking of a playboy pad. But you mature as you get older."

The family room has an inside bathing pool with a large palm tree on one side and a spacious bar on the other. The roof opens and closes at the push of a button. A display area of feudal relics includes a fully armored knight and dueling swords. Antique furniture and elaborately carved wood abounds. There are secret passageways and a dungeon, which resembles a disco with antique musical instruments recessed into the walls.

"A Canadian just offered me $1.5 million for the castle," says Dr. Copenhaver, "but no way. How do you put a price on 12 years out of your life? Right now, I'm arguing with the city appraisers over its tax status. I'm hoping they value it at no more than $300,000. I'd work on the castle for a while, then have to get back to my practice to make some money to pay the bills and catch up on my social life. One wife left me because she couldn't stand all the time I was spending up on the mountain."

The castle has common touches: a handsome den-library off the dungeon, a gourmet kitchen set off with heraldic emblems, a game room with pool table, a two-car garage. The final touch will be a tennis court now being built below the castle.

"I used to play a little tennis in college," says Dr. Copenhaver.

"You should see him snow-ski and water-ski," says the dentist's friend, Bev. "I'm pretty hard-working myself, but I've never seen anyone as driven as Mort is."

The dentist adds, "As a farm boy, I learned that it is often necessary to do whatever has to be done. From time to time, I had help building the castle. High school boys, friends who could be conned into working with the promise of all the beer they could drink. One of my sons helped out, but he broke his neck swinging a sledge hammer. The gas tank on a tractor exploded once and I got burns over 20% of my body. But I kept on. One friend showed me how to install plumbing. Another gave tips on electrical wiring. Phoenix city inspectors kept watch on the construction."

The castle is virtually part of the mountain, expanding and contracting as the mountain does. Because of the building material, it requires little heating or cooling. Dr. Copenhaver uses solar energy for most of his heat, and a 10,000-gallon water tank—made from the solid rock—is a coolant in summer and a heat-storage unit in winter. Depending on the season, hot or cold water is pumped through the radiators.

"I've never had any architectural training," Dr. Copenhaver says, "but I would read a lot at the library, including everything written about the pyramids. My idea of a great time is going to the library. I'd rather go to the library than go dancing. And I'm a slow reader. But once I'm through, I've got it. I used to make little drawings of how I wanted the rooms to look and then I'd go ahead and build them."

The castle is basically built of 100-pound rocks jackhammered out of the building site. The 100-pound size was best because one man could lift it, yet it was still adequate for building. The major expense was the 50,000 bags of cement required to hold those rocks together.

"I was taught to finish whatever I started," says Dr. Copenhaver. "Once I finished the access road (after three years), I knew I could build my castle. I would wake up every day before 6 a.m. and pound away until noon, then head for the office. Whenever I got bored or tired, I would just take a little time off and recharge myself. Everybody has a hobby. Building this castle was my hobby."

Dr. Copenhaver, 45, considers himself "somewhat of a recluse," and the decision to allow reporters into his castle was made only "to help raise funds for my foundation to provide orthodontia for children. I hope to make this program nationwide. And I've had some interest from Mexico and Guatemala. Up to now I haven't provided orthodontia for anyone outside my practice. Except for Bev, of course. And, come to think of it, I straightened the teeth of my last girlfriend, too. But I'd like to help people all over. I was going to retire at 42, but for right now this orthodontia thing is it for me." He intends to show his castle on Alveolar Ridge ("that's Latin for jaw; I'm high enough up to name it whatever I want"), aptly located at 5050 Red Rock Dr. ("that's how it was built, by chiseling away at this red rock") on behalf of preventive orthodontia.

Despite his playboy appearance and appurtenances, Dr. Copenhaver is a man of serious bent. He is apt to interrupt his long silences with learned comments about the curvature of teeth ("the need for orthodontia goes back to human evolution. . . ."), mechanical intricacies ("this mountain slope is a 25-degree grade, which means it's on an angle of . . ."), and physics ("the water tank provides a cooling-heating system by collecting water and then . . .").

Friend Bev says, "A woman has to be a strong person to have her own interests, or else Mort would drive you up the wall."

Dr. Copenhaver now wants all Americans to have straight teeth. It's a challenging goal. In fact, it's a little like building a castle atop a mountain. But he hopes that this time he won't have to go it alone.□

Chris Chandler

They really do climb the mountain "because it's there."

That, and for a few other reasons, explains Chris Chandler, MD, who in 1976 as part of the U.S. bicentennial team reached the summit of Mount Everest.

IMAGES FLASH BY. Men moving up the mountain.

It is the American Bicentennial Expedition taking on Mount Everest. Late last year, the expedition put two men on the top of Everest—one of them a physician—the first Americans to conquer the peak since 1963. The event was featured in a TV network special this January.

On this spring day in 1977, however, the images are flashed on the refrigerator door of Chris Chandler, MD, who, with Bob Cormack, reached the summit.

Dr. Chandler, 28, is a free spirit, both as a climber and a physician.

In many ways, he is the personification of the American bicentennial effort—an expedition that came about purely by chance. The expedition hastily flung together climbers who were friends but who had no previous climbing experience in the Himalayas. TV filmed it, strictly on a hunch.

Dr. Chandler is bearded, with long, blond hair falling to his shoulders. He is dressed in jeans, clogs, sweatshirt, and plaid outdoorsman jacket.

He is between 24-hour shifts at Seattle's West Seattle emergency room ("at first, they got on me a little bit about my appearance, but actually we do a pretty good job for them—most of the time. It's just something you don't pay too much attention to.")

The physician lives in Vashon, Wash., a ferry ride across the bay from Seattle. His small cottage sits above the water. He shares it with a cat and a female blues singer, currently out of work. Posters of music and mountains cover the walls. A motorcycle sits in the driveway ("my only transportation—the two old cars aren't working"). Below, bobbing in the water, is his 10-foot dinghy.

A potbelly stove serves in lieu of a fireplace; the rug is a memento from Nepal. The stereo alternates from blues standards to Himalayan chants. Laidback is the West Coast vernacular for Chris Chandler, MD. Soft-spoken but iron-willed.

As he flashes the carousel of slides against his refrigerator door, Dr. Chandler recalls the unusual way in which his climb to fame came about.

The leader of the expedition, Philip Trimble, a 39-year-old State Dept. lawyer, wrote a law school friend in the U.S. embassy in Nepal, asking permission to climb in the Himalayas.

Mountain climbers, Dr. Chandler noted, like to talk about the "eight-thousanders" (peaks that are 8,000 meters or 26,247 feet). There are only 14 in the world and most are in the Himalayas.

Trimble had asked permission in March, 1976, to attempt one of several Himalayan peaks smaller than the two giants—Mount Everest (29,028 feet) and K2 (a mere 778 feet lower, and considered by many the toughest climb in the world).

The mountains Trimble had specified were not available (Himalayan mountains are booked seasons in advance), but would he like Mount Everest instead? The king of mountains is booked through 1985, but the French had cancelled their expedition for the fall of 1976 (because of the fierce weather, there are only two times each year when one group only can attempt Mount Everest: "pre-monsoon," in the spring, and "post-monsoon," in the fall).

Trimble booked the vacated fall slot, and quickly put together a climbing team of 11 Americans and one Dutchman. Two were women. The group was thrown together almost casually, consisting mostly of friends who had climbed together previously. Dr. Chandler took a leave of absence from West Seattle Hospital, and prepared for the climb in a matter of months.

It was this element of adventure that convinced a television network to risk its resources on the Everest climb. Barry Frank, producer of the show for CBS-TV, told the *New York Times:*

"What first struck me about the idea was that the people were not professional climbers, not astronaut-like automatons. They were interesting in and of themselves—one of them working for the State Dept., another a chemical engineer, a teacher of modern dance, two doctors (the other, Dee Crouch, MD, Boulder, Col., did not get to attempt the summit). And here they were, going off on every man's dream. I didn't want a mountain show, I wanted a people show."

Dr. Chandler was to be one of those people.

A native of Wenatchee, Wash., he started climbing in high school as part of Boy Scout activities. He was also attracted to the mountains by his love of skiing and his service on the National Ski Patrol.

By 1976, his climbs included 15 ascents of Washington's Mount Rainier, the conquering of North America's tallest mountain, Alaska's Mount McKinley, and expeditions in the Sierra Nevadas, Canadian Rockies, Olympic and Cascade ranges, and in Peru and the European Alps.

Of his climbs abroad, Dr. Chandler said that a big part of the fun was "the trip itself, the chance to meet new people and see how different cultures live. This was one of the big advantages to the Everest trip, too."

While climbing, he also managed to earn his MD degree in 1973 at the U. of Washington Medical School, serve an internship in New York City's Harlem Hospital, and serve with the Kilimanjaro Christian Medical Center in Moshi, Tanzania.

A high school friend, writing in a Seattle newspaper, recalled his own jealousy that "he (Dr. Chandler) could come out for track in his senior year and qualify in the mile run, nearly breaking a long-standing school record, while I struggled to just place in meets after having turned out for years."

The physician-to-be managed this, the friend recalled, by running on golf courses at 6 a.m. every day. "yet, when offered a chance to go skiing, he took the risk, jumped training, and went. The coach was furious, but Chris just grinned his good-natured grin and all was forgiven."

After some shakedown climbs on Mount Rainier and the Colorado Rockies, Dr. Chandler and the expedition left for Katmandu, where they underwent additional acclimatization and, then, on Sept. 1 started the six-week push for the summit.

Dr. Chandler was a relative unknown among Northwest climbers— "a young Turk" in the mountaineering set, according to veterans such as Willie Unsoeld of Olympia, Wash.

Months later, Dr. Chandler recalled, he had his chance to prove himself.

"This is it," he thought as he set off with Cormack for the nine-hour trek from the last camp to the summit.

"Finally, we've cut the cord between the rest of the camps. The whole reason we've come to the mountain was to experience that feeling of being above the last camp and going for the top, knowing that you're really pushing it.

"As we came over the south summit and took a look along the summit ridge, it was our first view . . . from the summit to the top, and both of us felt our stomachs sort of sink. We said, it looks bad. It's a long way, it's fluted ridge, the winds are really heavy. It's super cold. The weather does not look very inviting, and the ridge was steep, and we were very pessimistic at that point."

Dr. Chandler's partner, Bob Cormack, recalled, "It was a crummy day to climb Everest. The wind was so strong that we had to squat down for a few minutes every 10 steps."

Above 18,000 feet, Dr. Chandler said, human tissue begins to deteriorate from lack of oxygen. The fragile brain tissues that control thought and judgment are the first affected. One grows weary ("it takes an hour or so just to put on your boots at those kind of altitudes," Dr. Chandler said).

After Dr. Chandler and Cormack broke camp for the last 1,528-vertical-foot climb, observers lost sight of them in clouds after they crossed the last main obstacle, the dangerous "Hillary Step."

The Nepal Foreign Ministry reported to the press that they were following the traditional southeast ridge route pioneered by the first climbers of the mountain, England's Sir Edmund Hillary and his Sherpa guide Tenzing Norgay, in 1953. The ministry noted, "We have every reason to believe they are going to make it."

Drawing on a table napkin, Dr. Chandler sketches what it looked like at the south summit, just 278 feet short of the top.

"The winds have for centuries been blowing the snow and ice up across the ridge. That ice has formed a cornice overhanging the ridge. Judging what is the mountain ridge and what is the cornice—and not venturing out onto the cornice, which can break off—is critical."

Everest overlooks four countries, Dr. Chandler noted, and a misstep might plummet the climber into one of them.

"It was almost surrealistic," he said. "It was like we were living a dream. It was steep. We looked down to our left. It was a good 8,000 feet down to advance base, and we looked down on snow fields . . . and on the other side, there was the glacier . . . it was very steep."

"I felt like I was in a moon suit. It was an intense feeling of suffocation. I felt like I was going to faint. My vision began to get narrower and narrower, until it was almost like looking down a tunnel. I remember actually enjoying it because you could stop and rest, lean on your axe, regain your breath. They were nice rest periods, and slowly it would all come back."

It was 4:15 p.m. on Oct. 8 when Dr. Chandler and Cormack finally stood on the summit, shooting photographs and TV film.

And what did he feel like after scaling a peak thrown up maybe a hundred million years ago?

"Well, here we are. It's all downhill from here on out," Dr. Chandler says.

Dr. Chandler said that he came up to the summit fairly quickly in four or five steps and "brought my hands up in the air like victory. It was too much. There was no oxygen left. I totally collapsed with my arms around the tripod (placed by a previous Chinese delegation) to keep from slipping down the slope."

Cormack took some photos of the physician, but the film was ruined (and the photos of Dr. Chandler taken from the TV footage are fuzzy).

As they looked around the edge of the world while hurricane winds howled, the two had sobering thoughts. "I better get the hell out of here," is the way Cormack recalls it. "We could hardly stand up," Dr. Chandler said. "I asked myself, 'what am I doing here?' "

Roped together on the summit for half an hour, the two weary climbers became preoccupied with survival. As they turned away, they left no U.S. flag on the summit. It was in Cormack's pocket, "but it was just too cold and complicated to get it out." Ever the romantic, Dr. Chandler pulled out the scarf given to him by his girlfriend and blessed by a lama. The two wrapped it around the tripod and took a picture. "It seemd fitting," Dr. Chandler said.

Expedition leader Trimble called off a second summit attempt by a team of three men because of the continued high winds and numbing cold.

Dr. Chandler recalls that he was originally scheduled for the second summit attempt, but was paired with Cormack when another climber slotted for the first team became slightly ill and decided he would be at maximum strength if he waited for two days and went on the second three-man team. The wait for this climber, Dr. Chandler observes sympathetically, may be forever.

An encore to Mount Everest is not easy, but Dr. Chandler has one in mind: assaulting K2 in the summer of 1978. Already, he is making plans with another Seattle physician, Robert T. Schaller, MD, 41, a pediatric surgeon.

Mountaineering, like politics, makes for strange bedfellows. Consider Drs. Chandler and Schaller.

Dr. Chandler seems casual and laidback. Dr. Schaller seems compulsive and buttoned-up. A Yale graduate who once did the mile in 4:01, and who still can run 15 miles in an hour and a half, Dr. Schaller dresses in pinstriped suits, button-down shirts, and rep ties. His shoes are shined and his hair closely shorn in the Ivy look. But he and his younger colleague are as one in their addiction to the mountains.

Dr. Schaller started to climb in the early 1960s as a medical student.

The surgeon reflected on his hobby:

"I love it," he said, "because when you're in the mountains you know that's as close as you're ever going to get to—I won't say God—but as close as you're ever going to get to the world. I quit going to church when I started to climb. I can't describe the feeling when I come upon a virginal slope that's been there long before us and will be there long after we're gone.

"All I can tell you is look at the photos. That tells it all."

Dr. Schaller has had nine years of residency training in surgery, moving from thoracic to orthopedic work to pediatrics. He has little time for his speciality, however.

Dr. Schaller took six months from his practice when he attempted to climb the forbidding K2 with an American group in 1975 (foul weather and a porters' strike foiled the effort; the peak in the Karakorum region of the Himalayas has been mastered only once—by a two-man Italian team in 1954. Mount Everest, by contrast, has been climbed by 55 people). "I grossed maybe $10,000 that year," he recalls, "not enough to cover liability insurance.

Climbing has already cost Dr. Schaller one marriage, and he refers to rumblings by his second wife. He says his professional career also suffers from the sorties into the mountains. But, climb he must, he says.

Dr. Chandler, likewise, would make his living climbing mountains— if only he could. Physicians are always in demand for climbing expeditions—whether superb climbers or not—and offers are coming in.

During the Mount Everest expedition, Dr. Chandler treated fellow climbers and young Nepali children. He himself made it to the top without as much as a case of frostbite ("My biggest health problem was diarrhea brought on by the food in Katmandu").

Money is not important to Dr. Chandler, but he notes that "I need to earn $20,000 just to begin to think about breaking even. I like to practice medicine and I like to climb mountains, but I wish the ratio would work out a little more even. Right now, I can only squeeze in a weekend climb every three months or so."

The two physicians animatedly discuss the assault on K2 that is more than a year away. "But we're running out of time," Dr. Schaller asserts.

It is a strange business, mountaineering, Dr. Schaller says, fraught with—of all things—politics. He would like to climb K2 from the Sinkiang province of China, but politics make this entry doubtful. A big factor in the foiling of his earlier K2 climb was the unreliability of the local porters, whose enthusiasm for the mountains is not equal to that of the skilled Sherpas, who shepherd the Everest expeditions. Recently in Uganda's Mountains of the Moon, an American expedition was hassled at 20,000 feet or so by Swiss and Zairean authorities looking for a fee.

Both Drs. Chandler and Schaller are interested in the medical aspects of mountaineering, and have researched metabolic changes at high altitudes and the performance of essential equipment such as oxygen masks.

The two could talk all night, but tomorrow morning marks another 24-hour shift for Dr. Chandler. Dr. Schaller has a surgery scheduled (he recalls the emergency operation he was prepared to do at 18,000 feet on K2 when a helicopter due the week before fortuitously arrived and took the patient back to sterile conditions at base camp).

On another medical matter, Dr. Schaller notes that the Karakorums are often referred to as cancer-free, presumably because of their vegetarian diets. They do have cancer, he said, "that is, the few of them who manage to live beyond 50. Most appear to die before then."

Outside the restaurant, there are a few last words about the need to assure compatibility among the K2 climbers (the earlier K2 effort, Dr. Schaller believes, suffered from a lack of the teamwork essential to tough climbs).

Teamwork is the cardinal virtue among the fiercely individualistic mountain climbers. Dr. Chandler's girl friend recalls that as a child one of her babysitters used to be the now-legendary Pete Schoening of Seattle. It was Schoening who accounted for one of the most memorable mountaineering feats in K2's history.

While clearing a tent platform for the night, six climbers, roped together, slipped, and five of them fell over the edge. Only Schoening remained on his feet. He hooked his rope around a convenient ice projection and held the swinging five for more than an hour while they worked their way up to safety. One was later swept away by an avalanche. Schoening, who has lost parts of several fingers to frostbite, says, "If you haven't lost a finger, you haven't really been on a climb."

Both Drs. Chandler and Schaller still have all their fingers, but, clearly, the risks are there (six lives have been lost on the 10 K2 expeditions). It accounts for Dr. Schaller's alternating humor, seriousness, and sardonicisms.

"You know," Dr. Chandler said, "sometimes I'll be walking about in Seattle and the feeling will just come over me:

"I have to get up in the mountains."

Postscript

On Jan. 15, 1985, Dr. Chandler, then 36, died while trying without oxygen to reach the summit of Nepal's 28,208-foot Mount Kangchenjunga, the world's third-highest peak. A spokesman for the Nepal Tourism Ministry said that the climber died at about the 25,000-foot level on Kangchenjunga, on the Indian-Nepalese border.

His widow, Cherie Bremer-Kemp, a 38-year-old cardiac nurse, was with him on the mountain and suffered frostbite as she struggled to get her husband down the mountain after he was struck by cerebral edema, the most severe form of altitude sickness. She herself faced amputation of most of her toes and fingers above the knuckles.

"I am not angry at the mountain," she said. "I am just angry at myself that I couldn't have done more to help him. I miss Chris."

The Australian-born nurse vowed to return to a village near the base of Kangchenjunga to set up a clinic and school as a memorial to her husband. "The people of the village are desperately in need." she explained. "One of the last things Chris and I talked about was setting this up."□

The AMA Story

James H. Sammons

The American Medical Association is a large, powerful, diverse organization whose real strength is to be found in its thousands of members who year after year volunteer their time and talent on behalf of improved patient care.

The true legacy of the AMA is that, unique in the Western world, American medicine remains free of undue governmental interference. The AMA position is, and always has been, that care of the patient must come first. In brief, the AMA message is: Medical care is provided by physicians, not by government agencies.

The AMA sees itself as the doctors' advocate and as the patients' advocate, and a fair appraisal of the record will demonstrate that it is on behalf of this philosophy that the Association has committed its power and its prestige.

Over the decades, the AMA has spoken with thousands of voices, through its board of trustees, house of delegates, hundreds of councils and committees, staff officials, publications, and Washington office. However, when all is said and done, one among the thousands has left a vital imprint upon the organization:

James Harris Sammons, MD, who was appointed Executive Vice President in 1974 and 12 years later remains as the Association's chief executive officer.

It is a little-known fact that back in 1974 the AMA almost went bankrupt. Years of deficit financing and a sudden upsurge in the cost of publishing—paper, printing, and postage—had the organization reeling and for the final three months of 1974 the AMA had to borrow to meet payroll! AMA's reputation in Washington was at an all-time low. It all came to a bitter showdown in December, 1974, when angry delegates, shaken that the nation's most-affluent professional group could have fallen into such a predicament, demanded answers from their trustees and staff.

It was Jim Sammons who engineered the turnaround, a turnaround so dramatic that, today, the AMA is a $200-million-a-year operation, with $150 million in reserves. Much of the reserves are in prime Chicago real estate that soon will be transformed into an AMA-powered redevelopment of the Association's extensive land holdings just west of

322

Michigan Avenue. The AMA also owns its own building in Washington, D.C., and the new structure is graced with a $1.2-million corporate art collection. For years to come, the AMA will be a "big player" on the medical scene.

Many people, of course, share in this revitalization of the world's largest medical organization, but, make no mistake about it, Jim Sammons' fingerprints are all over the place.

BACK IN 1943, when he was 16 and growing up in the small Alabama town of Clayton—population maybe 2,000 if everybody were at home— young Harris Sammons, as he was exclusively known in those days, set off in a Model A Ford with his good friend Tommy Lassiter for the town of Eufaula 21 miles down the road.

Eufaula was where the girls were, but by the end of their double-date Harris and Tommy had a problem. The Model A, which came for $35 complete with a rumble seat, had been in the garage only that morning to get it running and now the forward gears had burned out. The boys walked the Eufaula girls home, and then young Harris folded down the windshield, straddled the steering wheel—which included sparks and throttle—threw the car into reverse, and with Tommy as navigator proceeded to drive the recalcitrant car for the entire 21 miles to make it home the only way he could. Backwards.

Even then, young Harris was a man who knew where he wanted to go, who was interested in direction, not driving style, who wanted his own hands firmly at the steering wheel, and who had to get moving. Immediately.

The determination stayed with him over the next 41 years, and today, in March, 1984, upon his 10th anniversary as the chief executive officer of organized medicine, James Harris Sammons, MD, can look back with pride upon driving the AMA forward from the dark days of virtual bankruptcy in 1974 to today's colossus as the most powerful medical organization in the world.

It was not an easy ride.

December, 1974. Portland, Ore.

Of the hundreds of meetings, large and small, private and public, that accompany an AMA Interim Convention, few are as boisterous as the exclusive "SOS" session for top staff. The acronym may or may not stand for "Save Our Staff," but it honors such efforts. In Portland in 1974, the mood was somber.

Beset by a financial crunch that threatened to eat it alive, the AMA was suddenly reeling from the effects of years of deficit financing. The high costs of publishing—paper, postage, printing—had dealt a particularly heavy blow. For Dr. Sammons, who had been selected executive vice president (EVP)-designate only the past March in a controversial and stormy meeting that required 15 ballots by the Board of Trustees, the subsequent months had been a baptism by fire.

That June, at the Annual Convention, angry delegates, misinformed in part by a lurid article in *Medical World News* that portrayed a scenario of sinister scheming to enable the forces of the American Medical Political Action Committee (AMPAC) to seize control of the organization, had lashed out. An 11th-hour candidacy for AMA president-elect was mounted by Richard S. Wilbur, MD, the former AMA deputy EVP and the man who after 15 ballots had been bested by Dr. Sammons in the contest to replace the retiring EVP Ernest B. Howard, MD. Dr. Wilbur came within two votes of upsetting the previously unopposed Max Parrott, MD, a Sammons supporter, in the race for the AMA's highest elected office. Seven new trustees were elected and two incumbents who had voted for Dr. Sammons, physicians Donald Wood and John Chenault, were denied re-election, a rare event. The House of Delegates' actions were widely perceived as a vote against the stormy nature of Dr. Sammons' selection.

Dr. Sammons remained unperturbed; he had more important things to worry about. Asked earlier by the *Medical World News* writer what he made of the controversy over his selection, the new EVP-designate replied, "What this means to me is that I am delighted that the present and future leadership of the organization want me in this job." He added, "We have many problems to solve and I did not seek this job to preside over the demise of the American Medical Association."

By July, the storm clouds were gathering. Board Chairman Raymond Holden, MD, was summoned to Chicago to confront a rapidly growing financial problem. "The hole was growing deeper by the day," Dr. Holden recalls. "It looked as if we might have to padlock the building."

In September, Dr. Sammons remembers, AMA Finance Director Sam Miller walked in and quickly came to his point.

"Sign this, if you want to meet the October payroll."

The first of three monthly $1-million notes from Continental Bank was required to enable AMA to pay its 1,000 employees.

"It was a bolt out of the blue," Dr. Sammons says. "One day, Sam just walked in and said, 'Here it is. We ran out.' Three times, I had to sign loan notes. Just like that."

Dr. Sammons grabbed the steering wheel. That October he tackled the issue upfront. "Gentlemen, we're going to go broke unless we take some immediate actions," he told the board. The "designate" had been dropped from his title, and he was now in command of a sputtering vehicle.

The new EVP made three controversial recommendations: Raise the dues ("Every doctor in this country could pay five times the current dues and not begin to pay back what this organization has done for them.") Reduce the vast number of AMA committees and councils ("We need to get rid of the Tinkertoys. We can no longer afford all our proliferating fiefdoms, each going off on its own ego trip.") Discontinue the acceptance of advertising in AMA publications ("The net gain is not worth the cost.") Right down the line, the board supported its EVP in his determination to balance the budget and build up reserves.

But, in Portland that December, it was to be another shootout. In their attempt to give the house the most up-do-date information about AMA finances, the board and staff succeeded only in confusing the already upset delegates, who could not believe the sequence of events that had made the AMA financially vulnerable. Trustees were accused of lying. Some delegates called for "management heads to roll."

So, at the 1974 SOS session, the booze flowed, but the good times did not roll.

At one point, the entire board had discussed—though briefly—resigning en masse. Dr. Sammons' principal deputy, Joe D. Miller, recalls attending a dinner one night in honor of President-elect Dr. Parrott, a friend and a Portland native, and being absolutely depressed. Miller, a social man, says, "I walked into that room, looked around, and left. The way I was feeling there was nobody in that room I felt like talking to."

Later one night, Miller and Dr. Sammons, the two top staff executives, huddled together for several hours and almost gave in to their combat fatigue.

Ten years later, Dr. Sammons reminisces:

"I guess that's just about as down as I have ever been in my life. To have worked so hard for so long and to be accused of dishonesty. The speculations were patently false, but the delegates were unwilling to believe their board and staff. The house had a vendetta against the board and staff.

"I actually gave very serious thought to saying, 'Fine, you can have this damn job and struggle out of it yourself.'

"Oh, I thought about it, but not very long. That's not my nature. I told Joe:

" 'No, damn it, I'm too mean to resign. That's the easy way out and I've never taken the easy way out. And I'm not going to start now. Let's go get 'em.' "

That week in Portland, one of the worst in the AMA's history, actually proved to be a blessing in disguise, Dr. Sammons believes. "In fact," he says now, "it was probably the best thing to have happened to AMA in 50 years. The fiscal crisis motivated us to bring AMA into the 20th century and turn it into a modern corporation."

The first steps were mixed and modest.

The house approved a $60 assessment to bail the organization out of the immediate cash-flow problem, but declined to raise the dues, slash committees and councils, or discontinue advertising, until its own committee had studied the situation and was satisfied. By June the committee was satisfied, and a $140 annual dues increase (to $250) led the Association out of the fiscal woods. In subsequent years, the board would pare 100 AMA committees down to eight councils, plus ad hoc panels as needed. Advertising was retained and for 1984 was projected at a record $25 million, but the Association also saw in 1975 a steady parade of those large publishers who compete with the AMA (including the publisher of *Medical World News*) beat a path to the AMA's door to urge the world's largest medical publisher to stay in the business of publishing pharmaceutical ads.

In the meantime, Dr. Sammons did what he believed he had to do. For starters, that meant a 20% across-the-board cutback in staff budgets. This was a dramatic move for an organization as accustomed to prosperity as the American Medical Association, and it did not entirely endear Dr. Sammons to his co-workers in the first weeks of his tenure as EVP. But the cut was essential.

Jim Sammons had used revolution, not evolution, to put the AMA back on its feet. The low point, he says, was "that Black Friday in May, 1975, when we had to terminate scores of employees. Truly, that was wrenching, but it had to be done."

In subsequent years, the AMA would reorganize its staff along corporate lines, install sophisticated budgeting, planning, and administrative controls, and build its reserves to $100 million. By the end of this decade, the Association very well may be a $250-million operation, the size of a medium corporation. A new AMA building went up in 1982 in Washington, D.C., and a new AMA-powered real-estate development will soon go up in Chicago. For decades to come, the AMA will be "a big player" in the medical ballgame.

Through it all—through dozens of new trustees and hundreds of new delegates, through five changes of Congress and three changes of U.S. presidents, there has been one constant—Jim Sammons. He has been the glue that has held the pieces of the puzzle together. Former AMA President Hoyt Gardner, MD, says, "It's been a great venture and I've been privileged to be part of it. But Jim's fingerprints are all over the place."

March, 1984. Washington, D.C.

Dr. Sammons is in town for a series of meetings and media appearances. The main purpose: promote the voluntary freeze on physician fees proposed by the AMA, and head off a move in Congress to make mandatory the assignment of Medicare claims and to make hospitals police physicians who choose not to comply. Of course, there will be other business to attend to as well.

Dr. Sammons insists upon being well-briefed, and he is a walking encyclopedia of AMA policy and programs, a superb spokesman for the needs of the practicing physician, the community and university hospital, and the quality medical school. He is, in short, a one-physician information explosion.

Rising early after a late meeting the night before, his legislative and media briefings completed, he is now good-naturedly sleep-walking through a photo session to lay a new plaque over the door at Needham House, the Association's elegantly refurbished four-story brownstone at 1710 N St., N.W.

Already, the strong-willed AMA director of communications, Toba Cohen, has persuaded the AMA executive to trade in the plaid suit (a modest plaid by his standards) in which he had breakfast for a dark-gray number for the photo shoot. Everything is proceeding smoothly—if slowly—while the photographer strains for the right angle, the right lighting, and the right poses. Dr. Sammons is becoming visibly bored when the phone rings.

Chicago is calling for Dr. Sammons. "I need the boss," says Dr. Sammons' executive secretary of seven years, Elizabeth Novak. Chicago needs a decision.

Dr. Sammons snaps to attention. A friend once observed that when challenged, the AMA leader's IQ "jumps about 50 points." Feet spread at a 45-degree angle, his right fist resting on his hip, his jaw clenched and his eyes blazing, Dr. Sammons listens patiently while the situation is explained to him. It takes about three minutes for the answer:

"Well, I say, 'Go!' Let's get on with it."

That's the way it's been for the last 10 years. Jim Sammons doesn't go to the ballet, enjoy the symphony, or read Proust. He lives for the AMA. He runs the AMA 99%-plus of his waking hours, pounding upon organizational opportunities like a dog pounces upon a bone. It is a 24-hour-a-day, seven-day-a-week job.

Now, dressed in his dark-gray suit, sporting an AMPAC pin in his lapel, a striped necktie with the AMA seal, and AMA-embossed cufflinks, he climbs into a waiting limousine for a series of television shows.

He will be tough with a right-to-life hardliner arguing for "Baby

Doe" legislation ("These agonizing decisions should be left where they belong," he says, "between the parents and their physicians. If you don't think they're qualified to make the decision, you're crazy."), but tender with a representative for senior citizens ("The American Medical Association wants to make sure that the *needy* elderly of our country will always receive the medical care they need."). With a TV anchorman, he will patiently explain the facts ("You know, many people believe that the elderly have a contract under Medicare with their physicians. That's not so. They have a contract with the government, and the government is not willing to pay today what it promised 20 years ago. And, as you know, physicians only account for 19 cents of the health care dollar.").

At lunch with Abigail Trafford of *U.S. News & World Report,* he discusses a danger confronting American medicine, the threat of rationing posed by the organ-transplant bill before Congress.

"This bill will give the government the absolute right to ration not only organ transplants but all medical technology. It stipulates who can get what care at what facilities. Now, I'm 57 years old and if I have the money to pay for it and I'm not eligible for care at Stanford or Pittsburgh, or wherever the government wants me to go, I ought to be able to shop around for it."

He adds, "Another problem you shouldn't forget is the high cost of professional liability. It's forcing some of our finest physicians to restrict their practices or to get out altogether or to move to different parts of the country."

At the end of the lunch, Trafford says she will be back in touch for a story or two.

And so it goes. Dr. Sammons will spend the afternoon in the White House talking to presidential chief of staff James Baker. He will spend the evening dedicating a new Yvonne Jacquette oil painting. "Night Panorama with Jefferson Memorial," an aerial view of the nation's capital that at $36,000 will be one of the cornerstones of the AMA collection inside the building.

Outside, there is the AMA-commissioned work by the grande dame of American sculpture, Louise Nevelson. The sculpture, "Sky Landscape," was valued initially at $350,000. This night's dedication includes a reception for congressmen and local artists. Afterwards, there is a dinner at the posh Georgetown Club. The AMA started the art collection to help American artists, and tonight they are the guests of honor, improbably strewn among AMA lobbyists and congressional staffers.

The AMA vice president for Public Affairs, Wayne Bradley, notes, "Sure, Washington can be B.S. and tinsel, but that's a real part of the game. Image counts, and AMA's image is way up. The new building, the art collection, our new corporate presence in Washington all help say that AMA is a big player, a big player that's here to stay.

"The tinsel, though, is only part of the program. We need image, but we also need the work of the AMA Council on Legislation and the AMA legislative staff, we need the legislative alerts sent out to the nation's physicians, and we need the visits to Washington by MDs from county, state, and speciality societies. It's all part of the program."

At dinner, Dr. Sammons finds himself seated next to a physician he first met during an AMA trip to China. Talk naturally turns to the Chinese-language edition of the *Journal of the AMA*.

The EVP keeps his dinner remarks brief and social. The time to talk will come later, about one month later, when Dr. Sammons can report to the board that the Medicare mandatory assignment bill has been blocked in Congress, largely due to the voluntary fee freeze recommended by the AMA. This latest AMA legislative victory follows successes over the years in preventing broad federal bills for health maintenance organizations, professional standards review organizations, and caps on hospital reimbursements, not to mention the AMA's success on the overriding legislative war—keeping American medicine free from national health insurance.

But Dr. Sammons is not complacent. He later will warn his Washington staff that the Medicare bills will be back and that they have only won the battle, not the war. But, this night in Washington is purely social, a small footnote to the legislative chapters that unfold over the years. Immediately after the dinner, Dr. Sammons heads for the waiting limousine and the short ride to Needham House. Tommorrow will be more of the same.

The physician moves through his world of power and privilege as if he were to the manor born, but, of course, it is not that simple and it was not that easy.

He calls it a "love affair—a love affair that has grown better and better and deeper and deeper over the years." Jim Sammons fell in love with the AMA the first time he saw it—in 1949 in St. Louis.

"It was a hot summer day in June, and the AMA Annual Convention was being held at Kiel Auditorium. I was a junior medical student at St. Louis U., and the dean of the medical school, Father Alphonse Schwitalla, MD, insisted that the students go and see what the AMA was all about.

"This was when the scientific and socioeconomic meetings were held together and it was a massive meeting, with the exhibits alone filling half the auditorium. I looked at all these physicians coming from all over the country to help educate each other and I thought, 'Boy, this is really one hell of an organization!"

"It was a moving experience. It never occurred to me not to belong and not to participate. I could hardly wait. I fell in love on that hot summer day and I've never fallen out."

He graduated in 1951 and after a one-year internship in Mobile, (Ala.) City-County Hospital, he joined a cousin, Karl Sammons, MD, to do general practice in Highlands, Texas, a small town that sits high atop the San Jacinto River midway between Baytown and Houston.

He got involved in organized medicine for the simplest of reasons—self-survival. In the Southwest, as in the rest of the country, general practitioners had to fight to maintain the scope of their hospital admitting and surgical privileges. It is a battle that continues today, but in 1952 Dr. Sammons joined the East Harris branch of the Harris County Medical Society to do something about it.

He would go through the chairs of Texas medicine so fast that, in the words of one observer, "they never saw him."

He held almost all offices in the Harris County Medical Society (HCMS), served 11 years on the Texas Medical Assn. (TMA) Board of Councillors (the association's ethical and disciplinary body), 14 years on the TMA Executive Board, ran the HCMS' business foundation, the Houston Academy of Medicine, and in 1971, at age 44, became the TMA's youngest president. He helped found the Texas Political Action Committee. On the national scene, he joined the AMPAC board in 1964 and served as its chairman in 1969–1970. In 1970, he was elected to the AMA Board of Trustees, the youngest physician ever accorded this honor, and he also became the AMA board's youngest vice-chairman (1972) and chairman (1973–74).

The meteoric rise was not accidental. The term "Type A" appears to have been coined to describe Jim Sammons.

He was never one to agonize over long philosophical dilemmas. Jim Sammons was always one to cut, not untie, the gordian knots. When one of his medical partners developed a vision problem and had to switch from general practice to psychiatry, it necessitated the partner's leaving to undergo a psychiatric residency. It also meant a potential legal problem, since the Texas statutes of incorporation required an elaborate dissolving and reassigning of corporate assets. Paperwork. Red tape. Dr. Sammons found an expedient soluion: "We broke out the bourbon, built a large bonfire, invited all our friends, and put to flame about $300,000 in group receivables. Our partner could get on with his medical training and we could get on with our medical practice."

His Texas friends can describe why he made it from a town of 2,000 in the red clay soil of Alabama and a town of 3,000 on the banks of the San Jacinto River to the pinnacle of medical power.

Haden McKay, MD, a Houston physician, offers one clue. "He is the most mentally organized person I have ever met in my life. He is always organized, he is always prepared, and he always takes immediate action. Jim and I were active in TMA at the same time, and I was constantly amazed at how he never let up, he never put anything off. We'd be in the back of a car after attending a medical meeting, and Jim would be dictating notes about what needed to be done next. He doesn't have a lazy bone in his body.

"He piloted his own plane in those days and once he called in weather-bound and asked me if I could make a speech he was scheduled to give. Well, I just picked up the phone and called his son. I said, 'Jimmy, go look on your dad's desk and get the speech he's written for tonight.' Sure enough, he had written the speech weeks ago. I delivered Jim's speech and it was the best speech I've ever given. And it had Jim Sammons written all over it."

In 1965, as an alternate delegate to the AMA from Texas, the 37-year-old Jim Sammons sat through a special session of the house that had been called to deal with the imminent passage of Medicare. The AMA board had countered by proposing "Eldercare" legislation, and house ratification of the board action was required.

Throughout the morning, disgruntled delegates, upset by the prospect of the coming federal intrusion, sniped away at the board's action. Believing that the board deserved praise, not brickbats, for responsible action, Dr. Sammons rose to propose a standing ovation for the trustees. When the delegates rose to applaud, the endorsement of Eldercare was assured, and a new medical-political star was in the making.

In 1970, as a newly elected AMA trustee, Dr. Sammons came to an AMA briefing for senior medical society executives and heard the constant carping about the failures of the AMA. He asked the execs:

"Well, if AMA doesn't represent you, then tell me, who in the hell does?"

A familiar sight at AMA meetings is the movement of Jim Sammons, driving with a full head of steam, toward a microphone. One Texas physician observes, "No one would ever think of taking a [surgical] knife away from Mike DeBakey, and no one would ever think of taking a microphone away from Jim Sammons."

What drove Jim Sammons through Texas medicine to the executive vice presidency of the AMA is the same thing that drives him today.

"We have one overriding purpose at the AMA, and that is to preserve the individual physician's right to make his or her clinical judgments based upon his or her experience and decisions as to what is best for the patient. That right has to be totally free from interference by any third party, whether government, insurer, or businessman. Taking care of sick people is the job of the physician and the hospital—and the physician and the hospital alone. And this same kind of thinking applies to medical education and medical peer review. Our emphasis has to be on maintaining high quality, as well as expanding access and working for reasonable cost. That's what I'm all about and that's what AMA is all about."

A workaholic virtually from birth, young Harris Sammons skipped two grades, graduated from high school at 16, studied around the calendar to get through college (at Washington & Lee, Lexington, Va.) and medical school. He took off only for 1945 ("There was no way I was going to miss the war, so I enlisted for a year as a hospital corpsman"). The pattern continued when he set up medical practice in Texas.

"I was having such a great time that I thought I was indestructible," he recalls. "I thought I was Superman. When my activities in TMA and AMA began to really pick up about 1968, I had to try to figure out how I could be involved in organized medicine and still have a medical practice. I insisted on taking my own calls and giving my patients first-class service. Fortunately, I had some understanding partners, and they agreed to cover for me. So, my medical practice went down by about one-third, but my days became longer by about one-third. I was flying around the state on TMA business, around the country on AMA business, and was still running a hands-on medical practice in Baytown."

Dr. McKay says that Jim Sammons "was a damn good doctor. He cared about medicine, he cared about his patients, and he had a large practice that required a lot of hours. His patients came first and he always made time for them."

Today, Dr. Sammons recalls, "Oh, sure, sometimes I miss the patient contact. I loved taking care of people, especially little kids. I liked my patients and, over time, they became more than patients. They became my friends. I miss seeing them, especially the little ones. But once I took the AMA job, that was the end of practicing medicine. Being EVP is too demanding to have time for anything else."

In 1972, some 30 years of "living on coffee and cigarets and two hours of sleep a night" caught up with Dr. Sammons. He suffered a heart attack. It was reported that as he was wheeled into the coronary care unit, he asked his physician if he could have one last cigaret. The physician threw the pack away.

Typically, Dr. Sammons "shoved aside the temporary setback. It was a mild attack and afterwards I felt fine," he recalls. "Oh, I quit smoking and

I watched my diet, but I kept right on with my work. By 1973, when I decided to go for the AMA job, I had forgotten about the heart attack. I had been vice-chairman and chairman of the AMA board and had been running all over the place and I never felt better."

On St. Patrick's Day, 1974, in suite 1101 of the Washington Hilton, in an action immediately preceding an AMPAC meeting, he was named EVP-designate. "Sure, it was pretty stressful during the balloting," he says. "But I just sat outside the boardroom and read a couple of pocket mystery books. Somehow, in the back of my mind, I always knew that things would turn out right." It took him only two weeks to close down his Baytown medical practice, where he had been managing partner for a 10-physician group. On April Fool's Day, he reported to the AMA.

One of the men who helped engineer Dr. Sammons' election is Joe D. Miller, the man who was the first executive director of AMPAC, the first director of the AMA Division of Public Affairs, and for eight years the AMA's deputy EVP, helping to reshape the Association within the scope of a unique relationship that his boss, Dr. Sammons, calls "co-equal."

Miller, who retired in 1982 but remains a consultant to the AMA, addressed himself to "Landslide Sammons" during a 10-year anniversary testimonial dinner, and told the group:

"When Jim first got the EVP job, some of us on staff worried whether or not he could make the transition from being the board chairman to being an employe, even the No. 1 employe. We didn't know how well he would relate to the problems faced by staff.

"Well, it didn't take too long to find out. When the last day of his first board meeting as EVP finally ended, he called some of us into his office and broke out the bourbon. 'God,' he asked, 'are they finally out of town?' We knew then he'd work out."

Miller concludes, "Well, if it were part of my responsibility to make this man a good administrator, I think I've done a damn good job."

Proud and protective of their own, the people of Clayton, Ala., in the southeast corner of the state, say they knew all along that Harris would make his mark upon the world. And they are only too happy to tell you why. The very presence of a reporter in town rates a front-page story in *The Clayton Record,* headlined, "Medical news editor seeks Dr. J. H. Sammons profile."

The reporter's first stop, however, is 85 miles back up the road at the state capital, Montgomery.

George Wallace used to live in Clayton, four doors down from the Sammons' home. The governor was born in Clio (pronounced "clow"), a neighboring town in Barbour County, and he knew well the young Harris (who is five years younger than Wallace) and his parents. Confined to a wheelchair since he was shot in 1972 while campaigning for the U.S. presidency, the governor does not give very many interviews these days. But he has made an exception in honor of his fellow Claytonian, Harris Sammons.

The state legislature is in hectic session, with an abortion bill being furiously debated in one chamber and an auto insurance bill being languidly filibustered in the other. The summer seersucker suits of the various aides and lobbyists are drenched with sweat from the hot and muggy day and from a breakdown of the air conditioning system. But the governor is cool and dry as he sits in an enormous darkened room at the end of a long conference table. For 90 minutes, various youth groups have been run in and out of his office at five-minute intervals to have their pictures taken with a man who is a national newsmaker and a local legend.

Now, the photo sessions are over. The governor is alone. He doesn't hear well, but, for that matter, he doesn't need to listen, anyway.

"Anytime you meet a young man as brilliant and as ambitious as Harris," he begins, "you know he's going to go places. We expected his success.

"I haven't seen him much recently, but I know he's a very important person in the medical world and I'll never forget his kindnesses to me and my former wife, Lurleen, when we were down at M. D. Anderson Hospital in Houston so that Lurleen could be treated for cancer. He did everything he could for us."

The governor twists and turns as if he is about to lift out of the chair that imprisons him. Wallace was once an amateur boxer, and his forced immobility pains him. He settles for unwrapping and lighting a long cigar. "What's that? Why did Harris make it? I'll tell you why. He made it because he had the best upbringing a man can have, right here in the rural South. People cared about each other then."

The governor smiles. "You know, my granddad, Joe Wallace, was a country doctor. I was going through his diaries a while back and I came upon an entry he made for an appendectomy. He operated on this boy who was about 12 or 13 or so and after he closed him up the boy was taken by horsecart back to his farm. Five miles over a bumpy, rutted road. The boy was fine. Became a policeman here in Montgomery years later. Granddad charged his parents $3, according to his ledgers. Now, today, that kind of operation would need nurses and IVs and surgical assistants and so on and would cost maybe $5,000."

His political instincts rising, the governor concludes: "You tell Harris, now, that we public officials are looking to leaders like him to solve this problem of the high cost of medical care. It's a problem and we need a solution.

"You drop in again, now, you hear."

Today's AMA is dramatically different than it was a decade ago, and Jim Sammons says the changes of the past now make it possible for medicine to seize the opportunities of the present and meet the problems of the future.

Dr. Sammons thinks that his legacy so far has been "protecting the integrity of the Association, assuring its financial strength, and, above all, putting in place a marvelous staff. We have the greatest group of people assembled under one collective roof that I have ever seen. I am constantly amazed and pleased at the dedication and talent of the non-MDs we have at AMA who are working to protect the quality of American medicine. Many of them have never been closer to a medical center than to drive past it on the expressway, and yet, they are working hard every day to maintain the quality of those medical centers. They are a magnificent group and they are doing a magnificent job."

The AMA staff is now structured along taut corporate lines of command.

Assistant EVP Ted Chilcoat says, "The big administrative change of AMA over the past 10 years is that today, many more decisions are delegated. For the first four years or so, the financial crisis demanded that Dr. Sammons have his hands on everything. Every day, for three years, Dr. Sammons met at 9 a.m. with senior staff. Now, he has the freedom and staff to delegate."

Retiring deputy EVP for Business Services, Tom Hannon, remembers coming aboard in 1975 to try to rescue the Association's floundering publishing program and "wondering what have I gotten myself into." Within three years, however, Hannon had the publications back on their feet and was training his sights on bigger game.

He recalls, "Jim and Joe (Miller) were very candid with me upfront. They said they had a problem and they said, 'We don't know paper, we don't know postage, and we don't know printing. We're going to listen to you when it comes to publishing.' Well, they kept their word, they never interfered, and they supported me 100%."

By 1978, the rescue plan implemented by Dr. Sammons and Deputy EVP Miller had assured the survival of the nine specialty journals—which were almost sold in 1975—and both *JAMA* and *American Medical News* were on the upswing in advertising dollars. Dr. Sammons decided to look at other areas of the AMA that had "products" to sell. This idea was the beginning of a formal AMA marketing operation, which was begun in 1978.

"At General Motors," Dr. Sammons observes, "automobiles go out the door. At AMA, information about and for physicians goes out the door, and we decided that much of that information can be marketed."

From those modest beginnings in 1978, the AMA marketing operation rapidly grew until today the AMA's business activities bring in almost 60% of the $110-million annual budget and account for 60% of the employes. In 1975, 36% of the AMA's $56-million annual budget came from non-dues income. Dr. Sammons has restructured the entire 1,100-person Association into two broad areas—business and policy.

As a vast information center, the AMA's business activities feature the publishing program, including the foreign-language editions of *JAMA;* a computerized Medical Information Network, launched with GTE; the aggressive marketing of the AMA's unique Physician Masterfile; and an ambitious jump into the emerging field of elecronic publishing, including video clinics and cable TV.

On the drawing board are plans for a possible AMA travel agency, a possible AMA financial management and investment agency, and a possible AMA real estate management firm.

The Association's proposed "Grand Avenue Square" real-estate complex in Chicago will revitalize a prime area of the Near North Side and provide the AMA sliding equity positions in the new buildings scheduled to be built on the 12 acres of land the Association owns contiguous to its current headquarters at 535 N. Dearborn.

The proposed Grand Avenue Square development will feature as its cornerstone building a 790,000-square-foot tower conceptualized by distinguished architect I.M. Pei. This anchor building also may serve as the Association's new headquarters, occupying one-third of the space. The rest would be leased to commercial interests—offices, shops, and restaurants.

The key building block for this dramatic redevelopment is access to Michigan Avenue, and that access was assured when the AMA bought the 15-story 520 N. Michigan Ave. building. (Ironically, it was 23 years ago that AMPAC set up its first offices in only 400 square feet in that same Michigan Avenue building.)

Dr. Sammons believes that the AMA can reach revenues of $200 million within the next few years and that the vast majority can be non-dues. He acknowledges that there is a potential downside to the bullish projections.

"We believe," he says, "that the AMA business operation generates dollars to fund the policy and scientific activities and that whether the non-dues side of the equation of 60%, 70%, 80%, or 90%, the members will still control the organization and will still determine its direction. But, obviously, if dues account for less and less of the budget, I can see where some members might question whether or not they are losing control of their organization.

"The answer to that question is no. I am comfortable with the current 60-40 split of non-dues to dues income, but I believe that the split could be 90-10 and the members would not have to worry. We know who runs this organization—the House of Delegates and the Board of Trustees— and we know whose needs they serve—the members. That's never going to change."

Indeed, one reason the AMA got into the new math—non-dues income—in the first place is because of a chronic membership problem that has resisted countless cures. Dr. Sammons has tried everything—new membership sections for students, residents, and most recently, hospital medical staffs, an expanded Division of membership, and the allocation of a substantial chunk of the budget to membership recruitment—and, still, AMA membership has not kept pace with the growth of the physician population.

"One of every two physicians refuses to belong to any part of the medical federation—county, state, or AMA," he says. "And there are 50,000 physicians who join their county and state societies and refuse to take the next step and join AMA. These 'freeloaders' are riding on the backs of their fellow physicians. A recent poll shows that the vast majority of the non-members agree with what the AMA is doing, but will not pay their fair share. How short-sighted. But we're going to keep going after them."

The AMA Deputy EVP, Whalen Strobhar, describes Dr. Sammons' transformation of the AMA this way:

"He showed great foresight in making every conceivable effort to broaden AMA's decision-making base and to assure the widest possible impact for its policy. This includes his strong support for the Public Affairs Division, the American Assn. of Medical Society Executives (AAMSE) Advisory Committee to the EVP, the creation of new membership sections for students, residents, and hospital medical staffs, and the re-entry of AMA into the World Medical Assn.

"On the administrative side, he put into place sophisticated new budgeting, information, and planning systems. He strongly supported a staff reorganization to bring together the development of legislative policy in Chicago and the carrying out of that policy in Washington, along with necessary public relations and federal support, so that the goal—a legislative result—could be better reached."

Strobhar adds, "Dr. Sammons' strong support of the AMA Council on Scientific Affairs, his championing of AMA efforts in medical education and accrediting, and his commitment to the science of medicine, mean that AMA will continue to be a force in determining policy on medical education and technology."

Dr. Sammons says about his new staff structure: "I am very fortunate in having on board all the management talent we need to meet the challenges and oportunities of the future."

The medical problem of the present and future can be described in a single word:

Cost.

When Dr. Sammons began practicing medicine in Highlands, Texas, in 1952, it was a different world medically.

There was no such thing as a joint replacement, organ transplant, or artificial heart valve. No hypothermia treatment, no amniocentesis, no ultrasound. There was no heart-lung machine and no open-heart surgery. No polio vaccine, pacemaker, or anti-depressive drug. There was no microsurgery, no measles vaccine, and no coronary bypass surgery. No serum hepatitis vaccines, no CAT scanners.

Today, these marvels are common, but supermedicine means supermoney. American medicine can point to a cornucopia of riches, but there is one over-riding negative:

Cost.

Dr. Sammons poses the problem this way:

"We are faced with a vastly new challenge to the preservation of the quality physician and the quality hospital. The public is being led to believe that their expectations of ever-growing marvels and services will continue. The reality, however, will be a shrinking of services. Rationing. That's part of the vise. The other is that more and more limited-license practitioners will be competing with physicians.

"The federal emphasis on reimbursement by diagnosis-related groups (DRGs) can have an extremely adverse effect. The pricing of medical services is not the same as preserving the quality of those services. Under DRGs, we may see the closing of some hospitals and a return to the old days of closed-panel hospital medical staffs. Physicians will be selected not only on the basis of how they practice medicine, but on how they price their services. That's one threat resulting from the cost problem. Another is that if medical school tuitions keep rising, only the rich will be able to go to medical school. After decades of trying to broaden the mix of MDs, we will be back to square one."

Dr. Sammons' solution: "A medical federation truly worthy of the name. We have to expand the federation from its legal definition and embrace the hospitals, medical schools, specialties, and others. We need a true 'Congress of Medicine.' We're all in this ballgame together."

He adds, "We have to come to grips with this startling fact—if you take all the housestaff and all the hospital-based physicians—who together comprise one-third of the profession—and add to them the physicians employed by health maintenance organizations (HMOs), group practices, and small two- and three-physician partnerships, you will find that the number of physicians falling under the definition of salaried is somewhere between *one-half and two-thirds of all the practicing physicians* in this country. That's totally different than it was 10 or 15 years ago.

"Our constituency has changed and we have to retailor our services to this new constituency. We are going to have several advocacies going at the same time—a smorgasbord of services. For example, we are going to need one advocacy position for those physicians who are hospital-based and must deal with the teaching institutions that employ them. Another advocacy position will be needed for physicians employed by HMOs and other forms of health care delivery systems that may be controlled by non-physicians.

"A third advocacy position will be needed in the way of consultative services to group practices. We must become a much stronger advocate of the medical schools than ever before. We must get rid of the "town-gown" split once and for all. Educationally, we will need a range of services. Not only in continuing medical education, but special programs to meet the needs of community physicians far removed from teaching institutions. AMA will be launching pilot programs to become an enormous, driving constructive force for all these new causes."

On the scientific side, Dr. Sammons points with pride to the AMA Council on Scientific Affairs, which is taking the lead in technology assessment; to the prospering scientific journals, particularly the expansion into foreign-language versions of *JAMA;* and to the vast amounts of scientific information that can be moved over the AMA-GTE Medical Information Network, including abstracts of articles and drug information.

He says, "With the hiring of Roy Schwartz, MD, 48, to direct our educational and scientific efforts, we have laid the foundation for AMA to assume an increasingly larger role in the educational and scientific arenas."

The EVP believes that the revolt will come from patients and physicians if and when the government uses cost as an excuse to ration services. He also believes that this revolt, "which may only be three to five years away," can be headed off if medicine "seizes the next few years as its best—

and last—opportunity to shape public health policy for the rest of this century."

The Association's hopes rest on the Health Policy Agenda (HPA), an ambitious attempt by the AMA and 100 other health organizations to chart the course of health policy. The HPA is successor to the AMA-convened Commission on the Cost of Medical Care (another Sammons idea), and the EVP believes that if implemented it can prevent the need for rationing, or at least assure that medical services and technology are rationally used. "This document has the potential to keep American medicine the best in the world," he says, "for the next five and the next 50 years."

The EVP will continue to have an "open-door" administrative style, with senior staff walking in and out of his office at will. He speed-reads ("I taught myself—I had to do it given the blizzard of paperwork that crosses this desk") his mail on two occasions when his concentration cannot be broken—early in the morning and late in the evening.

He adds, "I delegate most of this paperwork, but I have to know what it is I am delegating so that I can be sure later that it's moving along." His telephone "hot lines" connect to all AMA officers and trustees, HHS in Washington, the AMA's Washington Office, and key policymakers such as the American Hospital Assn., Blue Cross-Blue Shield, and the Joint Commission on Accreditation of Hospitals.

With staff, Dr. Sammons' style is much more like that of Gen. Dwight D. Eisenhower than Gen. George S. Patton. Despite his own formidable ego, the EVP has been known to yield to a superior argument from staff. He is forceful, but flexible. On issues in which he has a strong personal feeling, the EVP will go out of his way to listen to all sides of a problem, and if there is still disagreement, he will, in the way of the Old South, "ask my people to come into the office so we can reason together. Sometimes, I call it a prayer session."

He hopes for six or seven more years as EVP. "Oh, I know who wrote the contract," he says, referring to the Board of Trustees, "and I know they can unwrite it at anytime, but I hope they can find a use for me for awhile."

Just off the 14th fairway down in Grenelefe, Fla., ground is being broken for a Spanish-style golf house that will be the retirement home of Jim and Jo Anne Sammons. In August, in the middle of searing heat, he takes his vacation to play golf. He likes it hot. It was that way growing up in Clayton.

Jim Sammons started out many years ago with a golf handicap of 28 and today, after hundreds of lessons and hitting thousands of golf balls, he still has a 28 handicap. It is his only relaxation and it is his one failure to master the environment.

His friends complain about the high handicap, but former AMA President Hoyt Gardner, MD, sums it up: "To play good golf you have to relax. Jim attacks the courts."

Dr. Sammons intends to improve his golf game, but it won't be any time soon. Blue Cross President Bernard Tresnowski explained why in an eloquent comment at Dr. Sammons' 10-year anniversary dinner.

"When I woke up at 5 a.m. in Cleveland this morning," Tresnowski said, "knowing that I would be at this dinner tonight, I stood in the bathroom shaving and wondering, 'What more is there to say about Jim Sammons?' Well, when I think of Jim Sammons, I think of something you don't usually associate with the man.

"Poetry.

"Robert Frost had the key to Jim Sammons:

" 'The woods are lovely, dark and deep.
'But I have promises to keep.
'And miles to go before I sleep.
'And miles to go before I sleep.' "□

Gregory Hemingway, MD: "I never got over a sense of responsibility for my father's death."

Renee Richards, MD: "I think of myself as a woman physician, and that is a role with which I am very comfortable."

Photos (unless otherwise credited) by Dennis L. Breo.

Story Musgrave, first MD to walk in space: "It was an incredibly positive experience."

Photographer Roman Vishniac, MD, and his wife: "I wanted to save their faces, not their ashes."

John Rock, MD, father of "the Pill": "I was never afraid of the criticism."

Pied Piper of running, George Sheehan, MD.

Walker Percy, MD.

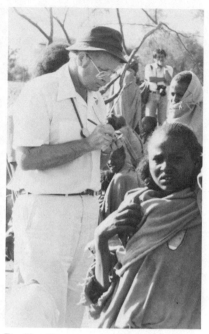

Siblings awaiting treatment at the
Alamata center, Ethiopia. World
Vision photo by Ross Arnold.

Dr. Jim Owens at the Alamata center.
World Vision photo by Ross Arnold.

Jim Owens, MD, in his Seattle office.

A celebrity as a result of his *Joy of Sex* books, Alex Comfort, MD, is also a noted gerontologist and novelist.

"It is a bit different," says Mort Copenhaver, DDS, of his hand-built castle.

Chris Chandler, MD, reached the summit
of Mt. Everest in 1976 as a member of the
U.S. Bicentennial team.

AMA Executive Vice President James H. Sammons, MD. Photo by Joe Fletcher.

Index

HOYT C. HARRIS, M.D., P.C.
RIVER PARK MEDICAL CENTER
McMINNVILLE, TENN. 37110